D1232687

BUSINESS COMMUNICATION

Online Materials for Instructors

This text has a companion website with resources for instructors.

Please visit:
sites.broadviewpress.com/
businesscommunication/

Your access code is:
bcrs2291w2

The site provides PowerPoint lectures, chapter overviews, additional business cases, and quizzes for each chapter.

Business Communication

Rhetorical Situations

Heather Graves and
Roger Graves

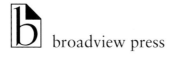

broadview press

BROADVIEW PRESS – www.broadviewpress.com
Peterborough, Ontario, Canada

Founded in 1985, Broadview Press remains a wholly independent publishing house. Broadview's focus is on academic publishing; our titles are accessible to university and college students as well as scholars and general readers. With 800 titles in print, Broadview has become a leading international publisher in the humanities, with world-wide distribution. Broadview is committed to environmentally responsible publishing and fair business practices.

Library and Archives Canada Cataloguing in Publication

Title: Business communication : rhetorical situations / Heather Graves and Roger Graves.
Names: Graves, Heather, 1958- author. | Graves, Roger, 1957- author.
Description: Includes bibliographical references and index.
Identifiers: Canadiana (print) 20210101466 | Canadiana (ebook) 20210101482 | ISBN 9781554815005 (softcover) | ISBN 9781770487789 (PDF) | ISBN 9781460407295 (EPUB)
Subjects: LCSH: Business writing—Textbooks. | LCSH: Business communication—Textbooks.
Classification: LCC HF5718.3 .G73 2021 | DDC 808.06/665—dc23

Broadview Press handles its own distribution in North America:
PO Box 1243, Peterborough, Ontario K9J 7H5, Canada
555 Riverwalk Parkway, Tonawanda, NY 14150, USA
Tel: (705) 743-8990; Fax: (705) 743-8353
email: customerservice@broadviewpress.com

For all territories outside of North America, distribution is handled by Eurospan Group.

 Broadview Press acknowledges the financial support of the Government of Canada for our publishing activities.

Edited by Martin R. Boyne
Book Design by Em Dash Design

PRINTED IN CANADA

Contents

Chapter 2: Argument in Professional Communication   51

Chapter 3: Style in Business and Professional Writing   97

Chapter 13: Design and Visuals in Business and Professional Communication 325

Preface

Writers in business and professional communication environments always write in response to the many and varied rhetorical situations they encounter in a dynamic, ever-changing environment. How can we best help students prepare to communicate in such a challenging environment?

This book is our answer. *Business Communication: Rhetorical Situations* supports more interactive and engaging pedagogies that students find motivating and enlightening. The rhetorical situations provide a framework for generating student discussion of the concepts in the chapter and how to apply those concepts to a real-world, specific context drawn from business and professional contexts.

The most prominent feature of this book is the focus on rhetorical situations that writers face. Each chapter has two or three rhetorical situations that challenge students to apply the business and professional communication concepts they are learning to a specific set of circumstances. These rhetorical situations are drawn from real-life communication situations. They are high-interest stories that invite students to think through a communication situation—such as having to write a difficult email message—and then to write that message.

In addition to the rhetorical situations printed in the book, we have supplied others on the instructor website. By doing this, we encourage instructors to select assignments that match the level of their students.

To understand the problem that a situation presents, students can discuss the case in small groups (or via chat in twos and threes), as part of a whole class discussion (synchronously or asynchronously), or online in discussion threads in a learning management system (Moodle, Canvas, Blackboard, Desire2Learn). The discussion leader for a group may make and post a short, unscripted presentation to the rest of the class—either in person or through video link. They might also present in person or post a short, five-slide formal case analysis to the class through voice-over PowerPoint (screencast) or video link. All of this discussion and sharing of perspectives helps students generate ideas for how to write the document that the rhetorical situations demand.

We invite you to work with our book and the many resources we have created (quizzes, slides, podcasts, and supplementary exercises) to support your teaching. Please consider listening to our podcast, *Teaching Writing* (https://www.podomatic.com/podcasts/rogergraves), for new ideas for teaching and assessment, and accessing our website, wecanwrite.ca, for supplementary materials to support you as an instructor. If you have ideas for other materials or questions you think we might be able to answer about teaching, reach out to us on Twitter @rogergraves or LinkedIn (https://www.linkedin.com/in/rogercgraves/).

Heather Graves and Roger Graves

CHAPTER 1

Audience, Purpose, and Genre in Business and Professional Communication

 ## LEARNING OUTCOMES

1. Differentiate between the types of audiences that read documents
2. Identify the purpose and goals for the message
3. Develop a persuasive strategy that motivates readers to respond to written requests
4. Identify genres and determine how to use them in business and professional communication

GETTING STARTED

audience: The individual(s) for whom a given document is intended

Who you write for, why you write to them, and the form you choose to convey your ideas are fundamental factors that affect your success as a writer in the workplace. **Audience** refers to the various individuals who will read a document that you have written. To address your audience (or readers) effectively, you should think about who your audience consists of and what kind of tone is appropriate when speaking to them. For example, in business, when you are writing a text or email to a coworker you can use a less formal tone than if you are writing a report to a manager, who has greater authority than you do. Some people who have not considered audience—that is, who might be reading—suddenly become acutely aware of this concept when they post something on a social media page and unexpected readers respond—parents, people from high school whom they had lost contact with, and others.

purpose: What you want your readers to learn, know, or do when they finish your document

The **purpose**—why you write—refers to your goals for the document: that is, what you want your audience or readers to learn, understand, or do when they finish reading your document. Before you begin writing, you should have a firm sense of why you are communicating to your audience. If you know *why* you are writing, you will be able to decide *what* to include in your message and, maybe even more importantly, what not to say. By being concise—leaving out unnecessary words—you enhance the power of what you do write.

genre: The type of document used in a workplace to accomplish the goals or purposes of the piece of writing

To accomplish different purposes, you should select an appropriate **genre**, or type of document, that will reach a particular reader or group of readers to accomplish a specified goal. The key genres of writing done in workplaces include email messages, text messages, memos, letters, and reports. These are the tools you use to communicate successfully in the workplace. Learn to pick the appropriate genre and you will find that your career advances much more quickly than those who can communicate through only one channel.

In this chapter you will meet three people facing three different situations in which they have to create a document to solve a particular problem. In the first Rhetorical Situation, Haylee Bostick, a part-time employee at a large commercial bookstore, has been asked to write a memo for her boss to initial before sending it to Head Office. In the second Rhetorical Situation, Mike Smith must explain his decision to exceed the limit on his corporate credit card without authorization. In the third Rhetorical Situation, Mevla Khan creates two documents to inform local residents of a new class at the community center for which they might be interested in registering.

AUDIENCE IN PROFESSIONAL COMMUNICATION

 Differentiate between the types of audiences that read documents

Audience refers to the groups of readers (intended or not) who will read a message. Readers of business and professional communication can vary widely. For the same document, you may have readers from diverse cultures, readers who speak different languages (not necessarily

English), and readers who have contrasting ideas and expectations about your message. For these reasons, you should know something about who will read your message before you write it. Most correspondence in business and professional communication will be read by more than one person. It is helpful to think in the planning stages of writing about the five different types of audiences who may encounter your document: the initial audience, the gatekeepers, the primary and secondary audiences, and the watchdogs.

Initial audiences are the first people to encounter your draft. If you asked coworkers to review an email intended for your boss to check your tone before you send it, they are your initial (meaning first) audience. The coworkers are not your intended (or primary) readers, but they are still readers of this text.

initial audience: The people who read your completed draft first

Gatekeepers are another type of reader. Gatekeepers can prevent your document from being distributed. For example, managers might ask you to draft a message to send out under their name. They will probably review your draft to approve it. If they do not like what you have written, they can veto your message and it will never be distributed. Therefore, your document may need to meet gatekeepers' approval to reach its intended audience.

gatekeepers: Readers who decide who else reads your document

A third type of audience is your intended or **primary audience**. Primary readers are those people who most need the information and whose names appear on the "To:" line of an email or memo. For example, if you write to inform employees in your organization about a change in parental leave policy, your primary audience would be those employees who fit into the child-bearing and -rearing demographic. They are the primary group that you want to persuade to accept the change; they will read and react to your message. Employees who are childless or whose children are grown up are likely going to have less interest (or none at all) in your message.

primary audience: The readers you think you are writing for

Often you have additional readers, known as your **secondary audience**. They may be like the group who are uninterested in a change to the organization's parental leave policy. But members of your secondary audience may also form the group that implements your message. For example, if you helped write the report that recommended the change to the parental leave program, you would have had the director who requested the study (and other decision makers) in mind as your primary audience. You would likely have focused on persuading decision makers that the change was reasonable and necessary. You likely would not have been thinking explicitly, as you wrote, about the team in human resources who would later transform your recommendations into organizational policy. But they are a secondary audience for the report, a group that reads the report with the goal of creating a new policy.

secondary audience: People who read your document but for different reasons than the primary audience

The last type of audience who may potentially interact with your message is the **watchdog**. Watchdogs are individuals or groups with political, social, or economic power who can comment on or criticize your message. For example, if people are offended by a particular advertising campaign, they might decide to criticize that organization in conversations with their friends or refuse to buy that company's products to express that disagreement. Such people can't change the organization's behavior, but they can speak out against it, so they join a watchdog audience that responds to the organization's actions.

watchdog audience: Readers who may obtain your document and read it for political, legal, or social reasons

Many organization websites address a variety of audiences. Others target a uniform group, such as the screen capture (Figure 1.1) from Capital Comets Dog Sports Club, an agility club website where the links are aimed at people interested in the sport of agility. Of course, there are variations among the individuals who constitute the primary audience (people interested in dogs and agility), but few people would visit this site who were not interested in either competing with or training dogs. In contrast, the homepages of city websites such as www.mendocino.com, www.edmonton.ca, or www.duluthga.net address diverse groups of readers. City residents are the primary audience of such sites, indicated usually by prominent links to "bylaws" or "dog licenses." City websites also include links that target secondary audiences composed of potential visitors to the city looking for information about attractions or individuals looking to relocate (so links to local jobs appear on many city websites). Other possible links to city expansion plans target watchdog audiences of lawyers or members from municipal governments of surrounding towns or counties.

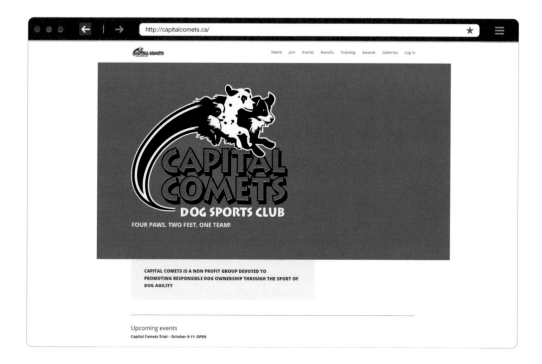

Figure 1.1 Many but not all organization websites address a variety of audiences.
Source: Home Page screenshot, Capital Comets Dog Sports Club, http://capitalcomets.ca/

Understanding Your Audience

Once you correctly identify the different groups who make up the audience for your message, consider what might be the best way to present your ideas to these groups. Your goal is to communicate your point so that it helps them accomplish the work they need to do. What aspects of your audience should you consider when preparing to write your message? Evaluate these five areas:

1. Readability and comprehension
2. Level of power or authority
3. Obstacles or objections to your message
4. Demographics
5. Communication networks

READABILITY AND COMPREHENSION

Your audience must be able to physically read the words on the page. If they cannot process your words, they will not receive your message, so choose words and sentences that match your audience's reading ability. To do this, you must understand your readers well enough to judge the level of language that matches their abilities. In addition to reading your message, your audience must also be able to understand and act on it. To do this, you must provide enough (but not too much) detail so readers can understand your message. Based on their understanding of your message, readers can act.

Sophisticated Audiences

The passage in Figure 1.2, taken from the City of Victoria, BC's Sustainability Climate Action webpage, addresses an educated reader—it contains six sentences and 113 words and uses a vocabulary somewhat above the reading level of many citizens. It also uses jargon such as "total GHG emissions" and conceptually dense language including phrases such as "space heating accounts for half of our energy consumption" and "low carbon buildings," as it outlines the vision, challenge, and plan to transform its current building stock into low carbon buildings. The use of "we"—as in "energy *we* all use ... *our* energy consumption" and "*our* homes and buildings"—draws readers into the plan (the page targets city residents), inviting them to join the city in reducing their greenhouse gas generation to make their homes, whether owned or rented, low carbon buildings.

Broader Audiences

The passage in Figure 1.3, taken from the City of Victoria, Texas's Victoria Main Street webpage, uses 92 words in three sentences to describe the city program's vision and mission. Although the sentences are longer than those in Figure 1.2, the level of language is more accessible: "quality of life," "personal enjoyment," and "small-town feel" are all phrases that most literate citizens can understand quickly. This short section of three sentences clearly communicates the city's mission and vision for its Victoria Main Street program.

Low Carbon High Performance Buildings

Vision
By 2050, Victoria will be home to efficient, renewably powered, high-performance buildings. Building design, operations and management will have evolved to deliver more sophisticated, comfortable, healthier, low carbon buildings, with far lower energy needs. Local industries will be recognized leaders in sustainable, high performance building design and construction.

The Challenge
The energy we all use to heat, power, and cool our homes and buildings makes up over half of the city's total GHG emissions. At home, space heating accounts for half of our energy consumption, while another quarter of energy is used to heat water. Many buildings rely on oil and natural gas and that is where most of these GHG emissions come from.

Source: City of Victoria, British Columbia, https://www.victoria.ca/EN/main/residents/climate-change/climate-leadership/low-carbon-high-performance-buildings.html

Figure 1.2 **Passage written for a sophisticated audience.**

About Us

Our Mission
Through leadership and the use of the Main Street Program, the Victoria Main Street Program will ensure that downtown contributes to the community's overall quality of life by providing opportunities for economic growth as well as for entertainment and personal enjoyment.

Our Vision
Just as they did on The Street of Ten Friends more than 150 years ago, residents and visitors continue to gather in Downtown Victoria. Today downtown Victoria is an energetic crossroads of multi-cultural activity featuring residential living with historic and emerging businesses, rooted in a vibrant and small-town feel.

Source: City of Victoria, Texas, https://www.victoriatx.gov/185/About-Us

Figure 1.3 **A document written for a broader audience.**

LEVEL OF POWER OR AUTHORITY

Assess the status and level of power or authority of your readers in relation to yourself. In some organizations, a flat organizational structure (where status and titles are not as important as outcomes) often results in informal communications. For example, in some organizations employees have met the CEO and address him or her by first name. In other organizations, there are many levels of managers between a lower-level employee and the CEO, a structure that often results in a more formal tone and level of language being expected. When writing to your boss or manager, adopt a level of language and tone appropriate to the different levels of authority. If your boss or manager supervises many people and is above you in status and authority, you should probably choose a tone and level of language that reflect this difference.

You will also write to coworkers who are your equals in status and power. Your language and tone should therefore reflect this relationship. For example, you might choose a more informal tone when writing to your friend in the next cubicle than to your manager in the corner office. Finally, when you are writing to subordinates, your word choice and tone may also reflect the fact that they hold less authority than you. However, your word choice and tone should always treat all your readers with courtesy and respect, whatever their status and level of power in the organization.

OBSTACLES OR OBJECTIONS TO YOUR MESSAGE

Think about how your readers' job responsibilities, attitudes, or experiences may affect their responses to your communication. Are there circumstances related to your request that might cause a negative reaction to it? For example, is this the third time you have written to ask for the same piece of information? Do you have a deadline of the end of the day? Does your manager, who is away today, normally handle these requests? If you can anticipate possible objections to your request, you can address these potential problems as you organize and present your message. If you can overcome possible objections as you deliver your message, you are more likely to achieve success. But to anticipate problems, you must understand your readers and their point of view and experience.

Figure 1.4 appeared taped inside the elevators in a condominium. It does not model good communication for a variety of reasons, including the fact that many people who would view the message rent the units and are not the owners. Because they rent, these readers may stop reading once they realize they are not the intended audience, so the age of the hot water tank in their unit will not be assessed. An objection that might be anticipated by owner readers is the expense of replacing a hot water tank. The writer attempts to motivate these readers to act by pointing out the inconvenience to *other* people if the tank malfunctions. To what extent will these readers be motivated by an appeal to their altruism? The legalistic direction to "relay same via email" increases the emotional distance between the Board of Directors and the unit owners and decreases the likelihood that owners will comply.

NOTICE TO RESIDENTS

The Corporation is currently dealing with a water damage loss which has affected some common element areas. This will result in some inconvenience while repairs are underway.

We wish to take this opportunity to remind unit owners that older hot water tanks should be replaced in a timely fashion.

NO ORIGINAL TANK SHOULD STILL BE IN USE

If you have any questions or concerns, please relay same via email or drop a note through the office mail slot.

Everyone's cooperation is appreciated.

Board of Directors

Figure 1.4 **Notice to residents. This notice does not motivate readers to comply.**

In the revised memo in Figure 1.5, the writer states the problem and its result in paragraph one. Paragraphs two and three elaborate the problem and give details to help residents determine whether their hot water tank may need replacing. The closing paragraph addresses the renter audience to explain how the situation affects them and aims to motivate readers to replace original hot water tanks by highlighting the consequences of further water damage to the building.

NOTICE TO RESIDENTS AND OWNERS

Water leaks from older hot water tanks continue to cause damage to common areas and other units. Repairs resulting from this damage are ongoing.

Original hot water tanks (tanks that were installed when the building was new) should be replaced immediately. Original tanks were all Bradford-White models; if you have a different brand in your unit, this notice does not apply to you. If you are unsure, please contact the building office and we'll be happy to take a look to confirm that your hot water tank is not an original one.

If you are not the unit owner, please contact the owner to ensure that the original has been replaced.

With everyone's cooperation, we can avoid unnecessary expenses and the resulting increases in monthly condominium fees.

Board of Directors

Figure 1.5 **Revised notice to residents and owners.**

DEMOGRAPHICS

Consider the major demographic categories to which your readers belong: race, class, culture, and gender. These aspects of an individual's social identity can affect how they communicate with others. Occasionally, these aspects can present obstacles for your readers in responding to your request. Considering how these aspects may shape your readers' response to your message can help you prepare your message to better fit their needs or expectations.

Demographic characteristics refer to such aspects of your readers as their age, their sex or gender, their socioeconomic background, their level of education, their ethnic background, and their ideological beliefs, including religion and political affiliations. Each of these categories contributes, to a greater or lesser degree, to making up the individual, along with his or her genetics and environmental factors. Demographic characteristics offer potential ways to gather or infer information about readers that make up your audience. For example, if an organization has updated its retirement benefits, you can infer and perhaps gauge the level of interest of its employees based on their age groups. You would expect those employees in mid- or late career to be particularly interested to learn about the changes and want to know in detail how those changes may affect them. Younger employees may be interested in the changes generally (or not), but because retirement seems a long way off, they may not want a detailed explanation of what the changes mean for them. Of course, individual responses will vary based on other demographic characteristics in addition to age (not to mention other factors).

It is easy to assume that readers might share your perspective on an issue and find persuasive those arguments that you are used to making or that would generally persuade you or your friends and family. But it is important to think carefully about your readers, if not individually, then at least as groups of perspectives, so that you can consider what your readers might value in order to decide whether they will find your points engaging. The term "engaging" is intended to draw your attention to the necessity in business and professional communication of motivating your audience to actually read your message. If you misunderstand what your readers think is important, they will abandon your message to do more pressing work. So gauging your readers accurately and then engaging them appropriately (that is, by framing your message so that they recognize its importance and relevance to them) help you increase the chances that your messages are at least read.

For example, if, as an employee of City Hall, you are creating a brochure about municipal dog-licensing information and bylaws for city residents, a primary underlying goal is not just to inform readers but to persuade them to buy licenses for their dogs. While dog owners generally all share some values (animal companionship), they differ widely in age, gender, socioeconomic status, ethnicity, and so on, differences that will affect their priorities. For example, to low-income dog owners the cost may be an issue, especially the higher licensing fee for unspayed or un-neutered dogs, a surgery that is also costly. To convince these readers to buy licenses, would it be more effective to tell them it is a bylaw offence to not license their dogs or to point out that a license will help them get their dog back if it gets lost?

Exercise 1.1: What Does Your Audience Value?

Read this list of benefits of owners buying licenses for their dogs:

- It allows owners to comply with a City bylaw.
- It helps fund the City Pound to provide food, shelter, and homes for stray animals in the city.
- It encourages animal population control.
- It enables staff at the City Pound to contact owners in case of emergency to make decisions regarding the care of their pets.
- It allows a member of the public to return owners' lost pets before they are impounded.
- It is cost-effective.
- It offsets the expense of animal services, including protection from dangerous dogs, shelter and care for lost dogs, investigation of dog attacks, and public awareness and education.
- It enables lost dogs to reunite with their families.

Individually, in pairs or in groups of three, discuss and order these benefits to reflect which ones you think would *most* engage and persuade readers to consider buying licenses for their dogs based on these demographic factors: age, sex/gender, ethnicity, socioeconomic status, level of education, ideological beliefs.

Are there some demographic factors that you think might affect dog owners' decisions more than others? Which factors? Why do you think those factors might be more important than others? Make a record of your group's discussion so that you can summarize and share it with the whole class, as your instructor directs.

How Might a Diverse Population Affect Communication?

To engage the members of a demographically diverse audience (for example, renters in a large city), you face a more challenging task because of the range of perspectives that need to be addressed. The message should contain the type and level of detail that each group wants while remaining clear and concise. Two strategies can help you to adapt your message to distinct readers. First, consider the range of perspectives among your groups of readers and include some information relevant to the major groups while directing them to additional sources for details (perhaps an attached PDF detailing the changes to renters' rights legislation in the city or a link to the renter information webpage). Second, consider whether you can create versions of the message that highlight different aspects of the information that different groups might want.

Audiences can also differ culturally and linguistically. In the United States, immigration may have declined slightly over the last few years, but in excess of one million people still applied for permanent residence status every year between 2016 and 2018. Similarly, in Canada, over one million people immigrated between 2011 and 2016 (the most recent statistics available). While some immigrants speak English (or French) as their birth language, many of them do not, and they come from countries and cultures that are significantly different from those of North

America. When you compose messages that address readers from a range of cultures, you need to consider the range of perspectives and attitudes that these readers may hold on the issues you are discussing and adapt your message to take these differing perspectives into account. When you respond to the diversity of your readers in organizing your message, you are more likely to find yourself communicating successfully with them.

Exercise 1.2: How Does a Diverse Population Affect Communication Processes?

North America's populations are becoming increasingly diverse. The statistics in Figure 1.6 (from Statistics Canada) and Figure 1.7 (from the US Department of Homeland Security) highlight this diversity.

1. In groups of two or three, review the statistics in both figures and identify which statistics you find most surprising.
2. Consider how the implications of this influx of immigrants might change Canadian and American society. Further consider the implications of these changes for professional and business communicators in the United States and in Canada.
3. Then discuss answers to the following questions:
   a. What implications do the statistics in both figures have for how we should communicate with each other in Canada and the United States, respectively?
   b. What kinds of assumptions should or can we make about one another when communicating?
   c. What kinds of assumptions might we have to abandon to communicate effectively with one another?
   d. What strategies might you use to learn more about the perspectives of your readers when communicating with them professionally?
   e. How might you use what you learn to create messages that engage and persuade readers?

Ethnocultural diversity

Immigrants (%)	21.9
Second generation population (%)	17.7
Visible minority population (%)	22.3
Number of recent immigrants (landed between 2011 and 2016)	1,212,075

Source: From the 2016 Census of Population, Statistics Canada, https://www.statcan.gc.ca/eng/subjects-start/immigration_and_ethnocultural_diversity

Figure 1.6 **Ethnocultural diversity in Canada.**

Region of Birth	2016	2017	2018
TOTAL	1,183,505	1,127,167	1,096,611
Africa	113,426	118,824	115,736
Asia	462,299	424,743	397,187
Europe	93,567	84,335	80,024
North America	427,293	413,650	418,991
Oceania	5,588	5,071	4,653
South America	79,608	79,076	78,869
Unknown	1,724	1,468	1,151

Source: Department of Homeland Security, https://www.dhs.gov/immigration-statistics/yearbook/2018/table3

Figure 1.7 Cultural Diversity in the United States: US Permanent Resident Applicants' Region of Birth, 2016–18.

COMMUNICATION NETWORKS

formal communication networks: People who are listed in a formal organization chart with you

informal communication networks: People you share information with at work but do not formally report to or work with

All organizations have **formal and informal networks of communication**. Formal networks spread information on the basis of who *should* know. Typically, formal networks consist of reporting structures that make information available through traditional emails and memos within work units. Informal networks move information around without regard to a particular person's status within the organization and tend to consist of chat sessions and email exchanges between workers who may not work in the same unit and have no formal relationship to the information being shared. Understanding where these networks exist and how to use them can help you when you need to spread information across an organization or, instead, keep something quiet. Knowing to which group or groups your readership belongs can help you decide whom to contact when you want a particular message to circulate or stay confidential.

Link Your Goals with Readers' Needs

If you think about your readers in terms of the five areas discussed in the previous sections, you can begin to understand your readers' needs and goals. For example, if you are requesting information from coworkers in another unit, they will be focused on their own work and on meeting their work-related deadlines for that day. Your request for information will interrupt what they are doing and delay or even prevent them from meeting their specific goals (for example, finishing drafting a report). You can motivate them to put aside their report draft to find or create the information you need and send it to you only if you write a message that shows them how helping you can also help them. That is, you want to communicate how doing what you request will help them meet other goals they may have, if not the specific goal of finishing that report. Therefore, by discerning the needs and goals of your readers, you can align your own goals with theirs to present your ideas in ways that motivate them to act on your request. Once you analyze your readers accurately, you can then focus on writing your message from their viewpoint. If your readers respond quickly and competently to your request, then it is likely that you have successfully linked your readers' goals with your own.

Figure 1.8 is a sample memo that communicates from the reader's viewpoint. The memo is annotated to highlight the strategies that the writer has used to align his request with his readers' needs.

MEMO

To:	Conference planning team members
From:	Bob Singh
Re:	Completion of first stage of planning
Date:	2015-01-27

Thanks again for stepping up to help out with the planning of this year's national sales conference. With your help, the number of possible locations has been narrowed to 4 finalists:

- New York, NY
- Montreal, QC   *Add lists*
- San Diego, CA
- Vancouver, BC   *Bold key items*

Our final selection meeting will take place on **Friday, February 7, from 1:00 to 3:00 in the first floor conference room (1–100).**

Preparing for the next meeting   *Headings*

For the meeting, please review the background materials for each site and identify your first choice and a second choice. We will discuss the rankings until we settle on one location. You may note that several of the initial sites did not make it to the final group, but the initial ranking process was important for us to narrow the choices.   *Anticipate questions*

Use "you"

I am looking forward to seeing you all on Friday the 7th. In the meantime, thank you for the time you have already put into this process. I'm sure that it will result in the selection of a site that the entire sales team will appreciate.

Figure 1.8 **Writing from the readers' viewpoint.**

HOW TO ORGANIZE YOUR INFORMATION IN RESPONSE TO YOUR READERS' VIEWPOINTS

Typically, the goal of professional communication is to transmit or elicit information. As a writer you will often be requesting that readers do something. However, before readers can comply with a request, they must understand what you need. If you link these goals to what your readers need, you are most likely to get readers to comply. One strategy is to look at the situation from your readers' viewpoint to ensure that you communicate your ideas in a way that is useful to them. For example, if you use language that reflects their viewpoint, they are more likely to understand why they need to act.

In Figure 1.8, the writer organizes the message to respond to his understanding of his readers' viewpoints. He starts by informing readers of an upcoming meeting (why have they received this message?). Paragraph one summarizes relevant information about the meeting: (1) its purpose (to select conference city), and (2) details about the meeting (day, time, place). Paragraph two informs readers about how to prepare for the meeting (that is, what the meeting requires of them), what the discussion will address (what they will talk about), and then anticipates and responds to potential reader objections/questions about the finalist locations ("Hey, why is New Orleans off the list?!"): "You may note that several of the initial sites did not make it to the final group." If you organize your message so that it takes into account their perspective, they will understand how to respond to your request.

Here are four ways to put your readers' needs first at the organization level:

1. Arrange the points in your communication to reflect their needs.

Answer the following questions to help you figure out how to present your message:

What will readers want to know first?

What might they object to in your message?

How might you overcome these objections?

What details might they overlook in your message?

Will your readers appreciate emphasis (use of bold, italic words) on the points they care most about?

Once you answer these questions, you have important information about how to structure your message to tailor it to your readers' viewpoints.

2. Emphasize the points that are relevant to your readers.

The writer in Figure 1.8 uses three formatting techniques to emphasize what he believes readers want to know:

a. he **lists** the four location choices so the white space highlights them;

b. he uses a **bold typeface** for the meeting details;

c. he inserts a bolded **heading** to inform readers how to prepare for the meeting.

3. Add headings and lists to visually emphasize main points.

Visual emphasis or changes of formatting are effective for drawing your readers' attention to the main points of your message. When you change the formatting by inserting a list or headings, you use the white space around the list or heading to make it stand out.

4. Anticipate questions readers might have and include answers.

As noted in 1. above, your pre-writing planning should have identified any possible objections readers might have to complying with your message and considered strategies for addressing if not overcoming those objections. In Figure 1.8, the writer suspects that some committee members may be upset about the list of final locations, so he explains why these cities are finalists: "the initial ranking process was important for us to narrow the choices"; that is, after the first round of votes, these four got the most support.

HOW TO CHOOSE WORDS AND STRUCTURE YOUR SENTENCES TO RESPOND TO YOUR READERS' VIEWPOINTS

In addition to structuring your message to respond to your understanding of your readers' viewpoints, you can further demonstrate that you understand their needs in your choice of diction and sentence structure. Here are five ways to put your readers' needs first at the sentence level:

1. Emphasize what readers receive, not what you are doing for them.

You may be tempted to highlight for readers what **you** are doing **for them**, but your message will be more successful if you rethink this approach and focus on highlighting what readers will receive. For example, the following sentence emphasizes the actions of city government staff: "If your dog is licensed, then if it has a health crisis while at the pound, our staff can call you to consult about your pet's emergency care." Revising this sentence emphasizes the readers' viewpoint: "If your dog is licensed, then if it has a health crisis while at the pound, you can be contacted and consulted about your pet's emergency care."

2. If you are replying, refer specifically to the issue or request raised by the reader.

3. Don't tell readers how *they* are feeling; don't tell readers how *you* are feeling.

For example, a message that begins "You will be thrilled to learn that your child has been selected to receive a free ..." tells readers how they should be feeling, but it may or may not accurately reflect the reader's emotions. What if the reader's child is gravely ill or even deceased? Misstating readers' reactions can make your message unsuccessful. Similarly, a message that begins "I am thrilled to inform you that ..." emphasizes the writer and de-emphasizes readers, a tactic that ignores the reader's viewpoint. Given the hazards associated with addressing feelings in your message, a good strategy is to omit any discussion of feelings (yours or your readers') altogether.

4. If your message is positive, use "you" more often than "I."

This strategy helps you to maintain emphasis on your readers and de-emphasize your own actions, resulting in a message that helps recipients focus on and appreciate your positive message.

5. If your message is negative, shun "you" to avoid assigning blame.

When writing a message that is negative, avoid explicit use of "you" to address readers because your message will not communicate successfully, obviously, if you blame readers for the bad news.

Rhetorical Situation 1.1: BookTime: Unspent Gift Cards

© Andrey_Popov/Shutterstock

Haylee Bostick has just finished setting up a feature table of books by regional authors at BookTime, a nationwide chain of bookstores. As a full-time college student, she juggles her classes at the nearby university and nearly full-time hours at the bookstore. She appreciates her manager, Gwin Patel, who allows her to schedule her work hours around her classes each term. Gwin has noted that when Haylee works a split shift of mornings and evenings with her classes in the afternoon, it benefits the store as well. Gwin approaches Haylee, nodding toward the feature table. "This display looks terrific, Haylee," says Gwin.

Gwin then explains Haylee's next task: an email has arrived from Head Office requesting information about the store's gift-card sales. The company chief financial officer wants figures on the cash value of gift cards sold during the previous year, as well as current redeemed dollar totals. Gwin then acknowledges that she has previously asked Haylee to collect and reshelve unpurchased books, but this new request means they have to reprioritize to calculate these statistics for Head Office.

Haylee agrees, and Gwin indicates that she will forward the email message to Haylee shortly. "Once you collect the details, you can also draft our response. Send me the draft after lunch so I can send you revisions ASAP. I want our report back to them today."

Haylee replies that she will do her best. She is familiar with the specialty sales function of the records database, so it shouldn't take long to pull out those figures. First, though, she will read the email (see Figure 1.9) to see exactly what Head Office is requesting.

To:	BookTime Store Managers
From:	Diego Battista, Assistant to CFO, Financial
Re:	Gift Card Redemptions
Date:	October 3, 2020

The table below shows sales and redemption figures for gift cards over the last four years. Note that for the gift cards sold in line 3, more than $42,000 is still outstanding (as of September 30, this year).

Year	Gift Cards Purchased	Gift Cards Redeemed
2017	$97,350	$96,975
2018	$102,800	$101,500
2019	$115,750	$72,500
2020	$147,375	$87,025 (to date)

BookTime has never had this large a surplus of unredeemed gift cards before. To reduce this amount, we are launching a marketing campaign in November targeting consumers with unused cards. We need to know which stores are logging the most unredeemed cards to target those areas. To help marketing develop its campaign, we need your sales and redemption figures for last year's gift cards ASAP. Please also determine whether or not you were the initial seller for redeemed cards.

We appreciate your prompt cooperation, and we anticipate your figures no later than October 8.

Figure 1.9 Email from Head Office requesting gift card redemption sales for 2020.

ANALYSIS: AUDIENCE FOR THE BOOKTIME GIFT-CARD MEMO

As you can see, the email from Head Office may have been directed to the store manager, Gwin Patel (the primary audience), but she is only *one* of the groups that reads it. Haylee also reads it, as a secondary audience member who assembles the numbers for Store 329. Before Battista sent it out, he had someone else review it—his boss, Jacques LaPlante, CFO at BookTime, whose priority it is to balance company books for the previous year. LaPlante is both the initial audience, who asked Battista to draft the message, and the gatekeeper, who approved the message before its distribution to store managers. In the case of the message from Head Office, there is no watchdog audience because this communication is an internal matter for the company. Watchdog audiences are present when an organization creates external public communications. For example, once the gift-card audit is complete, the company might create an advertising campaign to encourage gift-card holders to spend their cards. In this Rhetorical Situation, the watchdog audience for the campaign could include a customer who receives the promotional materials but responds, "I don't want to use my 2019 gift card to pay for this book for my brother-in-law. I'll use my gift card when *I* want to use it." The customer can postpone using his gift card, but he can't prevent the company's pitch to persuade customers to redeem their cards.

Memo from Book Time Head Office	
Writer of Memo from Head Office:	Diego Battista
Battista's Initial Audience →	Jacques LaPlante (He read Battista's draft)
Battista's Gatekeep Audience →	LaPlante (He approved Battista's draft)
Battista's Primary Audience →	Gwin Patel (Branch Manager)
Battista's Secondary Audience →	Haylee Bostick (Assistant to Branch Manager)
Response Memo from Store 329	
Writer of Response Memo from Store 329:	Haylee Bostick
Bostick's Gatekeep Audience →	Patel
Response Memo's Primary Audience →	Battista
Response Memo's Secondary Audience →	LaPlante

Figure 1.10 **Some audiences for the original memo from Battista (Head Office) and Gwin's response.**

UNDERSTANDING HAYLEE'S READERS

Planning is a crucial first step in preparing to write any message or document. To make sure you understand your rhetorical situation (what you are writing, why, and to whom), answer this series of questions:

- Who are your readers?
- What do these readers need to know?
- What are possible objections these readers may have to the message?
- How can you address and/or overcome these potential objections in your message?
- What unintended readers might this message reach?
- What tone and level of language are appropriate?

Business Communication: Rhetorical Situations

1. Who are your readers?

As part of her pre-writing planning, Haylee analyzes her audiences for the draft message. She notes that the ostensible primary audience for the memo is Diego Battista, whose name will fill the "To" line. However, before Battista ever sees the message, it will first be reviewed by Gwin, playing the role of initial audience, and then approved by her (thereby playing a second role of gatekeeper audience). She also considers that the message will probably move beyond Battista's inbox, to be read by his administrative assistant and maybe even Battista's boss (secondary and unanticipated audiences).

2. What do these readers need to know?

Haylee thinks about what information should be in the message. Battista will likely skip over the message itself to get to the figures quickly, she reasons, so this means she should probably present the figures so they are easy to find and to process. She has already copied the figures into a spreadsheet as an attachment, but she decides to also copy and paste the table into the email message so there are multiple ways in which Battista can find and process the numbers. By anticipating his desire to obtain the numbers quickly, Haylee has tried to understand his viewpoint and needs as a reader.

3. What are possible objections these readers may have to the message?

Haylee next considers possible objections by Head Office (or Battista) to the figures that she will present. She wonders whether he might be concerned or worried about the figures he receives. She wonders how her store's numbers compare to other stores' numbers—do we have more or fewer gift cards unspent? Without more information, she decides, she can't overcome this point if it is an obstacle. Thinking further, she decides that since Battista initiated this request and issued a tight deadline, he will likely be pleased to receive this message. She concludes that she should present Gwin's numbers as positively as possible.

4. How can you address and/or overcome these potential objections in your message?

After pondering possible objections by her primary audience, Mr. Battista, Haylee ultimately decides not to explicitly address those she identifies. However, there will often be reasons for your readers to delay in responding to requests that you make or object to information that you send. Figure 1.11 presents such an email message. V. Bhatia informs a client that the report prepared by his organization will be delayed, a situation that his reader will likely object to. To forestall the client contacting him to negotiate a faster response, Bhatia explains the reason for the delay, offers an updated timeline (next week instead of this week), and outlines the actions he will take to ensure the client has the report as quickly as he can manage.

> To: Client
>
> Subject: Final Step: Receiving approvals
>
> Dear [client]:
>
> I am writing to let you know that there has been a delay in obtaining the final release approvals for your request.
>
> We have the report prepared, and I expect that we should receive the necessary approvals to release it early next week.
>
> I apologize for this delay and, once we receive those approvals, will send you both an electronic copy of the report immediately as well as the signed copy by same-day courier.
>
> Thank you for your patience,
>
> V. Bhatia
> National Marketing Research Coordinator

Figure 1.11 **Email message that addresses the writer's objections.**

5. What unintended readers might this message reach?

Another aspect of your rhetorical situation to consider as you plan your message is whether unanticipated readers might read it. In the case of Bhatia's message in Figure 1.11, his client might forward the message on to her boss.

Further, in Rhetorical Situation 1.1, Haylee will probably mention her work with gift-card sales to her aunt the next time they talk. Aunt Helen manages another BookTime store halfway across the country. In discussing the request from Head Office (which Aunt Helen will have received as well) and the number of unredeemed cards at her store, Haylee serves as a **communication bridge:** she moves information from her store (or group) on the Atlantic coast to her aunt's group on the Prairie/Mid-West. Once you consider possible unanticipated readers, you can make decisions about how you wish to represent yourself to them—perhaps more formally than if you expect only your primary audience to read your message.

communication bridge: Someone who moves information from one context or work environment to another

6. What tone and level of language are appropriate?

As she starts to assemble the data, Haylee decides she should know exactly what figures Head Office has requested. When she realizes she hasn't received the email from Gwin, Haylee dashes off an informal message to remind her (see Figure 1.12). However, before she clicks "send," Haylee rereads the message, reflecting that Gwin Patel is her boss and clearly above her in status and power. Even if we do have a good relationship, Haylee reminds herself, I probably want a more formal word choice to create a professional impression. She decides to revise the draft (see Figure 1.13).

To: Gwin

Subject: Where's the message?

Hey Gwin,

I haven't gotten the email from Head Office. Did you forget to send it? Any chance you could shoot it my way shortly?

Figure 1.12 **What not to do.**

To: Gwin

Subject: Copy of Request from Head Office

Hey Gwin,

I haven't received the email that you were going to forward from Head Office. Would you be able to send it again?

Thanks,
Haylee

Figure 1.13 **What to do.**

Once she finishes her planning, Haylee reflects on what her analysis of the rhetorical situation implies as she composes her message. She is writing for Gwin, so she will expect a message that represents her viewpoint: formal, respectful language, because Battista is Gwin's boss and, further, the message will be read by others beyond him. Next, Haylee considers Battista as a reader. She decides that he will need little explanation with the accompanying figures because he is already familiar with the larger context; therefore, the return memo should be polite in tone, formal in language, and concise and informative in content.

Exercise 1.3: What Do Readers Need to Know?

In earlier sections, we discussed making sure that everything readers need to know is present in the initial communication. Examine the memo from Head Office (Figure 1.9) to determine whether Gwin and Haylee have all the information they need to respond to the request.

1. Review the memo.
2. Make a list of the specific requests made.
3. Do you need any additional information about this request?
4. Brainstorm a list of ways of organizing this memo to highlight the information requested.

Exercise 1.4: Might Readers Have Objections?

In earlier sections, we discussed possible objections or obstacles readers might have to a writer's request. Can you think of any objections that Gwin or Haylee might have to hinder them from responding quickly to Battista's memo?

1. Brainstorm a list of attitudes, events, or responsibilities that might slow them down.
2. Generate a list of ways in which Battista could motivate his readers (including Gwin and Haylee) to act promptly.

Exercise 1.5: Link Your Request to Your Readers' Needs

Reread the memo from Head Office to assess how well the request responds to readers' needs. Use the methods for meeting readers' needs at the sentence and organization levels to help you determine how the memo might better meet this objective.

1. What order of ideas would best meet your understanding of Gwin and Haylee's needs?
2. How might you visually emphasize the information requested?
3. What changes would you make at the sentence level—that is, revise the wording, etc.—so that it takes into account Gwin's and Haylee's viewpoints?

Professional Communication Challenges 1.1

1. Write the return memo to BookTime Head Office

Assume the role of Haylee Bostick from Rhetorical Situation 1.1 and draft the follow-up memo for Gwin Patel to send back to Head Office. Figure 1.14 contains the gift-card figures for Store 329. Use the information in earlier sections to help you analyze your readers and then develop an organization and presentation of information that will best meet your readers' needs. Use Haylee's figures as the data in your memo.

Audience: Diego Battista, manager at Head Office, is your primary audience; Gwin Patel, manager of Store 329 and your immediate boss, is your initial/gatekeeper audience

Purpose: To communicate clearly and concisely the information about Store 329 gift card sales

Genre: Informative message sent via email

Business Communication: Rhetorical Situations

Store 329 Cards sold in 2020: 215	
A	B
Total of gift cards sold at Store 329:	$24,575
Sales from gift cards bought elsewhere:	$4,376
Total value of gift cards redeemed:	$18,350
Value of unredeemed gift cards sold at Store 329:	$6,225

Figure 1.14 **Haylee's gift-card figures for Store 329.**

2. Rewrite Diego Battista's memo

Assume the role of Diego Battista and revise the memo that went out to all BookTime store managers (Figure 1.9). Use the discussion in the first part of this chapter to decide what aspects of the memo should be revised to make it better respond to the goals and needs of the readers (use Gwin Patel and Haylee Bostick as representative of the audience for the memo). Focus on presenting the information in a way that will motivate your readers to respond quickly with accurate data.

Audience: Gwin Patel, manager of Store 329, as well as managers of all other BookTime locations

Purpose: To persuade store managers to send the requested information as quickly as possible

Genre: Persuasive message sent via email

PURPOSE IN BUSINESS AND PROFESSIONAL COMMUNICATION

 Identify the purpose and goals for the message

In all business communication, you need to identify the purpose of your message. Sometimes you will have to reply to communications that ask questions or request information; in these cases, your purpose is clear: to **inform** your audience. In some cases you will have to reply to a message that requires you to justify or explain a situation, cases in which your goal is to **persuade** your readers to accept or do something.

Most business and professional communication is motivated by some combination of these main goals: to persuade, to inform, to build goodwill, and to minimize follow-up communication. Writers communicate to provide information, to persuade readers to do or believe something or to sell an idea or product, and to create a positive impression of themselves or their company with their readers. A fourth goal may be to ensure that the communication is complete, to forestall any follow-up. Good writers also aim to build goodwill for themselves as employees and for their organizations.

inform: To use language strategies (including definition, statistics, and facts) to help your audience understand your topic in detail

persuade: To use language strategies (including logic, emotion, and credibility) to convince your audience to agree with you

Motivating Readers to Grant Your Request

Part of success in business organizations results from motivating readers to read your messages. If you constantly write long-winded email messages that do not get to the point of the message, readers will learn to avoid reading your emails. Motivate readers to read your messages by meeting their information needs. Earlier in this chapter we introduced the concept of meeting such needs; in this section we discuss that idea more thoroughly.

WHAT MOTIVATES YOUR READERS?

Generally, humans are motivated by needs. For example, most people work to earn money to buy food and pay rent. These are basic needs; more advanced needs might include feeling competent, being capable of looking after oneself, or even feeling good about accomplishing important work. Basic needs must be fulfilled before people can worry about more advanced ones. For example, if you haven't eaten for two days (a basic need), it's difficult to finish a work project (a more advanced need), let alone feel good about it (the highest level of need).

People are motivated by extrinsic factors (external to an individual) and by intrinsic factors (internal to an individual). Extrinsic motivators come from the outside. For example, if your workplace offers a cash bonus for the employee with the highest sales figures, you might work extra hard serving customers in order to win that prize. If the manager discontinues the bonus, you may no longer exert yourself to out-sell your coworkers. The bonus is an extrinsic motivator that shapes your performance at work.

Intrinsic motivators are internal; you derive inner satisfaction from doing something because of your personal beliefs or values. For example, you may believe that it's important that you give your best possible effort to everything you do, so you work hard at selling your company's products and you feel good about yourself whether or not you win the cash bonus because you know that you did your best. Your sense of satisfaction comes not from an external cash bonus but from meeting your intrinsic need to always do your best work.

As the examples show, intrinsic factors are more motivating than extrinsic ones. If an extrinsic motivator or need ends, the behavior it generates often ends too. In the context of writing persuasive messages in professional and business communication, you can achieve success if you can link your message to your readers' needs. As we mentioned in our earlier discussion of audience in this chapter, your readers are focused on their own goals and needs. They are not motivated to drop everything and do what you ask. However, if you can show them how helping you also helps them achieve their goals, they will be more willing to do what you request.

But first, of course, you must understand who your readers are well enough to identify their possible needs. For more information about analyzing audience (that is, understanding who your readers are), see earlier sections of this chapter. Once you understand who they are, you may infer some of the factors that motivate them. If you take these factors into account as you plan your message, you increase the chances that they will respond to your message, helping you to communicate successfully with them. Remember that intrinsic motivators are more effective than extrinsic ones, so aim to link your message to that type of motivator.

HOW DOES YOUR REQUEST MEET YOUR READERS' NEEDS?

As noted, once you identify possible needs that may motivate your readers, the next step in planning your message is to connect your request to those needs. For example, many bosses put a priority on saving time and money. If you see a way in which your company can save money by changing one of its current practices, you might pitch your idea to your boss, proposing that you develop the new procedure. Your idea helps make your boss look good by improving company processes, and you get approval to work on a new and interesting project.

Figure 1.15 illustrates one writer's attempt to link her request to the needs of her reader. The reader, Marcia Espinoza, has requested information about Laurie Stewart's research service. In her request, Marcia notes that she wants to get the research project under way quickly. Since Laurie knows that the client hopes for speed, she replies by requesting that they schedule a teleconference call, so that Laurie, her manager, and Marcia can exchange information about the research project more quickly than through email communication. The request for a conference call communicates to Marcia that Laurie values her project and understands her desire for prompt action.

To: Marcia

Re: Possible meeting times to discuss your research request

Dear Marcia,

Would you be available to speak with my manager and me at a time starting between 3:30 and 4:30 (Eastern time; 12:30 to 1:30 Pacific time) this afternoon? I expect that the conversation should only be about 30 minutes.

During this call we can cover the details of your research request, the outstanding documentation that we need from you, and the details of a specification sheet for your research request. *Reader needs*

If this time is not convenient for you, we are also available during these times:

- Between 11:30 and 12:30 (Eastern time) today (8:30 and 9:30 Pacific time)
- Between 3:30 and 5:00 (Eastern time) Tuesday (12:30 and 2:00 Pacific time)

We would be happy to call you. Could you please provide a phone number where we can reach you?

Thank you,

Laurie Stewart
Account Representative

Figure 1.15 **A message that responds to readers' needs.**

In the email, Laurie motivates her client to respond by making a clear request for a telephone call to clarify the details of the research request. The specific times she offers for the call and the clear statement of the call agenda both work to motivate Marcia to make time for this call. By offering to place the call, Stewart also removes a possible reason for Marcia not wanting to schedule it (the cost of a long-distance telephone call).

▲ Rhetorical Situation 1.2: Arena Boards North America: Unauthorized Employee Expenses

Arena Boards North America (NA) designs, manufactures, and installs the dasher boards for hockey rinks and indoor soccer fields. Their plexiglass and aluminum boards have revolutionized the industry. Based in a small city near the US–Canada border, they have sold and installed boards in hockey rinks and soccer fields in Canada, the United States, Russia, the United Kingdom, and the Middle East. Now several investors are interested in buying either part or all of the company. Arena Boards NA could definitely use the additional capital. It has taken a huge initial investment to install and program the robot to manufacture the arena boards to precise specifications.

The phone rings and Paul Zehr, the majority owner of Arena Boards NA, hears Mike Smith on the line. Mike is a summer intern who studies robotics at the local college and the son of one of their first employees. He wants to work on programming the new robot, but Paul prefers that summer students spend the first half of the summer on an installation crew. If Mike excels there, he can then join the coders to write manufacturing programs.

"What's up, Mike? This has to be fast because I have a meeting starting right away."

Mike explains that he has a problem. The trailer axle broke yesterday, and the repair shop wanted $1,500 to fix it. They both know the company credit card limit is only $500 so, Mike says, he had to put it on his personal credit card. Paul interrupts that the company credit limit is $500 for this very reason—so employees *can't* charge large unauthorized expenses to it. Paul demands to know why Mike didn't call yesterday to ask how to handle the problem before spending the money.

Mike tells him that he just didn't think about calling. He thought he needed to get back on the road to make it to the job in Spokane, Washington, by Tuesday. Mike's explanation does not satisfy Paul. He has potential investors waiting at the meeting so he tells Mike to send an email with all the details about what had happened. Paul says he will read Mike's message after the meeting and then figure out what to do.

Paul hangs up the phone and thinks, "Mike is a hard worker but he lacks judgment." Six months ago, the company was nearly bankrupted by employees like Mike purchasing supplies without oversight. Paul solved the problem by issuing small-limit credit cards so installation crews can buy small stuff while they are working on a job. For any expenses over $500, they must call the office and get his permission. $1,500 is way out of line for fixing a trailer axle, concluded Paul. What was Mike thinking?

ANALYSIS: AIMING TO KEEP THE JOB

When he writes his message about the axle repairs to Paul Zehr, owner of Arena Boards NA, what does Mike Smith want to accomplish? He needs to do several things:

1. Explain what happened
2. Justify his decision not to call the office
3. Get reimbursed for the cost of the trailer repairs
4. Keep his job so he can work on the robot later

His message will need to explain (or inform), justify (or persuade), and placate (or build goodwill). In this situation, he does *not* wish to end further communication with Paul Zehr, but he *does* want to include a full discussion of what happened so that Paul can understand and sympathize with Mike's predicament and decision-making process.

Exercise 1.6: What Is Mike Smith's Purpose in Writing?

Consider Mike Smith's purpose in the email he must compose to Paul. Discuss his writing situation using these questions as a guide:

1. To what extent is Mike's message an informative task? A persuasive task? What other goals do you think Mike should have for this message? Do you think one of these aims is more important than the others? Explain which one(s) and why.
2. How important do you think it is that Mike express his thoughts and feelings about the incident in his message?
3. Outline the informational elements Mike's message should contain. Then list the persuasive elements. Number these elements to reflect what you regard as their relative importance in helping Mike achieve his goals in his message.
4. How should Mike organize his points in this message? What advice would you give him about structuring his explanation to achieve the goals that you identified as important in #1 above?

MOTIVATING READERS TO GRANT MIKE'S REQUEST

 Develop a persuasive strategy that motivates readers to respond to written requests

Mike's two primary goals for his message are to *inform* Paul Zehr of what happened to the trailer axle and to *persuade* him that the decisions in handling the repairs are justified. The most challenging part of his message is the second part, persuading Paul that Mike made the right decisions. To be successful, Mike needs to show how his decision-making actually benefits Paul and the company. He needs to explain clearly why Paul should ignore company policy this once and refund the repair costs so that Mike can pay his personal credit card bill.

To accomplish his goals, Mike should follow these two steps:

1. Carefully analyze his audience to determine what motivates his reader: How does Paul feel? What does he fear? What does he need?
2. Clearly explain to Paul how retroactively approving and reimbursing his expense will meet Paul's needs.

What Motivates Mike's Reader? Mike must identify the intrinsic and extrinsic motivators that will help him to persuade Paul. What kinds of intrinsic and extrinsic needs might Paul have that Mike can try to meet in his email? As the owner of a relatively small manufacturing business with huge capital overhead, one of Paul's primary needs is to stay in business and make a profit. Mike's expenditure may have jeopardized this need, at least a little, unless he can show how the repairs will help the company profit.

How Does Mike's Explanation Meet His Reader's Needs? Many bosses prioritize saving time and money. If we assume Paul Zehr shares this value, we have an option to explain (writing as Mike Smith) that we could not avoid hitting a piece of debris on I-94 on our way through Chicago, and the impact broke the trailer axle. We got a quote for the repairs from the shop that happened to be right across the street from the exit off the freeway, as well as three other local repair shops. We chose the quotation that best combined low price with fast repairs (saving time and money) so the breakdown did not affect Arena Board's arena installation schedule for May (saving more time and money). In reference to this value of saving time and money, this part of the explanation is potentially useful to show Paul that Mike was trying to look out for the company's interests.

How Does Mike Show His Boss that His Request for Reimbursement Meets Their Needs? When you are requesting that readers do something for you, your discussion must move clearly from stating your request to explaining the reasons for your request. In Mike's case, he needs to request that his boss reimburse him for the unauthorized repairs and then explain why Paul should. Through the explanation, Mike must convincingly argue why his decision to ignore company policy and initiate the repairs is ultimately in the company's best interests. These points must be concrete and detailed enough that Paul can see and (Mike hopes) agree with his problem-solving process.

Let's examine some of the details that Mike can use as evidence to demonstrate he made a good decision. Here are the four repair quotes that he got:

- Rockford Fix-It had the parts and quoted $1,500 with the job completed in 24 hours.
- Busy Bee Auto quoted $800 and a week or more waiting for parts. While Mike waited for the parts, he would also spend six nights in a hotel ($150 per night), plus food ($50 a day).

- Jake's Fix-All was $1,250 and three days to express-ship parts (plus living expenses).
- Northern Illinois Mechanics was $1,100 and a week's wait (plus living expenses).

To put these data in perspective, Mike might then explain that he speculated that Paul himself would have chosen the lower total cost and the faster repair job to ensure he arrived at the next installation on schedule. If he were late arriving in Spokane, he would disrupt the tight arena construction schedule for multiple other contractors as well.

 ## Professional Communication Challenges 1.2

1. Write Mike Smith's email

Using the chronology outlined in Figure 1.16, as well as the details discussed in both Rhetorical Situation 1.2 and the previous section, draft Mike Smith's email to Paul Zehr, explaining how Mike came to spend $1,500 of his own money to repair the axle on Arena Boards NA's trailer. Incorporate the relevant ideas from this chapter on both audience and purpose to help you make a convincing case for Mike's solution to the problem. Your message should achieve these goals:

a. Inform Zehr of the trailer axle problem and Mike's solution
b. Persuade Zehr that Arena Boards NA should reimburse him for the $1,500 repairs
c. Demonstrate that Mike made a good decision and is a conscientious employee

Audience: Paul Zehr, owner of Arena Boards NA, who will approve reimbursement of the expenditure

Purpose: See three goals above

Genre: Persuasive message in email format

05/07	Leave Arena Boards North America plant Hit debris on I-94 through Chicago, IL
05/08	Rockford (IL) Red Roof Inn: Trailer axle on ground in parking lot Got four quotes on repair time/cost
05/09	Flatbed truck took trailer to Rockford Fix-It
05/10	Trailer repairs finished Headed north on I-90
05/11	Called Paul Zehr to ask for refund of repair costs

Figure 1.16 **Chronology of Mike Smith's trailer repairs.**

2. Write a memo explaining new company policy on credit card expenditures

In response to the unauthorized expenditure by Mike Smith, Paul Zehr has decided to explain the company policy more clearly in a memo to distribute to all employees. He usually delivers such information verbally at meetings, but after the $1,500 trailer repair bill, he wants each employee to receive a clear personal copy of the policy. Writing as Zehr, draft the memo that explains the company policy on credit card expenses and employee reimbursement on expenses over their employee card limit. Use the information in this chapter to explain the policy to Arena Boards employees and motivate them to follow the policy at all times.

Audience: All employees at Arena Boards NA who have a corporate credit card

Purpose: To explain the policy clearly and concisely, motivate readers to follow the policy, and ensure that no one else makes a purchase that exceeds their limit without first gaining manager or owner approval

Genre: Policy memo and persuasive message. For more information about how to format a memo, see Chapter 1, p. 27. For more information about writing persuasive messages, see Chapter 2 and Chapter 9, pp. 233–47.

BASICS ABOUT GENRE AND GENRE SETS

 Identify genres and determine how to use them in business and professional communication

In addition to audience and purpose, genre shapes how you respond to a situation in business and professional communication. Genre refers to the kind of communication that fits a particular situation. For example, if you want journalists to report on your company's event or new product, you write a press release rather than a memo. Memos are documents that communicate information among employees inside an organization. Memos are less formal documents than letters that go to people outside an organization, usually on company letterhead. The memo, the letter, and the press release may contain the same information, but the information is formatted and presented differently, depending on the genre. Speaking and presenting in person also take place in a variety of genres, such as the impromptu conversation in an elevator, the formal sales presentation, and the webinar. In many ways the genre of a communication is the most important choice a writer makes because the genre then controls the choices made by writers and speakers.

Readers respond to a document based on its genre. For example, a customer expects a letter; an employee expects a memo. Members of a work group often receive email announcements from human resources, frequently in the form of flyers. Meet your readers' expectation by using the correct genre to communicate with them.

Business and professional communication genres are often related. They form **genre sets**. One type of genre set is a group of documents that share a social context and are related to each

A **genre set** is a group of related documents.

Business Communication: Rhetorical Situations

other by purpose. These documents result in action, that is, work being accomplished. Here are some examples of this type of genre set:

- Academic Genre Set: Assignment Description and Course Paper or Project

A request for a proposal, often referred to by its acronym, RFP, resembles a school assignment, with which you are likely familiar. An instructor distributes an assignment description that details the paper or project requirements. Students read the description and produce a paper or project. Occasionally, an initial assignment stage is a proposal that describes the student's plan for the paper. More often, students just produce a paper to match the assignment description. The assignment description and the finished paper are a genre set. The assignment description initiates important work in the class—that is, students use it to create documents that demonstrate for instructors their understanding of the course material.

- Professional Communication Genre Set: Request for proposal (RFP), proposal and report

Similarly, an organization may publish a request for proposals because it has a problem that needs a complex solution. The RFP lists the specifications or requirements desired in the solution and invites qualified individuals or companies to submit proposals describing their solution. The organization selects the proposal for the solution it prefers, and the winner then executes the plan outlined in the proposal and produces the solution, which often takes the form of a report. The RFP, the proposal, and the report or completed solution are a genre set because the three documents are connected by purpose: in this example, their need to solve an identified problem. Solving a problem is the action often initiated by this type of genre set.

- The job application package (advertisement, application letter, and résumé)

You are no doubt acquainted with the documents involved in applying for employment. Generally, an advertisement describes a job opening; individuals with matching expertise apply by submitting a résumé or CV (curriculum vitae) and often a letter. In this case, the genre set results in suitable candidates being invited for interviews (action initiated), and ultimately the hiring of whoever is the best fit (purpose of the documents).

A second type of genre set is a group of documents that share a social context and are related to one another by audience. For example, in Rhetorical Situation 1.3, summer intern Melva Khan is asked to create two different genres with similar information to advertise an upcoming English as an Additional Language class at the local community center to different types of audiences. The first version, an email announcement, will be distributed to the center's membership list. The second version is a poster that will be displayed on announcement boards around the town to reach the general public.

Why Should You Know and Use Genre Conventions?

Know and use genre conventions to show that you are a competent, informed, and credible professional. Readers judge your competence and credibility based on whether you present your ideas in a form that they recognize and expect. You demonstrate that you are capable by showing that you know the basics. Use the conventions of business and professional communication so that readers can focus on your great ideas rather than on whether your ideas are as flawed as your presentation of them.

Rhetorical Situation 1.3: Rocky Mountain Community Center: Advertising a Class for New Immigrants

Melva Khan sticks her head in the door of Risa Gomez's office. "Is there anything else that needs to be done?" Melva has worked her way through the items Risa gave her when she arrived at Rocky Mountain Community Center three hours earlier. Melva is a student from nearby Rocky Mountain University, majoring in business and professional communication, who works summers at the community center. Melva enjoys the varied work at the center and the fact that she can spend her summers at home in the mountains.

Risa, the center manager, notes that they are offering a new English as an Additional Language class starting August 1. "You have good writing skills, don't you? We need an announcement and publicity flyer created and sent to center members." She notes that they will print off a few posters and put them on message boards around the town. Melva suggests they could also publish a version in the local paper. "Good idea, Melva!" Risa agrees, searching for previous announcements that Melva can use as models for the new one. She forwards them to Melva. As for the flyer, Risa tells Melva to use a template from the word processing program—"Pick one you like! Just include the Rocky Mountain Community Center logo on it somewhere."

Melva examines the sample announcements and notes they use a similar format. She sketches out the basic format (see Figure 1.17) and then lists the information for the announcement.

To:

Subject: Concise, clear statement of message topic

CC letterhead
Address
Phone numbers

Title of Course

Description: Date, time, who might be interested, focus of course, where/room, costs

Registration information:
Email to events@rockymtncc.org

1. The news (the reason for the announcement)
2. Who cares, why you should care, where, when
3. Summary of event
4. Information about community center
5. Center contact information

Figure 1.17 **Basic format for electronic announcement.**

The task seems straightforward enough. She gathers her notes and heads to the staff computer.

ANALYSIS: CONSTRUCTING THE EAL CLASS ANNOUNCEMENT

The announcement and flyer that Risa asks Melva to create contain the same information but are formatted differently. The two genres target different audiences. The email message will reach members of the community center, many of whom the center staff may know. The poster, however, can reach non-members because it can be displayed in public areas around the town or as an advertisement in the local newspaper. The genre of poster extends the community center's reach beyond its membership to connect with the general public, some of whom may be interested in the class but not familiar with the center. As you select your genre for a particular communication, consider whether your choice fits your target audience and purpose.

The Alberta Writes 2 flyer (Figure 1.18) is an example of a communication about an event. It

Figure 1.18 **Flyer for Alberta Writes 2.**
Source: University of Alberta.

differs from an email announcement because it has very little text on the page. The email announcement contains much more explanation of what the event is about, who might want to attend, and why they should attend.

Professional Communication Challenges 1.3

1. Write the email announcement to advertise Rocky Mountain Community Center's English as an Additional Language class

Use the information that Melva gathers from her supervisor in Figures 1.17 and 1.19 to create the announcement for the Rocky Mountain Community Center's upcoming EAL class.

Audience: Immigrants in the community around the Rocky Mountain Community Center who might be interested in improving their spoken English skills

Purpose: To inform readers of the details of the course and to persuade readers who might be interested to attend the class

Genre: Email announcement

2. Create the poster to advertise Rocky Mountain Community Center's English as an Additional Language class

Use the information that Melva gathers from her supervisor to create a poster to advertise the upcoming EAL class at Rocky Mountain Community Center. Design the poster (or use a word processing template) to catch the eye of members and non-members alike. Make sure that the poster contains all of the information that interested people will need to sign up for and attend the session. Use the community center logo in Figure 1.20 as part of your poster.

Audience: Rocky Mountain Community Center members and members of the local community who might want to enroll in an EAL class

Purpose: To attract viewer attention, to inform about the details of the course, and to encourage viewers to enroll

Genre: Poster

English as an additional language class

Aug. 7 to 24 (weekdays)

1:00 to 4:00 p.m.

Rocky Mountain Community Center, Room 206

Cost: Members $120
               Non-members $150

Sponsor: Pacific Coast YMCA

Leader: Risa Gomez

Contact: 123-4567

Center Hours: 8:30 a.m.–9:00 p.m.

Figure 1.19 **EAL course information.**

Figure 1.20 Rocky Mountain Community Center logo.
Source: NasirGrfx/Shutterstock

CHAPTER SUMMARY

- Audience is a key factor that helps business writers decide what to include and what to exclude from their communications.
- Audiences vary from the primary reader of a document to various secondary readers; business writers need to keep these secondary readers in mind when they write.
- Identify your primary purpose for writing before you begin to write: purposes include persuading, informing, and building goodwill.
- Carefully select the genre or kind of document you will use for your communication; make sure that the genre is appropriate and will accomplish your purpose for communicating.
- Use more than one genre or kind of communication when you need your message to reach different audiences.

CHAPTER 2

Argument in Professional Communication

 LEARNING OUTCOMES

1. Analyze how to solve a problem or navigate a difficult situation to arrive at the best communication solution

2. Demonstrate expertise in writing on a subject so that readers will find you trustworthy

3. Develop argumentative claims to explain and create a convincing case for a recommended solution

4. Synthesize information from supporting documents to create strong arguments

5. Choose the appropriate method of creating an emotional appeal and present the solution in a way that makes readers care about the subject

GETTING STARTED

This chapter introduces you to the components of argument, an essential skill in business and professional communication. Because this type of communication is primarily persuasive, you need to be able to make a convincing case for your perspective. Most communication in this area requires writers to analyze a problem and present a solution. You need to be able to think through the problem to write clearly about it and make a persuasive case for the action you recommend. To make a persuasive case for your solution, you must be able to use the building blocks of argument: **credibility** (why should readers listen to you?), **logic** (does what you are saying make sense?), and **emotion** (why should readers care?). Of these building blocks, credibility is most important. If readers do not view you as a competent speaker on the subject, they will not be persuaded, no matter how good your logic is or how well you appeal to your audience's emotions.

In the first Rhetorical Situation in this chapter, you meet Dan Cooper, who must manage his credibility in a letter persuading potential clients much older than himself to trust him with their retirement investments. This section shows you how to demonstrate your knowledge of the subject matter and show readers why they should trust you.

The second case introduces you to James Franklin, who has been asked to recommend whether the Prince Edward Island Department of Health Board of Directors should sell the waterfront between a nursing home and the ocean for commercial development. To recommend a course of action to the board, James must study the issues carefully, think through the implications of the sale, and understand the responsibility of the board in making this type of decision. This section explains strategies to help you analyze a problem and develop claims and supporting evidence (reasons) for the argument. It shows you how to motivate readers by linking your arguments to the readers' assumptions, values, and beliefs about the subject matter.

In the third section, Meijing Zhu, a summer intern in the hospitality industry, is asked to draft a letter to summer guests asking them to observe and abide by the resort's rules. This section shows you how to make readers more likely to care about the subject you are discussing. In this case, Meijing must use effective emotional appeals to persuade guests to follow resort rules while they are on vacation.

credibility: The sense of trust that you build in your audience through the way you present your document

logic: The reasons and reasonableness that you convey through what you say in your document

emotion: The passion, concern, or care you have for your topic

BASICS OF ARGUMENT

 Analyze how to solve a problem or navigate a difficult situation to arrive at the best communication solution

Argument is a central component of good business and professional communication. One of the main purposes of this type of communication is persuasion—for example, if you want coworkers to follow a new policy, issuing a command is unlikely to achieve your result. Instead, you should

present the policy and explain why it's important to adopt this policy. Argument or persuasion is about motivating readers to do something. If they want the outcome you are proposing, they may not need much motivation, but if you are proposing an action that they do not value or outright resist, you must work harder to persuade them to act. If everyone in the office wants a clean lunchroom, your message might require less in the way of passion to motivate them but more in the way of procedures about how to accomplish your shared goal of a clean workspace. In Chapter 1, we discussed this idea as one of overcoming reader objections to motivate them to do as you ask.

Logic, credibility, and emotion work together to persuade readers. Motivating readers often requires getting them to read the message. If readers don't care about the subject matter (emotion), they generally won't bother to read further. You need to use emotion to engage readers' attention so that you can explain why the change of behavior is important (logic) and what the advantages are to the change (logic and emotion). They are more likely to read the message if you present the basic information clearly and concisely so they understand the issue and your reasoning makes sense to them (logic and credibility). Once they trust your grasp of the issue, they are more willing to consider your request (credibility), and if you can show them how different behavior will benefit them and everyone else (logic), you can motivate them to follow the new policy (your persuasive goal). As you can see, the elements of argument (credibility, logic, and emotion) work together to achieve persuasion.

Credibility

Rhetorical Situation 2.1: ES Investment Group: Locating New Clients

Getting a position as an investment services consultant with ES Investment Group (ES) was a step up from his first professional job at the bank, and Dan Cooper was happy to leave for something that offered performance-based incentives and a real degree of freedom. ES offers—no, requires—that he develop his own group of clients. It is a little like starting up his own business or franchise. ES provides the office, the training, and the support network needed to provide a full range of financial consultation services. All Dan has to do is find the clients.

Finding the clients is turning out to be a challenge. In the six months since he started at ES, he's gone to all the training and marketing seminars. He's done three seminars on his own with groups of people generated from his immediate social network in the Burlington area—friends of his parents, his friends' parents, and people he knows from growing up in the area. In addition to these contacts, he's sent out a personalized letter (see Figure 2.1) to names he obtained from a marketing firm that ES works with. The contact list was limited to individuals and couples living in a section of Burlington with high real-estate values.

ES has a standard letter that he could have used, but Dan feels that it isn't aggressive enough. He knows he needs to get results, and he wants to show this potential group of clients that he can do the job and actively work for them to reach their financial goals.

To date, however, the letter's results have disappointed him. After sending out the first batch of 20 letters, he received emails from eight of them and phone messages from five more. None of them has wanted to set up a time for a meeting, and several of them have been aggressively rude in their responses. One even mentioned that they would never trust their financial future to someone who can't use a semicolon properly, as if that makes any sense!

With this as the initial response, Dan knows that he can't send the same letter out again next week. He needs to revise it, obviously, but first he needs to figure out why it isn't working. For help, he turns to his uncle Steve, a management consultant who runs his own one-man company.

Steve reads the letter and comments that he understands what Dan is trying to do in it. To help Dan understand how the audience reacts to the letter, he starts reading it aloud and saying what he is thinking as he reads. "If you want to get anywhere near my money, you'll need, first and foremost, to convince me that you know what you're doing and that you're trustworthy. It seems like every year there is another case of some investment advisor running off with the life savings of all-too trusting friends and relatives. How do I know I can trust you? Well, you work for Edward Schwab, which means you aren't an unvetted, independent financial consultant. Emphasize this point in your letter. After the letterhead, you don't mention anything about the company until the third paragraph. They are a great company—over 40 years in the business with a long list of clients. They sponsor baseball and hockey teams in the recreational leagues here. You need to draw more attention to their work in the community. And when you do talk about the company, you need to stress the network of professionals that you have behind you—independent advisors don't have that. It is another major advantage of yours."

Dan starts to stand up, but Steve gestures for him to sit back down. Steve makes the point that Dan also needs to show readers that *he* is qualified to advise them. Dan needs to give them a specific example of how he has helped someone. One example could be the tip Dan gave Steve about borrowing from his own RRSP/IRA rather than the bank for a short-term loan. Dan needs to talk more about specific examples of how his readers can organize their finances better. By providing help in this way, Dan doesn't have to be so aggressive about calling them. They will *want* to call him to see what other tricks he has.

© reedomz/Shutterstock

ES Investment Group

Dan Cooper
Investment Services Consultant
dan_cooper@edwardschwab.com

July 4, 2020

John and Joan Pleva
29 Beaver Street
Burlington, VT

Dear Mr. and Mrs. Pleva,

I am Dan Cooper and I am a consultant with ES Investment Group. I am looking to find people who are results-driven, open to new ideas, willing to take advice, and have the ability to look beyond the short term. Smart investors like yourself should be looking to improve your current financial situation by putting in practice innovative new ideas presented to you. These ideas have the potential to increase your overall wealth while reducing risk. To work with these ideas you should have some knowledge of investing. Here are the characteristics of the people who I can help the most; individuals with $400,000 in investable assets, have a mortgage, and have some specific financial goals in mind. Those goals could include paying off a mortgage or taking a vacation every year.

The real estate market over the last couple of years has been up and down but overall up. Increases over time in the city has trickled down and allowed even the residents of Burlington and the surrounding area to reap extraordinary growth in the value of their home. This growth however has caused some individuals to become over confident with this market. I'm as excited about the growth in the local real estate market as most homeowners but, as we have seen markets go up and down. My job is to help you navigate the turns in the markets through sound financial planning.

My promise is that working with me will bring you the best professional advice and service available. With an unlimited number of specialists, not just at ES Investment Group, but also with a network of professionals, I can assist you; i.e., Accountant, Lawyer, etc. Our goal will be to work as a team to create a financial plan and REACH these goals. Are you serious about creating wealth and reducing risk? If so then call me to arrange a ½ hour meeting.

I will be in touch on July 17th to set up a time for us to meet together and talk about how I can assist you and if appropriate create an investment plan. To avoid a phone call follow-up please respond via email or leave a telephone message at my office. I look forward to speaking with you in the near future.

Sincerely,

Dan Cooper

Dan Cooper

1159 New Street, Burlington, VT
PH: 123-123-4567 • TOLL FREE 800-123-4567 • FAX: 123-234-5678

Figure 2.1 **Dan Cooper's letter to prospective clients.**

Steve recalls that Dan was on the investment team at university that came third in the University/College Investment Challenge. He advises Dan to highlight that achievement. It shows that Dan knows what he is doing and may have new ideas that even experienced advisors haven't kept up with. Steve also mentions the semicolon and advises Dan to proofread the revised letter before he sends it out. Steve also advises Dan to have someone else look at the final draft as well. "My point is that people really do judge a book by its cover—or in this case its cover letter," he notes. "Faulty punctuation suggests that the writer may also be incompetent or sloppy in his financial advice. Right or wrong, this is how people make judgments."

Dan thanks his uncle. As he leaves, he heaves a huge sigh. What a brutal review of his first attempt at the letter! But Steve's insights have really helped him understand why his letter isn't working the way he expected. His next challenge is to revise it, and soon, before it costs him any more potential clients.

BASICS ABOUT CREDIBILITY

 Demonstrate expertise in writing on a subject so that readers will find you trustworthy

Credibility, or the readers' sense that writers know their subject matter, is the first element of a persuasive message. If readers are already acquainted with you, their response to your message is shaped by their prior knowledge, but if your message is their first point of contact, their only basis for judgment is your words and any additional details such as your email address, your job title, or your company letterhead. As they read your message, readers also assess your level of knowledge of the topic based on how you discuss it. They judge the reasons you offer for the statements you make and factor those judgments into their evolving sense of your credibility. That is, they extrapolate from your writing what you are like as a person. If you seem to know your subject matter and your discussion of the issues is clear and free of errors, they are likely to start believing that you are informed, have a grasp of the issues, and therefore can be trusted. Once readers believe that you are competent, they will pay attention to your actual message. On the other hand, if they decide that you are not a credible speaker, it doesn't really matter what you say: they will ignore your message if possible.

trust: The judgment that you can believe what a person says

This issue of **trust** is important, not only with financial advisors but also with writing in general. If readers don't trust what you say as a writer, you have no hope of persuading them of your argument. The key to proving yourself trustworthy in writing is demonstrating that you know what you are talking about. Here are four ways to demonstrate your expertise:

- include details to show your breadth or depth of knowledge of the subject
- describe any opposing viewpoints fairly and accurately
- show how you and your readers share common ideas about the subject
- create a feeling of identification (sameness) between yourself and your readers

Show Your Knowledge of the Subject

You can show your knowledge of the subject in several different ways:

1. *Using or defining the vocabulary that is central to the discussion.* One way for readers to judge your competence is in your use of the vocabulary associated with your topic. Therefore, use the terms necessary to discuss the topic but avoid using jargon. For example, how would you feel about being treated by a doctor that offered you "some stuff for your problem" rather than "some ciprofloxacin for your endocarditis"? Most of us would prefer to put ourselves in the care of medical professionals who demonstrate their competence by specifically diagnosing and treating our illness. This situation extends to business and professional communication, where readers at least partially decide to act based on the perceived competence of the writer.

Which passage do you think is more credible and trustworthy? Why?

A recently published government report shows that more people are working longer than they did 25 years ago. Various historical and cultural reasons account for this extended work life. Many people 60 and older work because they have to.

Statistics Canada reports that in 2017 Canadians were working nearly three years longer than they did in the late 1990s. Over the past 20 years, the rate of people 60 years and older still working has nearly doubled, from 14% in 1997 to 26% in 2017. A similar trend is also apparent among workers in the United States. Myriam Hazel, analyst for Statistics Canada, identifies several factors that explain this trend, including a healthier older population, better educated workers, early life choices impacting later life, and changes in the older population's finances. She elaborates this last factor, noting that global events such as the 2008/2009 recession and the shift from defined benefit to defined contribution pension plans in the late 1990s–early 2000s have hindered some members of this group from saving enough to retire. As a result, nearly half of those people aged 60 and older who work do so out of necessity.

Figure 2.2 Quoting data and experts helps build your credibility as a writer.

2. *Quoting data or statistics related to the topic.* Another area that strengthens your credibility, especially in business and professional communication, is including relevant data and statistics. Figure 2.2 illustrates how the addition of relevant data builds trust in addition to developing a logical argument. For example, instead of stating that "more people are working longer," your writing will be more persuasive if you give specific numbers (as in the example). If you also have a specific person to quote, give the details about that person, their job, and the company they work for, to increase the persuasive power of your message: "Myriam Hazel, analyst for Statistics Canada [or the Bureau of Labor Statistics in the United States]."

3. *Interviewing and quoting experts on the topic.* A third strategy for building trust is to consult experts on the topic and include quotations to illustrate your knowledge of that topic. Effective quotations must be connected to the specific point you are making. Make sure you clearly draw the connection for the reader. For example, if you received a mailing from an investment firm inviting you to contact them about managing your investments, would you consider actually contacting them if they illustrated their networks of professional support by quoting some of their experts? How motivated might you be to contact an investment firm if their promotional materials included the first passage in Figure 2.2? Often quotations can make facts and figures come alive and provide some narrative structure for readers to help them understand and connect the various points you are making.

The statements in the first version in Figure 2.2 are vague and contain no data or details to strengthen the writer's assertion. The second version includes data and an expert commentator who explains the significance of the statistics.

4. *Presenting new ideas about the topic that show your careful consideration of it.* A fourth way to demonstrate your knowledge of the subject is to include details that show you understand the issues. If you make a point about the topic that readers have not considered, you grab their attention while also showing them that you have given the subject matter some thought. For example, Figure 2.3 presents the promise of ideas in the first passage compared to a specific idea that illustrates the writer's ability in the second passage. The use of appropriate technical language in describing the idea also serves to build the writer's credibility.

Describe Opposing Viewpoints Fairly

A second way to demonstrate trustworthiness lies in summarizing and addressing viewpoints that are contrary to your own. By acknowledging contrasting perspectives, you show your broad knowledge of the topic. By summarizing them fairly and accurately, you show readers that you are a broad-minded thinker who is aware of and makes an effort to understand opposing viewpoints. Readers are more inclined to trust writers who are open-minded and sympathetic to new and different ideas. The argument about financial advisor fees (Figure 2.3) would be more effective if it acknowledged the opposing viewpoint (cheaper "robo advisor" software might make sense for people just starting out or who have accounts with less than $100,000). By acknowledging the opposing viewpoint, you demonstrate a level of sophistication in your own position, and that suggests you have thought deeply about the subject. If you show you think hard, you suggest that potential clients would find value in working with you.

Which advisor would you rather invest with?

Working with me I believe you will receive the best professional advice and service.	In the event of a market downturn, mutual fund management fees of 2 per cent or more can significantly reduce your investment returns. For this reason, I only recommend mutual fund companies with management expense ratios (MER) of less than 1 per cent.

Figure 2.3 **Demonstrate that you understand the topic by presenting new ideas.**

Show How You Share Common Ideas with Your Readers

A third way to gain reader trust is to show that you and your readers share similar beliefs (about how the world works) and values (ideas about what is important in life). Of course, to do this, you must know what kinds of values and beliefs your readers hold. Analyze your audience carefully to figure out what your readers probably value (for more information about how to analyze your audience, see Chapter 1). At the same time, it is unethical to pretend you share readers' values if you do not. Instead, you should keep thinking about the subject until you do find a point about which you and your readers can agree (see Figure 2.4).

Which writer do you find more trustworthy?

Global warming fanatics, horrified to see their global warming consensus destroyed by scientific facts, have desperately attacked the scientists who contributed to the study. They decry those scientists and engineers as biased because many of them are employed by oil and gas companies in the US or Canada. These global warmists also emphasize that because these geoscientists are not atmospheric scientists they are unqualified to understand the science or speak on global warming. Finally, they assail the skeptical scientists' objectivity while asserting that their own warmist scientists are immune to the influence of employment or sociopolitical factors.	Those who defend the theory of anthropogenic climate change have questioned whether the scientists and engineers who participated in the study could reach objective conclusions when many of them are employed by oil and gas companies in the US or Canada. They feel that those scientists may have been pressured by employers to express skepticism about the causes of climate change. Supporters also express reservations about scientists who speak out who are not specialists in atmospheric science and therefore may not understand the nuances of the science.

Figure 2.4 **Blatantly biased summaries of opposing viewpoints suggest that writers are narrow-minded and less trustworthy.**

Create a Feeling of Identification between Yourself and Your Readers

identification: The sense that your readers have moved beyond merely agreeing with you to joining your social group

Creating a sense of **identification** between yourself and your readers contributes a great deal to the process of creating a trustworthy impression and, with it, persuasion. If readers feel that they and you are alike, they are much more likely to accept your message. Here is a five-step method to create a sense of sameness between you and your readers (the list was created by Heather Graves, following Kenneth Burke):

1. List shared beliefs and values
2. Show how your interests are aligned
3. Show how you both "belong" to a privileged group
4. Identify points of conflict between your group and others
5. Invite readers to join you in taking common action

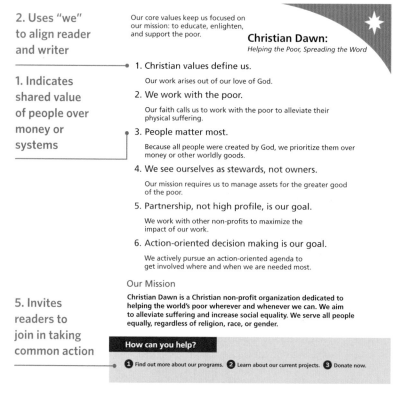

Figure 2.5 **This webpage creates identification to demonstrate the trustworthiness of Christian Dawn.**
Source: © Pearson Education, Inc.

List Shared Beliefs and Values: This strategy is similar to showing how you and your readers share common ground, but it goes beyond that method by detailing a discussion of the values and beliefs that underlie your claims. In Figure 2.5, the "Core Values" webpage of Christian Dawn explicitly identifies the six values to which the organization adheres. Although readers may not immediately identify with the first value, as they move down the list, they become more and more likely to share Christian Dawn's values. For example, most readers will agree that people should have priority over money, structure, or systems.

Show How Your Interests Are Aligned: In this step, you show readers how you and they can both benefit from your association. In Figure 2.5, Christian Dawn starts by emphasizing their values: "Christian values define us." The organization then elaborates these values, using "we": "*We* work with the poor" (emphasis added). Initially, the "we" may not include viewers, but as they move down the list, they are likely to see themselves, increasingly, as part of the "we" in "We see ourselves as stewards, not owners," "We work with other non-profits to maximize the impact of our work," and "We actively pursue an action-oriented agenda to get involved where and when we are needed most." Readers come to see themselves as aligned with Christian Dawn's compassionate interests—that is, to help alleviate the misery of the poor and less fortunate. As readers work their way through this text they become more and more drawn in to the vision and goals of the organization. That is, their viewpoints become more aligned with Christian Dawn, and, as a result, they come to see how having an association with Christian Dawn will benefit them.

Show How You Both "Belong" to a Privileged Group: Psychological research has shown that individuals feel a sense of closeness toward another person if they both share membership in the same group, whether formal or informal. For example, members of the same church (or religion) or service club often form business relationships because they trust one another based on their mutual experiences as members.

In business and professional communication, however, readers generally feel little connection to a writer or the organization when they first encounter a document or message. Consequently, writers must create the sense of connection through showing (not telling) readers that a special or privileged group exists to which they already belong—perhaps unbeknownst to them—or that they would benefit from joining. If writers can effectively build/create this sense of group membership for readers, they can successfully develop a highly persuasive argument/message.

Figure 2.6 presents an example of this step in action: the text box in the advertisement for Vulcan Youth Serum presents the series of stages of a typical "VYS user" experience: Skepticism → Reluctance → Conversion → Promotion → Rejection by friends ... The cycle repeats from 3 onward.

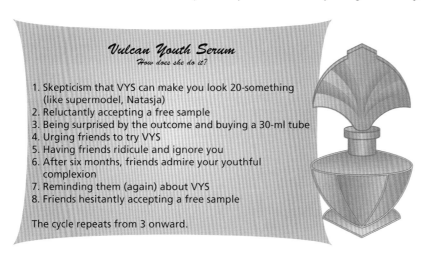

Figure 2.6 **Create a sense of identification with readers.**

In Figure 2.6, because many readers are going to be skeptical about yet another beauty product claim, the designers must disarm this response to capture potential readers' attention. They do this by creating a group of skeptical product users (of which readers are perhaps unwitting members) that the designers then show becoming converted into avid supporters. The trajectory suggests to actual readers that they join this latter group by trying VYS. The ad successfully enacts step 3 of creating identification by showing how readers are already members of one group associated with VYS and implicitly inviting them to join the unique group who found their skepticism about Vulcan Youth Serum misplaced.

Identify Points of Conflict Between Your Group and Others: The next step in creating identification involves building greater cohesion among the members of your group by showing how other groups are in conflict with them. Christian Dawn does not use this strategy in its webpage. Instead, the organization builds a partnership with viewers that brings them into the group based on their shared desire to help the less fortunate.

Invite Readers to Join You in Taking Common Action: This is the final step in creating identification and persuasion. When you feel you have established a sense of identity with your readers, you ask them to act in some way that brings your interests together and solves the problem(s) that you've described in your argument. In Figure 2.5, Christian Dawn concludes its list of values with a summary of "Our Mission," followed by the heading "How can you help?" The three steps invite readers to join Christian Dawn in taking common action to help the poor.

ANALYSIS: IMPROVING DAN COOPER'S CREDIBILITY

In Rhetorical Situation 2.1, Dan Cooper has 13 replies to his letter seeking new clients, all of them declining to meet with him. One of the callers notes that she would never trust her financial future to someone who cannot use a semicolon properly. Dan is stunned that what he regards as a trivial matter could be the deciding factor in rejecting his offer. But when the written document is the only point of contact between you and your reader (as it is in Dan and his prospective clients' cases), everything that you write becomes data for your readers to analyze in considering whether they find you trustworthy. Readers who don't know Dan use his faulty punctuation as evidence that he will also be careless of the details in handling their money.

As Dan reviews his draft, he realizes that he can improve his credibility by clearly showing his knowledge of investing and financial advising. He assesses his use of technical language in the draft and sees that, although he does use some financial planning vocabulary, he mostly avoids the kinds of specific terms that would demonstrate his extensive education in this area. For example, in the second last paragraph, he uses the phrases "financial plan," "creating wealth," and "reducing risk"—all laypersons' phrases associated with investment planning: "Our goal will be to work as a team to create a financial plan and REACH these goals. Are you serious about creating wealth and reducing risk? If so then call me to arrange a ½ hour meeting." He realizes that these phrases are not specialized, so they don't demonstrate his understanding of the technical aspects of investing. Readers are not convinced that he "knows his stuff." The challenge for Dan is to balance his use of plain language in his appeal to non-technical readers with the necessity to hint at the knowledge and value he brings because of his specialized and technical knowledge of investing. So while he might begin the letter with a more plainspoken approach, later in the letter he needs to indicate that he has greater knowledge to share. The key here is to use plain language as your default standard and then to add specialized vocabulary for emphasis.

Next, Dan notices that the only figure mentioned in the letter is the amount of assets the readers have to invest. Given that his letter is all about data and statistics, he decides he should probably add some attractive ones that will also demonstrate his knowledge. For example, he can quantify the increase in property values in the Burlington area over the last three years to show that he has done his homework on this point.

Another area that he can improve, Dan realizes, is his use of experts. He considers using a quote from a local investment banker as a way to show his knowledge of and connections with bankers and financial planners in the area. Dan decides he can go one step further by also using the local banker's comments to show that he has innovative and ingenious ideas that stodgy, traditional financial planners haven't considered.

Next, Dan considers whether there is an opposing viewpoint that he should include, but he decides that this strategy isn't relevant to this letter.

He also considers whether he shares common values with his potential clients and realizes that this is an important area. He sees that he did try to show his readers that they share similar goals with this statement: "Are you serious about creating wealth and reducing risk? If so then call me to arrange a ½ hour meeting." It demonstrates that he does share readers' goals of wanting to increase their wealth and minimize the risks inherent in doing so.

Dan also decides that he can improve his attempts to create a sense of identification between readers and himself. In his original draft, he does not really put into action this strategy for creating credibility. If he does, he can create a hugely persuasive letter. One way to create identification is to better demonstrate shared values. Dan decides to offer his readers a useful tip to help them generate more wealth (for example, Uncle Steve mentioned the point about borrowing from his own retirement rather than the bank for a short-term loan); this tip will demonstrate that Dan is serious about creating more wealth for readers. Giving away useful information backs up his claim to want to help readers increase their wealth. He demonstrates that they share the value of making money for the reader without taking big risks.

In Dan's case, he asks readers to trust him to use their money to make more money for them (and himself, indirectly). He needs to be subtle about showing how his and his readers' interests are aligned. He tried to get at this point in these two sentences: "My promise is that working with me will bring you the best professional advice and service available. With an unlimited number of specialists, not just at ES Investment Group, but also with a network of professionals, I can assist you; i.e., Accountant, Lawyer, etc." However, this wording just makes him sound self-important. Instead of *telling* his readers, he needs to *show* them what makes his among "the best professional advice and service." Then they will see how they can work with Dan to improve their investment portfolio. Dan might also show readers how he and they belong to a group by targeting a version of his letter to potential clients that share his religious or political affiliation. For example, he could refer to the volunteer work he has done offering financial consultation to clients of the domestic violence shelter sponsored by the Ben Ezra Synagogue. Another strategy that might be useful for Dan is to rewrite his letter to characterize his clients as a unique group gaining distinct advantages with him as their financial advisor. Readers will want to join this group and receive similar benefits.

Dan may also be able to show how investors working with financial groups other than Dan's form a group that is antithetical to his client group. For example, those investors will find their portfolios being "churned"—that is, assets (stocks or mutual funds) being bought and sold unnecessarily to create commissions for the advisors. The rival group of investors with churning portfolios causes increased fluctuations in the market that affect the volatility of Dan's clients' portfolios. Investors who respond to market fluctuations increase the risk of all investors. Readers will want to join the group with less risk, lower advisor commissions, and more stability, which Dan Cooper now represents (based on his argument in the letter).

Finally, Dan can end his letter by inviting readers to meet with him to review their portfolio, learn some new useful tips, and establish an ongoing financial partnership with him. Notice that he does take this step in his letter in Figure 2.1, but because he does not adequately establish the process of identification, readers are turned off rather than convinced to act. He has not adequately demonstrated his trustworthiness as a writer or investment advisor through the main body of the letter. He needs to more skillfully and tactfully create an emotional link or sense of identity between his readers and himself.

 Professional Communication Challenges 2.1

1. Revise Dan Cooper's letter

1. Reread Dan Cooper's letter in Figure 2.1 from the perspective of a new client. Underline all of the specific phrases and details in the letter that might have made some of the recipients aggressively rude in their responses to him. Note where you think the problem lies with each phrase and what revisions will solve it.
2. Then decide what specific kinds of evidence Dan could add to the letter to strengthen his credibility and trustworthiness.
3. Use details from Dan's résumé (reproduced in Figure 2.8) to develop accurate and detailed evidence that readers will find persuasive.
4. Then rewrite Dan's letter so that it can accomplish what he would like it to do: bring him new clients.
5. Draw upon all of the information in this chapter to create an effective letter that uses logic, credibility, and emotional appeals that demonstrate Dan's expertise and trustworthiness in the area of financial planning and makes readers want to hear what he has to say about their investments.

Your letter should be approximately the same length as Dan's original letter.

Audience: John and Joan Pleva, and other potential clients who are unclear on why they should trust him with their retirement funds

Purpose: To motivate Mr. and Mrs. Pleva (and other potential clients) to schedule an appointment with Dan to discuss their investments

Genre: Sales letter with persuasive message

2. Create an information card (6 inches by 4 inches)

Create an information card (postcard size) to include with the letter, listing the services that Dan Cooper provides. For details about what these cards look like, consult printing services such as Vistaprint. For details about what to include on the card, visit the websites of financial services firms. For an example, consider the one in Figure 2.7. Include an image or graphic that is interesting, and provide ways for potential clients to find out more about you through links to social media accounts and your professional website. By providing a paper card you hope that readers will be reminded to find out more because the card is sitting on their desk or counter. It thus accompanies your letter and business card, forming part of your mailing package to them.

Here are three models to help get you started:

- www.edwardjones.ca
- www.investorsgroup.com
- www.rbcwealthmanagement.com

Audience: Prospective clients who are skeptical of changing investment advisors

We can improve the writing in your organization in three ways:

1. Executive coaching (one-to-one)
2. Group writing workshops
3. Contact writing and editing

Email: roger@wecanwrite.ca
LinkedIn: www.linkedin.com/in/rogercgraves/
Twitter: (@rogergraves)
Listen: https://www.podomatic.com/podcasts/rogergraves

Figure 2.7 **Example of an information card.**

Purpose: To offer readers useful free advice that will increase their interest in meeting Dan to discuss their investment portfolio

Genre: Information card

Daniel A. Cooper

EDUCATION

2017   BComm, Economics and Finance (Joint Honours)
                        McGill University, Montreal

AWARDS AND HONORS

2015   3rd place, Canadian University and Colleges Investment Challenge
                        200 teams from colleges and universities across Canada entered, three
                        prizes awarded
                        Sponsored by Canadian National Trust

2013–2017   Dean's List

2012   Senior Economics Prize, The Integrated Arts Academy, Burlington

WORK EXPERIENCE

2020–present   **Investment Services Consultant**, ES Investment Group, Burlington
                        Manage individual portfolio of clients,
                        Offer innovative and effective financial solutions to maximize investment
                        potential

2018–2019   **Teller**, Community Bank, Burlington
                        Served bank clients
                        Prepared end-of-day statements
                        Headed courtesy desk for regular shifts responding to bank customer
                        inquiries

2017–2018   **Administrative Assistant**, Steve Cooper & Associates, Burlington
                        Document preparation services
                        Reception duties, supply management, book-keeping

2012   **Assistant to Small Business Advisor**, Community Bank, Burlington
                        Opened new accounts for new and existing business owners
                        Maintained paperwork
                        Data entry

2011   **Server**, Denny's, Burlington
                        Managed tables in section of restaurant
                        Took and filled orders, helped with food preparation

Figure 2.8 **Dan Cooper's résumé.**

Her face blank, Yasmin Blackwell pushes James Franklin's three-page memo report across the desk so that it sits in front of him. James's face registers surprise and concern; it is obvious that Ms. Blackwell is not happy. She says that she read the report last night to prepare for meetings on Monday morning next week. The problem with the report is that it doesn't tell her what she needs to know.

James is puzzled by this response. He did all the research that Ms. Blackwell asked for, and he thinks that he has laid the issues out clearly. He leans across the desk to pick up the report. He pages through it. He *knows* everything is there that she has asked him to do: comparative figures on similar properties; estimated revenue from the sale; a floor plan of the nursing home as it currently exists; even some figures that she hasn't asked for but that James knows are relevant and important.

Ms. Blackwell acknowledges that James did do the research, but notes that he hasn't provided her with a preliminary analysis or recommendations. She needs him to distill it for her. She needs him to make recommendations about what he thinks the board should do. As her administrative assistant, he needs to provide her with the tools to do her job. This means useful analysis *and recommendations*. Even if she does not follow James's recommendations, she points out, those recommendations are useful as a starting point for her own analysis of the situation.

Ms. Blackwell notes that she won't need the report until Sunday night or early Monday. This means that James has time today and over the weekend to rewrite the report. She emphasizes, "Your main priority is to add recommendations and elaborate your analysis of the situation. This report isn't bad—the information and analysis are solid—but it needs to be an *argument* about Islander Entertainment Group's proposal rather than a *description* of it."

James stifles a grimace and turns to go. He has plans for the weekend, so he will have to rewrite the report today unless he wants to still be writing it when he hits his friend's house in Sackville on Saturday afternoon. He enjoys working for the Department of Health, but the job of administrative assistant was more complicated than he had thought when he started back in June.

James sits down at his desk, flipping through the pages to see what he'd written. He starts to see what Ms. Blackwell means about the report describing rather than arguing a position. Isn't that a lot of responsibility for him—deciding what the board should do? Making a decision means he will have to think a lot more carefully about the information that he has collected.

About six weeks earlier, the Prince Edward Island Department of Health, which oversees the administration and management of Ocean View Retirement Community (as well as 12 other nursing homes across the island), had received an offer from Islander Entertainment Group for $100,000 to purchase the 25-foot-wide strip of shoreline between the nursing home and the water's edge. Islander Entertainment is proposing to build a large wharf, restaurant, amusement park, and marina out in front of the nursing home, using the waterfront strip as well as a 30-foot

right-of-way along the south side of the building that will give them access to the waterfront. The accompanying photograph came with Islander Entertainment Group's offer. It illustrates the proposed complex in relation to Ocean View, except that the building over the water would be located directly in front of the retirement community, blocking the residents' ocean view.

Logic

BASICS ABOUT LOGIC

One of the common mistakes that many people make in thinking about writing is that if the grammar is correct, the words are spelled properly, and the commas are where they should be, then it is a good piece of writing. And if the text also contains detailed and useful information about the topic, then it's a great piece of writing. Although these aspects of writing may be important in the final proofreading stages, they are secondary to the writing's content and thought, which is what really distinguishes good writing from bad. In Rhetorical Situation 2.2, James's report is well written and contains the basic content, but it lacks the thought that Ms. Blackwell expected and needs to do *her* job well. James has written a descriptive report but not an analytical one.

When you are asked to write a report in an organization, supervisors will rarely expect you to regurgitate the plain facts. Instead, they will be looking for you to take a stand on the topic, interpret the facts that you collect in your research, and present them with a viewpoint that demonstrates logical analysis, insightful ideas, and clear explanations. This process of analysis is the hard work of report writing, and it is achieved only after careful thinking about the topic.

In business and professional communication, thinking clearly and writing well are especially important because most communication involves analyzing a problem or situation and then presenting a solution. If your manager asks you to study a problem and collect all relevant information needed to solve that problem, they also usually expect you to analyze the information and propose an effective solution as well. Your logical analysis of the situation and your proposed perspective on it helps guide your manager's thinking too. Even if they disagree with your recommended solution, your writing helps clarify the areas of disagreement to help them think through the issue. As you think carefully and logically through the subject matter, you improve your own skills, and that will make you a better candidate for promotion.

In addition to thinking logically through the subject matter, you also want to take a stand on it based on your careful analysis. Taking a stand requires creating an argument. Creating an argument involves making claims about the subject and presenting evidence to support them. "Argument" is an abstract term and can mean many different things. In this book, we use the term to describe the activity of assembling information on a subject, analyzing it carefully, and presenting this information effectively to advance a position about that subject in a business and professional communication or workplace context. In this chapter, we focus particularly on analyzing information to write an argument suitable for a recommendation or analytical report in a workplace setting.

In general, argument as an activity can have many goals. They range from goading readers into, at a bare minimum, engaging with the subject (e.g., op-ed columns in the news), to persuading listeners or readers to think about the writers' perspectives on a subject (e.g., solutions to social problems), to convincing readers to do something (e.g., invest your retirement savings with Dan Cooper). In business and professional communication, writers generally create arguments to move readers to action or to assist readers in thinking through complex problems (as James must do for his supervisor in Rhetorical Situation 2.2).

How do you create an effective argument? As we discussed earlier in this chapter, a good argument is made up of three parts:

1. Credibility: The ways in which you demonstrate your knowledge of the subject. This topic was discussed on pages 56–62.

2. Logic: The claims and evidence that present your ideas on the subject. We discuss this topic in the following sections.

3. Emotion: The commitment the reader comes to feel toward your topic. This subject is discussed on pages 87–92.

In point 2 above, logic is defined as a series of related claims and supporting evidence that present your ideas on the subject. Readers must find your claims and evidence to be logical and interesting if they are going to finish reading your argument (emotion). Further, they must also be convinced that you know your topic well (credibility). All three of these aspects contribute to whether your argument is convincing.

ARGUMENT AND VALUES

The word "argument" is a technical term in rhetorical studies, but it has been used by the general culture and applied loosely to cover any kind of a strong disagreement. The term is often used generally as a synonym for "fight." However, in this discussion we must separate "argument" from this notion of "verbal fight" to explain how argument—in the sense of persuasive discourse—works. "Argument" in rhetorical studies refers to well thought-out and effectively supported discussions of subjects where different viewpoints are possible. The goal of this type of argument is to make a case for one of the possible perspectives on or solutions to a problem with the end of getting others, if not to change their minds, then at least to acknowledge that your viewpoint or solution is also valid.

In this type of argument, an essential component to reaching the goal is the common ground shared between the participants. Effective argument is possible when participants share at least one or two beliefs, values, or assumptions. If participants share no beliefs or values in common, their discussion is a fight. No resolution or solution is possible if none of the participants can agree on anything. In other words, an argument assumes that, through the exchange of claims and evidence, participants can see, acknowledge, or even convince each other that their perspectives are valid. The discussion can take place because the participants believe the same things are valuable. For example, a company pamphlet presents an argument for its field workers to take action to lessen their risks of developing skin cancer. The pamphlet exists because the organization believes its workers' health is important. However, it can reach its audience and influence them only if those workers share the belief that their health is important. This shared value of promoting the health of workers supports the pamphlet message. Beliefs, values, and assumptions enter an argument indirectly through these shared values that support the argument.

The logical part of an argument is constructed from a **claim** (a statement of a position), plus a **reason** (why you think this position on the subject is true) and some **evidence** (data, facts, research that supports the truthfulness or validity of your position). Beliefs, values, and assumptions also enter an argument directly through the reasons the speakers or writers present to explain their positions. In these reasons, we reveal what we believe in—what we value or think is important. We also judge the extent to which our listeners or readers share our beliefs or values and offer reasons that we expect them to also recognize as important or valuable. That is, we rely on our audience sharing our values to give our arguments some weight and importance. In this way, the logic of an argument depends on what society in general or individuals in particular believe in or feel is important. For example, during the coronavirus pandemic, some politicians and citizens argued that the lockdown should end and businesses open up again after only two or three weeks (their claim) because the economy was declining (the **stated reason**). Underlying this reason is the belief that improving the country's financial prosperity is the most important value. There is also an **unstated reason** implied in this argument: "We should end the lockdown and open businesses because most of the people who will die from the spread of coronavirus when we do so are old and therefore unimportant." Underlying both the stated and unstated reasons is the belief that the country's economy is more important than the lives of some of its citizens.

THE LOGIC OF YOUR ARGUMENT

 Develop argumentative claims to explain and create a convincing case for a recommended solution

The logic of an argument refers to its internal consistency. To create an argument that is internally consistent means that you develop a series of claims with reasons about the subject that cover its major aspects and do not contradict one another.

As noted, effective logic consists of three parts:

1. Claim: Statements that you believe to be true

2. Reasons: Reasons that accompany the statement or claim that explain why you think the statement is true. As noted earlier, reasons can also be unstated (or implied) rather than stated.

3. Evidence: Facts, narratives, other documents, and/or statistics that back up your claim that a statement is true

What Is a Claim? Claims, Stated Reasons and Unstated Reasons. A claim is a statement in which you give a position and then add a reason that explains that position. For example, the Canadian Cancer Society website (Figure 2.9) presents several arguments (that is, claims plus reasons) about preventing cancer.

Example 1: You can reduce your risk of developing cancer [the claim] *because* half of all cancers can be prevented through healthy living [the stated reason].

Example 2: You should learn more about healthy lifestyle choices *because* lifestyle choices can reduce your risk of developing cancer.

In both of these examples, the word *because* joins the claim and the stated reason. Usually, the claim plus a reason relies on a second reason that is unstated. For example, the claim "You should learn more about healthy lifestyle choices *because* lifestyle choices can reduce your risk of developing cancer" relies on the assumption (or unstated reason) that you want to avoid getting cancer. By making this claim, the Cancer Society assumes that you agree that avoiding cancer is a good move and something you are willing to work toward by changing your lifestyle. Writers usually assume that their readers share the value(s) implied in the unstated reason.

How Do I Develop Claims? Explore your topic. As we have noted, making an argument entails taking a position on a subject. Before you take a position, however, you should examine the subject from all perspectives. Only by carefully thinking through the subject can you arrive at an insightful conclusion. Think through the subject by generating as many ideas as you can about the subject from all perspectives. That is, think of as many claims in support of a particular action as you can think of against it. Brainstorm lists of reasons to accompany these claims for and against.

Here are five general strategies that you can use to help you come up with ideas for claims:

1. *Define or redefine key terms.* Examine the important vocabulary associated with your subject. What do those words or phrases mean? For example, in the arguments offered by the Cancer Society, what does it mean to make "positive lifestyle choices"? This could mean just switching from cream to milk in our coffee or removing the skin from our chicken before we eat it. It could also mean taking more explicit preventative action to avoid disease, such as eating a vegan diet or stopping smoking or vaping. We might also ask about whether making positive lifestyle choices includes promoting our choices to friends and family members. Asking these questions gives us insight that may help us define what "making healthy lifestyle choices" entails.

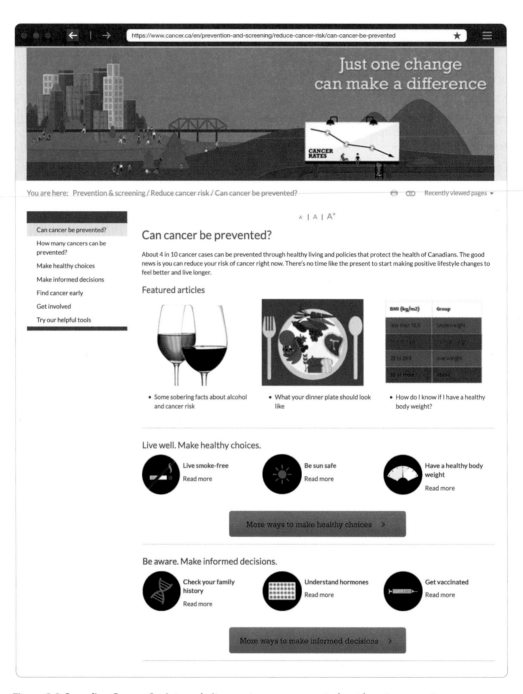

Figure 2.9 Canadian Cancer Society website creates an argument about how to prevent cancer.
Source: Used with permission of Canadian Cancer Society.

2. *Logically subdivide your topic.* To use this strategy in the planning stages of creating your argument, explore the numerous facets of your subject. Use logic to help you subdivide it into smaller associated points and ideas. Which of these points can be expanded into claims? Which are important to your subject? Identify the ideas and claims that seem most central to you, as well as those that are less central. Analyze both central and other claims to articulate less obvious aspects to them. The goal of this activity is to exhaust your ideas about your subject so that you can decide which position to argue and then select your most convincing claims for that position. Your goal is to create the strongest possible argument for the position you ultimately choose to promote.

The Canadian Cancer Society divides "Prevention" into three separate webpages, links to two of which are shown in Figure 2.9: "Live well" to examine making "healthy choices" in greater detail; and "Be aware" to discuss making informed decisions. By subdividing the argument into different pages, each with its own sub-claims, the Society develops a complex overall argument that educates website visitors on actions that may help them avoid getting cancer and attempts to persuade them to act.

3. *Decide based on precedent.* Another strategy for generating ideas about your subject is to research what others have decided when facing similar circumstances. That is, explore positions taken by others on the subject that precede your writing about it. You are likely to find in your research some perspectives and claims about your topic that you hadn't considered in your earlier explorations of the subject. When you consider what others have offered as solutions, you can assess and evaluate their claims and evidence. You can cite some of their ideas and solutions as evidence to support your own position, or you can critique their suggestions in light of your perspective on the topic. For example, you might interview a series of people who have survived cancer to discover their views on making healthy lifestyle choices. Their experience might provide inspiration and models for further actions people could take to prevent cancer so that you could add these to the argument by the Cancer Society.

4. *Use the consequences of something as a reason to do or not do it.* This strategy involves examining possible outcomes of proposed solutions to a problem and using the projected outcome as a reason to promote or avoid some of them. For example, pretend you work for a geological survey company, whose field workers spend long hours outside, and your human resources department has asked you to communicate with employees to remind them of company policy to reduce their skin-cancer risk in their outdoor work. You decide to update a pamphlet summarizing current research on skin-cancer risks. This leads you to research on sun blockers where you discover evidence of increased cancer risk associated with several brands. You worry that if you include this information in the pamphlet, some employees might decide to stop using sun block altogether, yet if you omit this research your information is incomplete and potentially harmful. You decide to include the research as well as a list of recommended sunblock products (and where to buy them) that proves extremely useful for company employees.

5. *Take a point of view that contradicts common opinion.* In this strategy you consider the various viewpoints that are possible on your topic. What do you think most people would say about, for example, making positive lifestyle choices? Perhaps they would complain that making such choices is boring: eating fruits and vegetables and lean meats, avoiding fast food, white sugar and flour and treats like donuts, pastries, and ice cream. You might consider the ways in which eating healthy food is interesting and tasty so that you could argue for the enjoyable aspects of healthy eating.

These five strategies can help you explore your subject matter from various perspectives so that you can see its complexity and nuances before you decide on the position you will argue. Of course, these strategies are useful for helping you generate some claims and reasons, but from there you need to expand these ideas into full-fledged, well-supported claims that build your overall argument. In the next section we talk about, among other things, ways to expand these ideas into claims.

EXPANDING CLAIMS

 Synthesize information from supporting documents to create strong arguments

A claim + a stated reason + an unstated (or implied) reason make a good *beginning* for an argument. To expand a claim into an argument, you need to add *evidence*. Evidence comes in many forms, including facts and figures, quotations, and testimony. Reasons are positions you advocate or things you want readers to believe. You use evidence (facts, data, quotations) to support the reasons you give for taking some action or believing something.

Let's expand an earlier example into an argument: The Canadian Cancer Society (Figure 2.9) provides evidence in support of its argument through a series of webpages devoted to Prevention. You can reduce your risk of developing cancer *because* half of all cancers can be prevented through healthy living. One way to expand this claim is to consider what values or beliefs are assumed in the stated reason. In other words, what does the Canadian Cancer Society value when it states "About 4 in 10 cancer cases can be prevented through healthy living and policies that protect the health of Canadians"?

1. It values quality of life—that is, the ability to live cancer-free.
2. It values taking action to achieve the goal of living cancer-free.
3. It values efforts made to reduce the risk of getting cancer.

How Are Values Present in the Evidence Used to Support Claims? In the series of webpages on "Prevention," the Canadian Cancer Society argues (makes the claim) that we, as individuals, *can* affect our chances of staying healthy and reduce our risk of getting cancer (outcomes that we, their audience, presumably value). The argument that the Society develops in these pages rests on the assumption that we share their belief in taking action to safeguard our health/lives.

Consequently, the site presents several pages on "Prevention" that both draw on these values and support the Society's claim. One page lists lifestyle choices that reduce our risks of developing associated cancers. These choices are actions that we can take to maintain our health/quality of life. The actions are *specific examples* that tell us what to do (the value of acting to stay healthy) and also support the claim that action is possible to preserve good health (we can act to do this). Interestingly, a fourth value underlies the evidence offered on this page to support this claim and that is the importance of education (learning/knowing). The page seeks to inform (educate) readers as to lifestyle changes they can make to reduce their risk of developing unhealthy lifestyle-associated cancers.

A second page presents *facts* about "alcohol and cancer risk" (https://www.cancer.ca/en/prevention-and-screening/reduce-cancer-risk/make-healthy-choices/limit-alcohol/some-sobering-facts-about-alcohol-and-cancer-risk/?region=bc). The lists of facts support the Society's claim that alcohol can contribute to cancer risk and that if we avoid or minimize contact with it, we can reduce our risk. By learning about these facts, we can recognize the risks alcohol poses and alter our behavior to avoid or minimize our exposure to it. Here again, this claim and presented evidence rely on readers finding value in being informed—that we will try to mitigate risks associated with alcohol once we know about them. Another link, "Canadian Cancer Statistics," connects us to research by experts (https://www.cancer.ca/en/cancer-information/cancer-101/cancer-statistics-at-a-glance/?region=bc). In this part of the argument, words in research articles by an expert on cancer prevention are used to support further the claim that we *can* act to reduce our risk of developing lifestyle-associated cancers.

In the discussion across their website of how the shared values about cancer prevention shape the kinds of evidence offered to support the Society's claims and reasons, three different strategies are used:

1. **Add specific examples** (vivid description: "If we act now, we can prevent thousands of cancer cases by the year 2042"). Specific examples such as anecdotes and vivid descriptions contribute details that sharpen your points and make the subject present for your readers or listeners. Detailed examples help you to improve the clarity and impact of your claims.

2. **Quote comments or research from experts** (doctors, World Health Organization, scientists). The words or research of informed people or experts is another important source of evidence, and quoting experts is a useful strategy for supporting your claim.

3. **Cite facts, data and statistics** ("32,700 new cancer cases are due to smoking tobacco"). Facts, data and statistics are the types of evidence that you would expect to be building blocks for a strong logical argument. Often you will need to do some research to locate the evidence that supports your claims and reasons. Any research you do to support your claims is worthwhile because data, examples, and quotations from experts strengthen the logic of your argument, making it more persuasive.

To develop an effective argument, consider what beliefs, values, and assumptions underlie the claims and reasons that you use in constructing your argument. Then select evidence that supports the beliefs and values that you draw on in stating your claims and reasons. During this process, also assess the extent to which your audience shares these beliefs and values. If they share your values *and* you offer strong reasons and compelling evidence to support your claims, they will probably find your argument persuasive.

However, if readers do not share your worldview, then you must find or create common ground (a value or belief that you both do share) and start there with your argument. For example, the Cancer Society webpage on "Prevention" starts with the claim, "About 4 in 10 cancer cases can be prevented through healthy living and policies that protect the health of Canadians," and then states the question that visitors may ask in response to this claim: "How many cancer cases can be prevented?" Underlying this question is the belief/assumption that we have no control over whether we develop cancer. But the writers refute this belief and then give an example to support their claim: "The good news is you can reduce your risk of cancer right now." Included in this statement is statistical evidence: "4 in 10 cancer cases can be prevented." Here the Cancer Society creates common ground by correcting a mistaken belief (lifestyle doesn't affect whether we get cancer) and then offers links where readers can learn more about preventing cancer.

STRENGTHENING YOUR ARGUMENT

Once you have developed a claim + stated reason + unstated reason into a well-supported argument, consider it from opposing viewpoints to see where its weaknesses lie. If you can figure out where the opposite perspective might criticize or refute your argument, you can decide how best to modify your ideas to take the opposing view into account.

For example, someone might rebut the Canadian Cancer Society's argument for taking action to reduce cancer risk by focusing on the other 50 per cent of cancers that are not lifestyle related. The argument may be made that we can spend our lives making healthy lifestyle choices but still develop a genetically caused cancer. In view of this position, we might qualify the earlier claim to acknowledge that action can prevent only some cancers but point out that it is better to take what action we can rather than wait around to develop a different cancer.

ANALYSIS: JAMES TRANSFORMS DESCRIPTION INTO ARGUMENT

James is shocked when his boss, Yasmin Blackwell, rejects his report because it doesn't include what *he* thinks about the proposed development of the Ocean View Retirement Community waterfront. He starts to realize that good writing is good thinking: logical analysis, insightful ideas, and clear explanation. Since he didn't carefully think through his topic, he could not write well about it—not in a way that was useful to his reader. He also realizes that he must move beyond just thinking carefully about his topic. He must also translate what he thinks into a form and presentation that communicate his ideas effectively to Ms. Blackwell to help them both achieve their purposes. She needs an analysis of the information about the Islander

Entertainment Group's offer. As chair of the regional Department of Health Board of Directors, she has to lead the board in making a decision about the offer. She has to attend the Monday morning meeting with a clear understanding of the offer and a carefully made decision about how best to respond to it. James's analysis and recommendations will be a shortcut in her own analysis of the situation.

To rewrite his report, James has to figure out what he thinks the board members should do. This means re-examining the data that he collected to decide what it means. Here are the major issues that he needs to consider as he decides whether is it better for the board to sell the land or keep it:

- What are the board's mission and responsibility in the larger community?
- How will the sale of this land affect the residents of Ocean View Retirement Community?
- What is the board's responsibility regarding the welfare of the retirement community's residents?
- Does the board need the money that the sale would generate?
- Is the offer realistically priced?
- What are the long-term negative and positive consequences to selling this land?

Figure 2.10 reproduces the answers that James jotted down to these questions. You can see that the answers themselves start to transform into arguments as he works his way down the list. The details that were neutral information in the descriptive version of the report become pieces of evidence in the argument that support his claims.

James's goal is to create a logical or internally consistent discussion of the proposed waterfront sale. To do this, he needs to develop a series of claims that cover its major aspects without contradicting one another. First, he develops a series of claims based on his answers to some of the questions he poses in Figure 2.10:

Example 1: The Board should sell the waterfront strip [claim] *because* the money from the sale will pay for improvements to the retirement home common room [stated reason].

Example 2: The Board should not sell the waterfront strip [claim] *because* developing this land will ruin the residents' spectacular view of the ocean [stated reason].

Example 3: The Board should sell the waterfront strip [claim] *because* the development will bring more tourists and local people to the town harbor to enjoy the waterfront [stated reason].

As you can see, examples 1 and 3 support the argument that the Board should sell the waterfront. Example 2 supports the opposing argument that the Board should keep it. If James decides to recommend that the Board sell, he can use examples 1 and 3, but example 2 contradicts this

What are the board's mission and responsibility in the larger community?
- Responsibility to provide quality health care to the citizens of the Atlantic region
- Responsibility to practice sound financial management of health care resources (including hospital lands)

How will the sale of this land affect the residents of Ocean View Retirement Community?
- Islander Entertainment's proposed structure will obstruct their ocean view
- Many won't notice because they are sedated for various health issues, including dementia, Alzheimer's, etc.
- Development adds someplace close for residents to go for entertainment (mental stimulation)
- Public right of way (road) on south side of building would increase road noise and traffic beside the dementia wing

What is the board's responsibility regarding the welfare of the retirement community's residents?
- Provide quality health care: does this include a quiet environment and a good view?
- Many elderly people lack mental stimulation: proposed development (Ferris wheel on wharf and restaurant/pub) would be increased mental stimulation for those residents that need it

Does the board need the money that the sale would generate?
- Some shortfall in funding in last year's budget
- Request for money to refurbish common room at Ocean View not allocated by Department of Health
- $100,000 offer would provide extra funding beyond refurbished common room for updating aging facilities at Ocean View
- Overall, though, the board/department/ministry does **not** need the money

Is the offer realistically priced?
- Conservative offer for oceanfront property
- Could ask for more $$$

What are the long-term negative and positive consequences to selling this land?

Negatives
- Board (and Ministry) would lose control of further development of land and its usage through selling it
- What if Islander Entertainment goes bankrupt? Board wouldn't control what happens to structure/additional development of the property
- Loss of valuable oceanfront asset: loss of $$ (long-term) and control

Positives
- Increased development of harbor community to draw tourists and locals to downtown center
- Potential activities for residents of Ocean View and their families/friends who visit
- I can't think of anything else!!!

Figure 2.10 **James Franklin's notes as he analyzes the Islander Entertainment offer.**

position. Similarly, if he decides to recommend that the Board refuse the offer, he will omit examples 1 and 3 because they undermine the internal consistency of his logic.

In each of these examples, the word *because* joins the claim and the stated reason. As noted earlier, a claim plus a reason relies on a second, unstated reason. For example, the claim that "The Board should sell the waterfront strip because the money from the sale will pay for improvements to the retirement home common room" relies on the assumption that improving the common room is important. It also assumes that other options for updating the common room are impractical or less desirable. To make this claim, James must believe that Ms. Blackwell agrees that updating the common room is a priority for the nursing home and, therefore, it will or should be for the board as well. As noted earlier, if Ms. Blackwell or the Board do not believe that improving the common room is important or if they believe other things are more important, such as the well-being of the residents, they will reject James's argument. For these reasons, it's essential that you consider the assumptions you are relying on when you make a claim *and* that you understand some of the beliefs and values of your readers.

James realizes that he doesn't know which side to argue on this issue. He can see arguments on both sides. He decides that he needs to carefully think through the proposal and its implications. He makes a thorough list of ideas from all perspectives. Figure 2.11 presents James's analysis using the five strategies discussed on pages 71–74, above, to explore the implications of both sides.

JAMES EXPANDS CLAIMS INTO ARGUMENTS

As noted, adding evidence to a claim expands it into an argument. Perhaps James wishes to expand the following claim by adding evidence: "The Board should sell the waterfront strip because the money from the sale will pay for improvements to the retirement home common room." He examines the stated reason and sees that it also implies two unstated reasons, one of which is that "Ocean View cannot fund improvements to the room from its operating budget." The other is "that updating the common room should be a priority" for the home.

James then analyzes the values and beliefs that underlie both the stated and unstated reasons. He asks himself, in choosing this particular claim and reason (plus the unstated reason), what values am I assuming are most important? He identifies these values underlying the stated reason:

- action (such as updating the common room) that improves residents' quality of life is most important;
- it is most important that the home update poor facilities;
- it is most important that the Board support the home's actions to improve residents' quality of life; and
- it is important to find innovative ways to overcome funding obstacles.

He sees that these values also motivate the unstated reasons. He also identifies an underlying assumption to this claim, which is that if money is not available to update the common room, it should be generated from other sources than the operating budget.

1. *Define or redefine key terms.* For example, what does it mean for the Health Authority to "provide quality health care"? Does this just mean providing doctors and facilities to citizens? Does it include taking preventative action to avoid disease? Does it include promoting mental health? These questions try to define what "health care" is. What about citizens' spiritual health? This question begins to redefine "health care."

2. *Logically subdivide your topic.* To explore the possibilities for action that the board could take, James writes: "The board has three options on this issue: 1. Refuse the offer to purchase and retain control of the waterfront; 2. Sell the land and lose control of the waterfront; and 3. Lease the land to Islander Entertainment and maintain control of the property." From here, he summarizes the case for refusing the offer. He lists the short- and long-term consequences for maintaining the current situation. He explores how these consequences intersect with some of his ideas about the definition of "quality health care" to consider the outcomes of these consequences. Then he subdivides the second option into a list of the short- and long-term consequences of selling the waterfront. He links up these consequences with some of the points he made in exploring the definition of "quality health care" to elaborate the outcomes of these consequences. Finally, he subdivides the third option as he explores the actions involved in leasing the land, as well as the short- and long-term consequences. Then he assesses the value of the three options for Islander Entertainment to decide which option provides the most value for all of the stakeholders (those affected by the Board's decision).

3. *Decide based on precedent.* To use this strategy, James decides he must research the decisions made by Health Boards across the country to discover what others have decided when facing a similar proposal. Depending on what he finds, he can use the decisions by other boards to argue in support of his position: "The Board of Directors for the ___ Health Authority, when faced with a similar offer to purchase the shoreline in front of The Peaks Retirement Village, decided to ___." He can thus use decisions made by other boards as a way to build a consensus to add weight to his recommendation.

4. *Use the consequences of something as a reason to do or not do it.* For example, in his analysis of the consequences of the three possible options he identified using strategy 2, he notes that a waterfront development will increase traffic in and around Ocean View. He sees two competing outcomes with the increased traffic: greater noise will disrupt the dementia patients (negative consequence) and provide perhaps much welcome mental stimulation and interest to healthier residents (positive consequence). James considers that what he chooses as his highest priority (most important value) also shapes whether he wishes to judge a particular consequence as a good or bad reason.

5. *Take a point of view that contradicts common opinion.* In this case, James assumes that common opinion would say to sell the land and use the money to improve the facilities for nursing home residents by hiring additional staff or purchasing new equipment that benefits the residents. In contrast, he argues for rejecting the sale, highlighting that the quality of the view and the health benefits that generations of residents will get from the peaceful setting are more beneficial than a few dollars that are soon spent. This argument relies on readers valuing the quality of life of nursing home residents from a spiritual perspective rather than purely a medical health standpoint.

Figure 2.11 **James generated some useful ideas using the five strategies of claim exploration.**

Business Communication: Rhetorical Situations

So if James wants to use this claim to make a convincing argument for selling the waterfront, he needs to include evidence as he expands it to persuade readers that these values (and therefore these reasons) are very or most important. For example, to show that updating the common room should be a priority for the home, he may describe its current condition, including vivid detail—the peeling, faded paint, the ripped fabric on the chairs, and the duct tape holding several card table legs together. He notes that few residents use the room because it is depressing (fact). He includes a comment from one resident about why she avoids the common room: "Daisy Ellis notes that in the common room these days, 'The sun shines right in there, and it gets too hot. We need blinds that block out the worst of the sun so it's comfortable to sit in there'" (comments from informed people or experts). James also adds a statistic: "Most mornings only two or three of the 125 residents will be sitting in the common room after breakfast." This evidence shows readers that the common room, in its current state, is not used. It demonstrates the importance of renovating the common room, supporting James's point that in this area the residents' quality of life is being neglected. The description and the details illustrate James's position that the renovation is a priority at Ocean View.

Another value that James may want to elaborate for readers as he expands this claim is the importance of the Board helping Ocean View to overcome its budget restrictions through an innovative solution such as selling the waterfront to create a budget for such expenditures.

Exercise 2.1: Analyzing the Values and Beliefs in a Claim Plus Reason

1. Examine the following two claims.

   Claim 1: The Board should not sell the waterfront strip *because* developing this land will ruin the residents' spectacular view of the ocean.

   Claim 2: The Board should sell the waterfront strip *because* the development will bring more tourists and local people to the town harbor to enjoy the waterfront.

   a. Analyze each to identify the unstated reason(s) the claim relies on.

   b. Create a list of the assumptions, values, and beliefs that the stated and unstated reasons rely on.

   c. Using the previous discussion, identify some specific pieces of evidence that you could use to support these claims.

   d. Identify an example of an audience that is likely to hold the assumptions, values, and beliefs that you listed in (b) and (c) and is thus predisposed to find your claims persuasive. Then identify an example of an audience that is unlikely to hold these assumptions, values, and beliefs, and thus is not likely to find your claims persuasive.

2. Generate your own claim plus reason that James could use in his argument. To do this, you may have to decide where you stand on the issue of whether the board should sell the nursing home waterfront. Then analyze your claim to identify the unstated reason or assumption and the values and beliefs that underlie them. Next, develop some evidence that supports your claim. Do some

research on the Internet or in the library, if necessary, to find appropriate facts or statistics that work as evidence. Then identify two audiences, one that would find them persuasive and one that would not find them persuasive.

Finally, James should consider possible rebuttals to this argument. In this case, an obvious rebuttal is to ask whether the land sale is the best way to fund the common room renovation. Opposing viewpoints might include the argument that updating the common room will increase the number of users but sacrifice the spectacular view from the windows, a questionable improvement. Users would lose an important reason to sit in there. To respond to this criticism, James could write a follow-up paragraph to this argument that addressed the value of the ocean view to nursing home residents. He could acknowledge the value of the view but argue that updating the common room is more important because of its larger and more real benefits to residents. He might argue that changing the ocean view at the nursing home will affect only a few of the residents because most of them are too ill to notice.

Figure 2.12 expands James's claim into an argument by adding evidence. Note that the italicized text in the figure identifies the various strategies used to assemble evidence to make the argument more convincing.

The board should sell the waterfront strip because the money from the sale will pay for improvements to the retirement home common room. Records show that over the last three years, the board has asked for but not received budget funding to improve the Ocean View common room [*Demonstrates that the improvements have been a budget priority not shared by the Department of Health*]. Since then, the quality of the furnishings has continued to degrade to the point that the worn patches of upholstery are actually becoming rips, with the stuffing sticking out. Several card table legs are repaired with duct tape [*Aesthetic reasons to update the room*]. The original curtains can no longer be drawn to keep out the early morning sun, so the room heats up quickly most days. Only a handful of residents (two or three of the 125 total) still use the room, mostly individuals in wheelchairs placed there by nursing home staff [*Statistical evidence*]. Daisy Ellis, a fifteen-year resident of Ocean View, no longer uses the common room [*Expert testimony as evidence*]: "The sun shines right in there, and it gets too hot. We need blinds that block out the worst of the sun so it's comfortable to sit in there" [*Practical reasons to update the room*]. One way to prioritize improvements to the common room is to use some of the proceeds from selling the waterfront strip. We have budgeted $10,000 for these updates in the past. The sale of the land would also provide $90,000 additional money for other projects at Ocean View or elsewhere.

Figure 2.12 **A claim plus a reason expanded to include evidence creates a convincing step in the argument. The italicized text identifies the strategies used to create evidence.**

However, he can make his argument stronger by refuting the claim in example 2 in his discussion. He could minimize it by pointing to the proportion of residents who are unaware of their physical surroundings, for example.

Instead he will refute these claims as part of developing his argument. He can explore other ways for the Board to find money to improve the common room and list these to reject the claim in example 1. He may elaborate the negative consequences of increased traffic on the waterfront to minimize the importance of the claim in example 3.

 ## Professional Communication Challenges 2.2

1. Rewrite James Franklin's report to make recommendations

Assume the part of James Franklin. Write a two- or three-page report to Yasmin Blackwell in which you summarize the offer to purchase the waterfront at Ocean View Retirement Community and argue a particular course of action for the director. Use the discussion in this chapter on how to create effective appeals to logic, emotion, and credibility to help you analyze the Rhetorical Situation and present your perspective in a convincing argument. Use the data in Figures 2.13 and 2.14 as evidence to help you support the arguments that you make. Add any additional material not explicitly stated in the Rhetorical Situation that you need to fully develop and support your claims into arguments.

Audience: Yasmin Blackwell, James Franklin's boss

Purpose: To outline a position about the proposed sale of the Ocean View Retirement Community waterfront that demonstrates careful consideration of the evidence and a well-thought-out plan that Ms. Blackwell can use as a basis for her own analysis and decision

Genre: Memo report

2. Write a memo to the Director of Ocean View Retirement Community

As a business communication co-op student working at Ocean View Retirement Community, you have been asked by your boss, Anthony Perkins, director of the facility, to draft a response for his signature to a letter he received from Yasmin Blackwell, Chair of the Board of Directors that oversees the facility, about a proposal to sell the waterfront access in front of Ocean View. She has requested advice from Mr. Perkins about how such a commercial development at the retirement community might affect the lives of its residents, and she needs a response by the end of the week. Mr. Perkins has told you that his gut reaction to the proposal is negative, but he is willing to listen to an argument about how it might benefit residents. Evaluate the information from Rhetorical Situation 2.2 to assess how the commercial development might affect the retirement community's residents. Decide whether you think it would benefit or harm residents.

Location of properties	Lot size	Water	No water	Asking price
Tignish	200 x 150		X	$26,900
Tignish	0.7 acres	X		$109,000
O'Connor sub.	0.34 acres	X		$60,000
O'Connor sub.	0.38 acres		X	$12,000
Cape Traverse	0.39 acres	X		$99,500
Cape Wolfe	0.5 acres		X	$7,900
Brooklyn	0.28 acres		X	$9,900
Seawood	0.28 acres		X	$29,700
Fernwood	various		X	$75,000
Fernwood	various	X		$100,000

Source: Based on Regional Real Estate Listings, August 2020.

Figure 2.13 **Real estate prices for waterfront and non-waterfront lots.**

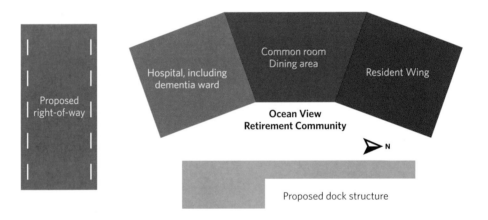

Figure 2.14 **Plan of Ocean View Retirement Community and proposed waterfront development.**

You have two options:

1. Draft the letter to Yasmin Blackwell explaining how the development will affect facility residents and arguing for a particular course of action.

OR

2. Draft a memo to Mr. Perkins trying to convince him that the commercial development will benefit facility residents.

Audience: For option 1, your initial audience is Mr. Perkins, your immediate supervisor; your primary audience is Ms. Blackwell, Chair of the Board of Directors of Ocean View Retirement Community. For option 2, your primary audience is your manager, Mr. Perkins, who is opposed to the idea but willing to entertain opposing viewpoints.

Purpose: For option 1, to educate Ms. Blackwell on the range of impacts that developing the waterfront will have on the residents and employees at the retirement community; a secondary purpose will be to demonstrate your competence and intelligence to your supervisor, Mr. Perkins, and finally, to make Mr. Perkins look good, because he will ultimately sign and send your draft. For option 2, your main purposes are to speak for the residents of the retirement community, to demonstrate your competence and intelligence to your immediate supervisor, and to provide an opposing viewpoint that will help Mr. Perkins explore the proposal more fully.

Genre:
Option 1: Persuasive letter
Option 2: Persuasive memo report

Rhetorical Situation 2.3: Persuading Guests to Observe the Rules at Brandywine Falls Inn and Cottages

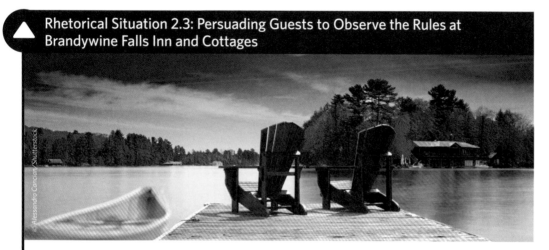

Meijing Zhu slams the car door shut and then inhales a deep breath of the cold, fresh air as she looks around. There is still more than a hint of winter in the knife-edged wind but the sun is shining brilliantly, lighting up the branches of the towering pine trees that surround her. There are worse ways of spending the summer than working at a vacation resort, she reflects, but in early May summer is definitely several weeks off yet. She shivers and retrieves her backpack from the backseat just as the black flies find her. Slinging it onto her back, she dashes to the main office at Brandywine Falls Inn, at that moment much too far away from the parking lot.

Meijing bolts in the office door, shutting it quickly and firmly behind her. "Boy, those black flies are vicious first thing in the morning!"

"Their appetites don't weaken as the day goes on," replies Helen Hurley, the wife side of the husband-and-wife team that own and operate Brandywine Falls Inn and Cottages, a popular holiday destination for nearby big-city residents. Mrs. Hurley rises from the desk behind the counter with a file folder that she holds out to Meijing.

Mrs. Hurley begins to summarize the materials in the folder. They have decided that every room should have a letter that tells guests about resort improvements over the winter and reminds them to follow the house rules. There had been a lot of trouble at the end of last summer with rowdy, thoughtless guests. The letter is one attempt to be firmer about the rules, as Brandywine risks losing its reputation as a family resort if they don't get the guests under control. Both owners agree that making sure guests have a clear list of the rules at the start of their visit is a priority. "The letters will be in the information binders in each unit," Mrs. Hurley finishes.

Meijing likes the idea and suggests that the letter could be given out at the registration desk as well as appear in the binder. She notes that she did an assignment like this in her college business communication course last year and offers to draft the letter.

That sounds great to Mrs. Hurley. She gives Meijing a list of some of the improvements made over the winter and directs her to the website for a copy of the resort rules. Mrs. Hurley notes that they do not want this letter to order people to follow the rules. That didn't work last year. She wants Meijing's draft to make them feel like they want to follow the rules. The owners hope that by explaining the reasons for the rules in more detail and appealing to guests' emotions about the rules, the resort will persuade more guests to comply with them.

Meijing stands in front of the computer, which has the Inn's main page onscreen, and clicks on the "rates and policies" link. After scanning the page, she notices that rules are combined with other information on the page. She opens a word processing file and begins copying the policies into the blank document. Figure 2.15 reproduces her finished list of rules; Figure 2.16 shows the list of renovations and updates to the Inn.

It will take a bit of writing to transform these terse statements into a persuasive argument, she decides as she works.

HIGH SEASON is from June 15 to September 21, all long weekends and holidays, and some additional weekends

TOWELS: Bring your own beach, pool, and whirlpool towels

HOT TUB: Skinny dipping permitted after 8 p.m.

VISITORS: Limit of four visitors per unit allowed at a time

PARKING: Please park in visitors' parking lot at entrance gate

OFF SEASON: Clothing optional permitted

HIGH SEASON: Clothing optional not permitted

REGISTRATION: For your security, all your visitors must register at office before going to any unit

PETS: Because some of our guests have pet allergies, we have had to strictly enforce our ban on pets. For this reason, we have a **no pets** rule at Brandywine Falls Inn and Cottages. Local kennels are available.

QUIET TIME: From 11:00 p.m. to 8:30 a.m. Please respect everyone's right to a quiet, peaceful holiday.

To ensure everyone's enjoyment, we reserve the right to accept, reject, or terminate a reservation at any time.

Figure 2.15 **Meijing's list of policies at Brandywine Falls Inn and Cottages.**

Improvements and Updates at Brandywine Falls Inn and Cottages

- ✔ All units painted and new blinds
- ✔ New awnings or porches on all cottage units
- ✔ Rec hall renovated, Oculus Quest headsets and games added
- ✔ Two computer terminals with email and computer game links
- ✔ Wireless Internet connection in all units, as well as rec hall lounge and library
- ✔ Addition of two trampolines and three barracudas for more water fun
- ✔ New marked and maintained hiking trail, increasing total to five different hikes of varying lengths
- ✔ Brand new white sand beach

Figure 2.16 **Meijing's completed list of renovations to Brandywine Falls Inn.**

Emotion

BASICS ABOUT EMOTIONAL APPEALS

 Choose the appropriate method of creating an emotional appeal and present the solution in a way that makes readers care about the subject

Although the logic of your argument and your credibility as a speaker on your topic are important, there is one other part to persuasion that is essential if you hope to have people act on your message: your emotional appeal to your audience. The **emotional appeal** refers to writing your argument in a way that makes readers care about your message. Your credibility, as stated, refers to whether readers think that you know what you are talking about—do they trust you? As well as establishing your credibility and developing a consistent and well-supported series of claims with evidence, you want to connect with readers on an emotional level so that they want to act in the way that you propose. To connect with readers, you can use several strategies to develop an emotional appeal:

emotional appeal: An argumentative strategy that uses emotions to sway your audience to your perspective

- ■ conscious word choice
- ■ concrete examples and vivid details
- ■ appropriate analogies or metaphors

Word choice. You are probably already aware that you can use a variety of words to talk about any particular subject. Some words add a positive slant to your topic (positive connotation); different words can convey a negative or critical attitude toward it (negative connotation). Let's look at an example of how word choice affects the development of the logic of an argument. Figure 2.17 is part of a pitch by the Canadian Automobile Association (CAA) to discourage readers from texting while driving. The CAA takes a logical approach, using facts and figures to convince readers: "Based on a recent CAA time trial, replying to a text message takes an average of 33.6 seconds. If you are driving on a residential road, this means that you may have missed 85 parked cars, 36 houses or 5 intersections. Maybe you didn't see the vehicle that was backing down a driveway or maybe it was the young cyclist who may have suddenly turned into your path. Just imagine what else you may have missed, and the consequences that could follow." In this passage, the word choice is neutral: "you may have missed ... you didn't see ... or maybe it was ... Just imagine what else you may have missed and the consequences that could follow." In this statement, the emotional appeal comes in the final sentence where readers must use their imaginations to confront possible catastrophic outcomes. Figure 2.18 presents an alternative version that replaces neutral verbs with descriptive ones, creating a vivid image of the catastrophic outcomes that leaves little to the imagination.

Figure 2.17 Note the primarily logical appeals in the CAA page on distracted driving.
Source: Text is reproduced from Canadian Automobile Association (CAA) website.

Business Communication: Rhetorical Situations

Neutral word choice	**Negative connotations**
If you are driving on a residential road, this means that you may have **missed** 85 parked cars, 36 houses, or five intersections. Maybe you **didn't see** the vehicle that was backing down a driveway or maybe **it was** the young cyclist who may have suddenly turned into your path.	If you are driving on a residential road, this means that you may have **side-swiped** 85 parked cars, passed 36 houses or run 5 intersections. Maybe you **T-boned** the vehicle that was backing down a driveway or maybe you **smashed** into the young cyclist who may have suddenly turned into your path.

Figure 2.18 Compare the connotations of the word choices in each passage.
Source: Text is reproduced and adapted from Canadian Automobile Association (CAA) website.

Exercise 2.2: Reflect on Effectiveness of Word Choice

Examine the word choice in both versions of the CAA appeal in Figure 2.18. With a partner or in groups of three, discuss the answers to these questions:

- What is the effect of the neutral word choice versus the more descriptive word choice in the two versions?
- What are the emotional impacts of the word choice in each version?
- Which version do you think is more effective?
- Why do you think it is more effective?

Put into words your emotional response to the more effective one. Explain why you think it works better for you. Write a paragraph explaining your analysis of the more effective version. You can collaborate on the paragraph, submitting one analysis per group, or you can each write and submit your own analysis.

Use concrete examples and vivid details. A second way to develop an effective emotional appeal in an argument is to use concrete examples and vivid details. Of course, these are also useful for fully informing your readers about the information you want them to know. But they also help readers to become more interested and invested in what you are saying. By "concrete examples" we mean specific examples with which readers will be familiar or that make an abstract idea concrete. By vivid details we mean using adjectives (as appropriate) to give readers a mental image of the concept. For example, earlier in this chapter James is considering an argument for updating the Ocean View Retirement Community common room. If he writes, "Renovating the common room is an urgent priority because the room is out of date," the lack of detail conveyed by this brief description doesn't justify his use of "urgent." Readers may dismiss his point as unimportant because "out of date" is vague. It could just mean that the room is painted in last

Figure 2.19 **Logical appeal appears in the text, whereas emotional appeal appears in both text and image.**

Source: iVegan.ca

year's trendy color. To communicate the actual state of the furnishings, he needs to give specific examples of problems ("broken card tables," "worn upholstery") and describe them using details ("repaired with duct tape," "horsehair stuffing spilling out of armchairs").

These two techniques allow readers to imagine the scene. As they do so, they feel connected to the topic. In addition, by imagining important elements of the argument, they also contribute to its development. In James's case, adding examples and details also allows readers to judge for themselves whether the common room needs renovating.

These techniques invite readers to participate in the argument, and these actions tend to encourage a greater emotional connection to the subject and the position being argued.

In Figure 2.19, note how the concrete details used in the advertisement, "Why love one ... but eat the other?" by www.iVegan.ca, persuade readers to shun pork. Context for the question comes from photographs of a Jack Russell terrier and a piglet, both smiling and making eye contact with viewers. The specific fact, "mother pigs sing to their piglets while nursing," for example, surprises viewers and demonstrates the writer's knowledge. Statistics, "26 million pigs" and "two-feet wide crates," also build credibility. Additional concrete details build emotional *and* logical appeals: "pigs are the smartest domestic animals, with intelligence beyond that of a 3-year old human child," "pigs dream, recognize their names, and form affectionate loyal bonds." These facts show that pigs are actually smarter and better companion animals than dogs, yet viewers are inexplicably repulsed at the idea of eating dogs but not of eating pigs.

 Exercise 2.3: How Concrete Examples and Vivid Details Create Emotions

1. Examine the advertisement for the humanity of pigs (Figure 2.19) and create a list of concrete examples and vivid details that add to its impact and its argument.

2. Analyze the phrases to determine the kind of emotion that each phrase or the phrases taken together are intended to create in the reader.

3. What other techniques does this advertisement use to pique the reader's interest in its message?

4. Write a one-half to one-page summary of your analysis of how the concrete examples and vivid details create an emotional appeal that builds interest in the argument.

Develop appropriate comparisons such as analogies and metaphors. The third way to develop effective emotional appeals in an argument is to use comparisons such as analogies or metaphors that make your subject come alive for your readers by creating vivid imagery. For example, telling us that "Mother pigs sing to their piglets" makes a bigger impact on readers' understanding of pigs than telling us that "pigs are very good mothers," because we know that human mothers sing to their babies. This analogy equates humans with pigs, and most of us would never dream of treating a human mother the way we routinely allow mother pigs to be treated.

Analogies are comparisons that emphasize the similarities between two things or situations. For example, the advertisement in Figure 2.19 uses an analogy to compare a pig to a dog (or human). The ad does this by posing this question and then detailing facts about pigs that viewers must measure against what they know about dogs. The facts about pigs summarized in the ad highlight their intelligence and inner lives, knowledge that also emphasizes ways in which pigs exceed dogs in intelligence, nurturing behavior, and emotional attachments. This comparison, where pigs exceed dogs in admirable qualities, creates cognitive dissonance in readers who believe they are entitled to participate in the mistreatment and consumption of these smart, sensitive animals. This strategy strengthens viewers' connection to the subject and creates an emotional appeal intended, in this case, to motivate readers to feel guilty about eating pork.

analogies: Comparisons that emphasize the similarities between two things or situations

Metaphors are comparisons that describe an unfamiliar idea in terms of a familiar idea. For example, the advertisement in Figure 2.19 illustrates through the extensive list of facts and information the ways in which pigs have human qualities: mothers pigs sing to their piglets as they nurse; they form affectionate bonds with one another and other species including humans; they are smarter than 3-year-old humans, and they understand some human language (for example, their names). These human-like qualities are then juxtaposed against the treatment that pigs receive in industrial pig farming, which is horrifying, especially if viewers, in light of what they have just learned about pigs, substitute dogs or humans into the photographs that illustrate some of the experiences of pigs as part of our food chain. The emotional content arises from the readers' response to the basis for comparison. Base your word choice on what you want to accomplish with the comparison: to educate, inform, persuade, entertain, and so on.

metaphors: Comparisons that describe an unfamiliar idea in terms of a familiar idea

The advertisement in Figure 2.20 uses a metaphor to enhance the emotional appeal of its argument. The advertisement juxtaposes an image of a glass of red wine that has been spilled on a white tablecloth with workers in green and red overalls cleaning up black, thick oil spilled on rocks and sand. The words "Red Wine Spill" appear above the spilled wine while the words "Kinder Morgan Pipeline Spill" appear above the oil spill. Both images appear in relatively tight focus so that no context appears for either the wine spill (a party? some violent act?) or the oil spill. Underneath each image is a contrasting image to suggest the solution to the problem the spills present. The solution to the wine spill is labelled "Red Wine Cleanup" and looks like soda water and salt; presumably a solution of those two products will remove the wine stain. The suggested solution for the oil spill is labelled "Kinder Morgan Pipeline Cleanup"; it is a computer-generated icon of a person shrugging their shoulders to suggest that they have no idea how to do this.

The metaphor aims to cause readers to fear the power of the oil-based energy companies to destroy their way of life and the natural world by suggesting that while there are ways to clean up some messes, there is no way to clean up environmental messes.

Figure 2.20 This advertisement uses metaphor to boost its emotional appeal.
Source: www.tankerfreebc.org

ANALYSIS: MEIJING MOTIVATES READERS TO FOLLOW THE RULES

Meijing knows that the logic of her argument will be important (see Rhetorical Situation 2.3), but it will be even more important to have readers act on her message. To have any hope of motivating them to follow the rules, she knows that she needs to develop her credibility and emotional appeals effectively—that is, readers will have to accept her argument and care about her request. Let's look at her audience and purpose first. Meijing wants guests to read and understand the resort's rules, but she also wants them to remember them and comply with them later (audience analysis). To persuade guests to follow the rules, she needs to convince them that it is important—that they *want* to act in those ways. First, she needs to develop good reasons to show readers why they should follow the rules (her logical argument). Not only does she want to present good reasons to follow the rules, she also wants guests to decide to act according to the rules. She wants to encourage those readers who were always inclined to behave appropriately as well as inform those readers who were unaware that there are rules, and she wants to sway readers who may have other ideas about the certain standard of behavior that is expected (her purposes).

To change or reinforce how readers respond to the rules, Meijing knows that she should pay attention to her word choice in the message, use concrete examples and vivid details, and, where appropriate, include analogies and metaphors—all strategies that will engage her readers. Meijing considers word choice: she has to choose carefully when to bring positive and negative slants to her topic. She selects one of the rules from her file and drafts two more versions of it:

- HOT TUB, bathing suits optional after 8 p.m.
- HOT TUB, nude bathing permitted after 8 p.m.
- HOT TUB, skinny dipping allowed after 8 p.m.

She considers how each phrasing conveys a different idea about the activity. The wording for "bathing naked" seems neutral in the first statement, hypercorrect in the second, and colloquial (informal or even slang) in the third one. She analyzes the emotions attached to each phrasing: "Bathing suits optional" seems least emotional, being mainly descriptive. "Nude bathing permitted" sounds stuffy and hoity-toity, whereas "skinny dipping allowed" sounds like harmless, adolescent fun. Meijing concludes that she can control and shape the impression of the resort that she creates in her readers' minds through her choice of phrase. She will have to ensure that whichever choice she makes reinforces the point that Brandywine Falls Inn and Cottages is a family resort.

Next, Meijing considers how word choice may affect how she develops the logic of her argument. Her rules list contains the bare bones of an argument explaining why pets are not allowed at the Inn: "Since some of our guests have pet allergies, we have had to strictly enforce our ban on pets. For this reason, we have a 'no pets' rule at Brandywine Falls Inn and Cottages. Local kennels are available." This rule informs and demands that readers follow the rule, attempting persuasion in an unforgiving way. Meijing decides that it needs rewriting if she is to persuade readers to board their pets. Rewritten, it should help readers understand and make them want to cooperate with the rule, she concludes.

She analyzes the argument to develop a more persuasive one. First, she identifies the claim and stated reason: "We have had to strictly enforce our ban on pets because some of our guests have pet allergies." The unstated reason underlying this claim is something like "We want to offer our allergic guests facilities that are not contaminated with pet allergens." If the owners want to make both pet-owning guests and pet-allergic guests welcome, they could designate some of their units as pet friendly and others as pet free. That seemed not to be the case. The target audience for this rule, Meijing decides, is guests who own pets, not guests with pet allergies. She contemplates various ways of expanding the claim into an argument to which pet owners might respond positively. Figure 2.21 reproduces Meijing's first draft attempt.

A number of guests at Brandywine Falls Inn have serious pet allergies, so we are maintaining our pet-free status at the Inn again this year. This policy is strictly enforced. At the same time, we do realize that it is often a problem for guests to find family members or friends willing to look after pets while they are on vacation, so we have arranged with two local kennels to provide excellent, loving care to your pets during your stay here at the Inn. Present one of our guest coupons to the St. Lawrence Country Club for Pets or the Four Paws Inn for a 15% discount on your kenneling fees. The coupons are available at the registration desk.

Figure 2.21 **Meijing's first draft of an argument explaining the no-pets policy at the Inn.**

Exercise 2.4: Analyze the Word Choice in Meijing's First Draft

1. Examine the words that Meijing has used in her first draft in Figure 2.21.

2. Underline the words that you think contribute most directly to creating the tone of the paragraph.

3. Classify each of your chosen words from question 2 according to whether it has positive, negative, or neutral connotations.

4. Substitute more negative or more positive words to change the overall tone of the argument.

5. Rewrite the paragraph emphasizing the negative tone.

6. Write it again emphasizing the positive tone.

7. Read through the positive and negative slanted versions. Which one do you think the inn's guests would find more convincing? Why? What effect does the word choice have upon an argument's persuasiveness?

Meijing further develops her emotional appeal by considering how she can incorporate concrete examples and vivid details. She considers whether prospective guests of Brandywine Falls Inn and Cottages who are exploring the activities available at the resort may be more interested in statement 1 or 2 as they research its facilities:

1. All guests may use the water and other recreational equipment.
2. All guests may use the paddleboats, kayaks, barracudas, canoes, rowboats, and mountain bikes.

She decides that 1 is too vague: "recreational equipment" could be anything from plastic donut floats to paddleboards to powerboats. The list of equipment goes much further toward persuading viewers to book a room because of its description and specificity. In fact, she thinks, potential guests may decide to spend a week's vacation at Brandywine Falls Inn and Cottages because they can kayak up the river and see the scenery on the mountain bikes. Or parents may want to tour the river below the falls in a paddleboat with their children.

Meijing also considers whether to use analogies or metaphors to develop effective emotional appeals in her argument. She jots down ideas: "You wouldn't hide your grandmother in the closet at the hotel to avoid paying for her, so why would you hide your dog to avoid the 'no pets' rule at Brandywine Falls Inn and Cottages? Instead, get Grandma her own adjoining room and board Fido at the St. Lawrence Country Club for Pets, so both they (and you) can enjoy a comfortable, stress-free vacation." Meijing gauges the effectiveness of this comparison in motivating guests to follow the rule on pets: Will they respond positively to the invitation to avoid being someone who abuses their grandma or their pet?

Finally, she considers whether any terms needed defining. She considers someone being unfamiliar with the term *barracuda*: "What is a barracuda? A barracuda is a pedal-powered jet ski." She decides that most readers booking a holiday at a summer resort would be familiar with a jet ski. This metaphor isolates the main similarity (body design) as well as the main difference (human vs. engine-powered) between the two watercraft to introduce readers to the new concept.

 ## Professional Communication Challenges 2.3

1. Write the letter to Brandywine Falls Inn and Cottages guests

Assume the role of Meijing Zhu. Write the letter to resort guests telling them about the improvements that were made to the facilities over the last winter and persuading them to read and follow the resort's rules. Use the discussion in this module to help you develop a logical, well-supported, and persuasive argument. Refer to Figures 2.15 and 2.16 for summaries of the basic information you wish to convey in your letter. When you have written a first draft of the letter that you are happy with, revise the draft, paying special attention to the emotional and credibility appeals that you are creating through your word choice and argument strategies. Create letterhead for the resort, keep the letter to one page, and sign it as the owners of the resort.

Audience: Your primary audience for this letter is the guests who will visit the resort this summer; the secondary audience includes Mr. and Mrs. Hurley, whose voices will be represented in the letter

Purpose: Primarily to persuade readers (the resort guests) to follow the resort policies and to feel goodwill toward the resort; secondarily to demonstrate your competence and ability to your employers

Genre: Persuasive letter

2. Redesign the Rates and Policies webpage for Brandywine Falls Inn and Cottages

As Meijing Zhu noted after a cursory examination, the guest rules at Brandywine Falls Inn are presented among additional information and room rates, so there is no quick, easy reference for Inn guests to find and review the rules. Redesign and rewrite a "Rates and Policies" page so that the rates and the rules are presented separately on it. Find a resort on your own or use this link to search for resorts anywhere in Canada:

www.resortsandlodges.com/lodging/canada/index.html

and this link to search for resorts anywhere in the United States:

www.resortsandlodges.com/lodging/usa/

Using the resort rates and policies page that you selected from one of the websites above, remove any extra information that you think might confuse or distract guests from finding and reading the important rules. Rewrite any rules that you think could be improved or clarified. Your purpose in revising this page is not only to inform but also to persuade readers to follow the rules. Your revision should display the resort rules and policies clearly, prominently, completely, and persuasively. Hand in both the page you found and your revision of it.

Audience: Primarily potential and returning guests to the resort who will visit the webpage to review the rules and to decide whether to book a vacation there; secondary audiences could include rival resort owners checking out the resort's policies

Purpose: To provide a clear and quick reference to viewers to communicate the resort's rates and policies; to motivate viewers to choose this resort for their vacation destination

Genre: Webpage displaying resort amenities and policies

Using the strategies laid out in this module, you can create arguments that may move readers to respond in the way that you want. You greatly increase the chance that readers will do what you want when you give them a clear and well-supported argument with details that demonstrate your knowledge and expertise on the subject and that emphasizes the importance of the topic and their contribution to it through acting. Make your point through persuasive arguments tailored to your readers.

CHAPTER SUMMARY

- Successful arguments use three basic strategies to persuade readers: credibility, logic, and emotion.
- Writers build credibility through knowledge, fairness, and shared values or identification with readers.
- Writers create logical arguments by making claims and then supporting those claims with evidence such as experts, definitions, precedents, consequences, examples, and statistics.
- Writers employ emotion in argument through their choice of words, selection of vivid details or examples, inclusion of eye-catching visuals, and use of metaphors and analogies.

CHAPTER 3

Style in Business and Professional Writing

 ## LEARNING OUTCOMES

1. Analyze communication situations and create appropriate written responses to them

2. Use concepts and techniques from plain language to determine reader needs, present key ideas clearly, and eliminate jargon

3. Understand and apply methods for presenting negative information as positively as possible, while still presenting it clearly and ethically

4. Apply techniques for improving cohesion, concision, and emphasis

5. Read source texts carefully and use knowledge gained from them to create appropriate professional documents

GETTING STARTED

Style—the word immediately brings to mind images of colorful fashion, crazy hairstyles, and innovative music. In business and professional communication, style means writing in ways that help readers understand your message. In this chapter, we introduce you to five topics that will improve your written style in business and professional communication: plain language, positive emphasis when delivering bad news, cohesion, emphasis, and conciseness. Concepts from **plain language** help organize documents and present information so that it is clear and comprehensible. You will also learn how to use positive language to present your ideas and report bad news while also reporting it ethically. Further, you will learn how to improve the flow or cohesion of your sentences and how to add emphasis to the important information in individual sentences as well as paragraphs. Together, these techniques will improve the quality of your writing.

plain language: An approach to writing that emphasizes the needs of readers to make sense of documents through direct, simple, and unadorned prose and well-organized documents

In the first Rhetorical Situation, you will meet Dennis Chan, who finds that many of his clients are unable to read and understand their insurance policies because of the legal jargon they contain. He finds a solution in plain language, a global movement to make legal, medical, financial, and other important information more accessible to readers. In the second Rhetorical Situation, Toula Stephanos has to report a higher-than-average return rate for unsold eyeglass frames. Because her manager helped design some of the unsold frames, she has a challenging rhetorical situation: writing a report that puts as positive a spin as possible on bad news that directly affects her boss. The third Rhetorical Situation finds Jayson Morito revising a report to improve its style. Although the content is solid, it needs revision to improve its organization, its conciseness, and the cohesion of sentences within paragraphs. By working your way through these situations, you will learn ways to communicate clearly and concisely with your readers.

Rhetorical Situation 3.1: Plain Language, Insurance Contracts, and the Client's Right to Know

 Analyze communication situations and create appropriate written responses to them

Monday morning is never the easiest day of the week, but Dennis Chan has never had this many calls before. The callers share a common theme—everyone is asking questions that they should be able to answer by just reading their policies.

Sure, some of the questions are being asked by people who just can't be bothered to read the documents that the insurance companies sent, but some of the others—most of them, in fact—are real questions asked by very frustrated clients. Dennis knows that if he wants to keep these customers and grow his business, he has to find a way to help his clients locate information quickly.

All these calls are also cutting into the time he needs to spend looking for new clients. Also, referrals from his existing customers are an important part of finding those new clients. He needs to deal with the information problem, and soon.

For example, Mrs. Leung's question about the part of the insurance agreement shown in Figure 3.1 would puzzle just about anybody on their first reading.

AGREEMENT OF INSURANCE

4. In as much as the premium charged or as avowed in the Record of Automobile Insurance to which alteration form is conjoined, the indemnifier shall assure an entitled claimant for the pecuniary reimbursement to which he or she is lawfully permitted to recoup from a deficiently insured vehicle operator as recompense in response to the physical harm or the demise of the entitled claimant occurring from the direct or indirect use or maneuvering of a motorized vehicle.

RESTRICTIONS TO COVERAGE UNDER THIS ALTERATION FORM

5. The indemnified's fullest legal responsibility per this alteration form, despite the sum of entitled claimants or indemnified individuals physically harmed or caused to die or the sum of vehicles covered under the Policy, is the total by which the maximum familial unit protection coverage surpasses the sum of all constraints of automobile legal responsibility insurance, or bonds, or monetary deposits, or other pecuniary warranties as stipulated by law in place of such indemnification, of the deficiently insured vehicle operator and of any individual equally legally responsible with that vehicle operator.

6. Where this alteration form is ruled as surfeit, the indemnified's utmost legal responsibility under this alteration form is the total reckoned under Section 5 of this alteration form, minus the totals available to entitled claimants under any primary damage insurance mentioned in Section 15 of this alteration form.

Figure 3.1 **A passage from Mrs. Leung's car insurance policy.**

First of all, Part 4 is one long sentence—77 words. Dennis isn't a language expert, but he knows that shorter sentences are often easier to understand. He wonders how Mrs. Leung is supposed to sort her way through such a long sentence. The real problem, he decides, is that Mrs. Leung isn't supposed to be reading this document at all—lawyers are the real audience. He wonders why these companies cannot write a policy that their customers can understand.

Dennis decides that the policy writers probably forget about customers when they start worrying about the legal details. What his customers need, he realizes, is a guide or summary sheet of the policy that makes the agreement clear. When he offers to draft this document, Mrs. Leung responds that she thinks it would be wonderful—and the sooner the better, because she has to pay her bill by the end of the month. Dennis explains that it will probably take him a week or so, because he will have to get approval from company lawyers.

Dennis considers the policy language. It surely doesn't qualify as an explanation of how insurance works that is easy for his clients to understand. He knows there are codes of consumers' rights that describe the rights and responsibilities for all parties involved in the business–consumer relationship (see Figure 3.2). These codes protect consumers from having to sign a contract that they don't fully understand. One important consumer right is that contractual documents that consumers must sign and agree to abide by should be written in plain language that those same consumers can understand.

Codes of Consumer Rights

Many industries have developed codes of consumer rights to identify for both businesses and consumers what the rights and responsibilities are for all parties. These codes generally suggest that businesses have the responsibility to treat consumers fairly and to not drag out the process of responding for a long time. Federal courts in many countries have upheld these codes with recent decisions that outline the responsibility of businesses to act ethically.

These rights are balanced with consumer responsibilities to also act fairly in their dealings with businesses. This means that consumers must also act ethically by providing accurate and complete information when they sign contracts.

The details of fair dealing (which, as a legal term in the United States, means the commitment to act fairly in contracts) vary from one country and circumstance to the next, but the essence remains the same: both businesses and consumers have rights and responsibilities. For an example of the responsibilities of consumers, see Insurance Bureau of Canada, www.ibc.ca, click on Resources at the top of the page, Consumer Resources, and then Consumer Rights and Responsibilities.

Figure 3.2 **Many industries have developed codes of consumer rights.**

As Dennis continues reading the policy, he notes that all the text in the policy isn't impenetrable. The section "What We Will Pay For" (shown in Figure 3.3) is not bad, starting with the title. It has only two medium-length sentences and contains no specialized or abstract vocabulary. The second sentence is only 12 words long and a grammatically simple sentence (subject-verb-object). The problems that remain are the adjectives: "sensible" and "reasonable." These terms point to the kind of settlement that will have to be negotiated when a claim is made.

WHAT WE WILL PAY FOR

2.1 Once we receive payment for your insurance, we will refund any reasonable charges you incur when renting a similar vehicle. We will also refund any sensible expenditures for taxis or public transit.

Figure 3.3 **A passage from Mrs. Leung's car insurance policy that is written clearly.**

So it can be done, concludes Dennis. The legal language can be revised into plain language. But he also knows that the car insurance policy is a legal contract between the company and the client, so the obscure parts have to be revised carefully in the summary sheet so as not to jeopardize the legalities. The first step is to write a clear draft and then have the lawyers at Pacific Mountain Mutual verify that all legal points are covered and the summary sheet correctly reflects the contract.

STYLE IN BUSINESS AND PROFESSIONAL COMMUNICATION

 Use concepts and techniques from plain language to determine reader needs, present key ideas clearly, and eliminate jargon

Plain Language in Professional Documents

Plain language is language that is clear. It contains specific information that is relevant to readers, and it is logically arranged and easy to follow. Governments, including the Government of Canada and federal and state governments in the United States (see Figure 3.4), the legal and medical professions, and businesses have grown increasingly interested in using plain language after recognizing that many of their documents were too difficult for the average person to understand. The plain language movement evolved to promote the rewriting of important public documents so that intended audiences could access the information they contained. Legal documents, insurance contracts, tax documents, medical information, product information, and guarantees are some of the targets of this movement to ensure that ordinary readers can understand and follow them.

An institution's duty to inform the public includes the obligation to communicate effectively. Information about policies, programs, services, and initiatives must be clear, relevant, objective, easy to understand, and useful.

To ensure clarity and consistency of information, plain language and proper grammar must be used in all communication with the public. This principle also applies to internal communications, as well as to information prepared for Parliament or any other official body, whether delivered in writing or in speech.

Source: Communications Policy of the Government of Canada, http://www.tbs-sct.ac.ca/pol/doc-eng. aspx?id=12316&section=text, Treasury Board of Canada Secretariat, 2012. Reproduced with the permission of the President of the Treasury Board of Canada, 2014.

Figure 3.4 **Using plain language is the official policy of the Government of Canada.**

Plain language is also a good and effective business communication style. When you are writing business documents, use these principles to help you communicate effectively with your readers:

- use short sentences and simple words
- write so that readers can understand your message in one reading
- be simple and direct, but not simplistic or patronizing

To apply these principles to your document, follow these four steps:

1. Determine the needs of your audience: Consider who your primary audience is. Are there different groups of readers who will need their own version of the document?
2. Organize the information to meet these readers' needs: Is chronological order suitable, or should you use another organizational pattern?
3. Check the accessibility of the vocabulary: See stylistic advice in this chapter.
4. Test your draft: Who might give you useful feedback to determine whether the message is clear?

DETERMINE YOUR READERS' NEEDS

To determine the needs of your readers, approach the document from their point of view. What do they want to know? For example, if you were writing a message to employees in your organization to remind them to renew their confidentiality agreement for the upcoming year (see Figure 3.5), what would the different groups in your organization need or want to know? Regular employees will have signed this agreement in previous years, so they will be familiar with the form and the request. New employees may not have encountered this practice before, so they may need more detail than established employees. The contract workers (e.g., external consultants) may want to know whether they need to sign this form since they are not permanent employees.

Good morning,

[1] As announced by President Dustin Pearce earlier this month, all employees, including external consultants who work with Marbury Associates' data, are required to renew their annual *Confidentiality Agreement* at this time. [2] This is part of our obligation to data providers, and it serves as a way to demonstrate to them our commitment to maintaining their privacy and security.

[3] Close to 70% of staff have already completed this agreement. [4] If you've not already done so, please renew your *Confidentiality Agreement* here. [5] It only takes a few minutes and the deadline for renewal is **January 31**.

[6] Please also take a few minutes to visit our new webpage, January is Privacy Awareness Month at Marbury, on the MarburyFreeway and download and read the latest edition of MarburyNews. [7] We invite you to join us in celebrating Privacy Awareness Month!

[8] Thank you for continuing your commitment to maintaining and strengthening Marbury's ongoing reputation as a culture of privacy.

Alex LeCourt
Director of Privacy
Privacy and Legal Services/Vie privée et Services juridiques
Marbury Associates
123, rue Champlain Road, Ste. 123
Ottawa, ON K3L 4R9

Figure 3.5 **Plain language and determining your readers' needs. [Note: the sentence numbering is for ease of reference in a later exercise]**

As you examine the needs of your readers, consider whether they form a homogenous group. Will a single version of the document serve all readers' needs, or should you think about readers as different groups? For example, are the needs of contract employees identical to those of permanent employees when they contemplate signing the agreement? How might the differences affect how you write the request? To write to different audiences, many organizations ask readers on their websites to identify themselves (university and college websites have links for students, staff, and alumni) and then serve up different pages for each group when they click to identify themselves.

ORGANIZE THE INFORMATION TO RESPOND TO READERS' NEEDS

After determining your readers' needs for a particular document, you must decide how best to organize information to meet those needs. You can choose from several organizing principles:

- chronological order
- most important to least important
- general-to-specific or specific-to-general

Use a principle that best organizes the information your readers need. For example, in requesting that co-workers renew their confidentiality agreement, you might use a specific-to-general pattern of organization. This organization works because employees must comply; starting with specific information about how to comply helps most readers get the task done and move on. Those who want more information about the general context for the agreement and more detail can continue reading. On the other hand, if you were asking for their cooperation for a non-compulsory task, you might begin with the more general information to convince them of why this would be in their best interests.

In the case of Figure 3.5, LeCourt begins by reminding employees that the agreement must be renewed by month's end, describes the process for renewing it, informs them of more general information associated with privacy in the organization, and concludes by thanking them for their cooperation.

EFFECTIVE STYLE IN WORKPLACE WRITING

Writing effectively means attending to what you say at the level of word choice, sentence structure, and paragraph organization. Avoid abstract terms, keep sentences short, and focus each paragraph on a single idea.

Words

Here are some tips for good business writing at the level of words.

Use active voice: Active voice means putting people and things into the subjects (usually at the beginning) of your sentences. For example, the following sentence uses active voice:

Mrs. Leung requested *that Dennis Chan explain paragraph 4 of her insurance policy.*

This sentence uses passive voice:

An explanation of paragraph 4 in her insurance policy was requested by Mrs. Leung *of Dennis Chan.*

Note that the passive sentence structure is longer (17 words instead of 13). It also makes readers wait until the end for all the details they need to understand the sentence. Use active voice to improve conciseness and clarity.

Use present tense: Present tense is the simplest form for a verb in English. Using the simplest form reduces wordiness and makes ideas clearer and more immediate. For example, using the conditional tense (verbs using *would* and *should*) makes readers work harder to understand: "If you would need to make a claim, you should contact one of our insurance adjustors at 123-123-4567." Instead, say "If you *need* to make a claim, *contact* one of our insurance adjustors at...." Using present tense makes the point fast and easy to grasp—the whole point of good business communication.

Use "you" to address readers: Using "you" to address readers creates a closer relationship between writer and reader, and it produces clear, concise prose. For example, which sentence would you rather read?

1. Policy holders should verify the details of their auto insurance policy before submitting their payment.
2. Please verify the details of your auto insurance policy before you pay your bill.

In the first version, the writer addresses someone else ("the policy holder"), not me. I have to place myself into the third person (they) to see whether this directive applies to me or not. In the second version, I immediately know I should read through my policy before I pay the insurance company.

Use short, simple words: English has many words for the same ideas and concepts. When you choose a word, use the shortest and simplest one for a particular concept. For example, both these sentences mean the same thing:

1. Peruse all documents in advance of any submission of remuneration.
2. Read this form before you pay your bill.

Many readers have to read the first sentence twice to understand it. Some may use a dictionary to look up one or two words. Most readers will read the second sentence once and understand it. When you have a choice, choose the short, simple word.

Use the same word to refer to the same object: In some writing situations, you may want to show your rich and varied vocabulary (in an academic essay for your history class, perhaps). In most business and professional communication, avoid using synonyms: use the same word for the same object, concept, or idea throughout a document. Synonyms can confuse readers because they wonder if the different words mean the same thing or something else. To inform readers of specific information clearly and concisely, reuse the same terms. In real estate, refer to either a title or a deed, but do not alternate using the terms.

Avoid jargon but not necessarily technical language: Jargon is specialized language used to impress, not to inform. According to Dictionary.com, one meaning of jargon is the vocabulary specific to a group (for example, "medical jargon"), but it is more accurate to describe these vocabularies as technical language because they have developed to enable specialists to discuss sophisticated concepts ("herd immunity," for example). That they tend to exclude non-specialists and lay people is inadvertent. When you are speaking to other specialists in your area, by all means use technical language to demonstrate your knowledge of the area, but when speaking to lay readers or the general public, limit your use of technical language to only those one or two terms that you cannot speak on the subject without (for example, "GHG" or greenhouse gases when speaking of climate change) and define them clearly and simply.

The word "jargon" emphasizes the exclusionary properties of the vocabulary. In business and professional communication, jargon generally refers to pretentious language that is vague and hard to understand. For example, the first sentence below uses jargon (in bold typeface) and technical language (in italics). The second uses just technical language with definitions where needed (underlined):

1. The purpose of the *consultation* was **to dialogue with** the communities and **key** *stakeholders* of Perth-Grand Valley and the Northern Townships on the need for a *Regional Hospital* **Service Delivery model** with **in-depth discussion** on how this could best be achieved.
2. The purpose of the *consultation* was to talk to communities and *stakeholders* (elected officials and health administrators) of Perth-Grand Valley and the Northern Townships on whether they needed a *Regional Hospital* and how best to achieve it.

Technical terms are often essential to a topic. For example, the terms "consultation" and "stakeholder" and "Regional Hospital" are essential in example 2 above. However, neither "consultation" nor "regional hospital" need be defined for most readers. If you can, and where necessary, translate a technical term into simpler language ("*elected officials and health administrators*"). Avoid using jargon to impress in good business communication.

Sentences
Here are some tips for writing effectively at the level of sentences.

Keep sentences short (between 14 and 22 words): Long sentences tax reader memory. If readers get lost, they may not reread to follow your point. They may also lose interest when they forget the beginning of the sentence. Most short-term memories can process only about 25 words in a chunk, so use 25 words as your limit for sentences. Aim for lengths of between 14 and 22 words. One exception is a topic that only makes sense in a longer sentence. In these cases, revise to make the sentence as clear and readable as possible. Use parallel grammatical structure (for example, start all bullet points with verbs) and lists, and avoid interruptive phrases (for example, definitions you provide in parentheses after a technical term).

How do you shorten sentences? Limit yourself to one or two topics per sentence. If you need to qualify or modify an idea, do so in separate sentences. Break complex ideas into smaller units. Avoid coordinating conjunctions such as *and*, *but*, *yet*, *or*, *so*, *for*, and *nor*. Conjunctions encourage long sentences because they enable you to connect ideas into one long sentence.

The paragraph in the left column of Figure 3.6 is composed of four sentences that contain 128 words—31 words a sentence on average, which is too long if we are aiming to write in plain language. Each sentence contains 23 words or more. The paragraph uses four coordinating conjunctions to join ideas that make the sentences long. If these conjunctions are used as points at which to separate the ideas or if they are removed altogether, the four sentences become eight, and each idea is contained in a separate sentence.

Coordinating conjunctions can create long, complex sentences.	Revising coordinating conjunctions can simplify and clarify sentences.
[1] Many people do not think of writing as a technology, **yet** it is a tool that humans have used for several thousand years to develop, record, and communicate their thoughts, ideas, and knowledge about themselves and the world around them. *(40 words)* [2] Scholars believe that humans use writing as a way to think, that writing facilitates complex thought **and** that it has enabled our species to make the advances that we have in science, medicine, technology, and the arts. *(37 words)* [3] **And yet** writing is rarely mentioned in wide-ranging discussions of technology, the more likely focus being on the Internet, artificial intelligence, or nanoscience. *(23 words)* [4] At the same time, writing makes possible many of the innovations that humans develop, **and** it also makes possible the dissemination of knowledge around these innovations. *(26 words)*	[1] Many people do not think of writing as a technology. *(10 words)* [2] However, it is a tool that humans have used for several thousand years. *(13 words)* [3] They have used writing to develop, record, and communicate their ideas about themselves and the world around them. *(18 words)* [4] Scholars believe that humans use writing as a way to think. *(11 words)* [5] They argue that writing helps humans think complex thoughts. *(9 words)* [6] It has also enabled humans to advance our knowledge of science, medicine, technology, and the arts. *(16 words)* [7] Yet writing is rarely mentioned in discussions of technology. *(9 words)* [8] Instead, discussion focuses on technology related to the Internet, artificial intelligence, or nanoscience. *(13 words)* [9] Writing makes possible many of the innovations that humans develop. *(10 words)* [10] It also makes it possible to inform people about this new technology. *(12 words)*

Figure 3.6 **How do you shorten long sentences?**

Business Communication: Rhetorical Situations

In the paragraph on the right of Figure 3.6, the coordinating conjunctions have been divided to shorten the sentences and simplify the language. The same passage is now 10 sentences between 9 and 18 words long, 14 words on average. The ideas from the coordinating conjunctions (*but*, *yet*, *and*) have been placed in separate sentences.

However, write longer sentences if a longer sentence is more direct. And do not omit transitions as a way to shorten sentences. Transitional words help readers connect ideas and follow your points.

Exercise 3.1: Shorten Long Sentences

Use the advice on shortening sentences to revise the long sentences in Figure 3.5.

1. Count the number of words in each sentence and decide which ones are too long.

2. Use the techniques described previously to shorten those sentences that you decide are too long.

3. Make any other changes to the letter that you think make the content clearer and easier to understand.

4. Be prepared to explain what you revised and why.

Vary the length of your sentences: When every sentence is 14 words, your writing becomes boring. Include short, medium, and long sentences (up to 25 words) to keep your ideas fresh and interesting. For example, the sentences in the revised version of Figure 3.6 contain sentences between 9 and 18 words long.

State ideas positively and avoid negatives: Introducing negatives into your writing increases the complexity of the ideas and the mental gymnastics needed by readers to understand your thoughts. Stating points positively and negatives clearly can keep your writing clear and comprehensible. For example, in Figure 3.5 the clause "If you've *not* already done so" can be stated positively and more clearly: "If you have already done so, thank you. Otherwise, please renew your Confidentiality Agreement here." A further example from Figure 3.6, "Many people *do not think* of writing as a technology," may be revised as "Many people *overlook* the fact that writing is also a technology."

Paragraphs

Cover one topic in a paragraph: Discuss one idea or topic in a paragraph. Subdividing your ideas helps keep your paragraphs short. Short paragraphs help you create a page that is clearly laid out with lots of **white space**. White space refers to the area on a page that contains nothing, such as the margins, the ragged end of left-aligned text, and the space between paragraphs and around headings, figures, and visuals. Short paragraphs also invite readers into your writing. For example, the writer of Figure 3.5 uses short paragraphs for each topic: the first paragraph reminds readers to renew their confidentiality agreement. The second paragraph asks readers to act and emphasizes the deadline. The third paragraph informs readers where they can learn

white space: The space not occupied by text or images on a page

more about the privacy policy, and the last paragraph thanks readers for acting. Allotting one point to a paragraph also visually organizes the message and aids in scanning.

Use short paragraphs (150 words, 3 to 8 sentences): Keep paragraphs short—between 3 and 8 sentences and no more than 150 words. When you are revising a document, scan for long paragraphs. Often a longer paragraph will signal a change of topic within that paragraph that means you need a new paragraph. As with sentence length, vary the length of paragraphs. Varying paragraph lengths adds visual interest to the page. It gives you a chance to add more white space, and it allows you to include more headings that help readers and create an inviting layout. Sometimes the occasional one-sentence paragraph will add emphasis and visual impact to your writing.

Use topic sentences: A topic sentence states clearly and simply what the main subject is for that paragraph. When the topic sentence appears first in a paragraph, you aid readers by enabling them to skim your document, reading only the first sentence and still getting an overview of your subject. In Figure 3.7, sentence (a) in each paragraph is a topic sentence. The rest of the paragraph then elaborates on the ideas introduced in the topic sentence. For example, in paragraph 1 the topic is "I have handled all KWIK messages quickly and accurately." Sentence (b) then defines what the writer means by "quickly and accurately." Sentence (c) further explains her actions on messages where a one-week complete response was not feasible. This sentence ends with a specific example of one such occasion. Sentence (d) supplies information about the writer's interactions with co-workers to whom she has delegated some messages to ensure that they too respond efficiently and consistently.

transitions: Words and phrases used to connect one paragraph or idea to another

Use transitions: Help readers follow your shifts of thought by including transitions between paragraphs. **Transitions** are words that forecast to readers where you are taking the discussion next. Time-based transitions—*first*, *second*, *third*, *in conclusion*—help readers track the progress of your argument or discussion. Each transition signals that you have finished one part of the subject and are moving on to the next. Other transitions such as *also*, *in contrast*, *in addition*, and *however* help readers understand the relationships between your ideas. Transitional words and phrases have been highlighted in Figure 3.7 using bold text. Like transitions between sentences, transitions between paragraphs help readers predict and anticipate what follows in the discussion. Paragraph 2 begins with a transitional sentence: "A second important area in which I have excelled has been to consistently review...." This longer transition reminds readers of the document's goal of presenting a self-evaluation and signals a shift from one area of accomplishment to another one. Don't sacrifice transitions to keep your sentences or paragraphs short.

[1] (a) Over the past year I have handled all KWIK messages quickly and accurately. (b) I have acknowledged all KWIK messages within 48 hours and followed up with a full email response within 1 week where possible. (c) In cases where a longer response period was necessary, I provided as much information as possible to the client as soon as it was available and communicated the expected timelines for a full response (**for example**, Healthy Pathways, Lianna Garcia's request for updated information on a readmission JxL produced by Marbury). (d) I **also** consult with team members to whom KWIK messages have been delegated to ensure they are handled efficiently and consistently, especially around interpreting the mandate section of the data request form and producing timelines.

[2] (a) A **second** important area in which I have excelled has been to consistently review all data requests assigned to me for potential problems with the data requested. (b) **For example**, in Raymond LaFrance's (MRAD) request for Spinal Stenosis Mobility, I identified a problem with the RES-16-MN/ABC codes provided by Data Control before we sent out the data. (c) This change resulted in additional work for both teams, but ultimately provided the requestor with much higher quality data that was usable for his study. (d) I have **also** worked with Augustus to mitigate any risk associated with supplying client data that is sensitive (NWT Support Life) or that requires aggregate data in a very tight timeline (CSPHL).

[3] (a) **In addition**, I have developed procedures to reduce potential errors in process. (b) **For example**, I have created two checklists for the data request process: one for aggregate and one for record-level requests. (c) I have updated these checklists with common errors that have been made in the process previously to ensure that the same mistakes do not continue to be made. (d) I have shared these checklists with the new analysts on the team.

Figure 3.7 **An excerpt from a sample year-end self-evaluation.**

Page layout and effective communication: Use document design to present information effectively. Put some thought into how and where you place information on the page to help readers follow and understand your ideas. Lots of white space around headings, paragraphs, and visuals can emphasize the important elements of your document. Formatting elements such as headings and lists can also add emphasis and visual interest. Part of the challenge of getting people to read government forms, medical information, legal contracts, and insurance documents is extending the invitation into the document. An attractive page layout can invite readers in and good business style can encourage them to continue reading.

ANALYSIS: DENNIS WRITES A SUMMARY OF THE INSURANCE POLICY

 Analyze communication situations and create appropriate written responses to them

Dennis remembers learning about writing and plain language in his business communication class a few years ago. A quick Internet search turns up some relevant websites, a definition, and some useful pointers. After a quick tour through several plain language sites (see Figure 3.8), Dennis plans four steps for writing a summary sheet to help explain the auto insurance policy:

1. Determine the needs of my audience (Mrs. Leung and others like her): Will different groups of readers need their own version of the policy?
2. Organize the information to meet these readers' needs: Is chronological order suitable or should I use some other organizational pattern for the policy information?
3. Use stylistic advice to revise the policy language.
4. Test my summary of the policy: Which two or three current clients should I ask to read my summary to see whether the message is clear?

Dennis considers what his readers will want to know about the auto insurance that they are purchasing. Then he generates a list of questions his readers will want answered as they read through their insurance policy: Will a single summary sheet serve all his readers' needs, or would it be more effective to think about readers as forming different groups? Will the needs of non-native speakers of English be the same as those of native speakers of English? How may any differences affect how he writes the summary?

Exercise 3.2: Determine the Needs of Auto Insurance Policy Readers

 Read source texts carefully and use knowledge gained from them to create appropriate professional documents

1. Before beginning this exercise, review Rhetorical Situation 3.1, and reread Figures 3.1 and 3.3 closely, if you need to.

2. In groups of two or three, discuss Rhetorical Situation 3.1 to determine what owners of the insurance policy would want to know as they read through the passages reproduced here. As a group, generate a list of questions that you think policy holders would have about their insurance coverage (related to these excerpts).

3. Identify the topics that the excerpts cover. Do these topics answer the questions that policy holders would have about the information in the excerpts?

4. Is there any additional information that readers would want about these topics?

5. Using points raised in your discussion, summarize the needs of Dennis Chan's auto insurance policy readers.

- www.plainlanguage.gov: This is the website of the American government's Plain Language Organization. It contains a wealth of valuable and useful information about plain language, including definitions and some history.
- www.plainlanguagenetwork.org: This website is sponsored by the Plain Language Association International. It provides information about projects, conferences, and many other topics associated with plain language in several different languages.
- http://en.wikipedia.org/wiki/Plain_language: Wikipedia's definition of plain language provides a quick overview of the movement and its goals.
- www.centreforliteracy.qc.ca/node/188: This page contains an excellent overview of the controversy surrounding readability and tests for readability, one aspect of plain language.

Figure 3.8 **Sources for additional information about plain language.**

Professional Communication Challenges 3.1

1. Revise the excerpt from the insurance policy

Revise the text in Figure 3.1 so that it is written in plain language and clients like Mrs. Leung can understand it. Use the discussion about style and plain language covered in this module to help you revise the excerpt. Also be sure that your revision fulfills the promise to the consumer described in the Codes of Consumer Rights in Figure 3.2. Because you are probably not a lawyer, you can't reasonably assess whether your revision maintains the legal integrity of the original policy, but do your best to clarify the excerpt without radically altering the intent of the original.

Audience: Clients such as Mrs. Leung who wish to know what they are paying for in their insurance coverage

Purpose: To clearly and concisely communicate important details about insurance coverage

Genre: Excerpt from an insurance agreement

2. Revise an insurance document for yourself or a family member

Find a copy of an insurance document of your own or of a family member and revise a 500-word chunk of it. Use the information in this module to help you with your revision. Hand in a copy of the original excerpt from the insurance policy along with your revision. Make sure you clearly mark the section that you revised.

Audience: You or your family members who want to understand the insurance coverage that they are purchasing

Purpose: To clearly and concisely communicate important details about insurance coverage

Genre: Excerpt from an insurance agreement

Rhetorical Situation 3.2: Style! Eye Fashions: Selling Bad News

 Analyze communication situations and create appropriate written responses to them

Irina Nemcova explains to the visiting sales representative that the whole product line is unpopular—nobody likes these eyeglass frames. Patients try on a set of frames from the Casanova line, but they end up choosing something else. The eyeglass frames look good on the display, but when the customer puts them on, the fit or proportion just isn't right.

Toula Stephanos grimaces and notes that her manager had had high hopes for that collection when it came out. She starts putting the small pile of rejected eyeglass frames into her leather display cases. Irina points out that perhaps the name, the Casanova line, is part of the problem.

Toula quickly responds that Marketing names the lines, not her. But she is glad that Irina wants some of her other frames. Those are some of her favorites from the new fall collection of the Cool Dudz line. Irina points to the group of frames that she has selected from the samples of new styles during the sales presentation. She explains that she likes the unusual but subtle details that make the Cool Dudz line attractive.

Irina asks Toula how her sales trip is going so far. Toula admits that it is disappointing. The optometrists across the prairies and the Midwest are also returning the Casanova line. She notes that Dr. Bhathal in Fargo has sold several frames, but she only ordered 12 pairs. Toula snaps the clasps shut on her display cases and places them on the floor. The order for the Cool Dudz line is a bright light. Toula reflects that she will have to start her trip report this evening. She must submit the report before she catches a plane to Milan for European Fashion Week on Sunday.

Toula is more disappointed with this sales trip than she has let on to Irina. She knows her manager, Gaston Papineau, will be particularly upset because so many units from the Casanova line are coming back to them. He has pushed her to sell that line because he was involved in some of the designs. At least the Cool Dudz and the MyFrames lines have interested nearly all of the doctors that she's visited on this trip. Maybe their orders will soften the return of—how many unsold frames? There are four or five dozen, at least. Style! Eye Fashions is a relatively small company compared to the competition. Returned frames won't cause financial problems, but no one looks good when they miss the mark on designs or sales.

Positive Emphasis and Bad News

 Understand and apply methods for presenting negative information as positively as possible, while still presenting it clearly and ethically

As a professional business person, you will sometimes have to communicate bad news to customers, clients, or colleagues. No one likes to send or receive bad news, but there are ways of making readers feel better about the information that you send them. Generally, readers respond more favorably to descriptions of events that are depicted positively rather than negatively. One strategy is to put a **positive emphasis** on the discussion while also remaining clear about the unfavorable news.

One example of this strategy occurs in Figure 3.9, a sample message declining an offer of employment. In the first paragraph, the writer thanks his reader for inviting him to apply to her organization's open position. In the second paragraph, he notes the two reasons that underlie his decision to decline the offer. In the third paragraph he expresses his continuing interest in the organization and seeks to maintain the goodwill of his reader by remaining positive and appreciative of the opportunity he was offered. Although he sends bad news to his reader, he states his refusal as positively as possible. The writer uses three strategies in this message to present negative information in a positive way:

positive emphasis: A writing strategy that emphasizes positive news and downplays negative information

1. He uses positive language as often as he can.
2. He links the negative information (his refusal) to a reason.
3. He de-emphasizes the negative point and states it briefly.

Hi Marianne,

First of all, I would like to thank you for thinking of me for the position that you are trying to fill within First Financial. The projects that your team is working on are quite exciting.

Given my current position on my team, however, and the timing of the contract that you are trying to fill (eight months, with no possibility for extension) I don't think that it makes sense for me to pursue this position at this time.

Thank you again for thinking of me, and I hope you will keep me in mind for future openings in your organization because I find the collegial work environment and the interesting projects very attractive. You have a great team, and I hope to have the opportunity to work with you in the future.

Best Regards,

Paul

Paul Li
Senior Analyst
Epsilon Zeta Accounting
Phone: 123-123-4567
Fax: 123-234-5678
pli@eza.com

Figure 3.9 **Sample email that uses positive emphasis to decline an offer of employment.**

USE POSITIVE LANGUAGE

Positive language is most easily defined by identifying what it is not, which is any mention of something negative. There are several ways to maintain positive language. These include avoiding the words listed in Figure 3.10, avoiding negative linguistic constructions (*"I cannot send you x"*), and, in negative messages, avoiding constructions that use "you" when it might be construed as blaming your readers. Therefore, using positive language means developing a sensitivity for the connotations of words, the importance of word choice, and the subtlety of positive linguistic constructions. Positive language means emphasizing what you *can* do for readers and taking into account your readers' viewpoint. In the discussion that follows, we explore these topics and strategies in greater detail.

Figure 3.10 reproduces the sentence from Figure 3.9 that contains Paul Li's refusal, which uses some negative language that could be revised to use more positive language.

Negative: Given my current position and the fact that you are offering an eight-month contract with no possibility of extension, I don't think it makes sense for me to pursue this position at this time.

Better: Given my current position and the fact that you are offering a contract limited to eight months, it makes more sense for me to remain in my current situation.

Better yet: Given my current position and the fact that you are offering a contract limited to eight months, I prefer to wait until you have a permanent position so that I could join the team permanently.

Figure 3.10 **Negative language revised to be more positive and include the reader's viewpoint.**

LINK NEGATIVE INFORMATION TO A REASON OR READER MOTIVATOR

Readers can accept negative news more easily if they know the reason for it. If you can include a reason that clarifies the negative, do so. Similarly, if you can, show readers how the negative might benefit them (this reason becomes the reader motivator). Of course, make sure readers would agree that your suggestion is an actual benefit to them. In the revised example, the writer gives two reasons in advance of stating his refusal (in bold typeface):

> "**Given my current position** and **the fact that you are offering a contract limited to eight months**, I prefer to wait until you have a permanent position so that I could join the team permanently."

The writer identifies the eight-month contract as the main reason for his refusal, and when that detail is linked to his continued enthusiasm for First Financial as a potential employer, the message is intended to motivate the reader to look for permanent positions to invite the writer to apply for in the future.

afraid	fault	lacking	problem
anxious	fear	loss	reject
bad	hesitate	missing	sorry
delay	ignore	mistake	terrible
difficulty	impossible	neglect	unfortunately
dissatisfied	inadequate	never	unpleasant
error	incomplete	no	unreasonable
except	inconvenient	not	unsure
fail	injury	objection	wrong

Figure 3.11 **Avoid using several of these negative words in one message.**

DE-EMPHASIZE THE NEGATIVE AND STATE IT BRIEFLY

Using positive language doesn't mean omitting negatives. Sometimes you have bad news that readers must know. However, you can present the negatives clearly and simply without emphasizing the negative aspects, as the revisions in Figure 3.10 illustrate. De-emphasizing rather than obscuring or omitting may seem like a subtle distinction, but it is an important one. You may not put the negative information in a headline, but you still have to include it.

Figure 3.11 lists words that communicate a pessimistic viewpoint. Sometimes we write without realizing that we have used these words, resulting in an overly pessimistic account of the subject matter. For example, Figure 3.12 presents two messages: one where the writer conveys disaster through repeated negative words, and another that conveys the same point more positively.

You can also de-emphasize the negative by placing it in the middle of a paragraph. Locating it at the beginning or end of a message or paragraph makes it stand out because the start and the end are points of emphasis (see Emphasis in Rhetorical Situation 3.3 below).

In Figure 3.12, the revised text builds goodwill by demonstrating concern for the owner's pet in the first sentence. The last two sentences also add to goodwill by reproducing the clinic phone number to make booking an appointment easy and by using the pet's name to personalize the message.

ORIGINAL	REVISED
Dear Mrs. Graves,	Dear Mrs. Graves,
According to our records, your dog, Finn, has **sadly missed** his annual wellness examination and appropriate vaccines. **Unfortunately**, this area has a **terribly** high incidence of diseases such as rabies and distemper, so we urge you not to **neglect** your pet's welfare and good health any longer. If you **fail** to schedule an appointment promptly, your **delay** may compromise his health and the health of your whole household. We are certain that you are anxious to avoid this possibility of **injury** and **death**, so we urge you to address this **problem** immediately.	According to our records, your dog, Finn, is due for his annual wellness examination and yearly vaccine boosters. Given the high incidence of diseases such as rabies and distemper in this area, it is important that Finn's immunization remains current. Regular vaccinations and a yearly inspection will protect your pet by helping him maintain a strong resistance to disease. Please call us at (123) 123-4567 to schedule an appointment. We look forward to seeing you and Finn soon.

Figure 3.12 **The highlighted text emphasizes the use of negative phrases that convey a pessimistic impression to readers.**

Exercise 3.3: Revising for Positive Emphasis

Rewrite the following sentences to state the negatives as positively as possible. As you revise, keep your readers in mind and work to build goodwill with them.

1. I am afraid that your payment reached us too late, so we will have to charge you a 10 per cent late fee.

2. Because your file was incomplete, we were unable to consider your application.

3. Unfortunately, due to the hideousness of this frame line, most of our clients sent them back for a refund.

4. If you are dissatisfied with the resolution of your claim, do not hesitate to contact our customer service line.

5. I'm so sorry to be three days late responding to your request. I had to wait for our legal department to get back to me. According to our lawyers, there's nothing we can do about your injuries or lost work time. We recommend that in future you carefully read and follow all usage instructions.

ANALYSIS: RETURNED EYEGLASS FRAMES AND POSITIVE EMPHASIS

 Analyze communication situations and create appropriate written responses to them

When Toula Stephanos begins her report on her trip to promote the fall line, she plans to emphasize the positive outcomes—in particular, the popularity of the Cool Dudz and MyFrames lines. She also has to report the high rate of return of the Casanova line, but she decides to phrase these returns as positively as possible. She knows that readers respond more favorably to positive than negative descriptions of events, so she will use that approach. She considers the options and decides to use positive language, to link negative information to a reason, and to de-emphasize any clearly negative points. She also decides that there may be one or two trivial negative points that she could omit from the report altogether. First she considers the range of choices available to talk about her trip positively. She jots down two negative points that she will have to make (Figure 3.13). Her first draft of both points is too negative, she decides, so she revises to give them more positive emphasis. Figure 3.13 shows several examples of how to change negatives into positives.

Point 1: Higher than average return rate of Casanova frames

Negative: Sales of the Casanova line failed to meet our expectations.
Better: Sales of the Casanova line were smaller than expected.
Better yet: Although returns on the Casanova line were generally higher than expected, six clients also ordered additional frames from this line.

Point 2: Low sales on Hectic frame lines

Negative: Unfortunately, sales of the Hectic line are also disappointing, missing sales targets by 50 per cent.
Better: Sales of the Hectic line achieved 50 per cent of targets.
Better yet: Hectic line sales started slowly, but we expect them to build in the last quarter.

Figure 3.13 **Toula revises two points to make them more positive.**

Second, Toula knows that her boss will want to know why the frame lines didn't sell as antici-pated, so she reflects on her conversations with clients for clues. She knows that if she can explain why the frames were returned, her boss will be more willing to accept this bad news. She also considers whether there are any ways that the company might benefit from knowledge about why the frames are being returned. Figure 3.14 presents the reason and the benefit that Toula develops for her report.

Reason: Several clients suggested that the Hectic designs are too contemporary for their patients.

Reader benefit: This feedback from these initial sales of the Hectic line is invaluable because it suggests we may need a more conservative line of eyeglass frames at Style!.

Figure 3.14 **Toula links the negatives to a reason or reader benefit.**

IF THE NEGATIVE IS TRIVIAL, LEAVE IT OUT

As Toula scans the data in Figure 3.15, she notices that only two of her clients who returned Casanova frames ordered additional frames from this line. She jots this point down for inclusion in the report but then thinks further about it. She realizes that if she mentions this point, she will draw her readers' attention to it. She decides that emphasizing this point is probably not necessary; her boss, Gaston Papineau, will probably look closely at the return data so he will see this point for himself. If not, it probably isn't that important; she decides, after thinking further, to omit it from her report. Figure 3.16 presents two examples where writers could omit the negative point because it is unimportant.

Office and Location	Casanova		Cool Dudz		MyFrames		Hectic	
	Order	Return	Order	Return	Order	Return	Order	Return
Ngô (Brandon, MB)	2	5	7	0	6	0	3	1
Vemulakonda (Brandon, MB)	0	7	9	1	7	1	4	0
Polizzi (Winnipeg, MB)	3	0	5	0	5	0	1	2
Lemanski (Winnipeg, MB)	0	7	9	0	9	0	7	0
Lopez (Winnipeg, MB)	0	10	10	0	10	0	3	2
Vogler (Grand Forks ND)	0	9	12	0	7	1	3	0
Ilioviciu (Grand Forks, ND)	3	0	2	0	3	0	2	1
Bhathal (Fargo, ND)	5	0	6	0	5	0	3	0
Blanchard (Fargo, ND)	0	5	7	0	5	1	5	0
Shah (Bozeman, MT)	0	8	6	1	8	1	4	1
Krizek (Saskatoon, SK)	2	0	2	0	12	0	7	0
Quansah (Saskatoon, SK)	0	10	15	0	5	0	0	0
Nemcova (Regina, SK)	0	12	15	0	7	0	5	0
Brown (Billings, MT)	1	9	6	1	7	1	4	1
Pereida (Billings, MT)	0	4	9	1	8	1	7	1
Totals (Sales and Returns)	**16**	**79**	**130**	**4**	**104**	**6**	**58**	**9**

Figure 3.15 **Sales and merchandise return figures for Year to Date.**

Negative Point 1: Most of the clients who returned Casanova frames ordered additional frames from this line.

Better: Leave it out.

Negative Point 2: Clients who buy five or fewer frames from a particular line pay 25 per cent more than if they bulk ordered (took six or more frames).

Better: Clients who bulk order (buy six or more frames from a particular line) save 25 per cent over smaller orders.

Figure 3.16 **If a negative is trivial, leave it out.**

Before we leave this point, we should clarify that while trivial negative information may be omitted, you should never omit *important* negative information. For example, Toula cannot submit her report and remain quiet about the numbers of returned frames. This is essential negative information that her boss must know.

Communicating ethically in business and professional writing means that you must share negative information clearly and concisely to ensure your readers are aware of it.

 Read source texts carefully and use knowledge gained from them to create appropriate professional documents

 ## Professional Communication Challenges 3.2

1. Write a status report on Toula Stephanos's sales trip

Assume the role of Toula Stephanos and write a status report for her sales trip to optometrists' offices in Manitoba, Saskatchewan, North Dakota, and Montana. Use appropriate sales and return figures from Figure 3.15, as well as any other relevant information from Figures 3.17 and 3.18. Address your status report to her manager, Gaston Papineau, and in your summary of accomplishments, report the poor sales along with the new sales. Use positive emphasis where possible, without glossing over the negatives of the situation. Use the discussion in this chapter to help you write a short (500–750-word) memo report (use the structure of a memo, with To:, From:, Subject:, and Date: headings) that will create a positive impression of Toula Stephanos and demonstrate the ways in which she is trying to earn her sales bonus this year.

Audience: Gaston Papineau, Toula's manager

Purpose: To inform him of the high rate of returns on two lines of eyeglass frames that he helped design, while maintaining his goodwill

Genre: Status report (for more information about status reports, see Chapter 11).

Casanova	Cool Dudz	MyFrames	Hectic
111 Advantage $119	121 Sick $87	221 Enchanté $110	071 Pic-man $78
112 Outré $134	122 Wow $96	222 Absolute $125	072 Bongo $88
113 Oh la! $159	123 Play $104	223 Mystical $135	073 Corsica $99
114 Nonpareil $189	124 Just $110	224 ZsaZsa $155	074 Retreat $99

Figure 3.17 **List prices for assorted frame lines this year.**

Optometrists	Frame line	Comments
I. Nemcova (Regina, SK)	Casanova (12 pair)	"Patients tried frames, chose something else. Frames display well but fit or proportion is not right."
R. Quansah (Saskatoon, SK)	Casanova (10 pair)	"Clients refused them, saying 'Not me.' Styles don't suit our clients."
J. Lopez (Winnipeg, MB)	Casanova (10 pair)	"I couldn't find a face shape that these styles flattered. Neither could Brenda (our frame salesperson)."

Figure 3.18 **Toula's notes on doctor comments for top three returns.**

2. Write the email to report that Toula Stephanos can no longer go to fashion week

Based on the extensive return rate of several of Style! Eye Fashions' newest frame lines, Style! has to reduce expenses, including the planned trip of its top salesperson to Milan for Fashion Week. Writing as Gaston Papineau, draft an email to Toula Stephanos informing her that her planned trip to Italy has been canceled. Present this news as positively as possible, using the discussion in this module to help you draft a message that will maintain Toula's commitment to her job and goodwill toward the company.

Audience: Toula Stephanos, top salesperson for Style! Eye Fashions

Purpose: To explain why Style! Eye Fashions cannot send her to Milan, Italy, for Fashion Week this year, while maintaining her positive attitude and goodwill toward the company

Genre: Email conveying bad news

Jayson Morito is feeling great. He has just finished a huge product promotion that was extremely successful. He stretches out his legs and clasps his hands behind his head, smiling broadly up at Dorian Alvarez, his boss. Dorian stuck his head in the door a few minutes ago to chat. Dorian agrees that Jayson should be feeling good about this latest success. He explains that corporate is quite pleased with how well the promotion event went. Apparently, Arva Springs' president, Jonas Crosby, called raving about how ecstatic they were about everything. That kind of feedback might even lead to a job offer here at Paragon Promotions when he graduates.

In fact, this is exactly what Jayson is working toward. Dorian points out that Jayson has worked 80 hours a week for the last month getting the details right for that event. Jayson has been working since April as an intern at Paragon Promotions, Ltd., in connection with his college program in Business Management. In addition to the Arva Springs Brewery promotion, he has also worked on events for the local American League hockey team and the junior soccer team. He enjoys putting the theory from his classes into action at Paragon Promotions. Jayson responds that he loves putting such events together and that he would love to do it 24/7.

Putting the events on is the fun part of the job. Dorian pulls a document out of the stack of paper he is carrying and places it on Jayson's desk, asking him to draft another version of the report (see Figure 3.19). The smile fades from Jayson's face as he sees the red circles and slashes on the page.

Dorian explains that while the event was fantastic, the report is difficult to follow because of its organization. Jayson keeps changing topics, Dorian observes. He continues, explaining that Jayson's writing could be more cohesive and concise. He mentions that the president of Paragon Promotions, Albert Barker, will definitely read the report, so Jayson will want it to make as positive an impression on Barker as the feedback he is getting from the event itself.

Report on the Arva Springs Honey Cream Ale Promotional Event at the Caribbé Festival

On Saturday, July 5, Toronto Promotions kicked off the Arva Springs Honey Cream Ale promotional event at the Carribé Festival with an 14-hour extravaganza, featuring live performances, giveaways, free samples to anyone over 19, and a "surprise" visit by two players from the Marlies. Tomas Giordano and Alexi Poporov wowed the crowd with their appearance, and they spent more than 45 minutes talking to fans, signing autographs, and sampling the new honey cream ale. *Purple Hurricane* performed some of their most popular songs, and so did Alina Markova, and the city's newest hip hop sensations, *The Boardwalk Poets*. Their performances were scheduled to start at 7 p.m., and they raun until quite a bit past midnight. We also arranged to give away baseball caps, t-shirts, and beach balls with Arva Springs Honey Cream Ale name and logo on them.

Everyone really like the beer. We gave it out in 2 oz. plastic cups, made of recycle plastic. For underage drinkers we had soft drinks like grape or orange soda and some coke, so they weren't left out. We gave out wristbands to all 19- year -olds and older. If they didn't have a wristband, they got pop. We set up the tent on the west side of the Railway grounds, which festival organizers assigned to us, luckily had a very popular rib restaurant tent on one side and snack foods vendor on the other side, so we had high traffic in front of and through our tent from the patrons visiting the other tents. The music also attracted lots of fans and their friends. The beer ran out before 9, but luckily we arranged for a backup truck from Arva Springs, so disaster was avoided.

Dashini estimated from the number of gallons of beer and soft drinks we gave out that we had about 7000 people through our tent in those fourteen hours. Oh, yeah, we limited people to five samples of beer. A lot of peoples came and stayed, listening to music, dancing, and talking. It would have been better if we had a few more boxes of hats and t-shirts to give away since we had so many visitors. We only gave out about 2000 freebies, so only 1/3 of visitors got something. But they did get the beer if they wanted it and were old enough to drink it. The people from Arva Springs Brewery, Mo and Carson, were really happy with how the event went and so we were happy too. The spoken word hour went really good too. It was before the musical acts, at 3 o'clock it started. Actually, a couple of *The Boardwalk Poets*—Transom and B.T.—read some new stuff at it, that they later did to music during their set. Everyone thought it was really cool. A lot of people came with something to recite, which surprised me. This means that they came to the Caribbé Festival with our tent as one of their event destinations. We should definitely do this again at similar kind of event.

Jayson Morito
Events Organizer

Figure 3.19 Jayson Morito's report.

Jayson sees immediately that Dorian's evaluation is accurate. He does jump around from one topic to another. He concludes that Dorian is right: he should have revised it before he submitted it.

Cohesion, Emphasis, and Conciseness in Business and Professional Communication

 Apply techniques for improving cohesion, concision, and emphasis

Cohesion in writing grows out of how your prose "flows" to readers. For readers, "flow" or cohesion comes when the topic in one sentence is connected to the topic in the next sentence. There are two ways to do this:

1. Organize the paragraph around a central topic that all of the sentences relate to.
2. Repeat the subject matter from the end of one sentence at the beginning of the next sentence.

COHESION STRATEGY 1: ORGANIZE THE PARAGRAPHS AROUND A CENTRAL TOPIC

Examine the message in Figure 3.20. It is written as one long paragraph, and the sentences contain several complex ideas that make the message difficult to follow.

To: Larry

Subject: Please send a new data request form

Hi Larry,

We can certainly re-run this portion of your previous request following these new specifications, but you will have to submit a new data request form, which will be treated as a continuation of your previous request in that we will use as much of the code and documentation from your previous request as possible. This will minimize the time required for your request. Please see the attached sample Data Request Form that I've filled out for this re-run, based on your previous request and the information you provided in your email. I have also created a draft specification sheet (also attached). Make any changes to these documents once you review them to make sure they accurately reflect the information you are interested in receiving. It should take 2–4 hours of work. The cost will be $274–548 (excluding taxes). We will just bill you for the actual number to a maximum of 4 hours. You will receive an updated cost estimate if the new specifications result in significant changes. Once we hear from you we will extract your data. Likely the report will reach you in 2 weeks (10 business days) but first we need the form plus your approval. Please let me know if you have any questions or concerns about this information.

Have a great afternoon,

Carmen

Figure 3.20 **A message presented as one long paragraph may be unclear and difficult to understand.**

When a message is divided into paragraphs, each organized around a central point, the message becomes much clearer and easier to follow. In Figure 3.21, the message in Figure 3.20 has been revised to make the ideas clearer. First, it was divided into paragraphs. The first sentence of each paragraph acts as a topic sentence, introducing its main subject. Each sentence after the topic sentence then contributes some aspect of a logical discussion to the paragraph that relates to the main subject. The central topic is highlighted using bold typeface.

To: Larry

Subject: Please send a new data request form

Hi Larry,

[1] Please find attached an updated Data Request Form and Specification Sheet.

[2] [a] We can certainly re-run this portion of **your previous request** following these new specifications. [b] In order to do this, we require you to submit a new data request form. [c] However, we will approach this as a **continuation of your previous request** in that we will use as much of the code and documentation from **your previous request** as possible to minimize the time required to fulfill your request.

[3] I have taken the liberty of filling out a Data Request Form for this re-run, based on your previous request and **the information** you provided in your email. Also based on **this information**, I have created a draft specification sheet (also attached). Please review both of these documents and make any changes necessary so that they accurately reflect **the information** you are interested in receiving.

[4] Based on this current specification sheet, I estimate that this re-run will take **2–4 hours of work**. This translates to a **cost** of $274–548 (excluding taxes). We will, however, only **bill** you for the actual number of hours required to complete your request up to a **maximum of 4 hours**. If the **scope** of this follow-up request changes for the current specification sheet, I will provide you with an **updated cost estimate for** your approval.

[5] Once we have received your signed **request form and your approval** of the specification sheet and cost estimate for this work, we will proceed with extracting your data. Once we have the **form and your approval**, you should receive your updated report in 2 weeks (10 business days).

[6] Please let me know if you have any questions or concerns about this information.

Have a great afternoon,

Carmen

Figure 3.21 **To clarify how ideas are related and to create cohesion in your writing, use the strategy of repeating topics within the sentences in a paragraph.**

In Figure 3.21, the revision improves the cohesion of the message by using the strategy of repeating the central topic announced in each topic sentence throughout the paragraph. Each paragraph in Figure 3.21 has the main topic bolded so that you can see how it is elaborated from sentence to sentence.

1. Paragraph 1 announces the central topic of the whole message—the "updated Data Request Form and Specification Sheet."
2. Paragraph 2 explains that the writer requires an updated data request form to re-run an earlier project. It is organized around the topic of "your previous request," and some version of this phrase appears in each sentence (highlighted in the figure).
3. Paragraph 3 emphasizes that the writer has attached copies of the two forms that must be resubmitted to expedite the request. The central topic is "the information."
4. Paragraph 4 addresses the cost (in time and money) of the request. The central topic is "cost."
5. Paragraph 5 outlines the reader's next steps and the estimated time required to complete the request. The central topic is "request form and your approval," which links the ideas in the paragraph together.

The revised version of the message in Figure 3.21 more clearly and cohesively communicates the information that Larry needs to know. He can quickly scan the message because it is organized into paragraphs. He can easily identify what he must do so that Carmen can proceed with analyzing the data to match his new specifications.

As you can see, the priorities that drive good writing style in business and professional communication are clarity (the text communicates the message), conciseness (the message is succinct), and usability (the message or document meets readers' needs).

COHESION STRATEGY 2: REPEAT THE SUBJECT MATTER FROM THE END OF ONE SENTENCE AT THE BEGINNING OF THE NEXT

The second strategy for creating cohesion is to link sentence topics from end to start. In this type of cohesion, the idea at the end of one sentence is picked up and repeated to begin the next sentence. The repetition shows readers clearly how the ideas connect.

Figure 3.22 illustrates how this end-to-start linking can be done. The bolding indicates the relationship between the ideas and their location in each sentence. Note that in the paragraphs of the revised letter each sentence is structured in a particular way:

Old or known information at the start + new or unknown information at the end: "Your request to re-run the data extraction using these new specifications [old] + can certainly be done [new]."

To: Larry

Subject: Please send a new data request form

Hi Larry,

[1] Please find attached an updated Data Request Form and Specification Sheet.

[2] [a] Your request to re-run the data extraction using these new specifications **can certainly be done.** [b] **To do this**, we require you to submit a new data request form, but we will approach this activity as a continuation of **your previous request.** [c] As much as possible of the code and documentation **from your previous request** will be used to minimize the time required to process **this new request.**

[3] [a] A new **Data Request Form** for this re-run is attached, completed based on your **previous request and the new information** provided in your email. [b] Also **based on this information**, I have created a **draft specification sheet** (also attached). [c] Please review **both documents** and make any changes necessary so that they accurately reflect the information you are interested in receiving.

[4] Based on this **current specification sheet**, I estimate that this re-run will take **2–4 hours of work. This time** translates to a **cost of $274–548 (excluding taxes). The bill** will cover the actual number of hours required to complete your request up to **a maximum of 4 hours**. If **the scope** of this follow-up request changes, I will ask you to approve an updated cost estimate for the **current specification sheet**.

[5] Once we have received your signed request form and your approval of the **specification sheet** and cost estimate for this work, we will proceed with **extracting your data**. Once **data analysis** is complete, we will prepare our updated report, which you should receive within 2 weeks (10 business days) of the form and approval reaching us.

[6] Please let me know if you have any questions or concerns about this information.

Have a great afternoon,

Carmen

Figure 3.22 The bolding indicates the relationship between the ideas and their location in the sentence.

In Figure 3.22, the end-to-start linking strategy improves message cohesion by explicitly and logically connecting the ideas in a paragraph. Here we unpack the structure of Paragraphs 2 and 3 to show you what this strategy looks like in action:

Paragraph 2:
In sentence [a], "your request" is the old information drawn from the previous paragraph, and it ends with the new information in the verb "can be done." In sentence [b], the new information from the end of sentence [a] ("can be done") is repeated as old information and the subject of [b]:

"*To do this [now old], + we require you to submit ... of your previous request [new].*"

Sentence [c] then takes the topic "your previous request" and opens the next sentence with a reference to that previous request:

"*As much as possible of the code and documentation from your previous request [old] + will be used to minimize the time required to process this new request [new].*"

Paragraph 3:
Paragraph 3 explains to readers that they need to review and approve the attached form. Here, sentence [a], the topic of "new request" (new information at the end of sentence [c] in Paragraph 2) is repeated as the subject, but "Data" and "Form" are added to emphasize how this topic connects to the previous paragraph:

"*A new Data Request Form [old] + based on your previous request and the new information provided in your email [new].*"

In sentence [b], the writer summarizes "your previous request and the new information provided in your email" as "this information" at the beginning (to show how it links up):

"*Also based on this information [old] + I have created a draft specification sheet [new].*"

Sentence [c] condenses "Data Request Form" and "draft specification sheet" from sentences [a] and [b] into the phrase "both documents" and instructs the reader to "review and make any changes."

The two strategies for improving cohesion both work. The first one, repeating a topic, is easier to use. You probably already use it without being fully aware of it, but if you use it consciously you can greatly improve your readers' experience of your document as clear and easy to read. The second one, end-to-start linking, is better suited to logic-based arguments but is also more complicated to apply. However, once you practice end-to-start linking you will find it useful in helping you to detect where you have omitted important ideas that readers need to follow your ideas. Use the one that you can employ successfully.

Exercise 3.4: Revising for Cohesion

Using the pattern of end-to-start linking, revise these paragraphs to improve their cohesion.

1. Sales in the fourth quarter made up for the slow start in the first and second quarters. Our promotional efforts in the second and third quarters were mainly responsible for the 110 per cent increase in November and December. Television advertising, mass mailings, newspaper advertisements with discount coupons, and displays in distributing stores were our main promotional efforts. In addition, we gave free samples away to further promote our new products. Our outstanding results for the fourth quarter indicate these efforts were very successful.

2. None of us knows when illness, catastrophe, or plain bad luck might cause us to lose our comfortable homes. Many clients that Bar Harbor House serves never expected to find themselves homeless either. But if we all work together to provide a reliable safety net that provides temporary and longer-term shelter for members of our community who need it, we can be sure that such services will be available should the unthinkable happen and we find ourselves in need of just this service. We are our brothers' and sisters' keepers and if we all do our part by making a cash donation or volunteering our time, we can help build and maintain a safe, caring community in the town of Bar Harbor. Help Bar Harbor House help those who need a hand up, not just a handout.

EMPHASIS

When working toward cohesion, the first few words of a sentence are important because they announce the topic. The topic of the sentence gives readers a firm base from which to understand the rest of the sentence. The end of a sentence is equally important. Because readers remember the information they find at the end of the sentence, give important points and ideas emphasis by placing them at the end. Use the ends of your sentences to introduce one of the following:

- new information or difficult technical terms
- complex phrases and clauses

Here are three ways to give your sentence endings more impact:

1. end sentences concisely.
2. shift qualifying phrases to the start.
3. shift new information to the end.

End sentences concisely: Trim excess words away so that sentences end with emphasis. For example, doesn't everyone who lives in Bar Harbor know it is a town? Probably, so in the following sentence we could delete the unnecessary phrase "in the town of":

Wordy: If we all do our part by making a cash donation or volunteering our time, we can build and maintain a safe, caring community in *the town of* Bar Harbor.

Shorter: If we all do our part by making a cash donation or volunteering our time, we can build and maintain a safe, caring community in Bar Harbor.

Wordy: Their performances were scheduled to start at 7 p.m., and they ran until *quite a bit past midnight*.

Shorter: Their performances were scheduled to start at 7 p.m., and they ran until *3 a.m.*

Shift qualifying information to the start: In the following sentences, the information at the end of the sentence creates a weak conclusion because it is unimportant. The revised version moves the qualifier to the start and ends with emphasis.

Original: Canvassing the riding for Gina Marconi, the Green Party candidate in Prince Albert North, was unsuccessful *despite our best effort*.

Revised: *Despite our best effort*, canvassing the riding for Gina Marconi, the Green Party candidate in Prince Albert North, was unsuccessful.

Original: We are going to need a new strategy *if we want to convert more people than we did when we were canvassing last month*.

Revised: *If we want to convert more people than we did when we were canvassing last month*, we are going to need a new strategy.

Shift main ideas to the end: In the following examples, the main idea is buried in the middle of the sentence. Shifting it to the end allows readers to recognize that it is the essential point.

Original: We are going to need *a new strategy* to reach the sparse population.

Revised: To reach the sparse population, we are going to need *a new strategy*.

Original: It's hard to build sympathy among *voters who are farmers and potash miners* when banning pesticides and chemical fertilizers makes up a central plank of your party's platform.

Revised: When banning pesticides and chemical fertilizers makes up a central plank in your party's platform, it's hard to build sympathy among *voters who are farmers and potash miners*.

Exercise 3.5: Revising for Emphasis

Rewrite the following sentences to place the most important information into a position of emphasis. If you can, shorten or rewrite sentences as well to improve cohesion and clarity.

1. Response to our new fall fashion line has been encouraging, believe it or not. All of our customers have ordered a broad range of sizes and styles from the casual line, and eight out of 10 have ordered a range of sizes in the business professional line, which exceeds projected targets. We believe that the partnership with Scoundrel Gold and Silver is partially responsible for the surge in orders because the buttons and fastenings that we purchased from them have increased our new styles' interest and appeal across the board with so many of our customers. Though the partnership resulted in increases in garment pricing, we are finding that customers are more than willing to pay a little extra for elegant styles and tailored finishing.

2. Our good news story of the year was receiving the $25,000 grant from the United Way, which allowed the shelter to stay open until midnight every night through the coldest part of the winter from December 15 until March 15. Being able to stay open those extra three hours each evening resulted in a 35 per cent increase in clients who visited the shelter last winter. We are proud to note that not a single citizen from Cuddy's Cove or Totem Bay died from exposure last winter, even though we had night-time temperatures that were 10 per cent colder than those measured during the previous five years. We believe that this improvement is directly related to our extended hours at the shelter as well as our outreach work with local and regional law enforcement agents.

CONCISENESS

Conciseness refers to using the fewest words necessary to express your ideas clearly. When writing a first draft, ignore ideas about conciseness and focus on getting down what you want to say. When you are happy with your draft, then worry about conciseness. Read through the draft carefully and delete any words that you don't need. Use these principles to help you see and remove unnecessary words:

- cut words that add nothing to the meaning
- delete words that repeat other words
- use a word in place of a phrase
- state negatives positively

Cut words that add nothing to the meaning: Words such as "really" and "very" can increase your sentence length without adding much to your meaning—they add empty calories. These words also add length without meaning:

- kind of
- basically
- sort of

- generally
- usually
- virtually
- particularly
- various

If you find you have used these words in a passage, consider deleting them or, if necessary, replacing them, to tighten up the flow of your prose. For example,

Original: In *virtually* all cases, customers chose a *particularly* speedy delivery of their *various* orders.

Revised: In most cases, customers chose overnight delivery.

Delete words that repeat other words: We have habits of speech in English that encourage us to double up words for emphasis. The following lists some of the doubles that add length to a sentence; note that both words mean the same thing:

- first and foremost
- here and now
- any and all
- various and sundry
- true and accurate
- fear and trepidation
- hopes and dreams
- basic and fundamental
- short and concise
- surprising and unexpected

It is easy to revise this type of wordiness by deleting one of the extra words, as demonstrated in the following example:

Original: *First and foremost*, I request that you submit a *true and accurate* account of the *basic and fundamental* experiment that yielded such *surprising and unexpected* results.

Revised: First, I request that you submit an accurate account of the basic experiment that yielded such surprising results.

Even better: First, I request an accurate account of the experiment that gave such surprising results.

Use a word in place of a phrase: This strategy is more challenging than the earlier ones because it requires that you reread your prose alertly, looking for places where you can distil your ideas into a few words. Draw on your vocabulary and creativity to make your writing more concise. Here are some examples:

Original: We *are seeking* a *highly motivated* and creative person who *is capable of* working independently to prepare the *complete layout and design of the* book.

Revised: We seek a motivated and creative person who can work independently to prepare the book's layout and design. (25 words reduced to 18)

Original: *The people I have found whom I can be of the most assistance to are* individuals with $250,000 in investable assets or the potential *to have* $250,000 in investable assets, *have* a mortgage, and *have some* goals *they wish* to achieve.

Revised: I find that I can most assist individuals with $250,000 in investable assets (or the potential for $250,000 in investable assets), a mortgage, and goals to achieve. (41 words reduced to 27)

State negatives positively: Using negatives adds extra words and slows reader comprehension. For example, how many times do you need to read the following sentence to understand it?

Original: Your ideas do not lack sparkle or shine, nor is your meaning unclear, but your spelling is without that precision and correctness that must thoroughly impress your readers.

Readers must slow down to follow double negatives and translate them into positives.

Revised: Your ideas sparkle and shine and your meaning is clear, but your spelling lacks the precision and correctness to fully impress your readers. (28 words to 23)

Even better: Your ideas sparkle and your meaning is clear, but your poor spelling mars your readers' admiration. (28 words to 16)

Note that the phrases in this example that state something negative are *not* revised to be positive. Only revise phrases that use negatives unnecessarily, such as "If your application is not complete, it will not be funded." Instead, say, "Only complete applications will be funded." It says the same thing clearly and concisely.

Exercise 3.6: Remove Wordiness

Revise the following passages to make them clearer and more concise.

1. It is in the best interests of all and sundry that a true and accurate account of those events is widely circulated. It helps no one if fiction and fable misinforms the general public and innocent readers misunderstand the true state of business affairs at our organization. A press release will not be amiss to set the record straight. Although our President and CEO is not present and available, this does not mean that first and foremost he will not contact us and explain his recent actions in light of the accountant's report that was carefully evaluated and assessed.

2. Profits in the third quarter were not unrewarding. Consequently, the CFO was not unhappy to approve a one-time bonus of 15 per cent for all employees who work more than 25 hours a week. In point of fact, he also approved a one-time bonus of 10 per cent for employees who work less than 25 hours a week. All employees should therefore check their forthcoming paycheck to ensure that they do not go unrewarded for their not inconsiderable efforts over the third quarter of this fiscal year.

3. Our recommendations are not insubstantial in fact. There are three of them. We suggest that all volunteers receive copies of the organizational newsletter delivered to their home addresses to inform them of what is happening at the museum. This should improve the sense of disconnect volunteers feel with the current paid staff. Second, we suggest that the newsletter editor does not fail to initiate a staff profile in each issue that features both paid and volunteer members to increase the visibility and profile of all members of the organization. Third, we urge the board of directors to consider the starting up of a small staff rewards and recognition program to ensure that hardworking volunteers, as well as paid staff, do not go unnoticed in their exemplary efforts to improve the service and morale of the museum organization. We believe that these three initiatives, if not implemented in an untimely fashion, could go a long way toward resolving the staff–volunteer issues that were the impetus for this report.

ANALYSIS: IMPROVING JAYSON'S STYLE

 Read source texts carefully and use knowledge gained from them to create appropriate professional documents

Cohesion in writing grows out of how your prose "flows" to readers. In Rhetorical Situation 3.3, Jayson's draft felt disorganized to Dorian because of the topic changes from sentence to sentence. Readers experience a text as cohesive if the information in individual sentences is presented so that the topic talked about in one sentence is connected to the topic in the next sentence.

To use emphasis effectively, examine the final phrase or clause in a sentence to determine whether it contains an important idea. If it does, then the sentence doesn't need revision. But if it ends with a trivial phrase or clause, reorganize the sentence to emphasize the central point. Figure 3.23 reproduces a sample paragraph from Jayson's report.

> (1) The Arva Springs Honey Cream Ale promotional event was a resounding success. (2) Attendance peaked at 7,000 visitors over 14 hours. (3) We gave out 2,000 t-shirts, baseball caps, and inflatable beach balls stamped with the Arva Springs Honey Cream Ale name and logo. (4) Musical performers entertained the crowd. (5) Celebrity visitors signed autographs and chatted with fans. (6) We gave away 10,000 liters of product to legal-aged drinkers.

Figure 3.23 **A sample paragraph from Jayson's draft report that is not cohesive.**

This paragraph seems disorganized because each sentence contains new information at the beginning and ending of each sentence. As readers, we reel from the constant shifts in topic as we try to organize and process each piece of information. If the information was arranged and presented differently, we would begin to see connections between the ideas. Note that in the revised version in Figure 3.24, end-to-start linking strategies have been used to highlight how one idea is related to the next across the five sentences.

> (1) The Arva Springs Honey Cream Ale promotional event welcomed 7,000 visitors over 14 hours. (2) These visitors took home 2,000 t-shirts, baseball caps, and inflatable beach balls stamped with the Arva brand. (3) Arva Springs Honey Cream Ale also gave away more than 10,000 liters of product to legal-aged drinkers. (4) While legal drinkers enjoyed the new beverage, under-age visitors were served a variety of soft drinks. (5) While visitors enjoyed their beverages they also listened to the musical performers and chatted with celebrity visitors. (6) Both performers and celebrities graciously autographed caps and shirts at visitors' requests.

Figure 3.24 **A revision of the sample paragraph to improve cohesion.**

Jayson rereads his report carefully and decides that he can improve both the style of his report and its argument. After assessing the endings of his sentences, he sees many wasted opportunities to emphasize important points he should be making. He also realizes that he claims people had fun but he doesn't include specific evidence to support these claims. For example, he could add more detail about some of the participants. He drafts the paragraph in Figure 3.25, adding information about three visitors to the tent, and then he underlines the final phrases in each sentence to assess their impact.

He realized that the end of each sentence needed some revision to highlight his main ideas. Sentence 1 could be improved, he decided, if he shifted the qualifying information to the start: "At the event, I interviewed three guests." He reviewed sentence 2 and decided that it could be more concise: "Fifteen-year-old Terry said he came with three friends and they were having a sweet time." After reviewing sentence 3, he saw that its ending was weak and repetitious: "I asked Joanne why she came and she said she loves a party." Next, he considered whether to combine sentences 3 and 4. Ultimately, he decided the point was probably better in its own sentence, and he shifted the main point to the end: "She said she wanted to read a poem but the crowd intimidated her." Jayson decided sentence 5 could also be improved by moving the main point to the end: "I talked to Gil, who said he hoped to meet a celebrity or band member." Finally, Jayson looked through his draft for phrases and words that he could delete to make it more concise (rephrase "some other celebrity person" as "a celebrity" and state "she decided not to because she was scared when everyone was looking at her" as "the crowd intimidated her").

> [1] I interviewed three guests <u>at the event</u>. [2] Terry, who said he was 15, says he came with three other friends and they were having a really sweet time even if they can't score free beer samples, <u>which they were really hoping to</u>. [3] I asked Joanne why she came and she said she loves a party <u>when there is music and drinking</u>. [4] Plus she wanted to read some of her work but she decided not to because she was scared <u>when everyone was looking at her</u>. [5] I talked to Gil who said he was hoping to meet some of the band members <u>or some other celebrity person</u>.

Figure 3.25 **Jayson examined the phrases at the end of sentences to determine their impact.**

 ## Professional Communication Challenges 3.3

1. Rewrite Jayson's report

Use the discussion in this chapter on plain language (including paragraph organization and transitions), positive emphasis, and elements of style, including cohesion, emphasis, and conciseness, to rewrite Jayson's report. Aim to present the account of the promotional event as professionally as possible, so reword some of the casual and colloquial expressions that Jayson has used and correct any grammatical or spelling errors you see. Think of this report as additional evidence toward a possible job offer at the end of the internship.

Audience: Dorian Alvarez (Jayson's boss), Albert Barker (president of Paragon Promotions)

Purpose: To describe the main events at the promotion and to demonstrate Jayson's ability and competence

Genre: Informational report

2. Write a report on a meeting or event that you attended recently

Report on an event or meeting that you have planned or attended recently. Direct the one- to two-page report to your imagined (or actual) supervisor. Use the information in this module to help you write a clear, concise, and cohesive account of the event that you choose. Use the report as a way to demonstrate your competence and ability as an employee so that you build goodwill and make your supervisor look good.

Audience: Your supervisor

Purpose: To describe the event and to demonstrate your competence and ability as an employee

Genre: Informational report (for a discussion of informational reports, see Chapter 11)

CHAPTER SUMMARY

- Business writing should be clear, concise, positive, and accessible to a broad range of readers.
- Plain language emphasizes short, direct sentences, words that most people use in their daily lives, and organizing messages to satisfy your readers' needs.
- Positive language and approaches build goodwill and credibility toward you and your communications.
- Connect your sentences so that readers can follow your thoughts with minimal effort.
- Write concisely so that the words that you do write stand out.

CHAPTER 4

Professional Writing in an Electronic Environment

 LEARNING OUTCOMES

1. Differentiate between when to use online/electronic communications and when to use print-only communications

2. Apply the conventions of business email to your writing

3. Assess business communications for personal privacy as well as the privacy of the people whose information you handle

4. Develop a writing style appropriate for online business communication

GETTING STARTED

The digitization of text communication has revolutionized how we interact with one another. Online instant message (IM) systems, social media, and text messaging on mobile devices have all created new ways to communicate using text. Mobile technologies like smartphones and tablets have expanded the reach of email as a communication technology. Facebook, Twitter, and LinkedIn extend communication to the web and encourage people to interact using technologies that combine voice, text, and image (including video calling). The electronic communication landscape changes quickly. How should you interact with it as a professional in a work environment?

One key component of your interactions will come through your social media pages. Consider this: when you apply for your next job, your potential employer may visit your Facebook or LinkedIn pages to evaluate your character. What level of writing will they find there? What pictures will they view? This new development—that employers can view webpages that were not designed for them—highlights a key aspect of electronic communications: electronic publication and distribution spread quickly and widely. Electronic communications circle the globe in seconds. Email, especially work email, may be forwarded to your boss's inbox even though you didn't write the message for him or her to read. In this module, you'll learn more about how to use new technologies for your own advantage while avoiding the problems they can cause.

This chapter outlines the basics of using digital communication media effectively and professionally. In the first rhetorical situation, Melania Wong needs to create an effective email message to persuade sales and marketing associates to try out her new software application. In the second rhetorical situation, Bart Steinberg and Emma Gilbert brainstorm the details of an annual retreat event for analysts in their division of the Canadian Tourism Association. Their challenge is to create an email invitation to the event that will excite the attendees and motivate them to read a report they might otherwise only skim. In Rhetorical Situation 3, Mansur Jain, owner of Center Cycle Center, is looking for ways to get customers to write appropriate reviews of products on his company blog and testimonials on the company website.

GOOD BUSINESS EMAIL MESSAGES: THE BASICS

 Differentiate between when to use online/electronic communications and when to use print-only communications

In business or large organizations, writing a good email message requires more thought and preparation than writing in a personal or informal social context. Unlike texting, which many people first used in a non-business context, email grew in the late 1960s out of organizational needs for military researchers to communicate with each other. Its origins in organizational communication show up in the headers for emails that prompt writers for memo-like information: "To"; "CC"; "BCC"; and "Subject." Texts and tweets do not prompt writers for that information because they were created to serve different communication purposes. Figure 4.1 is an example of a well-written email.

To: Rachel McGillivary

Subject: My participation in SEBC meetings

Hi Rachel,

I hope things have been going well with you.

I wanted to touch base with you about the working group meetings that I have been attending as a volunteer with the South Edmonton Business Community (SEBC) organization. I have found the meetings to be interesting, especially for the purpose of creating the demographic profile of south Edmonton for marketing purposes. The last couple of meetings, however, I have felt like I didn't have as much to contribute because of the nature of the topics.

I was wondering if you felt it was still a good investment of my time to attend these meetings. I am still more than happy to volunteer with the South Edmonton Business Community organization. At the same time, I'm wondering if the work of actually establishing your mission, values, and direction for the coming years isn't best left to those of you in the organization who really know it best.

Please let me know what you think,

Jerry

Figure 4.1 **Example email message.**

Emails include some or all of these elements:

- **"To"**: The person or group the message is sent to
- **"From"**: The person or group sending the message
- **"Subject"**: The topic of the message
- **"CC"**: People who get a copy of the message
- **"BCC"**: People who get a copy even though the people in the "To" and "CC" lines cannot tell that a copy was sent to them
- The **message** itself
- Any **attachments** sent with the message

The "To" Line

If you are replying to someone else's message, the "To" line will fill in automatically. You should also consider whom else you might include in the conversation. For example, if a topic comes up in an email that you think affects another person in the organization, consider adding that person to the "To" line. They will get a copy of the message, and because you have sent it to them directly (rather than adding them to the "CC" line), they are more likely to respond.

A note about "Reply to All": A common, sometimes critical, mistake people make is replying to all the people addressed to in a message. If you are replying to a specific question in the original message and only the person who wrote that message needs to read your reply, then double check to ensure that you are not replying to the whole group. Be particularly careful not to forward files that are attached to the original email on to others unless you have clear permission to share the information they contain.

In cases where you are beginning an email conversation, or "thread," choose whom to include in your "To" line carefully. In many cases, this may be obvious because you are asking a specific person something you know they can answer or comment on. For some other situations, such as when you are not sure whom to consult about a topic, you may need to ask others in your organization whom to send the message to. In addition, some messages may need to go to several people. For example, a draft of a new process for handling the budget may need feedback from several members of your team. You should probably include all the people you would like comments from in the "To" line.

The "From" Line

Usually a message that originates from your account will be marked as coming from you. In some cases, however, you might want to set up a separate email account for a project or work-group. Messages sent from this account would show the group name in the "From" line. This technique allows several people to manage communications on a project—they could all share access to that account. If one person is out of the office or moves on to another project, the account continues uninterrupted.

The "Subject" Line

The subject of the message often determines how quickly readers open the message. In Figure 4.1, Jerry writes a specific subject line: "My participation in SEBC meetings." It communicates the topic of the message clearly and concisely. A less informative subject line that Jerry might have used is "Your opinion, please." Rachel would be unable to judge from this subject line what Jerry is writing about or how important the topic is. She would need to open the message to find out whether she needs to reply immediately or leave it until after lunch. Figure 4.2 lists some other poor subject lines.

- Your opinion [Opinion about what?]
- toolkit [What kind of toolkit? For what purpose?]
- See attached [What is attached?]
- numbers [Budget numbers? Attendees at seminar?]
- draft [Of what document?]
- (no subject) [This is automatically inserted if you do not include a subject]

Figure 4.2 **Poor subject lines.**

The subject lines in Figure 4.2 are too short and too vague. Readers cannot tell what the message is about. In many cases, the lack of information may cause readers to ignore the message and not respond. Good subject lines indicate what the message is about. Figure 4.3 lists some examples of subject lines that give readers a good idea of the main point of the message. They all inform readers of the specific topic of the message and summarize it in a few words. Readers can judge the importance of the message as well as its subject matter.

- Upcoming seminars in March and April
- Ultimate Web Hosting can build your mobile app or website
- Please rate your recent interaction with Information Systems
- This afternoon's meeting times
- Technical question regarding SBUD

Figure 4.3 **Good subject lines are specific and detailed.**

The "CC" Line

Traditional memos within organizations included the CC: line. Originally "CC" referred to "carbon copy," a reference to carbon paper, which enabled business communicators to make immediate copies of their messages, both for storing and for sharing with one or two people. In an electronic environment, however, this copy feature expands almost infinitely.

Use the CC: line to communicate the message to people not directly affected by it but who might need to be aware of it. For example, when you write an email to an instructor on behalf of a group of students asking for clarification on an assignment, you should copy the other members of the group so that they know the message has been sent. This keeps the entire group involved and limits misunderstandings about exactly what you asked the instructor. In turn, when the instructor responds, everyone in the group will receive the reply. Note the social function of using the CC: line—in this case it keeps communication channels within the group open.

In other cases, however, you may want to use the CC: line to ensure that the person to whom you send the email understands that other people within the company are aware of the situation that is discussed in the email message. By using the CC: line in this way, you bring other people into the virtual conversation. That act changes the nature of what is said and how it is said because others are there to witness it. If you think that the topic of the email is going to lead to disagreements about how to proceed on a project, then using the CC: line to invite others into the conversation might help keep the communications professional.

The "BCC" Line

The BCC: line refers to "blind carbon copy" (see Figure 4.4). This means that the people who receive your email do not know whom else it was sent to. Use this line to send multiple email messages without displaying the addresses of all the people who received it. By using BCC:, you can protect the email privacy of individuals in the group. If you are circulating a newsletter at work to dozens of people, use the BCC: line to avoid filling the top of the email message with email addresses. You can also use the BCC: line to send a copy of the message to your other email address without revealing that address. This allows you to make sure your message really did get sent.

To:	H. Brodie
From:	R. Graves
CC:	roger.graves@depauluniversity.edu
BCC:	[not listed]

Thank you for registering for the Writing Across the Curriculum Reading Group on Teaching and Evaluating Writing. Sufficient numbers of people have registered for the reading group that we have opened a second session. This second group will meet in Lincoln 145 at the identical dates and times of the first group.

Since you are part of the second group, we are requesting that you join us in Lincoln Park Building Room 145 from 3:30 to 5:00 p.m. on Thursday, October 31, Nov. 7, Nov. 21, and Nov. 28.

If you would like to get started preparing for the reading group before our first meeting, please contact my administrative assistant, Jane Bennet, at jbennet4@depauluniversity.edu about picking up the text (John Bean's *Engaging Ideas*) or receiving it through campus mail (please email your campus mail address). We look forward to meeting you and talking with you about teaching writing over the next several weeks.

Figure 4.4 **Appropriate use of the BCC address line.**

Resist the urge to use the BCC: line to send messages to coworkers without letting them know that you sent the message to their supervisor, for example. Unless you have a very good reason to hide the fact that others will also receive copies of the message, this practice will create distrust when it becomes known.

The Message Space

Email messages should start with a salutation if you are directing the message to someone in particular. Using "Dear Ms. Lemay," for example, is formal; using "Hi Odette," on the other hand, would be informal and conversational. Using just a first name suggests that you know the person you are emailing fairly well. If you have never met the person to whom you are writing, you should use a formal salutation ("Dear Dr. Khan," "Hello Ms. Rodriguez").

The body of the email should be direct and concise. Although email messages offer the ability to extend to just about any length, only rarely should you write an extensive message. Keep the message to the topic you identified in the subject line. Say what you have to say about that topic, and then end the message. If you need to communicate with the same person about a different topic, consider creating a second email message with a different subject line. Sending separate messages helps recipients deal with issues separately and file the messages so they can be found easily later, if necessary; such practices help colleagues manage their email workflow.

Figure 4.5 is a personal message that uses nonstandard spelling and informal salutation and closing. Avoid sending messages at work using this level of informality. Always keep in mind that workplace communication can circulate beyond the individual to whom you sent it; if you always use a professional tone and language, you will demonstrate your abilities as a competent and professional employee. Figure 4.6 presents a short email that uses a more appropriate and professional tone.

To: Donna, Oscar, Jordan
Subject: Vegas idea

Hey Guys,

Would u want to go to this? Sounds cool and based on that I think u guys liked the illusionist movie I thought u might want to go?

The deal expires tonight tho ...

Doing okay. Got my antibiotics + pain killers and just icing my face from wisdom teeth extraction.

E

Figure 4.5 Informal message that is not appropriate for professional communication.

To: Robert Graves

Subject: Change of address confirmation

Dear Mr. Graves:

Please accept this email as confirmation of receipt of the completed "Change of Address" form, which we received on February 04. We have now completed the process of changing your address (all three accounts) as you requested. All future communications will be sent to your new address.

If you require any further information, please let us know.

Many thanks,

Omar Saludin

Figure 4.6 **Maintain an appropriate tone for professional email messages.**

Endings for email messages should mirror the introductory salutation. If you begin the message informally, then end it informally: use "Hi Pete" with "Talk to you soon" and "Dear Ms. Lemay" with "Best wishes," for example.

Attachments

Consider attaching a file when you need to communicate about complicated or extensive topics. These topics might include a report or a draft of a letter or document. In your email, refer the reader to the document and explain what you need from them—comments about the style or the accuracy of the figures in it, for example. Use the email message as the cover letter in which you explain what is in the attached document. However, avoid sending large files (over 1 megabyte). Most text files will be well under this limit.

Rhetorical Situation 4.1: Getting Coworkers to Respond to Your Email Messages

 Apply the conventions of business email to your writing

After a lot of trial and error, the new Sales & Marketing Support system application is ready to go. Melania Wong, a junior employee in the Information Systems division of Architectural Ecosystems Products, has spent the past year developing and perfecting the pilot project. The system is a digital tool that offers various help to the sales force: sales projection documents; reports based on actual sales in real time; and trip accounting software, among other features. The value in those features comes mainly from centralizing already existing information into one web-based interface. The system features a social media function, Sales Buddy (SBUD). SBUD, in essence, creates an internal Twitter feed: texts from any sales or marketing employee worldwide are fed into this online space, and members can post questions, strategies, information they gain about competitors, and successes. As a result of feedback from the 40 sales and marketing specialists who had volunteered to participate in the pilot trial of the system, the finished system is ready to launch.

The next step, one that Melania Wong knows will be difficult, is to write a company-wide email to promote SBUD. She recognizes that the sales and marketing people are busy and work under a lot of pressure. She had learned this a year ago when trying to recruit volunteer users to develop the pilot study. She received a fraction of the responses she needed to the message she had sent out then (see Figure 4.7 for a copy of her unsuccessful message) and had to work hard to convince enough people to help her. She also knows that the sales and marketing teams are smart readers of marketing material, so this time her pitch for promoting SBUD's useful features is going to have to be effective to convince them to try it. "First I should figure out where I went wrong last time," Melania decided. "So I won't make the same mistakes again." Her task is clear: Review the earlier email and draft a new message that will get better results. The success of the entire year-long project depends on this.

To:	SalesForce@AESystems.com
From:	Melania Wong mwong@AESystems.com
Subject:	A favor
CC:	Reid Simpson, Technical Systems Manager, Information Systems Division; Prashant Sharma, Manager Information Systems; Hyun Kim, Vice President, Sales

I am writing to request your help with a project. I am a relatively new employee in the Information Systems Division of AEProducts. I have enjoyed my first year and like working for the company. Although it is a large company with many people working throughout the world, it seems very open and welcoming to me. One of my main responsibilities for the coming year will be to develop a new system. It will be a virtual interaction and communication electronic chat system, web-enabled, and compliant with SSI standards for network systems, including the IEEE 802 standards for wireless networks. When we have a prototype of the system ready to test, it would be great if some of you would consider using it to help me find ways to improve it.

Thanks for reading this far and I hope to hear from some of you if it isn't too much trouble.

Warmly,

Mel

Figure 4.7 Melania's first recruiting email for the SBUD project.

Analysis: Melania Revisits Her Unsuccessful Recruiting Email

Melania rereads her earlier draft of the recruiting email. After the months that have passed since she wrote the draft, she can easily place herself in the position of reader, which she had difficulty doing when she first wrote it. Immediately, she notices the generic listserv in the "To" line. She feels her eyes wavering as she reads because she recognizes that it resembles those batch emails she receives daily that are usually irrelevant to her job responsibilities or interests. She understands that this choice depersonalizes the message for the recipient.

Next she reviews the "From" line and sees her own name and email address. This seems like a good choice because recipients can quickly see that the message is from her, not a generic or group address with no clear human sender.

She rereads the subject line, "A favor," and grimaces. She realizes that readers cannot tell the subject of the message beyond the fact that she is asking them to do something for her. Questions flood her mind: What is the favor for? Is the favor personal? Reflecting on her past year's experience, she admits that she herself would not jump to read this email when it's clear the writer is going to ask her to add one more activity to her already overfilled schedule. The subject is too vague, she decides. It also does not help readers know whether the message is important.

She sees that she copied her boss, his boss, and the head of sales at AESystems on her original message. She decides that copying them on the message was a good decision, and she considers whether she should add anyone else for the next mailing.

Next, she contemplates the possible use of a BCC: in a subsequent message. If she uses the BCC: function, she can address each recipient individually without filling the first screen of the message with all those individual email addresses. She also wonders whether she should worry about publicizing all those employee email addresses or whether they are readily available throughout AESystems—something she could ask Reid, her boss.

Then she examines the content of the original message. She is shocked to realize that the first four lines of the message are totally about her: Who she is, how she feels, what she is doing. The next point she notices is that only three sentences discuss the project itself, and she has used so much technical jargon that her readers probably didn't understand the subject matter or what she wanted them to do.

Finally, Melania reviews her concluding paragraph and closing, deciding that the deferential tone and weak request would be unlikely to motivate even herself to participate. She sees that there are many areas where she can improve the recruiting message. She also feels that her critique has given her some good ideas as to how to write the message to publicize the launch of SBUD as a useful application for the company sales force.

Professional Communication Challenges 4.1

1. Revise Melania Wong's initial email

Use the details in the case to revise the initial email (Figure 4.7), as Melania Wong, to recruit volunteers to work on the pilot project. Remember that she wants to show them that the end product will help them increase their sales and market AEProducts more effectively. Keep in mind that most readers of this email do not understand technical language related to computer applications.

Audience: Sales and marketing professionals within the company

Business Communication: Rhetorical Situations

Purpose: To persuade readers to participate in piloting the proposed new software application

Genre: Persuasive and informative email message (for more information on writing informative and persuasive messages, see Chapters 7 and 9)

2. Write Melania Wong's email announcing the SBUD application

Use the details in the case to write a new email from Melania Wong to the sales and marketing agents in the company. The message needs to be concise but also persuasive. It should be formal because Melania does not know many of these agents. It also should have an informative subject line so that the agents will open and read the message. Consider copying the message to other, more senior people in the organization to encourage the agents to open the message.

Audience: Sales and marketing professionals within the company

Purpose: To persuade readers to use the proposed new software application

Genre: Persuasive and informative email message (for more information on writing informative and persuasive messages, see Chapters 7 and 9)

TONE, LEVELS OF FORMALITY, AND PRIVACY IN ELECTRONIC COMMUNICATION

 Assess business communications for personal privacy as well as the privacy of the people whose information you handle

Electronic communication differs from printed versions of memos and letters in several particularly important ways. Electronic communications can be

- distributed widely
- shared quickly
- copied effortlessly
- forwarded indiscriminately

These characteristics mean that you, as a writer, must choose your message carefully. If you have a message that you do not want circulated widely (such as a password), consider sending a paper copy of the memo or conveying the message in person or through a phone call. Similarly, if you need to communicate information that should not be shared until after a particular time period passes (including, for example, the names of winners of a competition), consider alternative ways of sharing that message (perhaps a phone call).

Text Messaging and Chat

"Work appropriate" is a phrase that can be applied as fruitfully to clothing as it can to the language you use at work. In professional contexts, employees usually are expected to behave according to rules and norms that the company sets. There is a wide range of formality between companies, with some being famous for their informality (WestJet encourages their flight attendants to tell jokes) and others being famous for their lack of it (Air Canada). Politeness helps people get along by creating ways to converse that show respect for the other person. In online exchanges, professionals need to observe a set of rules that reflect the business culture of the organization that employs them. In Figure 4.8, Paul uses a formal style for his email message. Formal style has been a standard in larger organizations and functions as part of building and maintaining work relationships. In other, non-work contexts—such as texting between friends—different language standards apply. Take care to use the appropriate style for your communication purpose and context.

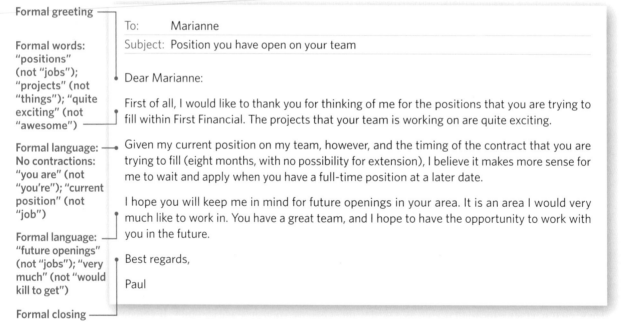

Formal greeting

Formal words: "positions" (not "jobs"); "projects" (not "things"); "quite exciting" (not "awesome")

Formal language: No contractions: "you are" (not "you're"); "current position" (not "job")

Formal language: "future openings" (not "jobs"); "very much" (not "would kill to get")

Formal closing

To: Marianne

Subject: Position you have open on your team

Dear Marianne:

First of all, I would like to thank you for thinking of me for the positions that you are trying to fill within First Financial. The projects that your team is working on are quite exciting.

Given my current position on my team, however, and the timing of the contract that you are trying to fill (eight months, with no possibility for extension), I believe it makes more sense for me to wait and apply when you have a full-time position at a later date.

I hope you will keep me in mind for future openings in your area. It is an area I would very much like to work in. You have a great team, and I hope to have the opportunity to work with you in the future.

Best regards,

Paul

Figure 4.8 **A professional tone in a letter or email.**

© oatawa/Shutterstock

Electronic Mail

 Develop a writing style appropriate for online business communication

Readers make judgments about writers based on the correctness and clarity of the message. In professional settings, you are judged by how you express yourself, even in something as simple as an email message. At the very least, you should always proofread before you click "send." Even if email can be an informal method of communication for many people in their personal lives, it is also an important means of communication in business, where it is generally neither informal nor personal.

Email is fast and direct. You can ask a question and receive a response within minutes. You can dash off an explanation to a customer that resolves the problem quickly and efficiently. Of course, the speed and directness of email can also create problems. If you react emotionally to a word or phrase in the original message, you might send off a **flaming** retort that could embarrass you later or even get you fired. A message written and sent too quickly can encourage you to say what you really think rather than what you should have said. Let's look at some tips for negotiating email in the business and professional world:

flaming: A response to an email that is emotional and potentially verbally abusive

1. Email is not always private.
2. Humor rarely travels well electronically.
3. When a message reaches you that makes you angry or defensive, do not respond immediately.
4. Use standard edited English when writing email in a professional or business setting.
5. Before you send, reread carefully to catch errors.

EMAIL IS NOT ALWAYS PRIVATE

Employee email is not always private. Supervisors at all levels can legally access and read any message that you compose and send from a business or professional account, particularly if you use a device that belongs to the company. For this reason, you should not use work email (or the equivalent) to transact personal business or to make comments about your colleagues, coworkers, or organization that you would not want your boss or some other member of the organization to read.

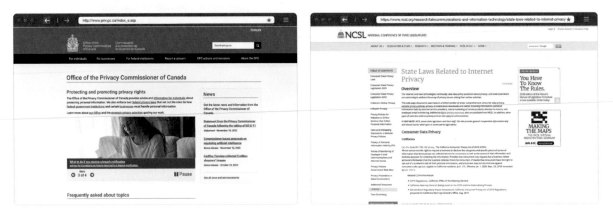

Figure 4.9 The Privacy Commissioner of Canada's website is an authoritative guide to privacy issues for individuals and organizations in Canada. In the United States, the National Conference of State Legislatures provides a good overview of state laws.
Source: http://www.priv.gc.ca/index_e.asp, Office of the Privacy Commissioner of Canada.
Source: https://www.ncsl.org/research/telecommunications-and-information-technology/state-laws-related-to-internet-privacy.aspx

Instead, use your personal (not company-issued) smartphone to check and respond to personal emails, texts, and chats. At some organizations, employee email is routinely monitored; at others, supervisors rarely review it. Don't take the chance with your career. Free email accounts are available from Gmail, Outlook, Yahoo!, and others, and many Internet providers also offer email accounts as part of their services, so use one of these types of email accounts for your personal communications. Reserve your work email for matters related to work, and don't use work computers to view your personal email accounts.

HUMOR RARELY TRAVELS WELL ELECTRONICALLY

Be careful about making jokes online in a business or professional environment. The humor does not always travel safely across the electronic divide. Some people circulate and forward jokes through email (see Figure 4.10), but you should ask friends and family not to send such messages to your work account. Given the lack of privacy and workplace discrimination laws, you can be held responsible for sending or receiving inappropriate material online.

A variety of **emoticons and emojis** have evolved to help writers convey emotion electronically (see Figure 4.11). However, the number of icons available in any instant messaging program can quickly become overwhelming. If you know your reader well and you share similar status levels at work, you can probably safely use the occasional emoticon. If you are writing to someone of a higher status level, avoid using emoticons. They can make you look unprofessional.

emoticons and emojis: Symbols that are used to convey emotions within email and text messages

DO NOT RESPOND IMMEDIATELY TO AN INFLAMMATORY MESSAGE

If you receive a message that makes you angry or defensive, by all means, write the response you'd love to send back, but first, clear the "To:" line (so you can't accidentally send it), and instead of sending it, click the "discard" button. *Never send that inflammatory reply back*. These types of unconsidered responses usually make you look unprofessional and mean-spirited, especially if your reply is then circulated widely around the organization. Often the message doesn't actually need a reply. If you do have to respond, wait 24 hours so that you can carefully think through what you should say. Take the time to compose a response that is logical, carefully argued, and avoids using inflammatory language in return. Always aim to be calm and professional in your replies.

To: Shawna, Apurv, Tate, Lucy
Subject: Alternatives to foul language

Dear Employees:

It has been brought to management's attention that some individuals throughout the company have been using foul language during the course of normal conversation with their co-workers.

Due to complaints received from some employees who may be easily offended, this type of language will no longer be tolerated.

We do, however, realize the critical importance of being able to accurately express your feelings when communicating with co-workers.

Therefore, a list of 18 new and Innovative 'TRY SAYING' phrases has been provided so that proper exchange of ideas and information can continue in an effective manner.

Number 1
TRY SAYING: *I think you could use more training.*
INSTEAD OF: You don't know what the f___ you're doing.

Number 2
TRY SAYING: *She's an aggressive go-getter.*
INSTEAD OF: She's a f___ing bit__.

Number 3
TRY SAYING: *Perhaps I can work late.*
INSTEAD OF: And when the f___ do you expect me to do this?

Figure 4.10 **Do not forward inappropriate messages like this one.**

Figure 4.11 Avoid emoticons in professional email exchanges.
Source: stas11/Shutterstock

To: All

Subject: Pierre's insulting and sexist comments

Dear All:

Re: my report on work/life balance that was circulated this week, I want to say that I find the comments Pierre made about my report to be **insulting and degrading**. Work/life balance is not a "women's issue" and it does not mean that if a woman brings it up as a significant factor affecting work that she is not serious about her career. **Pierre's comments show just how little he cares** about issues that don't affect him personally.

Sonya

Figure 4.12 Avoid writing emotional and accusatory email messages.

Do not write an email like the example in Figure 4.12! If you receive or are the target of an email like the one in Figure 4.12, do not respond to it immediately, and perhaps do not respond to it at all through email.

USE STANDARD EDITED ENGLISH IN BUSINESS AND PROFESSIONAL EMAIL

Your friends may not mind phonetic spelling or abbreviations when you invite them out for dinner, but your coworkers will not appreciate receiving an email such as the one in Figure 4.13 because of the time they may have to take to decipher it. Use standard edited English in all professional electronic communication to make your message as clear and easy to understand as possible (see Figure 4.14). Demonstrate your competence and strong literacy skills by always using standard edited English when you write in any kind of business or professional situation, whatever the medium. If you are unsure about a point of grammar, consult a handbook or someone whose knowledge of English grammar is solid and trustworthy.

REREAD CAREFULLY TO CATCH ERRORS BEFORE YOU SEND

Proofread your text before you click "send." Too many people skip the review and send off a message with letters missing or words misspelled. If your email program does not have a spell checker, then copy and paste your text into a word processing file and turn on the spell check feature to catch obvious errors. Never rely entirely on spell-checking programs to find your errors. Instead, read your message carefully to help you catch mistakes.

To: salesvp@healthsolutions.com
Subject: ready for lift-off

Okie, thanks! I'm thinking to reply tonight and see if spacey has time to meet up this week for coffee, and ask her a few questions, to make sure this ptential foray away from work isn't a disaster like the last one (if possible!) . . . Then, get that cover letter + updated resume off before I fly to montreal :)

Figure 4.13 **Do not use texting language in work emails.**

To: salesvp@healthsolutions.com
Subject: Updated plans

Thanks for your reply; I appreciate it. My plan is to reply to that email tonight. I'll ask Cheryl this week if she has time to meet for coffee and to discuss a few things. I want to make sure that the leave I am proposing will accomplish my goals. My last leave didn't do that. Once I have met with her, I'll write the cover letter for the position I am applying for and update my resume.

Figure 4.14 **An example of appropriate use of Standard English in email.**

Rhetorical Situation 4.2: Communicating to Create Anticipation and Excitement

"Okay, we have the date, the venue, the food, a schedule of activities, and manager approval of our plan," summarizes Bart Steinberg. "What we are missing is the invitation to the branch retreat."

Emma Gilbert, the other analyst assigned to plan the retreat, agrees that it is a good time to start publicizing the event. Bart and Emma have been tasked with organizing the branch retreat for the North American Tourism Association (NATA), where the junior and senior associates gather yearly to take stock of the previous year's work and to set out their plan for the short and long term. Although it is intended as a team-building exercise that inspires the group to work cohesively for another year, it often turns out to be dull and uninspiring. Emma and Bart have set as a main goal in their preparations that all attendees will enjoy themselves this year. To that end, they have reserved the Hockey Hall of Fame in downtown Toronto as the location, and they have planned games and

Figure 4.15 The venue: Hockey Hall of Fame.
Source: Gheorghe Roman/Shutterstock

contests with prizes to encourage everyone to share information and develop and contribute ideas for the strategic plan.

Emma volunteers to draft a copy of the email invitation and send it to Bart for editing before distributing it. Bart offers to brainstorm a list of information it should contain to make the drafting easier. They create a list of information they need:

- The date: December 4
- The time: Coffee and breakfast at 8:30 and festivities full on at 9 a.m.
- Location: The Hockey Hall of Fame (the address plus a map link)
- Dress: Wear your favorite team gear

Bart mentions that perhaps not everyone will have a hockey jersey and wonders if they should allow people to wear other sports paraphernalia. After a few minutes of discussion, they decide that they should limit the gear to hockey because of the venue, since it should be possible for anyone to borrow a jersey, T-shirt, or ball cap if they don't actually own one. T-shirts with a team logo aren't expensive, Emma points out. Bart concedes her point and adds that it will also be important to create excitement for this retreat in the message. From his point of view, most employees dread these events, especially after last year's retreat.

"Well, I don't think anyone will be bored at our meeting," says Emma. "At least, I sure hope they aren't. With all of these activities, everyone should be able to keep their eyes open."

To prepare for the retreat, all members of the branch are supposed to read the annual report, circulated one month earlier, and to familiarize themselves with the central accomplishments of the branch during the past year. Usually, no one does more than flip through it briefly. To encourage their coworkers to read the report more carefully, Bart and Emma decide to stage a contest with trophies and prizes. They plan to divide the unit into three or four teams of people who will earn points by answering a series of questions based on the contents of the annual report. Trophies will be awarded to the two teams with the highest scores, and the individuals with the two highest personal scores will receive hockey-themed prizes. Emma and Bart decide that it will only be fair to warn their colleagues in the invitation that they will benefit from taking more than a cursory glance at the report this year. They don't want to give them too much information. They do want them to read the report but not necessarily know *why* they should read the report. Emma and Bart decide that they should at least hint at why attendees should do more than skim it.

Next they debate the extent to which the catered lunch is a selling feature that should be highlighted in the invitation. The Stepping Stone Café, a local-fare restaurant near the Hockey Hall of Fame, has recently revamped its menu, and Bart has arranged for the chef to prepare gourmet lunch boxes based on some of its most popular new offerings. They decide that including a brief mention in the invitation is appropriate.

Finally, they discuss whether the invitation will be sent as an email or as a text message. Emma argues that an email with an attachment will allow them to design the page layout to ensure its visual appeal, but Bart points out that an in-text message will make sure everyone can access the invitation from their cell phones and prevent them from printing out multiple pages for the invitation.

After a few more minutes of discussion, Bart and Emma agree that they have covered what seem to be the obvious details that should be included in the message. Bart passes his notes across the desk to Emma and then the two of them turn to her computer to start drafting the invitation.

Analysis: Creating Excitement among Emma and Bart's Coworkers

Before they begin writing, Emma and Bart discuss their readers for a few minutes. Bart makes several suggestions of possible approaches that will catch their readers' interest about the branch retreat and how the email might increase their enthusiasm for what, in the past, had been a long, dull meeting. Emma also points out that they will need to use a **formal tone** in the email, because it is going to go to the branch manager, their own manager, and the senior analysts in the branch, not just the other junior analysts whom they know quite well. Although some of their readers are good friends, others they do not know that well. Bart agrees, noting that they aren't just dashing off an informal message to friends; the tone should be professional in order to build their credibility in the organization. Emma points out that in many cases their readers will make judgments about the writers' competence based on this message.

formal tone: In writing, the use of language to convey a respectful and serious approach to business communications

1. Write the invitation to the branch retreat

Use the details in the case to draft the invitation to the annual retreat, as Emma Gilbert or Bart Steinberg, to the other employees of the branch at NATA. Remember that you want to stir up excitement among your coworkers for the day-long event, so try to persuade readers to read the annual report, to wear some hockey-related gear, and to look forward to an enjoyable and interesting meeting. As you write your invitation, incorporate the discussion from this module to help you draft a message that is appropriate to the business context. Where appropriate, use visual aids (this might include an electronic map to the site and maybe an image from the Hockey Hall of Fame website) and include links that will give readers more information about various aspects of the meeting (e.g., links to the café website or the Hockey Hall of Fame website). Remember that your message should take into account the difference in status between you and many of the senior employees at the branch.

Audience: The branch manager, the unit manager, junior and senior analysts at the branch

Purpose: To ignite interest and excitement in fellow employees for the upcoming annual branch retreat; to demonstrate Emma and Bart's ability and competence as employees at NATA; and to convince employees to read the annual report

Genre: Persuasive and informative email message (see Chapters 7 and 9 for more information about writing informative and persuasive messages)

2. Write an email to Bart and Emma's boss requesting budget increase for annual retreat

Bart Steinberg totals up the projected expenses for NATA's annual retreat and realizes that they are $200 over their allotted $1,000. After reviewing the costs for food and coffee, the facility reservation, and other expenses, he realizes that the only area where they could reasonably reduce their costs is that of the prize budget. He and Emma discuss alternatives and decide they can make some tacky trophies with plastic goblets and spray paint, but they also want two or three good prizes such as restaurant certificates. They decide to ask their boss for an additional $100 so they can purchase two $50 gift certificates for their grand prize winners. Write the memo to Bart's boss, Michael Banner, asking for a $100 increase to the NATA retreat budget to buy prizes.

Audience: Michael Banner, manager of data analysts at NATA

Purpose: To convince Michael Banner to approve the budget increase

Genre: Persuasive message (see Chapter 9 for more information about writing persuasive messages)

PUBLISHING ON THE WEB: TWITTER, BLOGS, FACEBOOK, AND LINKEDIN

 Assess business communications for personal privacy as well as the privacy of the people whose information you handle

Handling Other People's Private Information

One special aspect of writing in electronic environments involves handling the personal information of customers and clients. In addition to two federal laws, all provinces and territories in Canada enforce laws governing how personal information—much of it collected electronically—is stored. Links to these laws can be found on the website of the Office of the Privacy Commissioner of Canada (www.priv.gc.ca/index_e.asp). In Europe, the General Data Protection Regulation (https://gdpr-info.eu/) provides guidance on privacy. In the United States, the laws are more specific to particular areas, such as health care (see this source for an overview: https://termly.io/resources/articles/privacy-laws-in-the-us/).

When you communicate as an employee of a business or government organization, you need to be aware that strict rules apply to the use of personal information. For example, do not send email messages with someone's confidential information in it (social security number, birth date, credit card information) outside the business's secure intranet. Regular email is not secure, so unintended readers might gain access to this information and compromise that individual's privacy. If you handle this kind of information, always lock your screen when you leave your desk so that coworkers or visitors do not gain access to it while you are away. Do not store personal information on a portable memory stick that could easily be lost or left on another computer.

Email attachments may contain private information about clients and potential customers. In one-to-one communications, you may choose to write and attach copies of documents to messages to explain a procedure, share a proposal, or supply an image. To take advantage of this feature of email, become familiar with how to create attachments. Word processing documents can easily be attached to email messages, but the default file format can only be read by someone with the same word processing software on their device. Unless you know what kind of software your recipient has, choose a file format that is more generally supported. For example, when a new version of Microsoft Word was issued, no one could open the new .docx (document) file format unless they had the latest version. To ensure that your word processing attachments are widely available, save them as .rtf (rich text format) files or, better still, as .pdf (portable document format) files. Although all of these file formats can be posted to a website for people to download, you might consider using an .htm (hypertext) file instead, if that is your most likely use of them.

Writing Online: Principles and Strategies

Though email may be the primary method for communicating with coworkers and clients online, other electronic tools work better for extended and repeated communications. Many companies have websites, of course, but social media such as Twitter, Facebook, LinkedIn, and blogs also provide opportunities for online publication. In this section we focus primarily on writing for blogs. The principles we discuss in connection with writing blogs also apply to writing posts for Facebook and LinkedIn. Writing for Twitter requires a more extreme application of these principles aimed at producing an arresting point as succinctly as possible.

Online publication tools such as these provide a variety of ways to communicate with potential customers and clients. Although it's unlikely that you will do the design work for these pages, you may be asked to write copy for them. When you write for web publication, keep these principles in mind:

- shorten your message; create separate, printable files for longer messages
- write short paragraphs
- use visuals where possible
- write short (12 to 20 words on average), simple sentences
- use bullets for lists
- add links to other pages

Several practical realities of electronic communication explain these principles. First, messages may be read primarily on portable devices such as cell phones. Longer documents and documents with long paragraphs demand that readers keep scrolling. Paragraphing is, to some extent, a visual phenomenon. The act of breaking texts into paragraphs gives readers clues about how the ideas within the paragraphs are related. However, when readers cannot see the paragraph breaks, they can no longer visually determine the point of the paragraph.

People reading on electronic devices have less patience for reading longer texts. To help them read and process information more quickly, write shorter sentences (12 to 20 words). Also, write mostly simple sentences—that is, contain one main clause (main subject plus a main verb). Use dependent clauses and phrases sparingly. If you have an opportunity to include a visual, take it.

Blogs

Like most new online communications, blogs (short for weblogs) are an evolving genre. They range from personal (https://dooce.com/) to political (www.macleans.ca/rss-feeds) and beyond (see Figure 4.16). If you are an aspiring journalist, writing your own blog offers you an opportunity to write and publish as a way into the profession. This also holds true for the fields of public relations and marketing communications.

informal tone: Written communications that employ conversational, relaxed, colloquial language

Writing style for blogs tends to have an **informal tone**, even in "professional" blogs sponsored by major media outlets such as *Maclean's*. You'll find words like "sucks," nicknames ("Arnie" for former politician Arnold Schwarzenegger), contractions ("How's" for "How is"), rhetorical questions ("You know what?"), and other kinds of language meant to mimic conversation between people. Sentence lengths tend to average under 20 words, and paragraphs tend to be shorter—five lines or fewer. In keeping with the conversational style, the tone is often personal:

writers talk about their feelings, what is outside their windows, or their personal reactions to events. If you write a blog for work, keep these stylistic characteristics in mind.

COMMUNICATION | **MOTIVATION**

Top 10 Best Blogs Around the World That Will Inspire Your Life

Jordan Fried
Read full profile

| 🛐 Share | 🅿 Pin it | 🐦 Tweet | 🔗 Share | ✉ Email |

Figure 4.16 **The Lifehack site provides a useful way to find good blogs.**

▲ Rhetorical Situation 4.3: Center Cycle Center's Blog for Returning Customers

Center Cycle Center, or C3 ("C cubed," as the locals say it) was established in 1935 and has long been the top merchant for local cycling enthusiasts. The business has been sold a couple of times since the original owners parted with it, but the brand remains strong locally. Cycling clubs, a store-specific discount card, and charitable donations to just about every fundraising event all help to keep C3 in the public eye. Big box stores on the edge of town have managed to cut into the sales of low-end products, but Center Cycle's devoted following and focus on high-end equipment help them stay profitable.

The most recent buyer of the business, Mansur Jain, knew all of this when he made the purchase. The previous owner had developed a basic website, but Mansur saw an opportunity to increase sales by building out the website into a destination for cycling enthusiasts. Expanding the site started modestly two years ago, and so far sales have indeed gone up. Expanding and maintaining the site has proven to take more time than he had thought, but by hiring a sales assistant with marketing experience to help develop the site he has avoided the headaches that often cripple such online marketing efforts.

All the same, he feels that sales can be increased. He was pleased to learn that in-store customers use the site frequently, and in talking with them he often hears the complaint that although the information on the site is good, it could be better written. A recent example involves what cyclists call a trainer—a machine to hold your bike so that the back wheel spins and you can ride the bike indoors during the winter. The current text on the website had been largely lifted from the manufacturer's site. Several customers noted that the site information pitched the trainer without helping them assess its strengths and weaknesses or compare it with the competition.

Mansur feels that the manufacturer's site, although not perfect, is good enough—he could include a link to it from the C3 website. But he finally decides that what he needs is an online journal or comments from customers about the products, perhaps a blog. That way, customers will stay on his site; they can engage with the information on his site or return to it, and that will make them more likely to purchase from him. He decides to ask the organizer of the Center Cycle Riding Club, Cahya Pham, to see if one of the members would like to try out the trainer in exchange for writing something about it for the website. If he posts reviews of the equipment he sells on his site, his customers will have the additional information and perspectives they have asked for to help them decide which products to purchase.

Analysis: Planning the C3 Blog Entry

Cahya Pham agrees to write the first blog entry for Mansur's page on the MySpinner trainer. The chance to try it out was a powerful incentive for volunteering to write. Obvious angles to discuss will include how easy it is to install the bike on the trainer; how durable it is for regular use by multiple users, including Cahya's three teenaged sons; and how realistic the trainer is as an exercise option once the streets become icy and snow-covered in winter. Having posted regular observations about the city cycling culture on a personal blog over the past year or two, Cahya knows what she has to do to make her blog post a success: Let your personality come through in your conversational tone; keep sentences and paragraphs short; add visuals from the manufacturer's website; make some interesting observations about the trainer that other cyclists will enjoy.

 Professional Communication Challenges 4.3

1. Write a description of the trainer as a blog entry for the C3 website

Mansur Jain has asked you to write something you think the other members of the club, as well as other cyclists, would be interested in reading about cycling trainers generally, and the MySpinner ones specifically. He sells the complete MySpinner line, and as part of the deal with the manufacturer he is able to sell them online across Canada as well. If the blog helps increase sales, he is willing to compensate the writers with free and discounted equipment. Using the principles described earlier in this chapter, write a blog entry about cycling trainers, focusing on the Minoura line for your examples and for pictures. Consult YouTube videos and the Minoura company site for information about cycling trainers.

Audience: Current and potential customers of Center Cycle Center (C3)

Purpose: To evaluate cycling trainers generally, Minoura trainers specifically, and to motivate readers to visit the blog site regularly

Genre: Evaluative blog posting

2. Write a blog entry based on a current fashion topic

Identify a current topic in fashion design and write a blog entry in a style appropriate for a fashion blog. Be sure to use an informal tone and language, contractions, rhetorical questions, conversational phrases, short sentences, and short paragraphs. Begin by reading several fashion blogs: try the *New York Times* site (http://runway.blogs.nytimes.com); Fashion Salad (www.apparelsearch.com/fashion/Fashion_Blogs.htm); Canadian Beauty (www.canadianbeauty.com); or final fashion (http://finalfashion.ca). Then write an entry in that style.

Audience: Friends and family members who are also interested in fashion

Purpose: To express your opinion and insight about the fashion topic that you chose and to motivate readers to return to your blog site regularly

Genre: Evaluative blog posting

CHAPTER SUMMARY

- Email messages should be concise, direct, and sent to the right people in the organization.
- Email messages should be professional in tone: use formal language, not slang, and avoid contractions and humor.
- Electronic communications at work are not private, and they may be forwarded and copied to others both inside and outside the organization without your knowledge.
- Blog posts, tweets, Facebook posts, and public comments on websites that are made from a company account must represent the organization well. Posts made from your own personal accounts enable you to decide how you want to be represented.

CHAPTER 5

Writing in Teams

 LEARNING OUTCOMES

1. Identify the kinds of projects that are usually completed in teams
2. Describe the two types of collaboration and their characteristics
3. Identify activities teams can engage in to help promote their group's success
4. Avoid behaviors that sabotage group success
5. Develop four different strategies for resolving group conflict

GETTING STARTED

Although some instructors may discourage you from working with others on course material and assignments at school, you will find the attitude toward collaborating in the workplace is completely different. Employers welcome employees combining their talents to efficiently and effectively complete work projects. In fact, you will be viewed as a less desirable worker if you cannot work well with others. Take every opportunity while you are still in school to develop your interpersonal skills so that you can work positively and productively with others.

This chapter outlines tips and strategies that you can use to improve both your interpersonal skills and your productive abilities. It also provides opportunities for you to work with your classmates on discussion-based as well as document-based exercises and assignments. In the first rhetorical situation, Howard Kent assembles a group to write a report about organizing a conference for a client. The group works in both a hierarchical style, with Kent in charge, and a dialogical style when they meet without him being present. In the second rhetorical situation, you meet a group of individuals who are not functioning well as a team; you will apply what you have learned about group dynamics in this chapter to analyze why that group doesn't work and what could be done to help them work better together.

WORKING AND WRITING IN GROUPS

 Identify the kinds of projects that are usually completed in teams

In the rhetorical situation that you will read shortly, the employees of an event-planning group have been asked to organize and run a government-sponsored conference for academic research-ers, scientists, and industry partners. The timeline for holding this conference is quite short, so a group of people is needed to gather the information necessary to plan the conference, a task that would be impossible for one person working alone. However, when all of the tasks are distributed among the group, the short timeline is not an issue.

These are the kinds of projects that are often done collaboratively:

- projects that are too large for one person to complete at all
- projects that require expertise from different areas that no one person has
- large projects that need to be completed quickly
- projects that are especially important, so many people contribute; therefore no one person is responsible for whether the project succeeds or fails

Many large projects require team members to work and to write individually and collabora-tively. If you have had bad experiences collaborating on school projects, with team members who did not complete their assigned tasks or did them poorly, you may hesitate at the prospect of contributing to a large, important work project. If you have had good collaborative working groups, then you know that such group work can also be energizing and enjoyable: when everyone does their tasks well and on time, it is a recipe for success and possibly promotion.

In addition to doing your assigned task well and finishing it before the deadline, here are other ways to help the group succeed.

Request Knowledge and Opinions

Ask questions to figure out what the group needs to know. Figure 5.1 displays a list of brainstorming questions posed by a collaborative group in their first meeting. The group begins with questions to identify the target audience for the event they are planning. By learning the characteristics and needs of their target attendees (as well as secondary groups who might attend), they can figure out what activities to include in the event, as well as the additional arrangements that might be necessary. Once they thoroughly discuss the questions that they need to answer, they can divide up the list and assign tasks to committee members.

What do we need to know?

Who is going to come to this event?

What is our main and secondary demographic in this audience?

What kinds of activities do they enjoy?

What amenities are there locally that our target audience might enjoy?

Who/what will attendees bring with them? (Children? Pets? Other?)

Will we need to arrange childcare? Pet care?

What age groups? Activities? Kind of care?

Figure 5.1 **What does the group need to know to get started on the project?**

Offer Information and Opinions

Answer questions when they are asked if you are sure of the answer. Another role that you can play in a group is to suggest answers as a way of brainstorming, even if you are not sure if the answer is appropriate or correct. For example, one member of the group generated a list of types of people who might want to attend the event that they were planning. Two others logged onto a company laptop to check out the Chamber of Commerce website in the city where the event would be held, to find out what activities and amenities were advertised in that region. When they noted the town's location on the lakeshore, several people suggested they look for water equipment rentals and boat tours to add to the list.

Summarize

Restate major points that are made. The role of summarizing in a group can be helpful for reviewing the highlights of the discussion and ensuring that all members agree on what topics have been covered. By restating major points, the group can assess its progress as well as review the direction of the discussion. Toward the end of the meeting, pull ideas together by reviewing notes, summarizing key points, and allowing group members to ask questions, point out problems, and so on. At this point, everyone should focus on whether something important has been forgotten and evaluate the progress they've made toward their goals for the meeting as well as the larger project.

Review Decisions

Often summarizing a meeting provokes a recognition that some decisions have not been made or should be re-thought. The review of decisions can be important to ensure that everyone shares the same understanding about the plan. Often a review of key decisions can uncover misunderstanding or disagreement about the group's final position. The group can clear up any problems before proceeding.

Evaluate Decisions and Ideas

groupthink: The tendency of group members to immediately agree with each other and not really evaluate an idea or direction

Reflect on group decisions. Evaluation of the group's process is important. It raises the issue of quality, which can head off potential problems with **groupthink**. Groupthink refers to a group process in which members rush to decide on an action without thoroughly discussing it. Often, the group stifles disagreement to avoid unpleasantness, but thoughtless agreement results in an inferior outcome. Step back from group decisions to evaluate whether they are, in fact, the best solution or the best action to take.

Measure decisions against group goals. Group members should look at decisions that have been made and assess further whether these decisions are good ones that will contribute to the group accomplishing its goal(s). Thinking critically about group decisions will usually help the group to arrive at the best solutions.

Coordinate

Plan work: A group coordinator uses the decisions that the group makes to figure out how best to subdivide the work to accomplish the goal. It is a valuable contribution to the group to plan or work out in greater detail how something should be done. If one member of the group makes detailed notes about what needs to be done, the tasks can be assigned around the table and a workable plan can be developed for what needs to be done by whom. Of course, planning work can also be done verbally with several members contributing.

Give directions: Someone in the group should take the leadership role and supervise the division of responsibility for the work. The leader may sketch out a timeline for completing the various stages.

Figure out how all group members will contribute. The group that generated the list of questions in Figure 5.1 collaboratively decided who would research each topic. Everyone had a subject and knowledge of what in particular they needed to find out when they left the meeting.

MODELS OF COLLABORATION

 Describe the two types of collaboration and their characteristics

There are two basic models for collaborating and writing collaboratively: hierarchical and dialogic. In **hierarchical collaboration,** one person assumes a leadership role and the rest of the team occupies subordinate reporting roles. Hierarchical collaboration takes place within a well-defined system of reporting and authority. The leader directs the meeting, gives instructions, and assigns deadlines. Members complete their tasks and report back to the leader.

In contrast, **dialogic collaboration** is characterized by the absence of a clear single leader. Instead, team members share the common goal of compiling the research and drafting the report. They act as peers and share the authority and decision-making process.

hierarchical collaboration: Collaboration where one person is clearly in charge and the others report to that person

dialogic collaboration: Collaboration where a group of equals decides collectively how to proceed with their work

Group Behaviors That Create a Successful Collaboration

 Identify activities teams can engage in to help promote their group's success

ENCOURAGE PARTICIPATION
One goal of teamwork is to have everyone participate and contribute their ideas. You can encourage participation by demonstrating your openness to the ideas of others. Ask quieter team members what they are thinking and then respond positively and encouragingly to their ideas. As the discussion continues, give appropriate credit to team members for their ideas so that individuals feel good about being validated and appreciated.

RELIEVE TENSION
Such activities as joking can help everyone relax and remember to enjoy themselves. If you feel tensions are high because of disagreement or heated discussion, consider suggesting that the group take a short break or engage in a fun activity for a few minutes to give everyone a breather and a chance to reset their emotions to a more relaxed level.

CHECK FEELINGS
It fosters group loyalty, helps resolve conflicts, and keeps the group functioning smoothly if you check occasionally to see how everyone is feeling about the decisions being made and the

direction of discussion. You can encourage others to speak up about their feelings by sometimes sharing your own feelings about the group's activities.

SOLVE INTERPERSONAL PROBLEMS

Sometimes interpersonal problems will develop between group members. Directly dealing with these problems by opening up discussion and suggesting ways to solve them can go a long way toward ensuring the continued smooth functioning of a group. Don't ignore or discourage discussion of problems, because, when unaddressed, they can escalate and prevent the group from successfully accomplishing its goals.

- respond to the speaker
- give feedback (for literal meaning and/or emotional content)
- ask for more information
- state your own feelings

Figure 5.2 **Active listening strategies.**

LISTEN ACTIVELY

Active listening signals to speakers that their ideas are being heard and understood (see Figure 5.2). It involves showing group members that they are being taken seriously. Active listening refers not just to hearing the sounds coming from someone's mouth but also to understanding and interpreting those sounds accurately. It means understanding the meaning of another person's comment as well as attending to the feelings that are being communicated along with the information. To be an active listener, respond sincerely and politely to the speaker. This means making such comments as "Yes," "Uh-huh," "I see," "Interesting idea," "Okay," and so on, to show that you are paying attention and thinking about what is being said. Remember to give feedback. Feedback can include paraphrasing what you believe the speaker said so that they can correct your understanding, if necessary.

Ask the speaker to elaborate on a point that is interesting or that you may not have understood. This shows the speaker that you are engaging fully with their ideas. Another method of listening actively is to share your feelings about what the speaker is saying. This demonstrates your response to what they are saying as well as how they are saying it.

Listening actively can help you reduce conflict that results from miscommunication in the group. Active listening allows you to hear and understand what others are saying. It provides a way to verify your understanding by foregrounding possible areas of misunderstanding. At the same time, active listening cannot solve all problems: it doesn't remove conflict when group members want divergent solutions or when one person has a conflict with another person.

© Matej Kastelic/Shutterstock

"Our contact at the Environmental Protection Agency [EPA] is Douglas Gervais." Howard Kent looks up from the sheet of paper and glances at his staff around the conference table. Gervais is supposed to be running the First North American Conference on Water Quality, but he is too oversubscribed to handle it, so he has asked Mueller Kent Events to step in and take over. If Mueller Kent Events can do a stellar job putting this conference together, then they definitely will have a shot at signing other contracts, not only with the EPA but with other government bodies as well. Kent reminds everyone how important it is to get some government referrals. There have been a few lean times at Mueller Kent Events while Howard Kent and Rebekah Mueller have been struggling to break into the events-planning business in the eastern US. The long-term picture is slowly looking brighter, but contracts with lucrative government offices have continued to elude them until now.

The conference is sponsored by the EPA and the North American Association on Water Quality. These two groups usually sponsor three symposia in regions across the country, but this year they also want to hold a three-day conference to bring together water-quality researchers from around the globe to network with American water-quality experts.

"Here's our first timeline for this project." Kent distributes around the table the handout that he's been reading from (see Figure 5.3, Items A and B). Item A in the outline lists contact information and a brief overview of the North American Association on Water Quality. Item B lists a timeline for the end of the week to generate several ideas and options for the conference. By the end of next week Kent wants a draft of the report outlining the plan for the conference to send to Douglas Gervais. Gervais wants the call for abstracts distributed widely by the end of the month, all proposals due by the end of November, and the conference held in the middle of January. This is a tight turnaround for this kind of event planning.

Kent asks whether anyone has been to one of these academic conferences before. One hand shoots up: Linda Johnson. As an undergrad she helped a couple of professors plan a history conference. She worked at the information booth but also helped with some of the arrangements.

A. Contact

Douglas Gervais, EPA, 000-123-4567, dgervais@enproag.gov

The North American Association on Water Quality (NAAWQ) was established as a voluntary not-for-profit organization in 1967 as a collection of individuals from industry, government, and academia who were interested in water treatment and pollution control in the US, Canada, and Mexico. Since that time, the organization has evolved to include engineers, scientists, and managers who are directly involved in issues surrounding water quality. The objectives of the NAAWQ are to:

- promote research on the scientific, technological, legal, and administrative aspects of water quality and of the control and treatment of water pollution
- further the exchange of information and practical application of such research for the public benefit
- promote the goals and objectives of the International Water Association (IWA)

(*Source: www.naawq.ca/en/about.shtml*)

B. Timeline

Monday, Sept. 16, Organizational meeting:
- brainstorm relevant topics
- assign tasks

Friday, Sept. 20, Research reports:
- email a copy of your research and recommendations to the other team members (as well as Howard Kent)
- read the reports you receive from other team members

Monday, Sept. 23, Decision and drafting meeting:
- discuss team members' research findings and recommendations
- as a group decide on a plan for the conference
- begin drafting longer report on plan for the conference for Howard Kent

Wednesday, Sept. 25, Conference plan report:
- email draft of team-written report to Howard Kent
- revise based on feedback received from Kent

Friday, Sept. 27, Final draft of conference plan report:
- submit final draft of conference plan report to Douglas Gervais

C. What we need to know

On Water Quality
- names and contact info (institution, email, phone number) of water-quality experts in Canada, US, Mexico outside of North America
- brief/paragraph summary of person's research focus and interests
- reasons why this person would make a good keynote speaker on water quality

- need information on two or three researchers in Canada, three or four from the US, two or three from Mexico, and two or three international researchers (i.e., outside of North America) (notes to self: remember gender and race of speaker, range of expertise, INTERESTING research topics)
- recommendations about who to choose and why (up to five suggestions)
- useful and relevant websites to start with:
  - www.cawq.ca
  - www.cawq.ca/en/links.shtml
  - www.earth.uwaterloo.ca/research/ucsigrc

Conference Locations
- conference facilities in town that can handle 100–120 participants on January 15–17
- hotel accommodations plus quotes for costs that can meet our needs for this conference (3, if possible)
- restaurant facilities near the hotels/conference center for lunch, dinner, conference banquet, plus cost estimates per person
- costs for morning and afternoon beverage service for three days
- NB. Who has deals for large groups?

Professional Associations and Related Groups Who Might Be Interested
- professional associations in Canada, US, and internationally who should be interested in water quality and pollution issues

Need director or president name, contact info (request mailing list?)
- activist groups interested in environment, pollution, water quality

Director or president name, contact info (request mailing list?)
- related academic disciplines? Science? Engineering? Humanities fields?

How to contact these people?

What are their professional associations?

Methods of Sharing Conference Information with General Public
- generate a list of documents we could create, ideas for how to create them, how to disseminate them to the public
- multimedia presentations for the public based on conference presentations: list of ideas for different types of media, possible content, etc.?
- general interest publications?

Ideas for how to publish them? Newspapers? Magazines?
- one or two innovative and off-the-wall methods of educating public re: pollution, water quality, etc.

Figure 5.3 **Timeline for planning the First North American Conference on Water Quality.**

Chad McMichael points out the need for keynote speakers. In the past, the EPA has invited two or three experts in the area to come and give a talk. McMichael suggests that they will need to know who the biggest people in water quality are. They might look for someone from outside of the United States, such as Canada or somewhere else where they do a lot of work in water quality.

Kent notes that Gervais has given him a list of water quality–related research centers in the US to get them started. Gervais says there is also some excellent work being done internationally, and that he wants to invite at least one international speaker. That is the main focus for the keynote speakers: To recommend three or four international researchers doing innovative or interesting work. Gervais will write the call for abstracts and take care of choosing the papers for the program, but Kent's team will do the organizational stuff.

After a few more minutes of discussion and brainstorming, Kent creates a list of areas in which they need more information. One of them is identifying the big names in water-quality research in the US as well as several names of international researchers. They decide they will also look for a couple of important Canadians.

Another area that they need to research is possible locations for the conference as well as accommodations for conference participants and attendees. Gervais wants a venue that will promote the involvement of the public and academics in related disciplines in the conference.

Dane Smith suggests that they should also figure out what professional associations exist that might be interested in attending or contributing to a discussion of water quality. This might include farmers' groups, environmental activists, manufacturing associations, and so on.

A fourth area to consider is outcomes for the conference—how to publicize the information presented at the conference, how to move from an academic discussion to educating the general public on water quality and conservation, what kinds of documents and/or media resources might be produced using information from the conference. Linda suggests that the local newspapers may also report on some of what goes on at the conference.

When they finish the list, Kent turns it over to the group to decide who will research which topic. After a minimum of wrangling, the topics are distributed satisfactorily. Kent begins giving instructions: Each of them will write a short report on the outcomes of their research. "I want you to email a copy of your report to everyone by Friday afternoon so that we can review these before the meeting on Monday. Unfortunately, I have to fly to Boston on Sunday night, so you will have to meet without me. I'd like you to pool your research and make decisions about where to go with this conference. When I get back here on Wednesday morning, I'd like the team to have assembled a draft of the report we'll send to Douglas Gervais. Any questions?"

Linda Johnson gathers up her notes (see Figure 5.3, Item C) and thinks to herself that in the next few weeks she will become a mini-expert on water quality in North America.

Analysis: The Mueller Kent Events Planning Meeting

Howard Kent has a tight timeline for organizing the First North American Conference on Water Quality. Four months is a short time for a conference to be organized and held. Kent's team needs to gather information and make decisions about how to run the conference in the next two weeks. When one part of the task is assigned to each person in Kent's group, the project becomes much more manageable. As a result, it is likely they will accomplish everything so that the conference turns out well.

Learning about and planning the conference requires Kent's team to work and to write individually and collaboratively. Not everyone on the team, however, works well together. Chad generally enjoyed working alone; he had had bad experiences working with others, mostly at school. He had completed huge projects by himself when the other members of his group either didn't do their work or did it poorly. He had to admit, though, that working with Dane, Liz, and Linda had been largely a positive experience in the past. They did their jobs and did them well—a definite recipe for success where collaborative projects are concerned.

WHAT DOES THE GROUP NEED TO KNOW?

The brainstorming session identified the areas that Kent's group need to research to develop a good game plan for the conference (the items under C in Figure 5.3). Each member of the work group contributed to this discussion with ideas, questions, and qualifications that resulted in detailed and relevant notes for them to work from on their individual tasks. Then Kent threw the discussion open to his team, inviting them to talk about what they knew about running or planning an academic conference. They each contributed new ideas that helped identify goals and areas of further research. In response to Kent's question about their prior experience with conferences, Chad provided useful information about keynote speakers, which helped the group to figure out what they need to learn about research in water quality, not only in the United States but around the world.

Linda made a relevant point when she noted that the conference will likely get media coverage that will advance Douglas Gervais's goal of educating the public. She thought further and said that newspaper coverage might inform readers about the conference but wouldn't necessarily educate them about their role in maintaining water quality in their area, which was the real goal of the group's discussion at that point.

As the meeting drew to a close, Kent started to pull their ideas together, going over what needed to be done in what order going forward. Linda played the part of group coordinator (coordinators help groups get organized but they aren't responsible for the group's outcome/work). Part C of Figure 5.3 displays her detailed notes about what the researcher in each of the four areas should find out. Each group member took her notes from the discussion to have a workable plan for what to find out, for example, about experts in water quality around the globe. Her efforts to coordinate were essential to mapping out a plan of work for each member of the group. After the group decided who would be responsible for each research area, Kent sketched out a timeline for completing the individual reports and then explained how the group should run Monday's meeting in his absence. He also outlined deadlines for the different stages of planning the conference.

This meeting is an example of *hierarchical collaboration*, with Howard Kent assuming the leadership role and his team of Linda Johnson, Dane Smith, Chad McMichael, and Liz Ahmad taking subordinate reporting roles. As leader, Kent directs the meeting, gives instructions, and assigns deadlines. Members complete their tasks and report back to him. Chad requests that Kent (and not his fellow team members) provide feedback on the individual reports the team will write.

In contrast, the Monday meeting where Linda, Dane, Chad, and Liz get together to draft the conference planning report is an example of *dialogic collaboration*. They share the common goal of compiling their research and drafting the report. They act as peers and share the authority and decision-making process.

Group Behaviors That Can Sabotage a Group's Process and Product

 Avoid behaviors that sabotage group success

Figure 5.4 describes a possible scenario for the Monday meeting where Chad, Linda, Dane, and Liz assemble their individual reports into a conference plan. As you read this scenario, note the interpersonal interactions among participants.

In this meeting, Chad behaves in a way that is potentially alienating. First, he did not circulate his report to the group in advance in the way that Howard Kent had instructed them to. As a consequence, they had to skim the report quickly, causing some confusion and misreading without the chance to review it carefully and plan questions. Chad also checks his email while the group reads, when he could have been reviewing his report with them or been available to answer questions. When the group has finished the report and begins the meeting, Chad continues to finish his email, signaling that his message is more important than his coworkers' time. These three behaviors distance him from the group (withholding his work, engaging in a non-group-related activity, and continuing the activity when the meeting begins). This type of behavior is called *withdrawing*, because Chad uses it to separate himself from the group.

Liz attempts to initiate a discussion of group procedure at this meeting, asking them where they would like to start, but Chad interrupts her. He ignores her question, rejecting the option of discussing group procedures, and begins to lead the group. He focuses group attention on his report. He summarizes his conclusions briefly without explaining them, apparently expecting everyone to agree instantly. Chad's behavior as he assumes leadership is called *dominating*. Dominating refers to one person insisting on controlling the meeting and running the project. When Dane asks a question about his recommendations, Chad becomes defensive, interpreting the question as blocking or disagreeing with everything he said. He responds to what he perceives as *blocking* by withdrawing, refusing to discuss the issue further. See Figure 5.5 for a full list of negative behaviors that can undermine group success.

"Okay, Chad," said Linda as the group sat down in Howard Kent's office to assemble their plan for the conference. "I didn't get a copy of your report yet. Did you bring one with you?"

"Yeah," responded Chad, sliding a copy over to each person. "I wanted to hear from Howard before I sent you guys copies, but he didn't get back to me until late last night."

"I'd like to take a few minutes to read Chad's report before we get started," commented Dane as he started to read. The others followed his lead, except for Chad, who started checking his email on his phone. Even when they finished reading and started talking, he continued to type a message. "I'll be with you in a sec," he said, not looking up. Linda and Liz exchanged glances.

"Where should we start?" asked Liz. "I thought that maybe we should start with the location of the—"

"I'll start," interrupted Chad, as he clicks "send." "Since you've all just read my report, it will be fresh in your minds. I'm researching the guys who are experts on water quality, remember? Now, there's a guy in Sri Lanka who is doing some interesting work. We should include him as a keynote speaker. There's also a guy at the University of Waterloo who would be good. And I recommended that guy in Australia, as well. They have a huge groundwater research center there so he's a good choice."

"Correct me if I'm wrong, but I thought we were going to choose one international person and one Canadian?" commented Dane. "Not three international people and no Americans."

"Well, I did the research on this," Chad said defensively. "Look, if you don't like who I recommend, then do it yourself!"

"Whoa," responded Dane. "That wasn't a criticism. I was just asking for more information about what your rationale is for doing something other than what we talked about last week. For all we know, you've made a good decision."

"Oh," said Chad. "Well, mostly it's because I thought these three guys were doing really interesting research. See, if you look at the second page, there's a table that compares their research projects." He proceeded to lead them through a brief overview of how he chose the three experts he was recommending. As he continued, his three colleagues began nodding their heads in agreement with his explanation.

Figure 5.4 **Negative behaviors can undermine the group's chances of success.**

Blocking: Disagreeing with everything the other members propose

Dominating: One person appoints him or herself leader and tells everyone else what to do

Withdrawing: Not participating in meetings; remaining silent, or skipping work sessions

Clowning: Constant disruptive behavior that distracts and slows group productivity

Figure 5.5 **Negative group behaviors.**

Fortunately, Dane does not react to Chad's negative emotions; instead, he tries to clarify that he meant to ask for more information rather than to attack Chad's decisions. When this misunderstanding is cleared up, Chad begins to contribute to the meeting in a more productive way; he explains his ideas so that his coworkers can follow his thinking.

CONFLICT RESOLUTION

Negative group behaviors can grow out of conflict in the group. Individuals may feel that their ideas are not being heard and respond in negative ways, such as by clowning or withdrawing. Either way, they cease to help the group. To forestall negative behaviors, the group should address conflict up front. In Chad's case, he appears to have come to the meeting with some baggage: his past negative experience of working in groups at school, even though he has had positive experiences working with Dane, Liz, and Linda in the recent past. Perhaps the absence of Howard Kent to provide clear leadership caused Chad's anxiety. At any rate, his anxiety set up the conditions for a negative experience in this collaboration as well. Ironically, he could be the *cause* of the negative experience this time.

Four Ways to Deal with Conflict

 Develop four different strategies for resolving group conflict

1. *Check to see that everyone's information is correct.* "Correct me if I'm wrong, but I thought we were going to choose one international person and one Canadian?" Dane heads off further conflict in the meeting by explaining that this question was not intended as disagreement, necessarily, but checking his own understanding of what they had agreed on earlier as a group. In fact, his understanding was correct, but the incident provided Chad with the chance to explain why he came to a different conclusion than the one originally agreed on. Once explained, the group understood Chad's rationale. They may disagree with it, but at least they understand it first.

2. *Make sure the people involved really disagree.* Often individuals will use different language to talk about the same thing, so they think that they disagree when, in fact, they are on the same side. Exploring the point of disagreement further can reveal whether they do actually disagree. For example, when the group begins to discuss the list of possible locations for the conference, Chad argues that they should book rooms at the Hilton downtown, even though it will cost a little more, because the rooms are more comfortable and the coffee breaks are cheaper than the Ramada Inn near the airport. Liz explains that the extra cost of the rooms might discourage some attendance, but the participants would actually save on their trip to the airport over staying at the Ramada because the Hilton runs a free shuttle service. Linda eventually figures out that Liz agrees with Chad, although it sounds like she doesn't. The group can now move on to the next issue under discussion.

3. *Discover the needs that each person is trying to meet.* Sometimes conflict arises out of two people attempting to solve different problems that sound similar. Or people value different aspects of the problem so they work to make the others in the group agree that their view is a priority. If others in the group hold different values or priorities, conflict can arise over the order in which the group tackles different problems. If someone follows up to determine what needs each person is trying to meet in a conflict, the group may be able to re-establish priorities to minimize the conflict.

4. *Search for alternatives.* If people disagree on a particular solution, the group can take a creative approach to the issue and try to find alternatives that both sides can accept. For example, Chad thinks the three male keynote speakers that he's recommended are the best choices of those researchers he looked at, whereas Liz insists that at least one of their keynote speakers be a woman. After much discussion, Chad admits that he didn't search carefully through the options: he made his selection based on interesting projects rather than demographic characteristics. Dane suggests that Chad spend one hour looking carefully through the work of Canadian and American women researchers on water quality to see whether any of them have interesting projects going. Then he can choose one to add as a fourth option for Douglas Gervais to choose among. Chad agrees that this is a reasonable suggestion, and he is willing to spend one more hour doing a little more research. They find an alternative that both Chad and Liz can live with, putting the final decision about who to choose for keynote speakers in Douglas Gervais's hands.

Professional Communication Challenges 5.1

1. Research topics and write individual reports

Form groups of four people to emulate the four members of the collaborative group at Mueller Kent Events. Have each member of the group assume the role of one of the employees named in Rhetorical Situation 5.1. Decide amongst the group who will be responsible for collecting the information needed in each area. Although one person in the group will be responsible for deciding what information to include in his or her area, you can conduct the research collaboratively or individually. Use the Internet or school library to find the information you need. If you are researching possible conference venues, research locations and prices as if you were going to hold the conference in your city. When the research is complete, each person in the group should write up a short report on the results of his or her research. The report should not only summarize the information; it should also include recommendations about what the group should do. For example, of the experts on water quality identified, which two or three would the writer recommend as keynote speakers for the conference, and why? Use the notes included in the timeline handout (see Figure 5.3) to help you conduct your research and make decisions about what to include in your report.

Purpose: To report succinctly on your research in the area of conference planning assigned to you

Audience: The other members of your group, but ultimately Douglas Gervais, the client at the EPA

Genre: Short report (see Chapter 11 for details about short reports)

2. Write a collaborative report to plan the conference

When the four members of your group have completed their individual reports, each member should email a copy of their report to the others. Before you come to class, make time to read and think about the reports submitted by your group members. When you come to class, spend 15 or 20 minutes discussing the research and recommendations made by each group member, and map out a plan for the conference that incorporates each group member's contributions. As a group, begin drafting the report that Howard Kent needs to send to Douglas Gervais, a water-quality expert with the EPA and leader in the North American Association on Water Quality. Use the discussion in this chapter to help you work successfully as a team to draft this document. Each group should submit one report, containing the names of all the group members, to the course instructor.

Purpose: To combine group members' research into a coherent plan for running the conference

Audience: Your boss, Howard Kent, but ultimately Douglas Gervais, the client at the EPA

Genre: Short report

 ## Rhetorical Situation 5.2: Understanding Group Dynamics: DisplayWorks Prepares for a Client Conference Call

Bob looks around the conference table and decides to get started. Doreen over at Canadian Radiant Heat Specialists, their potential client, has agreed to a 15-minute call to answer questions about their Request for Proposals (RFP). They have to make the most of this opportunity.

Canadian Radiant Heat Specialists needs a sales display unit for the main North American construction trade show held in Las Vegas in March. The RFP notes that they want the display to provide an overview of their products, but also to focus mainly on their newest product, a radiant floor heating system that uses "hot water conveyed through flexible piping in the floors to heat the structure."

DisplayWorks manufactures custom trade-show display units consisting of collapsible lightweight matrix-like structures with magnetic plastic panels that adhere to the structure. The plastic panels are often graphically rich. Some of the panels are fabric, so brochure holders as well as laminated changeable content can be attached to them with Velcro. The client usually has up to six sales representatives at the trade show, circulating around the booth and interacting with clients, distributing product information, and giving out branded swag and other types of promotional items. These trade-show display units can cost between $25,000 and $50,000, and they are usually about eight meters long and two meters high. They can be disassembled fairly quickly and transported from one show to the next in lightweight plastic cases. DisplayWorks has created display units for a variety of different companies across North America.

Everyone around the conference table looks at the RFP, focusing on the part of the description that most closely matches their own expertise. There are six participants: Brianna, the graphic artist in charge of the unit's design; Bram, the structural engineer in charge of its materials and construction; Amita, Bob's administrative assistant, who will manage the conference call; Luanne, the chief writer, who will draft the proposal; Victor, the programmer and technical support wizard who will coordinate the electronic display; and, of course, Bob, the salesman at DisplayWorks, who has brought this team together to help prepare the proposal.

Victor speaks first, noting that the client wants a computer-controlled flat-panel display and slideshow to present their product details and description, so he needs to know who is going to be running this booth. How technically savvy are they? Does he need to set up this show as an endless loop or should it be indexed so that employees can locate a specific section to show a customer?

Brianna agrees and says that presumably DisplayWorks will be producing the presentation for the flat screen. She wonders aloud about the kind of access to Radiant Heat's manufacturing process that she and her group will have to create the video. Bob replies that he is not sure whether Brianna's group is creating the video. The RFP isn't clear on that point. They both agree that this issue is something that needs to be cleared up at the start of the conversation, because production of the video will be time-consuming and potentially costly.

Brianna nods and asks whether anyone knows the company colors. Amita said she visited Canadian Radiant Heat Specialists' website and made copies of their logo and homepage. They use a kind of pumpkin and hunter green in their logo.

"Oh," interjects Brianna, raising an eyebrow. "That doesn't give us the best palette of colors to work with, but if we use variations of...." Her voice trails off as she begins jotting down notes in the margins around the company logo. Everyone watches her for a few seconds, waiting for her to finish her sentence, but she keeps writing and then turns the paper over and begins drawing on the back.

Bob shrugs and looks at the other members of the team. "Any more questions? What about you, Bram? You haven't said anything. Is the RFP that clear on their structural requirements?"

Bram acknowledges that he could use a little more clarity about the size and nature of the content they want to display. He points to the RFP and notes that in the second paragraph, it sounds as if they want posters and digital photos of their products, but on page two, they are also talking about having a selection of actual products on site to handle. He has questions about where they want to display and store those products—on site or in a secure location off site. Also, he needs to know if they want to display some of the products on the unit itself, which will affect the unit construction. The more weight placed on the unit, the better designed and braced it needs to be so it won't tip over. The conversation continues for several minutes, with Bram explaining the technical aspects of unit construction and the others asking questions and making suggestions.

Luanne takes notes of the conversation. Amita asks Bram, Brianna, and everyone else to write down the actual questions that they want to ask because 15 minutes isn't very long. They need to ensure that they cover the most important questions first, and then if there's time left over, the ones of lesser importance. She asks them to rank-order their questions and be as concise and clear as they can.

Bob decides that the group hasn't gotten very far in this discussion. He suggests that they try individually brainstorming a list of issues or problems that each person sees with this proposal from the perspective of the area that they will be responsible for in this project.

A groan comes from Bob's right. "Why can't we brainstorm as a group?" suggests Victor. "That way I don't have to write everything down twice."

"I already did that," laughs Bram, a bit smugly. "It was part of my preparation for this meeting to write down the questions that I have about this RFP. I would have thought the rest of you would have gotten prepared before coming too."

"Well, not all of us are single and can devote every waking moment to our job," retorts Brianna, glaring at Bram. "I did prepare, by the way. I just didn't write everything down because I can't drive and write at the same time."

"What about red lights?" jokes Luanne. "My boss at Jazco answered letters by scribbling in the margins while she waited at red lights."

Bob sees the discussion going off track, so he intervenes by pointing out that they are supposed to place the call to Doreen in less than 10 minutes and they aren't organized yet. Victor suggests rescheduling the conference call, and after some discussion, Bob asks Amita to try to reschedule the meeting for 11:30, giving the group an extra half-hour to organize themselves fully.

Bob then suggests that Bram check out the sketch that Brianna has just finished to see if he can foresee any possible structural problems with the design. Then he directs the rest of the group to brainstorm at least three questions that they have about the RFP. After a few minutes, he gestures for the writers to pass their questions forward to him, and then asks Brianna to present her ideas for the display unit. In 15 minutes, Brianna's initial idea is quickly modified with input from Bram and Victor into a workable model over which the team expresses general satisfaction. During this time, Amita returns, announcing that the meeting has been successfully rescheduled for 11:45 a.m. While she was gone, Bob passed the group's questions over to Luanne, who reviewed them, rewrote two or three to make them clearer and more pointed, and then rank-ordered them according to complexity and importance. She now reads the questions aloud, noting who she has assigned to read them during the conference call. Victor and Brianna each add follow-up questions to the ones they were assigned. Luanne drafts a schedule on the whiteboard of the order in which each person will speak, how much time they can allot to each question, and what else they should ask if they finish up a bit early.

"Terrific work, everyone," announces Bob with satisfaction. They have a workable plan and a few minutes to practice their execution before placing the call.

Professional Communication Challenges 5.2

1. Analyze the group dynamics in Rhetorical Situation 5.2

Using the discussion in this chapter on working and writing in teams, analyze the meeting in Rhetorical Situation 5.2 to describe what is happening and why. Write a short report in which you present the following:

- your *summary* of the facts and events of the case, including theoretical concepts from this chapter
- evidence from the case
- your *interpretation* of what happened
- why you believe it might have happened
- how specific parts of the situation were or were not handled well

Include suggestions about how particular interactions might have been handled more effectively.

Purpose: To demonstrate you understand the concepts in this chapter and can apply them to a situation to analyze the group dynamics with an eye to understanding and improving them

Audience: Your instructor and classmates

Genre: Critical analysis essay or report

2. Analyze a transcript of a meeting that you attended

Attend and record a meeting (outside of your academic work or a meeting of students in a course or study group) and produce a transcript of the group dynamics. Be sure to secure permission to record the meeting in advance. Using the transcript that you created, analyze the group interactions and write a short report presenting that analysis. Use the discussion in this chapter to help you apply theoretical concepts to the interactions documented in the meeting transcript. Include evidence from the transcript to support and explain your analysis. Also evaluate the quality of the interactions, assess whether specific interactions were handled effectively, and make specific suggestions as to how the various situations might have been handled more effectively. Hand in the meeting transcript along with your analysis.

Purpose: To demonstrate you understand the concepts in this chapter and can apply them to a situation to analyze the group dynamics with an eye to understanding and improving them

Audience: Your instructor and classmates

Genre: Critical analysis essay or report

CHAPTER SUMMARY

- Use collaboration to complete large, complex tasks
- Help groups succeed by requesting knowledge and opinions, summarizing, evaluating decisions and ideas, and coordinating the group
- Use one of two models of collaboration: hierarchical (structured, with a well-defined system of reporting and authority) or dialogical (shared authority and decision making)
- Group behaviors that create successful collaboration include encouraging participation, checking feelings, and listening actively
- Group behaviors that can sabotage a group's process and product include blocking, dominating, withdrawing, and clowning
- Conflicts can be resolved by checking to see that everyone's information is correct; making sure the people involved really disagree; discovering the needs that each person is trying to meet; and searching for alternatives

CHAPTER 6

Communicating across—and within—Cultures

LEARNING OUTCOMES

1. Differentiate between national identity and cultural identity

2. Understand the importance of having many cultures in North America and identify the implications of this policy for business communications

3. Identify the components of cultural and business practices of intercultural business communication

4. Recognize that many people have multiple and shifting senses of their own cultural identity—they can be members of more than one cultural group

5. Adjust written documents to communicate well with audiences from a variety of cultural groups

GETTING STARTED

North America is composed of many subcultures, from Indigenous peoples to immigrants from across the world. Equity, diversity, and inclusivity initiatives at most major organizations seek to create an environment where all people in the country can bring who they are to the workplace and be accepted. Consequently, even as a business communicator writing to other people within North America, you will write and speak to people who have different backgrounds from your own. As a business communicator writing to others outside of North America, you will need to be even more aware of cultural differences. The bottom line: How well you communicate across cultural groups will greatly determine how far you advance in your career.

Take every opportunity that comes your way to seek out information about cultural groups you are not familiar with. Even informal exchanges around a barbecue can count as much as formal business meetings in conference rooms. Whenever you have a chance to meet someone who has a different background from your own, take that opportunity to learn more about them and how they see the world. You will find some of these individuals have ideas and experiences that may differ radically from your own, but you will also find that you share common ground, perhaps in surprising areas. When you feel comfortable working with people from diverse backgrounds you can work more effectively and do a better job of understanding them and meeting their needs. The more you learn about the lives of other people, the greater your understanding and acceptance will be of the variation that exists among people's ideas and assumptions.

When you talk to people whose backgrounds differ from yours, pay particular attention to **politeness, formality, and social interaction** practices. These are the ways in which those with backgrounds different from yours interact with other people. For example, when they address you or someone else, do they use honorifics—for example, Mr. Brown, Ms. Yusaf? Do they use first names from an initial greeting? Do they shake hands or incline the head in acknowledgement? Your knowledge of these practices is a prerequisite for building effective business communication practices.

In the first Rhetorical Situation in this chapter, you will meet Lauren Toews, a newly promoted commercial banking officer. In this new job she oversees client accounts, over 40 per cent of which are from China and southeast Asia. The **cultural values** and ways of doing business that she encounters provide challenges not only for her, but also for the people who need to do business with her. Specifically, she needs to learn more about the cultural backgrounds of her clients if she is to work well with them, and her clients need to understand her beliefs and values. In the second Rhetorical Situation, Daniel McMahon faces a common problem: he needs to reach beyond the borders of North America to build his business, but he doesn't know enough about how to interact with people from a culture distinctly different from his own. At the same time, it is important for you to understand McMahon's cultural background in order to determine ways to interact with a white, middle-class businessman. By researching other cultures—in this case, India—you will become familiar with the resources that exist to help individuals and companies

politeness, formality, and social interaction: These terms refer to social rituals people engage in to demonstrate their relationship to each other and to interact smoothly

cultural values: The beliefs people have about what is important in their society, including rules for speaking, interacting, and deferring to others

succeed internationally. Both these rhetorical situations require you to learn more about other cultures and subcultures and to adjust your writing and communication strategies to these readers.

COMMUNICATING ACROSS CULTURES

 Differentiate between national identity and cultural identity

 Understand the importance of having many cultures in North America and identify the implications of this policy for business communications

Business in North America crosses cultural borders every day. **Multiculturalism** is the most obvious sign of these borders: Canada operates with two official languages and promotes the use of many other languages, while in the United States, Spanish-speaking people account for almost 20 per cent of the population. In Mexico, 97 per cent of people speak Spanish. These facts alone suggest the reality of the many cultures that form our North American culture. But North American business also relies heavily on trade with other continents. Some of these other continents share aspects of their culture with some parts of North America. For example, we can group these nations by languages shared with large groups within North America:

- Spanish-speaking nations
- English-speaking nations
- French-speaking nations
- Mandarin- and Cantonese-speaking nations
- Hindi- and Urdu-speaking nations

As a student of business communication, you may bring to the classroom knowledge of more than one language or cultural group. This knowledge can be an important asset for you as a communicator because it gives you real insight into another cultural group.

What Constitutes Another Cultural Group?

Culture refers to social practices and objects that unite a group of people. Cultures can be identified many ways, including the following:

- the language used by members
- objects produced by members of the culture
- activities that members engage in
- beliefs and assumptions about how to understand the world
- geographical or national borders
- politeness and social interaction rituals

culture: Social practices and objects that unite a group of people

In many ways, North Americans have an advantage in understanding variations in culture because many languages are spoken there. North America today contains many distinct cultural groups: Indigenous peoples throughout the continent; the French-speaking majority in Quebec and the Spanish-speaking majority in Mexico; significant populations speaking those languages within Canada and the United States; and cities with large populations speaking many other languages. To communicate in an inclusive way with people who speak multiple languages and whose first language is not English means that you need to be sensitive to cultural values.

Communicating across Cultures within Canada

Many businesses operating in North America find it profitable to reach out to customers by adapting their communications to the languages of their customers. Communicating with other cultural groups involves more than translating from English or Spanish or French. Writers must also demonstrate knowledge of and sensitivity to the cultural values of the group they are communicating with. One way for students to learn more about the cultural values of some of the groups that they need to address is to visit the websites affiliated or associated with these cultural groups.

One large cultural group within North America is the Chinese community. In fact, more Chinese people emigrated to the United States in 2018 than did Mexican people.[1] To learn more about Chinese groups, consider visiting these pages:

- www.chinesebusiness.org
- https://www.everyculture.com/multi/Bu-Dr/Chinese-Americans.html
- www.ccbc.com

The Chinese Business Chamber of Canada, for example, runs a one-day course on learning about how to conduct commerce with Chinese businesses, both those located in China and those owned by members of the Chinese community in Canada. They emphasize the importance of having a sophisticated understanding of the variations in cultural practices and etiquette among subgroups. Among the topics they cover are cultural knowledge and etiquette. They begin with an overview of best practices in business communication, including appropriate business-writing style. Model documents serve to provide examples for participants to work from on their own writing projects. But in addition to the standard business communication knowledge you might expect, they have also added discussions of cultural etiquette that are specific to North American business practices. Finally, they introduce students to the typical ways in which North Americans tend to conduct business meetings, including how to follow up with meeting participants. A full description of the course is available by going to http://www.chinesebusiness.ca, selecting Business Training Centre, and clicking on International Trade Workshops.

As you can see, there is much to learn that goes beyond simple translation.

---

1   Carlos Echeverria-Estrada and Jeanne Batalova, "Chinese Immigrants in the United States," *Migration Policy Institute*, January 15, 2020. https://www.migrationpolicy.org/article/chinese-immigrants-united-states/

Exercise 6.1: Prepare a Presentation on Chinese Culture and Business Practices

Visit the sites listed previously for information about Chinese culture and business practices. Prepare a short (10-slide) presentation to give to your class. Focus on only one or two aspects—for example, Guanxi or deal-making—in your presentation. Alternatively, pick another culture and prepare a presentation on one or two aspects of that culture.

Within North America, you can see this kind of hybrid or complex identity in the example of the First Nations Bank of Canada and the Native American Bank in the United States. Among the core values of the First Nations Bank of Canada are these statements:

- We are a leader in the provision of financial services to Aboriginal People and an advocate for the growth of the Aboriginal economy and the economic well-being of Aboriginal People.

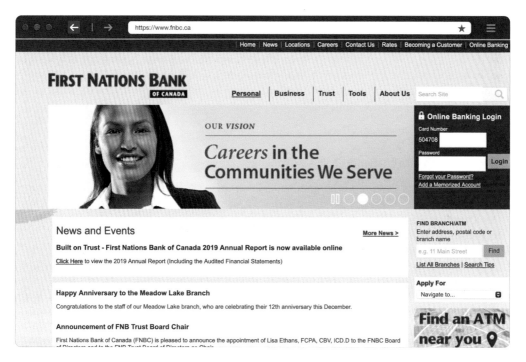

Source: https://www.fnbc.ca

- The Bank was conceived and developed by Aboriginal People, for Aboriginal People and regards itself as an important step toward Aboriginal economic self-sufficiency.[2]

---

2   First Nations Bank of Canada, The Aboriginal Bank, http://www.fnbc.ca/about-us/about-the-bank/. Accessed October 23, 2013.

These statements emphasize the need to speak to the cultural values of the audience: in this case, economic well-being and economic self-sufficiency are two of these values.

Currently, First Nations Bank of Canada has become over 80-per cent owned by Aboriginal shareholders. In articles written for Aboriginal readers, such as the one in Figure 6.1, the writing shifts in perspective to connect with Aboriginal readers of the *Globe and Mail* newspaper.

In the United States, the Native American Bank fulfils a similar purpose and mission:

> In 2001, twenty Tribal nations and Alaska Native Corporations set out with a dream to create a national bank to serve all Native people, communities, governments and enterprises across the country and established Native American Bank, N.A.
>
> We recognize that among the many issues facing Native Americans, the absence of access to financial capital and services has been a significant obstacle toward the realization of self-sufficiency and financial freedom across Indian Country.[3]

Exercise 6.2: Identify Some of the Cultural Values Expressed

Read the *Globe and Mail* newspaper article reprinted in Figure 6.1 and write a paragraph in which you identify three of the cultural values that Aboriginal readers would identify with. Focus on Martell's responses to the questions. Then write another paragraph in which you identify the business values discussed, for example, "drive for business."

How Canada's other national bank is expanding

Keith Martell runs Canada's other national bank, the First Nations Bank of Canada, whose mainly aboriginal clientele extends from the Yukon to Northern Quebec. With more than $300-million in assets, it is the only chartered bank with a head office in Saskatchewan, where it started 13 years ago. Based in a province where more than 15 per cent of the population is aboriginal—and projected to climb much higher—Mr. Martell has insight into the economic plight, and potential, of native Canadians. His bank has just expanded into Nunavut, opening a full-service branch in Iqaluit in partnership with an Inuit group.

Has the aboriginal population participated in the Saskatchewan boom? I think so. We do a lot of banking for first nations governments, which deliver primary social programs in many of these communities. You look at some of these remote reserves, and you can have 80-per-cent unemployment. But we did see a noticeable change in some social assistance budgets—they were beginning to decrease because more people were working out [of their communities]. There were more individuals with ... [earning] capacity.

---

3   Native American Bank, https://nativeamericanbank.com/about-us/. Accessed August 14, 2020.

But you have a long way to go? Definitely, but the other positive is that the median age of the First Nations population is still 18–19 years. So we have the same aging demographics of the employed work force, just like any other part of Canada, but we have this young growing engine that is ready to be engaged. The success will be in engaging them.

Don't you desperately need to get people to stay in school? I'm a chartered accountant, born in a first nations community in Northern Saskatchewan. Clearly, education does a lot. Every aboriginal person I know who has achieved an education is self-sufficient and functioning quite well.

I talk to companies looking for a strategy and they say "We go to the high schools and we don't see aboriginal people there. We go to universities and they are not there." I say you should spend all your effort and time getting to children in Grades 4, 5, and 6.

But they need to see there is a future for them, so they don't make the bad decisions you make once you become a teenager. If you can make them understand there is a future, they don't do things like having children when they are still children. They don't quit school early or take the easy route. They stay with it.

How did you get the education bug? My mother is not aboriginal and her family was all teachers, so she made sure we were getting education. My dad is Cree and went through residential schools—and one of the negative legacies of residential schools was that it lowered the importance of education for a lot of those folks. That's because it wasn't a very positive experience.

But he still understood the importance of education and he gave me my drive to work in business. He's always been a businessman and our family on that side goes back to the fur-trading days as traders and outfitters for the Hudson Bay Co. So I got my drive for business from the aboriginal side.

Does that really fit with the image we get? I regularly hear people say to me, "Aboriginal people don't have a history as being involved in business, and it's interesting that you have a bank." And I say aboriginal people actually ran the economy of this country for about 300 years.

When I talk to our young people, a lot of them don't know that history. That's really sad. I am of Cree background and the Cree stretch from the shores of James Bay all the way into Northeastern BC. They actually didn't dominate those areas throughout history—they moved with the fur trade. They were traders and they settled into this area. They were sort of the first imperialists—bad word, I know—because they ran out and started business going in these regions before the Europeans even got here.

So how do you connect with this tradition? Just through little things. In the 1990s, we weren't getting people working at the McDonald's and other fast food outlets. These aren't lifelong jobs but they are first jobs and they teach you how to work. At that time we would go down to local franchises, and even into neighborhoods that are predominantly aboriginal, and you wouldn't see one aboriginal person across the counter.

Figure 6.1 **This newspaper article from the** *Globe and Mail* **on the First Nations bank speaks from the perspective of Aboriginal Canadians.**

Source: "How Canada's other national bank is expanding" by Gordon Pitts, Globe & Mail, July 4, 2010. The Globe and Mail Inc. All Rights Reserved.

Rhetorical Situation 6.1: Banking and Culture

Lauren Toews knew what she was getting into when she accepted this transfer to the Central Region Commercial Banking Center: a big step up the corporate ladder—two steps, actually. Her last position with the bank had been as a branch manager in a small city. She enjoyed it—meeting customers in the branch, helping them negotiate the forms and requirements that the bank had for securing a loan. Managing the staff had taken most of her time, and although it had its challenges she did enjoy helping her team develop.

But this is a new week, and it presents new challenges. Commercial banking takes place out of a large office building in an industrial park in the north suburbs of a large city. Customers sometimes come into the office, but more often than not Lauren meets with them at their businesses. There are several advantages to this arrangement: she gets out of the office, she eats lunch at a variety of interesting restaurants, and she gets a first-hand look at how their businesses are doing. It is one thing to look at balance sheets and financial reports; it is another thing entirely to see how much inventory is on site and how many customers are in the stores.

But the biggest and most pressing challenge facing Lauren is cultural: 40 per cent of her accounts are companies run by people who have emigrated from China and Southeast Asia (Thailand, Vietnam, and the Philippines). Most of these clients speak passable English, and all have employees or relatives that speak English well. She knows that language will not present an insurmountable problem. Instead, she is more concerned with understanding their ways of doing business.

Lauren's visit to the Thai Noodle Pot highlights the need for her to learn more as she talks with Anand Shinawatra, the owner of the restaurant. Mr. Shinawatra begins their conversation by noting that Lauren is new to her job, and then he asks Lauren if she is married. Surprised, Lauren says yes, she is married. Mr. Shinawatra asks her if her husband objects to her having lunch with him. She replies that her husband knows that having lunch with clients is part of the job. Mr. Shinawatra then asks what her husband does for a living. Lauren replies that he is a lawyer at a big law firm downtown. Mr. Shinawatra says that lawyers make a lot of money and then speculates that the two of them must make a lot of money—even more since Lauren's promotion. This then leads him to the thought that Lauren can stay home and start a family if she wants to, and he is truly puzzled that she has not chosen to do this.

Lauren is speechless for a few seconds, wondering how to shift this discussion away from her personal life. But then she remembers why she is there and asks Mr. Shinawatra how things are going at the restaurant. She remarks that the soup is wonderful. She can't identify the seasoning—the sour flavor—and asks him what it is. He smiles and tells her that it is the tamarind, an important ingredient in many Thai dishes. That leads to more questions about food and how the business is progressing.

As she reflects on the lunch later, Lauren is surprised that Mr. Shinawatra seems to be excessively polite, on the one hand, while asking what she thinks of as personal questions about her life and recent promotion—a little too personal for her. She wonders if he means anything by it, but she also recognizes that she needs to learn more about Thai culture if she is going to be able to understand him.

1. Analyze Thai culture to understand how people behave.

Visit the following link to read about Thai society and culture: www.kwintessential.co.uk/resources/global-etiquette/thailand-country-profile.html.

Write a paragraph analyzing how what you learned about Thai culture applies to the exchange between Lauren and Mr. Shinawatra. Drawing on what you know about North American culture, explain potential reasons for Lauren's reaction to Mr. Shinawatra. What aspects of Thai culture and social interactions would explain his personal questions?

Audience: Your instructor and classmates

Purpose: To demonstrate your research into Thai culture and your analytical abilities in applying this research to Lauren Toews's experience

Genre: Critical analysis report

2. Reference notes on Thai culture for Lauren's replacement

Starting with the URL provided, do some research on Thai culture. Visit two or three other websites to gather information about Chinese or Filipino culture. Prepare a page of notes on Thai, Chinese, or Filipino culture and how you think these cultural attitudes and expectations would affect a business relationship that employees at the bank might have with customers from these cultures. Writing as Lauren Toews, draft notes for the next person who will hold this job so that they can quickly learn more about your customers' backgrounds. The notes should include advice about working successfully with them. These notes should be typed and organized neatly so that when you move on to another job in the bank you can pass them along to your replacement or share them with other bank employees.

Audience: Another bank employee who will replace Lauren

Purpose: To summarize and present important details about Thai, Chinese, or Filipino culture and to suggest ways in which they might affect business relationships so that readers (from the bank) can learn quickly and easily from them

Genre: Briefing notes

Communicating across Cultures outside North America

 Identify the components of cultural and business practices of intercultural business communication

Each country has unique cultural characteristics, but in the interests of classifying types of cultures, we can find categories of similarity. For example, one way to identify international business opportunities is to classify countries according to the nature of their economies:

- A fully developed, fast-paced market (Canada, Germany, the United States)
- A developing market with rapid growth (China, India)
- A development market (in many geographical areas)[4]

A country's type of economy affects the cultural practices and expectations of those individuals who conduct business there. For example, fast-paced, competitive economies and their societies value directness; business people from such countries see time as money, and their social practices promote productivity and profitability. They want to make a deal; if the deal is ongoing and beneficial, they may cultivate the personal relationship. Even nonprofit business in these economies is affected by culture, so while it may not prize profit to the same extent as private enterprises, it still values directness and efficiency in communication and action. In contrast, **relationship-based economies** value social interaction among people. Business people from affluent, relationship-based countries insist on building a personal relationship before discussing business details. They value trust and reliability first, and they establish these attributes before the deal is struck.

relationship-based economies: Economies that value personal relationships and trust as a precondition for business relationships

The *Step-by-Step Guide to Exporting*, a Foreign Affairs and International Trade Department document, offers this good advice to communicating with potential customers in other cultures:

> The usual Western business practice is to negotiate a transaction and then construct a buyer-seller relationship around it. In the business cultures of many countries, however, this process is reversed. One starts out by building a personal relationship with a prospective customer and, once that relationship has been established and everyone is comfortable with it, the actual business negotiations can begin.
>
> While the ultimate goal of all parties is to sign a contract, the immediate objective in a relationship-based business culture is to establish the personal connections. Your non-Canadian counterparts often see this as a necessary precondition for serious negotiations.[5]

This quotation from the *Step-by-Step Guide* highlights the possibility for cultural misunderstanding whenever people from varying cultural backgrounds assemble to do business. North American businesspeople may be frustrated at the slow pace of the deal as their counterpart seeks first to establish a comfortable relationship. Individuals from competitive cultures can view relationship building as wasting time and money. In contrast, a businessperson from Argentina may view Canadian or American impatience as rude and untrustworthy, undermining the goal of creating a solid working relationship.

Once you identify the kind of economy that your business partner works in, you can make decisions about the implications for your communication strategies. Many stereotypes abound in discussions of intercultural communication. For example, Asian countries such as China and

---

4 Foreign Affairs and International Trade Canada, *Step-By-Step Guide to Exporting*, https://www.tradecommissioner.gc.ca/guides/exporter-exportateurs/step4-etape4.aspx?lang=eng
5 Foreign Affairs and International Trade Canada, *Step-by-Step Guide to Exporting*, https://www.tradecommissioner.gc.ca/guides/exporter-exportateurs/step9-etape9.aspx?lang=eng

Business Communication: Rhetorical Situations

Japan have been described as **high-context cultures**, whereas North American countries (primarily Canada and the United States) are designated **low-context cultures**. The phrases *high context* and *low context* refer to the degree to which the context around a statement affects its meaning (see Figure 6.2). A low-context statement is stated directly and does not depend on outside information for meaning. For example, "I am angry because you did not answer my email right away" is low-context because the message is complete and unequivocally stated. In contrast, a high-context statement may not signal the speaker's emotion at all; instead, it communicates through contextual clues—for example, "Have you had the chance to check your email recently?" Couched as a question, this statement subtly directs attention toward the intended meaning: "If so, did you get my message? If so, why have you not answered it?"

high-context cultures: Cultures that communicate through indirection and suggestions

low-context cultures: Cultures that state directly what the speaker wants to communicate

High-Context Countries/Cultures	Low-Context Countries/Cultures
Asian countries such as China, Japan, Korea, Thailand, Vietnam	North American countries such as Canada, United States, Mexico
Middle Eastern countries such as Iran, Iraq, Afghanistan	European countries, including the United Kingdom
South American countries such as Argentina, Brazil, Chile, Ecuador, Colombia	Australia, New Zealand

Figure 6.2 **Countries/cultures typically designated as high- and low-context communicators.**

Traditional intercultural communication advice has stereotyped Asian communication as high-context and warned business writers to be aware and pay attention to the alternative meanings that any statement by an Asian businessperson might have. In fact, the recent boom in Chinese capitalism means that this advice may be a sweeping generalization. Although the use of high- and low-context statements may have some cultural basis, individuals within the same culture also use these contrasting styles of communication. Michelle LeBaron offers this advice to individuals with a preference for low-context communication who are working with high-context speakers:[6]

- Nonverbal messages and gestures may be as important as what is said
- Status and identity may be communicated nonverbally and require appropriate acknowledgment
- Face-saving and tact may be important, and they need to be balanced with the desire to communicate fully and frankly

6   Michelle LeBaron, "Communication Tools for Understanding Cultural Differences," *Beyond Intractability*, ed. Guy Burgess and Heidi Burgess (Conflict Research Consortium, University of Colorado, Boulder), http://www.beyondintractability.org/essay/communication_tools/

- Building a good relationship can contribute to effectiveness over time
- Indirect routes and creative thinking are important alternatives to problem solving when blocks are encountered

In contrast, she offers this advice to high-context communicators working with low-context speakers:

- Things can be taken at face value rather than as representative of layers of meaning
- Roles and functions may be decoupled from status and identity
- Efficiency and effectiveness may be served by a sustained focus on tasks
- Direct questions and observations are not necessarily meant to offend, but to clarify and advance shared goals
- Indirect cues may not be enough to get the other's attention

power-distance index: A measure of the cultural expectations between managers and workers

There are other important aspects to consider when communicating with people whose backgrounds vary from your own, including issues of power, distance, hierarchy, ethnicity, and gender. In his research into cultural differences, Geert Hofstede developed the **power-distance index** as one way to categorize cultural expectations between workers and their managers. A high power-distance culture expects managers and bosses to display their rank and for workers to seek direction from higher up and to take the blame if a problem develops. In contrast, in low power-distance cultures, managers and bosses treat workers with respect. Workers work on important projects, and if a problem develops, the manager takes the blame.[7] Examples of high power-distance cultures include Russia, China, India, and Arabic-speaking countries. Low power-distance cultures include Japan, Australia, and Canada.[8]

hierarchy: The degree to which social relations are managed from the top or elite members of society down through managers to the workers

Another issue that can affect intercultural communication is **hierarchy**, which is related to the power-distance index. The more hierarchical a culture, the more individuals perceive social and status differences between themselves and others. For example, Mexican culture is "steeply hierarchical. Persons can rank high on the social ladder by reason of family lineage, power, education, and wealth."[9] In a steeply hierarchical culture, higher-status individuals expect to be treated with deference by those they consider to have less status. In contrast, American and Canadian cultures have a flatter hierarchical structure because they emphasize the equality of all citizens. Novinger notes that Americans or Canadians who address high-status Mexicans too informally can offend by ignoring their status or not "maintaining a proper distance." Similarly, if they treat someone with less status than themselves as an equal, this "confuses or embarrasses the person because they perceive a clear status difference."[10]

7 Will Kenton, "Power-Distance Index (PDI)," *Investopedia*, https://www.investopedia.com/terms/p/power-distance-index-pdi.asp

8 "Geert Hofestede [sic] and Intercultural Communication," *Demography Resources*, January 28, 2008, http://demoblography.blogspot.com/2008/01/geert-hofstede-and-intercultural.html

9 Tracy Novinger, "On Contrasting Cultures," *Intercultural Communication*, November 19, 2009, http://culturespan.blogspot.ca/search/label/Mexico

10 Ibid.

A third area in which misunderstanding can occur in intercultural communication in business is **gender relations**. Expectations differ from culture to culture about appropriate roles for men and women in society and in business. When expectations conflict about the appropriate roles of men or women, misunderstandings can easily occur. For example, in cultures where men and women are viewed as more or less socially equal, the gender of those people negotiating a deal doesn't particularly matter. However, in cultures where women are prohibited from interacting publicly or professionally, expectations can prevent or undermine successful communication. For example, Lauren Toews wonders initially whether Mr. Shinawatra feels he can ask her personal questions because she is a woman. She considers whether he would still ask about her marital status and desire for children if she were a man. In this case, her sensitivity to gender bias (which arises from *her* cultural experience) results in her assessing whether his questions offend her.

gender relations:
Expectations about the appropriate roles of men or women

Of course, gender bias is not confined to specific cultures or societies. It operates on individual levels as well. Individual attitudes about gender can also interfere with successful communication. Although you have limited control over how elements like gender or hierarchy may affect the responses of people of different cultural backgrounds toward you, you can control your own reactions and responses. By intentionally pursuing chances to meet people with various cultural backgrounds, you can expand your own areas of experience and knowledge so that you can do your part to facilitate the interaction. By becoming sensitive to cultural practices and learning about how they differ, you can become more adept at interacting effectively with individuals you will meet in your work or personal life.

Learning to Communicate across Cultures

 Recognize that many people have multiple and shifting senses of their own cultural identity—they can be members of more than one cultural group

Given the multi-ethnic and multicultural nature of contemporary North American life, many people are members of more than one cultural group. Whether they were "born here," immigrated as children, or moved as adults, they are likely to speak one or more languages in addition to English, French, or Spanish, and they participate in various cultural groups at school, work, at home, or online. For these individuals, their sense of their own cultural identity shifts as they move among groups or switch languages. It can be impossible to judge based on appearances which cultural groups individuals might belong to.

In Rhetorical Situation 6.2, Daniel McMahon faces some of the most basic challenges for businesspeople starting out on a crosscultural venture in India: an almost complete lack of knowledge of Indian business practices, a lack of understanding of how critical it is for him to conduct meetings, and a lack of understanding of the amount of time the venture will consume. He does not, however, have to face one of the most basic challenges of communication across cultures: working in a language that he does not speak, because English is the language of business in India.

LANGUAGE

One of the most obvious markers of culture is language. By recognizing both French and English as national languages in Canada, Canadians make a political statement about the relative importance of these languages, both to each other and in comparison to the languages of other immigrant and First Nations groups. Similarly, by recognizing English as the national language in the United States, Americans make a statement about other languages, including Spanish, which is spoken by 18% of the population or nearly 60 million people.[11] As a business communicator, you will want to respect the values and culture of the person or group to whom you are writing. How can you communicate your respect? Try one of these strategies:

- Offer a salutation (such as "Nee Hau Ma," which is Mandarin for "How are you?") in the language of the person you are writing to
- Offer to provide a translation or summary in the language of the person you are writing to
- Limit your use of idiomatic words and phrases ("That's life"; "that's my word")

If at all possible, communicate in the language of the people you are writing to. If you are giving a presentation to a group whose English skills are not strong, consider presenting a slideshow handout that summarizes your talk in their language or using their language on the slides themselves. This will help them confirm their understanding of what you have said in English, and it will also demonstrate that you respect their language.

POLITENESS, FORMALITY, AND SOCIAL INTERACTION PRACTICES

Different cultures often have different ways of greeting people, different ways of introducing new people to a group, and different rules for interacting. In some residential areas of North America, politeness exchanges include saying "Hello" or "Hi" to people you walk past on the street. In a downtown business area, however, you are not expected to say hello to others unless you know them or have some business to conduct with them. At work, you might say "Hi" to a coworker but "Hello" to a superior (issues of hierarchy).

When you are writing to clients from a culture outside North America, assume a formal tone at first. Write "Dear Ms. Yousova" rather than beginning with "Dear Ingrid." After you have talked with the other person several times or exchanged several emails, you can gain a sense of how formal they expect you to be with them by studying their letters and emails.

Politeness and social interaction differences are particularly important when meeting people for the first time. In preparation for the summer Olympics in China, Beijing residents were advised to avoid asking foreigners about their age, religious beliefs, politics, or occupations. They were also warned not to ask foreigners about their health, love life, or marriages. These are all perfectly acceptable topics of conversation in Beijing, but Westerners might find them too intrusive for casual conversation with a new acquaintance.

---

11 "Hispanic Heritage Month 2019," United States Census Bureau, August 20, 2019, https://www.census.gov/newsroom/facts-for-features/2019/hispanic-heritage-month.html

ORAL COMMUNICATION PRACTICES

Oral communication practices vary significantly throughout the world. One general rule is to observe others in the culture closely. A second rule is to research the culture before you interact with people of that culture so that you have at least some general knowledge that you can draw on as you try to piece together rules for how you should behave (see Figure 6.3). You should try to determine these kinds of practices:

- Who opens and closes conversations?
- How do people determine who speaks next?
- Who may interrupt and how does this happen?
- How is silence used (e.g., to communicate respect)?
- Is humor appropriate or disrespectful?

BUSINESS PRACTICES

As you might expect, business practices around the world differ dramatically depending on how different the culture is from Canadian or American culture. The list of information that you should acquire about a target culture should include:

- language(s) spoken
- politeness (how to greet business partners, how to say no in a polite way, how to thank your business partners)
- what nonverbal actions communicate (which gestures are offensive, how close you should stand to other people)

Centre for Intercultural Learning
https://www.international.gc.ca/cil-cai/index.aspx?lang=eng

Kwintessential
www.kwintessential.co.uk/resources/country-profiles.html

International Business Etiquette, Manners, and Culture
www.international-business-etiquette.com

Geert Hofstede Analysis
www.cyborlink.com/besite/hofstede.htm

Figure 6.3 **Consult country-specific sources on business protocol.**

The best way to learn about the different practices in a particular country is to consult one or more of the Internet resources listed in Figure 6.3.

COMMUNICATING IN A CHANGING WORLD

 Adjust written documents to communicate well with audiences from a variety of cultural groups

Guidelines about cultures are just that: guidelines. For example, typical business communication advice about China will tell you that China is a "collectivist" culture—that is, Chinese people tend to work as a group. More recent commentators, however, suggest that this may no longer be accurate. Business owners in China combine elements of Chinese culture, such as collectivism and harmony, with elements drawn from Western culture, such as ambition and individualism.[12] Wei Wang describes this mixture of cultures:

> But in my years of experience in both the West and China, I have realized that, although Chinese individuals have a strong tendency to relate to each other, they do not necessarily work together towards a shared goal. In fact, on the contrary, the Chinese are much less collectivist than Westerners. For instance, inside Sino-Western joint ventures, I have found that, while Westerners debate vigorously among themselves about the best way to get something done, local employees neither communicate well with Western personnel nor discuss business issues adequately among themselves. When they do talk among themselves, they talk a lot about personal matters, and when they act, they tend to follow their own rules rather than those of the group.[13]

In essence, this research suggests that you need to have a complex understanding of people from other cultures. Of course, you need to learn as much as you can about politeness rituals (greetings, gifts, salutations, and so on)—that hasn't changed. However, you also need to recognize the complexity of people: many people are a mix of traditional values characteristic of their regional or national culture along with values from global influences (for example, American culture as depicted in movies or advertising). Individuals are also a mix of business values and cultural values outside of their business roles.

We encourage you to learn more about other cultural traditions, both within and outside your own country, and to apply what you learn from your research to your communications. This chapter has introduced you to a range of topics from social interactions and politeness rituals to business practices. We hope that you will extend the start you have made here by learning more about cultures outside your own. The more we all learn about the different cultural groups in our country, the richer we all will be.

---

12 R. Spence, "Nuggets from 'best in show' papers," *National Post*, July 21, 2008, FP4.
13 Wei Wang, *The China Executive: Marrying Western and Chinese Strengths to Generate Profitability from Your Investment in China* (2W Publishing, 2006), p. 20.

Business Communication: Rhetorical Situations

Exercise 6.3: Test Your Knowledge of Business Etiquette

To test your knowledge, take one of the international business etiquette quizzes at www.international-business-etiquette.com/besite/culture.htm.

Exercise 6.4: Summarize Best Practices

Using the information in Figure 6.4, summarize the basic advice you would give to a colleague traveling to India to begin the process of signing a contract with an Indian company.

Relationships and Communication
- Indians primarily do business with people they already know and have known for a long time.
- Mutual trust and respect are the foundations of relationships.
- To build credibility, get someone else to introduce you.

Business Meeting Etiquette
- Allow up to two months lead time to set up appointments.
- Confirm your appointment a week or two in advance and again the day before the meeting. Remain flexible and prepare for last-minute rescheduling of meetings.
- Arrange meetings in late morning or early afternoon.
- Arrive on time: punctuality is important.
- Share an agenda and supplementary materials and charts before the meeting.

Dress Etiquette
- Men should wear dark business suits and dress conservatively; in hot areas, less formal wear is acceptable.
- Women should dress in suits or conservative dresses.

Titles
- Address business peers using titles such as Professor, Doctor, and Engineer.
- If someone does not have a professional title, use the honorific title "Sir" or "Madam."
- Do not use someone's first name without their title unless they specifically invite you to address them by their name only.

Business Cards
- Offer your card with your right hand after the initial handshake and greeting.
- Business cards in English are acceptable.
- Hand your card in such a way that the recipient can read it as they accept it.

Figure 6.4 **Advice about cultural practices in India, intended to help travelers conducting business in that country.**

Rhetorical Situation 6.2: AccountSoft and the Patel Group

© Matej Kastelic/Shutterstock

Daniel McMahon, president of AccountSoft (a small but quickly growing accounting software company), considers his options. The first option is traveling to Mumbai, India, to meet Narendra Kulkarni of the Kulkarni Group to negotiate a deal to handle the customer relations side of his new product. The second option is for him to develop and manage it in-house. He doesn't like either option, but they are the only two he has.

AccountSoft's new software package, Accountant's Advantage, is the next generation of programming for the financial services industry in North America. One of its big advantages is that it can directly link up with (online, in real time) a client's financial records from the major brokerages, including E*TRADE and Questrade. The software can also download trading records from those sources and, with a few clicks of the mouse, save accountants huge amounts of time trying to reconcile trades and calculate the resulting taxes. The future of his company depends on this new product.

But his company's margins are also under pressure. He has to save on costs, especially support costs such as customer service call centers. It is this potential for savings that has led him to investigate the Kulkarni Group. He saw a presentation by one of their North American sales representatives at a recent technology conference in Buffalo, NY, and their name keeps coming up in the technology trade magazines he reads. They are leaders in providing customer services for smaller companies like his. In fact, they can do it in India for half the cost of managing it in-house.

Daniel likes what he read on the website, and from talking to the sales representative he feels like the Kulkarni Group might make a good match. However, he also feels that he really needs to visit their operations center in Mumbai to meet with their management. He wants to meet the people who might make or break his business before he commits to signing a contract with them.

It turns out that the Kulkarni Group also want to meet Daniel before they move forward. Adding AccountSoft will demand a significant investment on their part. They, too, want to know whom they are dealing with.

Daniel doesn't have much time to prepare for the trip, and what time he does have will be spent working out production schedules and timelines for the first release of Accountant's Advantage. But he knows next to nothing about India. He calls Pravnay Khera, one of the few programmers he has on staff who was born here but is connected to the Indian community through his parents.

He tells Pravnay that he is planning a trip to Mumbai in three weeks to work out a deal with the Kulkarni Group. Pravnay agrees that this is the right move financially, but notes that they do business differently over there. For example, he mentions that they probably will not want to sign a contract this trip. He explains that they will want to meet Daniel and make a judgment about him first. Then they will accept his spoken word as enough of a commitment. Daniel wonders aloud if maybe Pravnay should take the trip instead, but Pravnay points out that they will not deal with him because he is not the company president. Daniel has to go. Pravnay offers to put together a memo with some tips and pointers in it, together with some websites where Daniel can find more information. He suggests that a tip sheet may alert Daniel to the most obvious cultural differences. McMahon is interested in having this document and asks Pravnay to draft it as soon as possible.

 ## Professional Communication Challenges 6.2

1. Write the memo for Daniel McMahon

Daniel McMahon asks Pravnay Khera to write a memo outlining some tips and general information on how to conduct himself when he visits India in a few weeks. Write a one- or two-page memo in which you outline the most general kinds of things he should know, such as the value of an oral agreement over a written one, and that summarizes the most important information into tips. Use the websites on cross-cultural knowledge identified in this module as your sources of information. If you know anyone with previous knowledge, consider interviewing them and including that information in your memo.

Audience: Your boss, Daniel McMahon

Purpose: To orient Daniel McMahon to the important ways in which doing business in India differs from a North American context to help him achieve success in his business venture

Genre: Email memo

2. Advise McMahon to postpone the trip

One of the key components of successful business relationships with Indian businessmen is that they know who you are—that is, they either have a personal history of working with you or a mutual friend has introduced you. In this case, Daniel McMahon seems to be too eager to embark on this trip. Write a memo to him advising him to postpone the trip until he can do more planning and perhaps find a mutual friend or businessperson who already does business with the Kulkarni Group to write a letter of introduction.

Audience: Your boss, Daniel McMahon

Purpose: To persuade your boss to postpone his business trip to India so that he can establish a relationship with his Indian counterparts before appearing in person

Genre: Email message

CHAPTER SUMMARY

- Business communication must take into account subcultures within North America as well as cultures outside of North America
- Businesses in North America adapt their communications to the multiple cultures and languages of their customers
- Communicators can reduce miscommunication by identifying whether the people they are writing to belong to a high-context culture (where much explanation and relationship building is necessary) or a low-context culture (which requires more explanation through texts and contracts)
- Both cultural and individual tendencies employ context to make meaning in communication
- Key aspects of intercultural communication include hierarchy, power-distance relationships, gender dynamics, politeness, formality, and social interaction practices

CHAPTER 7

Positive and Informative Messages: Writing Letters, Memos, and Emails

 LEARNING OUTCOMES

1. Analyze a writing situation to decide whether a letter, a memo or an email is the appropriate genre of document to send

2. Differentiate between the purposes and ways of organizing positive and informative messages

3. Organize positive messages appropriately to build goodwill with readers

4. Adapt informative messages to emphasize positive elements and build goodwill

GETTING STARTED

Letters and memorandums (aka memos) are the oil that makes the modern corporate machine work. In fact, they are arguably the most essential tools for getting work done in the modern business world. The memo came into existence when the invention of the typewriter made it easy to communicate through paper. That ability to communicate through easily duplicated paper messages enabled corporations to grow to sizes that were previously unheard of. One hundred years later, the invention of the computer and then the Internet spawned a new genre: email messages. The ability to communicate through electronic messages in turn helped develop work arrangements that span the globe.

Organizations exchange information through letters or memos, whether electronic (email) or print form. Print memos generally communicate important information among employees within the same organization, whereas printed letters generally communicate information between individuals at different organizations. For example, the human resources manager of a medium-sized financial services organization might draft a memo to inform all employees within an organization of the new guidelines for submitting trip reports. When an administrative assistant writes to clients, they would use the genre of the letter to communicate outside the organization. Communicators in business generally use email for brief or informal transactions, but for communicating formal and important information or inquiries, they might send a print letter across town by courier.

Figure 7.1 What distinguishes a memo from a letter?

The generic conventions of formatting a letter or memo are easy to learn. It is also fairly easy to decide when to write a letter and when to write a memo (see Figure 7.1). However, organizing and presenting your message within the genre can be a major challenge. There are four different kinds of messages that you will find yourself writing frequently: positive messages, informative messages, negative messages, and persuasive messages. Positive messages deliver good news to readers. Informative messages convey neutral information. Negative messages deliver bad news to readers; writers of bad-news messages want to manage readers' emotions and maintain goodwill toward the organization. Persuasive messages present complex information that readers may react to with mixed emotions; this type of message requires writers to manage reader emotion or motivate readers to act when they might not particularly want to. In this chapter, you will read several examples of messages that deliver good news or information. This chapter also outlines patterns of organization that you can use or adapt to the different writing situations that you encounter. In the Rhetorical Situations of this chapter you will apply your knowledge of how to write short messages in the different contexts described there.

CHOOSING THE MESSAGE TO FIT YOUR SITUATION

 Analyze a writing situation to decide whether a letter or a memo is the appropriate genre of document to send

Communication tasks are not usually labeled as positive or negative (see Figure 7.2). Instead, you must analyze the **rhetorical situation** to determine what kind of message or response fits best. The main focus of your analysis should be your readers. Examine the situation from their viewpoint to decide how they will respond to your communication: Will they be happy to hear your news? Indifferent? Disappointed? Angry?

rhetorical situation: The context in which a writing or speaking event takes place, including information about the audience, purpose, and message

Informative messages: If you expect readers to respond neutrally to the information you communicate, the message is informative.

Positive messages: If you expect readers to be happy about the information you communicate, the message is positive.

Negative messages: If you expect readers to be angry or disappointed by the information you communicate, the message is negative.

Persuasive messages: If you expect readers to be resistant or opposed to your message, it is a persuasive one.

Figure 7.2 **Different types of messages.**

For example, if you were the administrative assistant in a medium-sized business that sponsored an academic award at the local community college, you might find yourself having to write to both successful and unsuccessful applicants for the award. Some of your readers should be pleased to hear that they have won. Therefore, this letter is a positive message. You will use the positive organizational pattern outlined in the next section of this chapter to develop your message. In contrast, when you write to unsuccessful applicants, your news is rejection, so you expect your readers to be disappointed or even angry at losing. To develop a bad-news letter to losing applicants, you will use a different organizational pattern.

To decide what type of message best fits your rhetorical situation, learn to distinguish one type of message from another. Use the checklist in Figure 7.3 to decide which pattern to use. For example, as you start to draft the letter to the successful award applicants, you might review the checklist in Figure 7.3 to determine that you are writing a positive message (sharing good news) as well as an informative message (informing the reader of details about accepting the award). You also know, based on your analysis, that you should format the messages as letters because they are going outside the organization.

ASK THE QUESTION	IDENTIFY THE RHETORICAL SITUATION	OUR RECOMMENDED MESSAGE PATTERN
What is the main reason for my communication?	To share good news	Use the **positive and informative** message pattern outlined in Figure 7.4.
	To communicate important information	Use, accordingly, the **positive and informative** message pattern outlined in Figure 7.4 or the negative message pattern discussed in Chapter 8.
	To communicate bad news	Use the **negative** message pattern. (see Chapter 8)
	To argue a particular point with which readers may not agree	Use the **persuasive** message pattern. (see Chapter 9)
What are the elements that I must include in this message?	My situation lacks some elements from the pattern	Omit those elements listed in the pattern.
		Discuss the elements you do have in the order recommended in the pattern.
	My situation has reasons from more than one pattern	Use the pattern that fits best with your **main** reason for communication.
		Adapt elements from other patterns as necessary.
Should I format my message as a memo or letter?	I am writing to someone who works for my organization	Use a **memo** format.
	I am writing to someone who works for a different organization	Use a **letter** format.

Figure 7.3 **Use this checklist to analyze your message.**

HOW TO WRITE POSITIVE AND INFORMATIVE MESSAGES

 Differentiate between the purposes and ways of organizing positive and informative messages

Like most business and professional communications, positive and informative messages usually have more than one main purpose. They generally aim to

- inform or share good news

- have recipients read the message, understand it, and respond positively to it
- downplay any negative elements

Simultaneously positive and informative messages have several secondary purposes:

- to have the reader think well of the writer and his or her organization
- to reduce or end further correspondence on this subject

Figure 7.4 is an example of a positive and informative message. Note the information that it contains and how it organizes and presents this information. The annotations in Figure 7.4 show how to organize a positive or informative message. If we examine the annotations, we quickly note that the sample letter could be improved upon to make a more effective positive and informative message. For example, the negative elements in the message are not stated as positively as they could be.

Exercise 7.1: State Negative Elements as Positively as Possible

Rewrite the negative sentences reproduced from Figure 7.4 so that the points are stated as positively as possible, while remaining clear and comprehensible. Review Chapter 3 for information about how to revise negative statements into positive ones.

1. Please note that your vehicle has been rated for personal use only, which does not include a commute to work.

2. We have confirmed that the vehicle is not modified or customized in any way, nor is it used for commercial purposes such as delivery, courier, etc.

3. If these conditions should change, please advise our office as soon as possible to ensure that your coverage is not negatively impacted.

4. Other than those drivers already listed on the policy, we understand that no one else is using the vehicle on a regular basis.

5. If you do have additional drivers in the household not currently listed, please contact our office to discuss.

Motivating Your Reader

The sample informative and positive letter in Figure 7.4 provides excellent additional details to motivate the readers, Horace and Bertha Baxtrom. The writer, Vivian, does this by requesting that the readers send her a copy of the new vehicle ownership to ensure her records are complete. Of course, the Baxtroms want her information about their insurance requirements to be complete. To continue the topic of complete insurance records, Vivian reports that the policy currently lists Horace as the principal vehicle driver. She invites the Baxtroms to inform her if there

ROBERTS & MANJIT INSURANCE / BENEFITS / FINANCIAL SERVICES

January 4, 2020
Horace and Bertha Baxstrom
10,972 S. Qu'Appelle No. 157,
R.R.# 4
Mclean, SK S0G 3E0

Dear Horace and Bertha:

1. Briefly present the main points and share any good news.

As per your request, we confirm that we have advised Southern Prairie Mutual to process the following change to your policy #0867143 effective January 4, 2020.

2. Add details, and include all information that Horace and Bertha need.

Add coverage on the 2020 Toyota Tundra as follows:

- Liability - $1,000,000 limit
- All Perils - $500 deductible
- Rental Vehicle coverage (SPCF #12/89)
- Waiver of Depreciation (SPCF #26)
- Claims Protection

3. Include any negative elements, but state them as positively as possible.

Please note your vehicle has been rated for personal use only, which does not include a commute to work. We have confirmed that the vehicle is not modified or customized in any way, nor is it used for commercial purposes such as delivery, courier, etc. If these conditions should change, please notify our office as soon as possible to ensure that your coverage is not negatively impacted.

4. Add details to show readers how they benefit (in other words, reader motivation).

To complete our files, we would appreciate receiving a copy of the ownership, which may be faxed, mailed, or scanned and emailed to our office. We have the registered owner and principal driver of the vehicle listed as Horace Baxstrom. Other than those drivers already listed on the policy, we understand that no one else is using the vehicle on a regular basis. If you do have additional drivers in the household not currently listed, please contact our office to discuss.

Enclosed are liability slips for your use. The documents amending your policy will follow from Southern Prairie Mutual in the next few weeks. Please review these, as it is important that all the information be correct.

5. Add goodwill ending.

Should you have any questions or if we can be of further assistance, please contact me at (123) 456-7890 or vivian.pierugi@romanjit.com. Thank you for continuing to entrust your insurance needs to Roberts & Manjit.

Sincerely,

Vivian Pierugi

Vivian Pierugi, CAIB
Insurance Advisor

Figure 7.4 **Sample informative and positive message.**

are more possible operators of the vehicle than are listed on their current policy. For example, if one of Horace and Bertha's family members has moved home (perhaps their son, while he helps out on the farm over the summer), they should notify Vivian so that she can make changes to their records. If their son crashes the new truck and it turns out he has been a regular driver of the vehicle over the summer but was never listed on the insurance policy, Horace and Bertha may find the insurance adjustor unwilling to process their claim. Vivian uses this argument as a motivator to prompt the Baxtroms to update their coverage details.

To decide whether you need to motivate your reader to accept your information, consider the following questions:

- Should you manage readers' responses toward the information or your organization? If you want readers to respond positively, include reasons why they should do so.
- Does your message present a new organizational policy? Often new policies are obvious as to how they benefit the organization; how they benefit the individual employee or customer is often less obvious. Highlight for readers how the new policy or change in an existing policy benefits them as well.

Concluding Positive and Informative Messages

 Organize positive messages appropriately to build goodwill with readers

Concluding a short positive or informative message gracefully can be a challenge. Some people fall back on the weak and negative invitation, "If you have any questions, please don't hesitate to call." Avoid this type of closing for two reasons: one, it invites readers to create more work for you (calling you with questions when your message should have answered them clearly), and it introduces a negative into an otherwise positive situation ("do *not* hesitate"). Alternatives are to end the communication without a closing or to use a goodwill closing that addresses readers directly. To build **goodwill**, close by referring to the business relationship that you have with your reader (rather than personal aspects).

goodwill: A positive disposition that the reader has toward you as the writer or your organization

In Figure 7.4, Vivian Pierugi uses a variation on "If you have any questions, please call," but her approach is successful because she phrases the invitation positively. It is feasible that her letter might prompt questions or notification of changes to the existing policy records. Her conclusion also includes a direct effort at building goodwill with readers by thanking them for their business.

Exercise 7.2: How Effective Are These Closings?

Evaluate the quality of the following brief endings for a positive or informative message. If you decide it is a poor conclusion, discuss ways to make it better.

1. Please don't be afraid to email me back if I've missed explaining something.

2. I'm really sorry that I won't be able to make it to the banquet, but when I return from my trip to Europe, I will definitely contact you to arrange to pick up my award.

3. I do hope we have the opportunity to meet at the banquet in May so that we can discuss further the ways in which Roberts and Manjit Insurance may contribute to the development of your knowledge of insurance and finance through our internship program.

4. Thanks for your consideration.

5. Together we can stem the growing disaster that the unchecked spread of the pine beetle represents to the timber reserves of this province.

Rhetorical Situation 7.1: Congratulations, You Have Won a Lily's Choice Award

© Rawpixel.com/Shutterstock

Dirk Pelham, administrative assistant to Lilian Fung, realizes he isn't done for the day the moment Lilian Fung, owner of the Lilian Fung Collection, Inc., sweeps into the room brandishing a three-inch stack of file folders. She asks him to draft letters notifying the three winners of this year's Lily's Choice Awards. She places the folders on his table and begins searching in the large bag that hangs from her shoulder.

Dirk picks up the top folder and looks through its contents. He had noticed the competition information on the company website (see Figure 7.5). The website describes the award and the contest rules and information about how award winners are selected.

Lilian explains that the company contacts the fashion program directors at post-secondary schools around the country every fall and invites their students to send in their designs. Students submit a portfolio of women's fashion designs, and she selects three students as "Young Designers to Watch" through her Lily's Choice Awards. Every year they get more submissions. This year they got 25 applicants; in the first year they started with just five. The contest is starting to catch on.

The three winners are in the green file folders on top. The rest of the folders contain the other submissions. From her bag Lilian extracts several pages of handwritten notes with her comments on the designs and her criteria for selection. Dirk's job is to make one or two specific references to the work in each letter using the notes. She advises him to look through the designs before drafting the letters. Lilian points out that the designs in the second green folder are particularly exciting, but warns Dirk not to spend too much time browsing through the entries. She wants the notification letters in the mail by early next week.

Dirk is unclear, though, about when she wants to see the letters: is Monday okay or does she want to read a draft sooner? Lilian replies that he should draft the first one and email it to her. She can look at it in the airport on Friday evening. Once Dirk receives her feedback, he can draft the other letters.

Dirk says this sounds straightforward. Lilian notes that in addition to knowing why they won, the winners also need details about the award presentation ceremony. The awards are usually given out at each school's formal awards banquet at the end of term. Lilian asks Dirk to contact the program directors at the three winners' schools for banquet details. He will also need to arrange for one of Lilian Fung's representatives to attend.

Once Lilian leaves his office, Dirk begins reviewing the winning student design portfolios with interest. He knows that the kind of recognition that comes from a Lily's Choice Award can really jump-start a young designer's career, especially because of the internship with the Lilian Fung Collection that comes with the award. He is also interested in picking up some cutting-edge ideas for his own work.

After a few minutes, he sets aside the design folders to begin the task of writing the letters. He will take them home with him tonight to study them more closely. He needs to check the Lilian Fung website for details about the awards and then make some phone calls for details on how and when the awards will be made.

Analysis: Writing a Letter of Congratulations

Before drafting the letter to contest winners, Dirk analyzes his writing situation. He quickly identifies his main reasons for communication—to share good news and relay important information about receiving the award. Next, he reviews the pattern outlined for writing positive and informative messages to determine which elements are relevant to his situation. As he jots down his ideas related to the analysis, he decides that, at least initially, there are no negative elements to receiving the award, unless the recipients are unable to attend the banquet ceremony. Then he makes a list of the information that must appear in the letter; as he brainstorms the letter's contents, he realizes that the challenge of this message will be ensuring readers have all of the details they need to collect the award (whether or not they can attend the banquet) and how to start arrangements for the winners' internships.

Suddenly Dirk realizes that an important component of this message is to ensure that recipients are motivated to contact him about setting up the internship part of their awards. Although he knows that if he were to win such an award he would be banging on doors to set up his internship, he also recognizes that different personality types might be nervous about contacting the Lilian Fung Collection, so this means he should analyze his readers' needs to determine the most effective means of prompting them to act.

 Exercise 7.3: Motivating Readers to Attend an Awards Event

1. Generate a list of needs that award recipients might have in connection with their education and the winning of an award that would be met by attending the award ceremony and promptly setting up their internships. Here are three to get you started:

- being a successful student
- distinguishing themselves from other students
- earning income

Add at least three or four more needs to this list that you think are relevant to the reader.

2. Expand the three that look most useful to you into two or three sentences of explanation that you might be able to use in a notification letter that will motivate your readers to attend an awards program event. Remember to choose reasons that your readers will find motivating.

 Professional Communication Challenges 7.1

1. Congratulations on Winning a Lily's Choice Award

Using the details presented in Figures 7.5 through 7.8, write a draft of Dirk Pelham's letter for Lilian Fung in which you inform one of the winners that they have won a Lily's Choice Award for innovative women's fashion designs. Make sure that your letter includes any information the recipient needs to accept the award, as well as Lilian Fung's feedback about the designs. If necessary, reread the discussion on writing positive and informative messages to review the important aspects of writing this kind of message and for pointers on how to organize and draft your message.

Audience: The three recent winners of the Lily's Choice Award

Purpose: To inform readers that they have won the award, which includes a cash prize and a six-month internship working at the Lilian Fung Collection, Inc.; to provide details on where and when they will receive the award (and what to do if they cannot attend the awards banquet); and to motivate them to contact Lilian about arranging their internship

Genre: Business letter (on company letterhead)

Lilian Fung invites all fourth-year students enrolled full-time in an accredited Canadian school of fashion apparel design program to submit a portfolio of between three and five designs of women's casual or work apparel for consideration for a Lily's Choice Award. The awards include a $1,000 cash prize, a commemorative brass plaque, and an opportunity to work for six months as a paid intern at the Lilian Fung Collection in its Toronto studio. Deadline for submissions: Nov. 30 (yearly).

Figure 7.5 **Lily's Choice Award description from the website.**

Scheduled for May 7, 6:00–8:00 p.m., at Fondini's Bistro, west campus (211 Spadina Rd)

Attendance by representative from the Lilian Fung Collection is now confirmed.

Send name and email address of representative [check this with Lilian?] to Anne Bechaumé, program administrative assistant (fshninfo@ryerson.ca), no later than April 15.

Figure 7.6 **Dirk's notes on details regarding one of the school program awards banquets.**

Rashana Develani, Apt. 807, 439 High Tech Rd, Richmond Hill, ON (905-123-4567)

Harcourt Van Sittart, 325 Queen St., Oakville, ON (905-234-5678)

Lami McTier, 22 Littlebottom Cresc., East York, ON (416-345-6789)

Figure 7.7 **Lily's Choice Award recipients.**

Rashana: Fascinating use of beading to add upscale elegance to casual weekender design. Textured fabric combination is arresting.

Harcourt: Flamboyant pantsuit design will give the working woman options. Stunning use of merino wool.

Lami: Functional yet elegant approach to basic jeans and t-shirt combination. This combination demonstrates understanding of contemporary women's need for style and comfort.

Figure 7.8 **Lilian Fung's commentary on Lily's Choice Award winners' designs.**

2. Accepting the award and requesting additional information

Imagine that you are one of the three recipients of a Lily's Choice Award (Rashana Develani, Harcourt Van Sittart, or Lami McTier), and draft a letter to Lilian Fung, the owner of the Lilian Fung Collection, thanking her for the award and notifying her of whether you are able to attend the awards banquet on May 7 to receive your award. In your letter, also request further information about the Lilian Fung Collection's internship program, a position that you have been offered as part of the award. Include information about your availability to accept the internship as well as your particular interests and goals for the internship. Use the information in this chapter about writing positive and informative messages to help you structure and draft your letter.

Audience: Lilian Fung, the owner of Lilian Fung Collections, Inc., who has just notified you that you have won an award sponsored by her company

Purpose: To accept the award and request additional information about the details of the internship that you will receive as part of the award

Genre: Positive and informative email message

INFORMATIVE MESSAGES

 Adapt informative messages to emphasize positive elements and build goodwill

Figure 7.9 is a sample letter written to inform a client of the details associated with a corporate move. As you read it, attend to how the message is structured, starting with the complete contact information for Cascades Moving & Storage. The message itself establishes a positive first impression by thanking the reader for his business and repeats the agreed-on dates for his move. The writer formats the letter using bold headings and white space to highlight the information of central interest to Dr. Wild: the dates for his move and important details associated with those dates. This formatting allows readers to scan quickly to check the details.

 Exercise 7.4: Analyze a Positive and Informative Message

Analyze the sample letter in Figure 7.10 to answer the following questions:

1. What pattern or organizational structure does this letter use?

2. How effectively does this letter present important details?

3. What suggestions can you make for changes in formatting to improve its presentation of information?

4. What stylistic changes can you make to move important details to positions of emphasis?

5. How could you rewrite the goodwill ending to improve its use of positive emphasis?

Cascades Moving & Storage
630 Industrial Road
Full contact information included in letterhead
Spokane, WA
Tel.: 123-123-4567
Fax: 123-123-4568
Email: move@cascadesmove.com

April 18, 2020

Dr. Robert Wild
2047 Pelkey Cres.
Duluth, MN 55802

Order Number: 0873004533033

Dear Robert,

Thank you for choosing Cascades Moving & Storage to manage your move. We're pleased that you've entrusted your valuable belongings to us and we look forward to serving you.

Your relocation is confirmed below. If you need to change these dates, please let me know at least one week ahead of time so that we may accommodate your new schedule.

From Duluth, MN **to** Corvallis, OR
Packing: 2021/05/13
Loading: 2021/05/14
Delivery: Your household goods will be delivered between 2021/05/21 and 2021/05/26. The exact delivery date will be the choice of York Van Lines. Your driver will advise you of this date 48 hours prior to delivery or, if possible, at loading.
Unpacking: Your household goods will be unpacked following delivery.

We appreciate your business and will do everything we can to get you settled quickly. If you have any questions prior to or during your move, please call us toll-free at 1-800-123-4567.

Yours truly,

Phyllis Simms
Corporate Relocation Coordinator

Goodwill opening identifies topic

Includes negative element as positively as possible

Presents main points

Adds details and includes all necessary information

Ends by building goodwill

Shows reader how he benefits

Figure 7.9 **Sample informative letter.**

Dear Cardmember,

Welcome to a new world where all those exotic locations on your bucket list seem much closer. You are packed and ready for an adventure that only North American Credit® FlyFreePlus® Titanium Card can offer.

Your new Card membership works like this. For each $1.00 purchase charged to your Card, you earn 1 FlyFreePlus® Mile. But FlyFreePlus doesn't stop there. Once you have reached $10,000 in purchases each year, you will start earning 1.25 FlyFreePlus Miles for every additional $1.00 purchase. If you use this Card for spending every day, you earn FlyFreePlus Rewards more quickly.

But this Card isn't just about earning FlyFreePlus Miles. It also gives you North American Credit's global service, plus the warm welcome of 5,000 fine establishments in the US, Canada and worldwide. Your unique North American Credit benefits include:

- No spending limit
- Travel assistance and insurance protection
- Our exclusive *NoMoreWaiting*® program

With FlyFreePlus, only your imagination can limit your travel options. Visit over 863 destinations in over 149 countries served by our member airlines. Whether it's short domestic flights or your round-the-world dream vacation, North American Credit FlyFreePlus Titanium Card has you covered. And your choices continue to multiply.

Redeem your miles online for hotel rooms, car rentals, or vacation packages. Reward yourself using hundreds of options for merchandise, gift cards, and FlyFreePlus experiences. Whether you pursue the heart-pounding excitement of heli-skiing in the Rockies or the quiet contemplation of an ocean fishing trip, North American Credit cards have something for you. For details on the FlyFreePlus program, please see flyfreeplus.com.

The enclosed Benefits Brochure will introduce you to all the nuances of your Titanium Card. If you have questions not answered in the brochure, do not hesitate to visit our website at namericancredit.ca or contact us at 1-800-NAM-CRED.

We appreciate you choosing the North American Credit FlyFreePlus Titanium Card. We strive to give you no less than the best possible service, whether you are in Toronto, Tulsa, or Timbuktu. We do not believe you can find a better business partner than us.

Sincerely,

Devrim Karga
Director,
Consumer Card Marketing

Figure 7.10 **Sample positive and informative letter.**

Filipa Dragovic, the customer relations manager for the Center for Skin Research (CSR), is always looking for ways to improve the services that CSR offers to their clients. The Center has thousands of clients in their database, but most come and go quietly. Most clients are nervous before their appointments and in no mood to complete a survey about their experience at the center afterward. The problem she faces is getting some insight from these clients about their experiences as patients.

Jayson Jacks, an internship student working on a commerce degree, thinks he can help. He is a marketing major, and getting this kind of feedback from clients is something that interests him. He recently received a request that he complete a customer feedback survey after his appointment at a physiotherapy clinic. That letter is short—just four paragraphs. The first paragraph talks about how the physiotherapy clinic is committed to providing the best health care possible. In the second paragraph they request that Jayson complete a two-minute survey as part of improving their services. To encourage him they offer to enter him in a draw for a $100 gift certificate—something he finds attractive because the odds of winning are much better than any lottery ticket he might buy. They end the letter by thanking him and assuring him that any information he provides will be confidential. He suggests this letter could be a good model for CSR to use in creating their own appeal for feedback from their customers. He notes that the chief physician of the clinic has signed the letter and thinks that maybe Filipa might ask their president, Dr. Mykyta Zelenko, to sign CSR's survey letter.

Jayson brainstorms the following list of items to include in the letter to CSR clients:

- an incentive for completing the survey
- some information about the online survey
- some idea of what the questions are about: info about wait times in the office, courtesy of the staff, cleanliness of facility, parking
- the URL for the survey (http://www.csr.ca/survey)

One of the key aspects of the letter from his physiotherapist that Jayson responded to is that it was short. He read the letter in less than one minute, and he could do the survey from his phone while waiting for the bus just by clicking a few buttons. This project seems like something he can handle.

Professional Communication Challenges 7.2

1. Write a letter to get clients to respond to the survey

Using the information in Rhetorical Situation 7.2, write a short letter (fewer than 150 words) to the clients of the CSR. Use the structure outlined in the sample letter in Figure 7.10 and described in the letter Jayson received to organize your message.

Audience: Clients of the CSR who plan to continue using the Center's services and have an interest in improving the services they receive

Purpose: Motivate them to visit the link in the letter and fill out the survey

Genre: Informative message sent as an email

2. Write questions for the online survey

Write the sample questions that would be included on the survey mentioned in Jayson's letter. Use the issues identified by Jayson in the Rhetorical Situation and add other questions that you think would be useful for the administration of the clinic. Limit the survey to no more than seven questions and include no more than one open-ended question (a question where the respondent has to write out an answer rather than click a box). For more information on writing good survey questions, see Chapter 12.

Audience: Clients of the CSR who plan to continue using the Center's services and have an interest in improving the services they receive

Purpose: Obtain information that can be used to improve the client experience

Genre: Short survey or questionnaire

CHAPTER SUMMARY

- Decide the best medium for the message that you have to send (email, print memo, letter).
- Analyze a situation to identify how best to pattern your message to accomplish your purpose.
- Organize positive and informative messages so that they present good news, include all necessary information, show readers how they benefit, and build goodwill.
- Motivate readers to respond to the requests made in informative and positive messages.

CHAPTER 8

Negative Messages: Writing Letters, Memos, and Emails

LEARNING OUTCOMES

1. Identify how to structure a negative message
2. Read critically to identify important information and make inferences
3. Develop the ability to write a good buffer to soften negative news
4. Demonstrate how to structure a negative message to recipients who have more or less status within an organization than you do

GETTING STARTED

We've all received them—the rejection letter, the phone call informing you that you did not get the job, or any one of the many other bad news messages. Nobody likes getting them, but some are clearly easier to deal with than others. Why? There are ways to break bad news that can make the situation easier to handle. In this chapter, we'll explore how to do that.

Negative messages deliver bad news to readers. Your goal in writing a negative message is to manage readers' emotions and responses to your message and to maintain their goodwill toward your organization. In this chapter, you will learn two ways of structuring a negative message to manage your readers' response, including using a buffer to open the message and giving a reason before your refusal. You will also learn how to structure your letter based on your relationship to the recipients, including coworkers, customers, and supervisors. Breaking bad news well can often mean the difference between maintaining clients and losing them, and between building relationships at work and finding yourself out of work. In the Rhetorical Situations in this chapter, you first meet Penelope Stefanopoulos, who must explain to customer Jared LeBlanc, who has improperly used a company product, why Pergola Products cannot refund the purchase price of his new shirt. In the second Rhetorical Situation you assess the quality of a letter to subscriber Fred Keynes from the city newspaper informing him of an upcoming increase in the paper subscription price.

HOW TO WRITE NEGATIVE MESSAGES

 Identify how to structure a negative message

Negative messages are ones to which you expect your reader will respond with displeasure: they will be unhappy to hear the news you have to communicate. Figure 8.1 is a sample negative message sent to a school-aged child whose book order is delayed while the book club waits for it to be restocked. Although it is a short message, Figure 8.1 uses the classic pattern for a negative message:

buffer: A neutral statement often used to begin a negative message

goodwill: A positive disposition that the reader has toward you or your organization

1. **buffer**
2. statement of disappointing news, plus reason
3. an alternative or compromise to soften the disappointment
4. a positive, **goodwill**-building closing

Business Communication: Rhetorical Situations

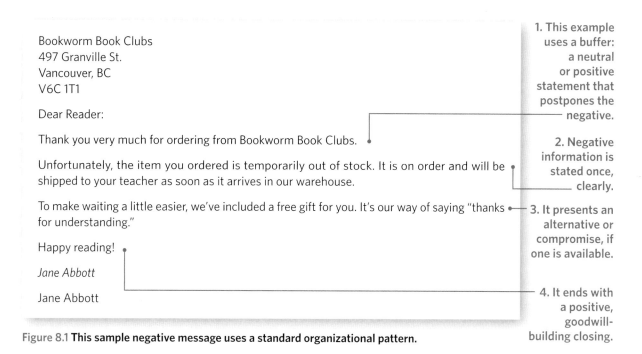

Bookworm Book Clubs
497 Granville St.
Vancouver, BC
V6C 1T1

Dear Reader:

Thank you very much for ordering from Bookworm Book Clubs.

Unfortunately, the item you ordered is temporarily out of stock. It is on order and will be shipped to your teacher as soon as it arrives in our warehouse.

To make waiting a little easier, we've included a free gift for you. It's our way of saying "thanks for understanding."

Happy reading!

Jane Abbott

Jane Abbott

1. This example uses a buffer: a neutral or positive statement that postpones the negative.

2. Negative information is stated once, clearly.

3. It presents an alternative or compromise, if one is available.

4. It ends with a positive, goodwill-building closing.

Figure 8.1 **This sample negative message uses a standard organizational pattern.**

In more complicated situations, you should expand each paragraph to elaborate your points and to manage your reader's response effectively. For example, later in this chapter you will meet Penelope Stefanopoulos, who is writing to a customer of Pergola Products with whom she is not acquainted but whom she would like to preserve as a customer, if possible. She will use a version of the first organizational pattern outlined in Figure 8.1. She has two options for the beginning of her letter (see Figure 8.2):

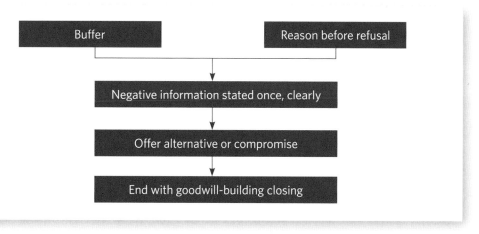

Figure 8.2 **A flowchart shows the standard organizational pattern for a negative message.**

1. She can use a buffer, as Jane Abbott did in her letter in Figure 8.1.
2. She can give a reason before her refusal.

In a case where you do not already know the person you are writing to, try to build as much goodwill as you can. After breaking the bad news, consider offering an alternative or compromise (if possible). End with a goodwill closing.

A primary goal in breaking bad news to readers is to manage their emotions in response to your message. If they are customers, you want them to continue to do business with your company despite your unwelcome message. If they are coworkers, you aim to maintain their cooperation (to follow a new but unpopular policy, for example) or positive attitude toward the organization going forward. Building goodwill and generating a positive (or at least not excessively negative) response to the bad news are important components of writing effective negative messages.

Buffers

 Develop the ability to write a good buffer to soften negative news

Good buffers can be hard to write. Figure 8.3 lists a few tips to help you write a good buffer.

When to Use a Buffer	What Makes a Good Buffer?	What Makes a Buffer Good?
When you know your reader values cultural indirectness (many non-North American cultures prefer indirect rather than direct statements)	Start with the positive	It should accomplish these things:
	Thank the reader for something he or she has done (see Figure 8.6)	■ Put the reader in a positive frame of mind
When you need to thank your reader for something	Describe what happened or list facts relating to the situation	■ Not give the bad news, but not suggest a positive response either
When openly stating the negative sounds too abrupt or rude	Refer to an enclosure in the message	■ Provide an effective transition to the negative news

Figure 8.3 **What you need to know about buffers.**

Exercise 8.1: What Is a Good Buffer?

Evaluate the following sample buffers to determine their effectiveness. Use the information in Figure 8.3 as your criteria to evaluate the degree to which each buffer is effective. Revise where necessary.

1. Dear Mr. Todd,
Thank you for your letter of May 7 in which you requested a replacement blade to your straight razor after extensive usage caused it to break.

2. Dear Mr. Sauron,
It is with great regret that I am sending you this replacement ring. We were unable to recover the original, as you requested, because it was recently destroyed after its bearer fell into an active volcano.

3. Dear Ms. Looser,
Congratulations! You have been selected as fourth runner up in this season's North American Idol contest.

4. Dear Mr. Vassani,
The members of the selection committee were very impressed with your credentials, your work, and especially your expertise in the area of groundwater contamination solutions, but they decided to offer the position to the other short-listed candidate. We felt the other candidate better suited our needs at this time.

5. Dear Colleague,
The process of organizing the program for the 2021 Business Communication Association Conference has been completed. With much regret, I am writing to report that your proposal(s) could not be included in the final schedule.

Rhetorical Situation 8.1: We Regret to Inform You …

 Read critically to identify important information and make inferences

Abdul Akbar rereads the letter that Penelope Stefanopoulos has just handed him (Figure 8.4). He doesn't know where to begin in his explanation about the errors the customer has made with the product. As a chemist in the research and development division of Pergola Products, Abdul is a first line of defense for administrative assistants like Penelope in customer service, who deal extensively with inquiries and complaints from consumers about Pergola's vast array of household products.

Penelope agrees that they can't refund the replacement cost of the shirt, but she also knows that she has to explain to Jared, the customer, why the Bleach'Em Out pen couldn't work when he used it in the way he described. She is wondering if Abdul can tell her anything about the chemistry of mixing together the different products Jared has used on his shirt.

Abdul nods. He says he may have to do some research to find out what is in the GooBGone formula, but the most immediate problem that he can see is that the dryer heat will set an ink stain (which is usually permanent unless it is an erasable formula), so Jared had been starting at a serious disadvantage. Abdul explains that the products that Jared has used first are all pre-treaters—meant to be done before the shirt goes into the washer the first time. The Bleach'Em Out pen is an on-the-go stain remover. It interacts on a molecular basis with the pre-treaters, so combining the two treatments risks potential discoloration or further setting of the stain.

Jared LeBlanc
479 Ponderosa Pine Cresc.
Fort Collins, CO 80524

February 27, 2020

Bonny Brite Bleach
Pergola Products
1089 State St. N.
Denver, CO 80012

Re: Your Bonny Brite Bleach'Em Out Pen Doesn't Work

Two weeks ago, I inadvertently left a marking pen in my new dress shirt pocket when I washed it. Unfortunately, I didn't notice the ink splotches all over the front until the shirt came out of the dryer. Since it's my favorite shirt, I didn't want to throw it away so I went through the products in my mother's laundry closet trying to remove the marks.

First, I soaked it with Spray 'n Wash, which lightened the black ink a little bit. Then I poured detergent directly on the stain and scrubbed away at it for five or ten minutes. This lightened the stains a little bit more, but they were still too dark. You could still see them. Next I tried "GooBGone," a citrus-based stain remover that my mom bought when she was shopping in Denver. It left a greasy stain around the ink, which I had trouble removing, so I applied more detergent directly onto the grease stain. Luckily that came out, but the ink was still there. As a last resort, I bought one of your Bonny Brite Bleach'Em Out stain removal pens, but it was no better than any of the other products that I tried. In fact, after I emptied half of the pen onto the ink stains, they seemed to get a little darker and turn a greenish color.

Needless to say, this outcome is extremely disappointing. Your advertisements show the person just wiping the pen tip over the stain and the mark disappears. This definitely didn't happen in my case, and now my favorite shirt is ruined. I have thought about complaining to the FTC about your deceptive advertising practices but instead, if you are willing to refund me the cost of my $70.00 Leo Chevalier Wrinkle-Free 100% cotton oxford cloth shirt, I am willing to let the matter rest.

You can send me my reimbursement at the address listed above. I appreciate your prompt attention to this matter.

Sincerely,

Jared LeBlanc
Jared LeBlanc

Figure 8.4 **Letter of complaint for Bleach'Em Out stain removal pen.**

The packaging instructions for the Bleach'Em Out pen are clear: they warn customers against using this pen on ink stains. The material safety data sheet of the citrus cleaner, GooBGone, states that its citrus and petroleum base is incompatible with oxidizing materials such as chlorine and strong acids. Abdul notes that the Bleach'Em Out pen contains chlorine bleach, so the interaction of the two substances likely caused the greenish color.

Penelope replies that what Abdul has told her should work well as the basis for the letter. She doesn't think the customer will need the actual chemical formulae—that would be too much detail. She decides to work up a draft of her reply and then see if she needs any more concrete data.

Abdul offers to email Penelope the website for the GooBGone product in case she wants to quote from it. He also suggests that the customer may package up the shirt and send it to him at the lab. He notes that he has a few things to try to remove the stain that Jared will not have access to, as a regular consumer.

Penelope agrees enthusiastically because his suggestion will allow her to offer the customer an alternative. She begins reviewing her options for writing the reply. She remembers that she also has some brochures about cleaning and some samples in her office of new cleaning products that are just coming onto the market. Another option is to send him some of those.

 ## Professional Communication Challenges 8.1

1. We Cannot Refund the Cost of Your Shirt

In the role of Penelope Stefanopoulos, write a reply to Jared LeBlanc in which you refuse to refund the cost of his ruined shirt. Use the information in this chapter to help you organize and draft the negative message. Use the details from the Rhetorical Situation itself and from Figure 8.5 to help you develop the content for the letter. Your main goals are to give Jared the bad news, to have him read, understand, and accept the bad news, and to maintain as much goodwill with him as possible.

Audience: Jared LeBlanc, the customer who ruined his shirt

Purpose: To convey the bad news that you will not be able to grant his request for reimbursement

Genre: Business letter

2. Documenting How to Handle Reimbursement Requests

Writing as Abdul Akbar, draft a memo to Penelope Stefanopoulos that outlines the problem from Pergola Products' perspective about why they cannot reimburse the cost of the shirt. Although you have already spoken to Penelope about the problem, this memo will serve as documentation of how the situation was handled internally. Use the discussion in this chapter to help you organize and draft your response to the request for reimbursement. Your main goals in writing this memo are to document the facts of the Rhetorical Situation and the reasons for not being able to agree to reimburse the customer.

Audience: Penelope Stefanopoulos, customer service representative at Pergola Products

Purpose: To describe the facts of the Rhetorical Situation and explain the reasons for not reimbursing the customer

Genre: Memo

Bonny Brite Bleach'Em Out Stain Removal Pen is not a pre-treater; it is an on-the-go stain remover.

DIRECTIONS FOR USE:

1. Remove excess food from stain.

2. Press the tip of pen onto the stain several times to release stain remover solution.

3. Rub pen tip carefully across the stain to remove it. If necessary, release more liquid onto the stain and continue to massage it in gently.

4. **Please Note:** If treated area comes in direct contact with sunlight, wipe with a damp cloth to remove excess solution from fabric.

Works Well On: Tea, wine, grape juice, chocolate, barbecue sauce, ketchup, coffee

Do Not Use On: Ink, grease, blood, lemon juice

Figure 8.5 **English instructions on the packaging of Bonny Brite Bleach'Em Out Stain Removal Pen.**

ANALYSIS: ORGANIZATIONAL STATUS AND REFUSING JARED'S REQUEST

 Demonstrate how to structure a negative message to recipients who have more or less status within an organization than you do

Organize your negative message according to your relationship with the recipient. In Penelope Stefanopoulos's situation in Rhetorical Situation 8.1, she is writing to a customer who is not part of the Pergola Products organization, so she will use the standard negative letter format (see Figure 8.1). In this instance, Penelope has no pre-existing relationship with Jared, but she does want to build as much goodwill with him as she can to retain him as a customer. Consequently, she is likely to offer him an alternative or a compromise following the refusal and then end with a strong, goodwill-building closing. If she were writing to a coworker with similar status to her own, or to a subordinate, Penelope would structure her message differently. She would structure it yet another way if she were writing to her boss.

For example, Figure 8.6 uses a direct approach to communicate bad news, the writer's resignation from a job. It also outlines one pattern to use when drafting a negative message to a superior. The annotations highlight the main attributes of the letter structure:

1. identify and describe the problem
2. give background, if necessary

3. describe options for fixing the problem
4. recommend a solution and offer assistance to solve problem

In cases such as the one in Figure 8.6, it is unlikely that the letter will announce the news; it is more likely that Armando will have spoken to or at least emailed Catherine about this transition. The letter is required for formal reasons, such as unit reviews within the company that look for patterns in people leaving a large organization, for example. The letter also has the effect of smoothing over the transition. The offer to help with the search for a successor, while unlikely to be accepted, shows a concern for the organization and reflects well on the writer.

June 17, 2020

Catherine Nugent
Western Regional Manager
Cellular City

Dear Catherine:

As you requested, I am writing to inform you that I have signed the contract for employment at AltaTel effective July 1, 2020, making that appointment official. Consequently, I am writing to formally resign from my position at Cellular City effective June 30, 2020.

I want to thank you for your support during my time at Cellular City. The Western Regional administrative team that you lead provided the training and support that I needed to increase our sales and improve our customer satisfaction ratings. I hope my successor can build on these improvements. I have enjoyed my time as a sales associate and lead product specialist for the Google Pixel XL platform. I have learned an enormous amount through this experience. The team of sales associates are starting to feel more like a group and less like a collection of individuals, and our sales successes continue to grow as I speak.

If I can be of assistance in the search for my successor, please feel free to call on me.

Sincerely,

Armando Juarez

1. Direct statement or description of the problem. Identifies a problem.

2. Statements that recognize the boss's contributions to the writer's achievements give background to the letter.

3. Lists employee's achievements in the job. Summarizes options for fixing problem (projects for successor to continue).

4. Offers assistance to solve problem (hiring writer's successor).

Figure 8.6 Sample letter conveys bad news from a subordinate to a boss.

Figure 8.7 is an example of the same bad news (the writer is resigning) conveyed to subordinates. The annotations highlight the organizational structure of the message:

1. describe the problem clearly and briefly
2. supply an alternative or compromise, if possible

3. ask for input or advice, if appropriate

As in the letter to his superior, Armando states the bad news directly. Although this situation offers no possibility of compromise, Armando does introduce an alternative. He notes that he will not be leaving before he arranges the client accounts—a direct concern for his readers who face an uncertain future with his departure from the job. He then invites his employees to take an active role in the search that will appoint his successor.

From:	"Armando Juarez" <ajuarez2@cellcity.ca>
To:	"Sales Associates" <salesteam@cellcity.ca>
Sent:	Sunday, June 14, 2020 3:03 PM
Subject:	My future at Cellular City

1. Describe the problem clearly and briefly.

Late last week I accepted a new job at AltaTel's office here in Alabama Hills to work as an international account executive.

2. Offer a solution.

3. Ask for input.

This, of course, means that the end of June will mark the end of my time here at Cellular City. It has been a pleasure to work with all of you; I can only hope that you feel the same way. In the next two weeks we'll need to reorganize our client accounts and make sure that our sales efforts continue smoothly after I depart. I hope that you will take an active part in this process.

I hope to see you around the office soon.

Armando

Figure 8.7 **Sample message conveys bad news to subordinates and peers.**

Rich Melnyk, publisher of the *Edmonton Moon*, had a problem. To reduce costs, in 2018 the paper had stopped delivering print subscriptions to the outlying areas in northern and central Alberta. They also had cut the size of the paper from 75 pages to 50 pages. Given this string of events, Melnyk had little choice other than to raise the price for subscriptions.

Figure 8.8 shows a sample letter that aims to inform subscribers of an increase in the cost of the *Edmonton Moon* newspaper while maintaining them as customers.

October 1, 2020

0763241
Fred Keynes
8443 90th Ave.
Edmonton, Alberta

Dear Subscriber,

In our booming province, prices are rising for all products, and the *Edmonton Moon* is no exception.

The huge increase in the price of oil, which has benefits for all of us in Alberta, has affected the cost of delivering your newspaper to your home. The price of newsprint has also jumped. We've absorbed these extra expenses as much as we can, but have now reached a point where we must pass some of these increased costs to our customers. Effective November 1, 2020, your subscription to the *Edmonton Moon* will be $21.50 per month plus applicable taxes. This still represents a saving to you of 10% off our regular price.

While no one likes to hear about increased prices, we hope you will understand this is necessary in order to continue providing you with the exclusive coverage of sports, city news, and popular culture only found in the *Edmonton Moon*.

Our hard-hitting local news commentary and award-winning sports reporting combine to deliver the best value of any newspaper in Edmonton.

As an *Edmonton Moon* subscriber, you will still have free access to our digital edition, a full online version of the newspaper that's yours to read anytime, anywhere.

If you have any questions or comments, please do not hesitate to contact our customer service center at 1-800-492-0000.

Thank you for reading the *Edmonton Moon*.

Rich Melnyk

Publisher, *Edmonton Moon*

1 Strathcona Road, Edmonton, AB T6G 5X7 Canada • 1-800-492-0000

Figure 8.8 **Sample negative message to subscribers.**

1. The price of your paper is going up

Read the letter in Figure 8.8 informing subscribers that rates for the newspaper will increase starting November 1. As you read, analyze the structure and strategies used to deliver the bad news and then evaluate the quality of this letter based on the discussion in this chapter.

How effective is this letter at informing readers of the cost increase while maintaining them as subscribers, and why?

What strategies does Melnyk use to manage readers' responses and emotions to the information?

What structure has Melnyk used to organize his negative message?

What makes this structure effective/ineffective for you, as a reader/subscriber?

What revisions would you make to the formatting, strategies, or sentence structure to improve the effectiveness of this negative message?

Audience: Course instructor

Purpose: Analyze the negative message and explain how it works

Genre: Memo from you to the course instructor

2. Discontinue your paper

Imagine that you are a subscriber to the *Edmonton Moon* and that you received a copy of this letter. After much consideration, you decide to discontinue your subscription to express your dissatisfaction with the price increase. Write a letter to Rich Melnyk breaking the bad news to him. Use one of the structures for a negative message outlined in this chapter to organize your letter.

Audience: Rich Melnyk, Publisher of the *Edmonton Moon*

Purpose: To express your dissatisfaction with the price increase and to try to motivate him to consider alternatives so that you could re-subscribe

Genre: Business letter

The letter in Figure 8.9 delivers bad news to parents of a class of Grade 7 students who will have to change teachers only a few weeks into the new school year. Read this letter and, using the information outlined in this chapter on writing effective negative messages, analyze and evaluate it. Decide which organizational pattern has been used as the basis for this message. Examine such details as whether the writer has used a buffer, as well as some of the other points from this chapter that create an effective delivery of negative information. Finally, when you complete your analysis, revise the letter to correct or improve any flaws that you noticed in your evaluation.

St. Xavier Senior School

October 3, 2020

Dear Parents/Guardians,

As your child may have told you, his/her grade seven math teacher has been absent for a week now. Unfortunately, this week, due to personal reasons, Mr. Jahvinder had to resign. To our students' credit they have expressed great concern for Mr. Jahvinder. Though I must respect Mr. Jahvinder's privacy, I want to assure the students that he felt a great responsibility to each of them, so his decision was truly based on what will be best for the children.

With that said, the focus needs to be on our next steps. Presently, Mrs. Maciaq is the substitute teacher and has been devoting many hours to catching up on the paper grading and planning of lessons. She has been available before and after school, as well as during lunch hour. In the meantime, we have begun the interview process to find the best person for this position. While we want to expedite the process, we will only hire the best qualified to teach Grade 7 mathematics to our children.

We appreciate your patience and understanding during this process. Please let Mrs. Maciaq or me know of any concerns you might have.

Sincerely,

Hazel Broadview

Hazel Broadview
Principal

1459 Carlton St., Omaha, NE 68108 • 123-456-7890

Figure 8.9 **Sample negative message to parents.**

CHAPTER SUMMARY

- The classic pattern for negative messages begins with a buffer, moves to a statement of the bad news, offers an alternative or compromise, and ends with a positive, goodwill-building closing.
- An alternative opening for negative messages begins by giving a reason before the refusal.
- Use buffer statements to soften the bad news; use them when you have an opportunity to thank the reader or to summarize the facts of the case in a neutral manner.
- Structure bad news messages depending on the recipient's status within the organization: use a direct structure and omit the buffer when dealing with people you work with regularly.

CHAPTER 9

Writing Persuasive Messages

 LEARNING OUTCOMES

1. Identify and distinguish between direct requests and diagnostic (or problem-solving) messages

2. Anticipate reader objections

3. Organize direct requests and diagnostic (or problem-solving) messages

4. Demonstrate that the proposed solution will benefit both the reader and the organization

GETTING STARTED

Sometimes the right thing to do is so obvious that it takes very little to persuade the rest of your team members to agree on a plan of action. Enjoy these moments—they are rare. More often than not, you will have to persuade your coworkers, your supervisor, and others that the plan of action you have in mind is the one everyone should follow. If you are new to an organization or are a junior member of the team, the burden of proof will be on you to persuade the rest of the team that yours is the right solution. In this chapter you will learn how to recognize and respond to communication situations where your readers may resist or oppose the message that you must deliver. This type of communication is called a persuasive message, and it includes direct requests and **diagnostic (or problem-solving) messages.**

diagnostic/problem-solving message: A message that diagnoses a problem and proposes a solution for the reader to approve or carry out

In the first rhetorical situation, you meet Sheri Safir, who is writing to the Ontario Assessment Review Board to ask them to reconsider their ruling of the Moonstone Valley Center for the Arts as a private club. In this message, she makes a direct request that members of the Review Board reconsider their earlier designation of the community service group as a private members' club. In the second rhetorical situation, Adam Zeleski solves a problem for his supervisor, Gerry Michaels—creating more storage space near the entrance to their office. Adam needs to write a persuasive message to convince the other employees to adopt the new policy and use the new space; he then has to consider an employee's request for an exemption from the new policy.

The discussion in this chapter shows you how to analyze and anticipate reader objections so that you can counter them convincingly. You will then learn how to organize your direct request message. Next you will learn about diagnostic or problem-solving messages, in which you identify a problem shared by you and your reader and propose a solution. In this type of message, the main challenge is to show your readers how your solution benefits them and to counter any objections they might have to your solution.

TYPES OF PERSUASIVE MESSAGES AND HOW TO WRITE THEM

 Identify and distinguish between direct requests and diagnostic (or problem-solving) messages

A persuasive message is one that you expect your reader to resist or oppose. Different types of persuasive messages include direct requests and diagnostic or problem-solving messages. In both types of messages, writers aim to persuade readers to act based on their message. Direct-request messages ask readers to do something. Generally, the request is something that readers may not want to do or that they believe will not benefit them. Writers of direct-request messages must anticipate where readers' resistance or opposition originates so that they can overcome those objections. Similarly, diagnostic or problem-solving messages also confront potential reader resistance or opposition. In a diagnostic or problem-solving message, writers identify a problem shared by writer and reader and propose a solution that readers must enact.

Direct requests are messages in which you ask your reader to do something for you. For example, you might want to change your readers' minds and prompt them to act by writing back to you. Persuasion involves getting readers to do more than think: it requires them to act.

direct requests: Messages in which you ask your reader to do something for you

Overcoming Objections

 Anticipate reader objections

Motivating readers to act takes more effort than persuading them to consider a different point of view (the goal of argument in most essay-writing situations). Inciting readers to action requires knowing how or what they think as well as understanding what motivates them (for more information about motivating readers to act, see Chapter 2). For example, barriers to action include objections that readers may have to the proposal or request. Successfully responding to and answering objections can make readers much more likely to grant your request. To discover what objections readers may have, ask them, if possible. If you are unsure if you understand, ask follow-up questions to clarify. If asking is impossible, then analyze both your reader and the situation to anticipate possible objections.

To anticipate objections your reader might have, you need to know that most people's objections are rooted in three areas:

- *Practical reasons.* Readers may object for practical reasons, meaning that they do not see how your proposal or request meets their needs or is advantageous to them. If you show how your idea benefits them, they are more likely to change their minds.
- *Misunderstanding or misinformation.* If readers are misinformed or misunderstand something about your proposal or request, they may object to it. By clarifying the misunderstanding, you can remove their reasons for resisting your message.
- *Emotional reasons.* Sometimes people object to your proposal or request because they are invested in keeping things as they are. By constructing a thorough argument, you can overcome objections based on emotional reasons.

 Exercise 9.1: Overcoming Reader Objections

For the proposals or requests described in the following examples, generate a list of possible objections that the following groups of people might have to them:

- your boss
- your coworkers
- your employees
- your customers

1. A new policy stating that the organization will no longer cover postage costs for employees' personal mail

2. A proposed increase in the wellness spending account for employees who have more than five years' service, from $500 a year to $750 a year; wellness spending accounts for employees with less than five years' service will remain at $500 a year

3. To qualify for full reimbursement of travel expenses, all employees must supply airline boarding passes for both departure and arrival segments of all travel taken on behalf of the organization

4. Any proposed expenses beyond the corporate credit card's $1,000 limit must be approved in advance by division managers

5. All customers who pay the full amount of their bill in advance of installation are entitled to a 4-per-cent discount on the total cost of their purchase

How to Organize a Direct-Request Message

Figure 9.1 is a direct-request letter that asks readers to fill out and return a survey to evaluate their recent customer-service experience. This message requires two actions of readers: to fill out the survey and to mail it back to the writer.

The letter uses the following organizational pattern for making a direct request:

1. Introduction:
   - gives background to request
   - delays request to avoid being abrupt
2. Asks for the requested actions
3. Gives complete information to allow the reader to act
4. Provides incentive to act
5. Counters possible objection to request

Adapt the pattern to best suit your message and context. For example, if you know your reader well and they are acquainted with the context for your message, you can skip the introduction by making your request immediately. Similarly, if you don't anticipate any objections to your request, don't include item 5 in your message.

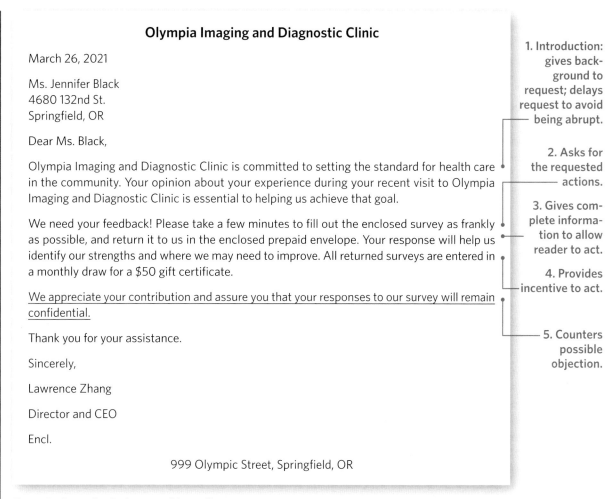

Olympia Imaging and Diagnostic Clinic

March 26, 2021

Ms. Jennifer Black
4680 132nd St.
Springfield, OR

Dear Ms. Black,

Olympia Imaging and Diagnostic Clinic is committed to setting the standard for health care in the community. Your opinion about your experience during your recent visit to Olympia Imaging and Diagnostic Clinic is essential to helping us achieve that goal.

We need your feedback! Please take a few minutes to fill out the enclosed survey as frankly as possible, and return it to us in the enclosed prepaid envelope. Your response will help us identify our strengths and where we may need to improve. All returned surveys are entered in a monthly draw for a $50 gift certificate.

We appreciate your contribution and assure you that your responses to our survey will remain confidential.

Thank you for your assistance.

Sincerely,

Lawrence Zhang

Director and CEO

Encl.

999 Olympic Street, Springfield, OR

Annotations:

1. Introduction: gives background to request; delays request to avoid being abrupt.

2. Asks for the requested actions.

3. Gives complete information to allow reader to act.

4. Provides incentive to act.

5. Counters possible objection.

Figure 9.1 Example of a letter making a direct request.

Exercise 9.2: Analyze and Revise a Direct-Request Letter

Figure 9.2 is a sample persuasive letter aimed at convincing a book-club member to make his selection for the trimester. Read and analyze the letter to answer the following questions:

1. What is the structure or organizational pattern of this letter?

2. How effective do you think the persuasive appeal is in this letter?

3. How could you reorganize the content of the letter to make it more persuasive?

4. What sentences in the letter could be revised for better cohesion, conciseness, and emphasis?

When you have identified the aspects of the letter that could be improved, revise it to make the appeal more compelling.

Book Lovers' Book Club

3/829711006

Mr. Hayden Mitchell
123 Whistler Point,
Colorado Springs, CO

November 4, 2020

Dear Mr. Mitchell,

A few weeks ago we sent you a letter mentioning that you had missed your deadline of October 19 for making your book purchase for the fall trimester. Attributing your lateness to forgetfulness, we then gave you a few extra days to make your reading choice at your leisure.

All the same, we have determined that, despite the extension, you have not made your purchase of the trimester, and we are concerned at your silence.

In our view, you are an important member of the book club and your satisfaction is our priority, which is why we decided to offer you additional time to make your purchase: your new deadline of purchase is November 16. If we haven't heard from you by this new date, we will assume that you wish to receive our selection of the trimester, chosen by our reading committee and we will then expedite it to you.

We continue to keep our promise of offering the best economical choices at 40% off the public price. I invite you to review our catalogue.

As soon as possible, please telephone our toll-free customer service number at 1-800-123-4567, or consult our website at www.bookloversunite.com. If you live near one of our stores, I invite you to pay us a visit where you will be impressed by the welcome and the exclusive products offered to members of Book Lovers' Book Club.

Be assured, Mr. Mitchell, of my best wishes,

Monica Pritchard

Director of Sales and Service

2244 4th Street, Aurora, IL www.bookloversunite.com

Figure 9.2 **Sample persuasive letter.**

When the phone rings, Sheri Safir knows the voice on the other end of the line: her accountant, Fred Johnson. Fred helped her set up her business, Tech Writing Solutions, including getting incorporated, and has given her valuable advice at many points along the way as her business develops. She feels he has done good work for her and that he is a valuable member of her professional network. Because she does not have any pressing concerns with her accounts, she asks Fred if there is something she can do for him.

Fred replies that there is, in fact, a favor he would like to ask. He is on the Board of Directors of the Moonstone Valley Center for the Arts, and the board is having a problem with the Ontario Assessment Review Board. They will not allow the Center for the Arts to designate itself as a non-profit service organization. As a result, they tax the Center as if it were a private club, so the organization is paying significantly higher taxes than it would if it were a community service organization. Fred is hoping that as a language expert at Tech Writing Solutions, Sheri might write a letter to the Review Board explaining that the Center for the Arts *does* qualify as a nonprofit service organization.

Sheri replies enthusiastically—this is something she is good at. She has a few questions, though. For one, why does the Review Board say the Center for the Arts is a private members' club? Doesn't it run art classes and other programs for the general public? Can anyone sign up for the classes?

Fred replies that, yes, it actually runs a large number of classes for all ages, from painting to sculpture to pottery. The classes draw people from across the community, and some teachers are not even members of the Center for the Arts, although many are. It is expensive to pay the higher taxes, and Fred notes that the Center is finding it increasingly difficult to operate with that designation, so it has become a priority to change it this year.

At this point Sheri is certain she wants to help. She asks Fred about the timeline for the project: how fast does he need the letter? His answer is October 23; the Board of Directors will meet the Assessment Review Board in Toronto on the 24th. He asks whether that date will work, given Sheri's busy schedule. He also notes that the Center for the Arts board would like to review a draft a day or two earlier so they can ensure it contains all the relevant information needed to make the argument.

Sheri sees that this timeline gives her three weeks to write the letter. She offers to send a draft by October 20, and Fred replies that that date is perfect. He also notes that the Center for the Arts wants to reimburse her for her time and asks her for her rates for this project.

Sheri replies that she will not charge for this project because it gives her a chance to give back to the community. She explains that she enjoys helping community organizations, especially when they contribute to the welfare of people in the community, as Moonstone Valley Center for the Arts certainly does. In one of her previous lives as a teacher, she notes, she taught service-learning courses, so she knows how such organizations contribute to the general well-being of the community. She explains that drafting the letter will be fun.

Fred is thrilled with Sheri's offer. He says that his administrative assistant, Delia, will email the regulations from the Assessment Review Board. That will give Sheri the exact wording to use in her letter.

Sheri hangs up the phone and turns back to her computer. A few hours later she receives Delia's email (see Figure 9.3).

This is the term being defined. ————

The bolding indicates the definition of the term. ————

> ### *THE LEGISLATION*
> ### *ASSESSMENT ACT*
> ### *ONTARIO REGULATION 282/98*
> *NON PROFIT SERVICE ORGANIZATION*
>
> 3(1) The residential class consists of the following:
>
> 2. Land not used for residential purposes that is:
> iv Land owned and occupied by ***a non profit service organization,*** a non profit private club, a non profit cultural organization or a non profit recreational sports club, other than land used as a golf course or ski resort.
>
> 2.1 "Service Organization" means an organization whose ***primary function is to provide services to promote the welfare of the community*** and not only to benefit its members.
>
> **Our Belief**
> The Moonstone Valley Center for the Arts meets this qualification fully.

Figure 9.3 Text from the *Ontario Assessment Act*, Regulation 282/98, defining what constitutes a nonprofit service organization.

Analysis: Argue Moonstone's Tax Status

 Organize direct requests and diagnostic (or problem-solving) messages

The letter that Sheri Safir will write is a persuasive message that includes a direct request. She wants the Assessment Review Board to reconsider its ruling. The board members have ruled that the Moonstone Valley Center for the Arts is a private club rather than a nonprofit service organization. Sheri's goal is to change the board's mind by showing how the Center serves the needs of nonmember citizens of the Moonstone Valley area.

Sheri Safir wants the Board to do two things for her: 1) change their minds about the Center for the Arts, and 2) act by revising the Center's designation. Next, Sheri Safir must persuade the Center for the Arts Board of Directors to rename the organization so that the mission of serving the community is more obvious. As mentioned earlier in this chapter, persuasion involves getting readers to do more than think: it requires them to act.

Although the standard advice is to ask readers to explain any objections that they might have to your proposed course of action, sometimes it is not possible to do so. Certainly, Sheri Safir cannot because she is not acquainted with members of the Assessment Review Board. In this rhetorical situation, she needs to analyze her readers and anticipate their possible objections. Sheri assumes her readers on the Review Board hold these attitudes:

Business Communication: Rhetorical Situations

- Not acting means more tax revenue for the board members' employer, the Ontario government
- They will consider an opposing viewpoint
- They want to do their jobs properly and well as members of the Review Board

To anticipate objections they might have, Sheri analyzes the three main areas where most people's objections are rooted:

- *Practical reasons.* Sheri quickly realizes that the primary practical objection her readers might have to her argument is also the crux of it: that nonprofit groups that provide benefits primarily for their members are not service organizations. She needs to show readers how the Center for the Arts serves a much broader community base than just center members.
- *Misunderstanding or misinformation.* Sheri knows that her readers do not understand the ways in which arts organizations provide community outreach to young people and how outlets for artistic expression can make a lasting impact on young people's lives. By explaining the less tangible aspects of experiences with fine arts, Sheri can show her readers that the Center for the Arts provides valuable service to the community.
- *Emotional reasons.* The Assessment Review Board has recently received a Ministry directive to apply the definition of "service" more selectively to private members' clubs. As a consequence, some board members may resist Sheri's persuasive appeal because they want to use her case to fulfill the Ministry directive. To ensure that her organization is granted the "service" designation, Sheri must provide detailed evidence to show how Moonstone Valley Center for the Arts completely fits the definition of "nonprofit service organization." By constructing a thorough argument, she can overcome this particular type of objection.

 Professional Communication Challenges 9.1

1. Write the letter for the Moonstone Valley Center for the Arts

Assume the role of Sheri Safir and draft a letter for Fred Johnson explaining how the Moonstone Valley Center for the Arts fits the Ontario government's definition of a nonprofit service organization. In your letter, include appropriate evidence to support your claims about the work that the Center for the Arts does, and make as strong an argument as you can for the Center's fulfilling the Assessment Review Board's own definition of the term. Use the information in this chapter to help you develop a convincing case for the Center.

Purpose: To convince members of the Ontario Assessment Review Board to designate Moonstone Valley Center for the Arts as a nonprofit service organization

Audience: Members of the Ontario Assessment Review Board, who rule on, among other things, whether a nonprofit organization fulfills a service function in its community

Genre: Letter

2. Write a persuasive memo

Write an email to the board of the Moonstone Valley Center for the Arts in which you argue that they should change their name to better reflect their community mission as a nonprofit service organization. In your letter, suggest a new name for the organization and provide arguments to support your position that the new name would be an improvement. Anticipate opposition from the board: they have used the current name for over 20 years, and it has a lot of brand awareness in the region. Using the information in this chapter, develop an argument that should persuade them to agree to your request.

Purpose: To show the board how they will benefit from having a new name and identity for the organization

Audience: The board is the primary audience, but members of the organization are an important secondary audience

Genre: Memo

DIAGNOSTIC (OR PROBLEM-SOLVING) PERSUASIVE MESSAGES

 Demonstrate that the proposed solution will benefit both the reader and the organization

A second type of persuasive message is a diagnostic or problem-solving message, which identifies a problem that you and your reader share to which you are proposing a solution. You have two primary aims: 1) to convince readers that the solution is good, and 2) to get them to behave differently to solve the problem. The main challenge in writing this type of message is showing your readers how your proposed solution benefits them. You must demonstrate that you and the reader are mutually benefited by solving the problem. This approach draws readers into the message to improve the chances they will consider your solution. As is the case when you are writing a direct request, you should also consider whether readers might have objections to the solution that you propose. Review the previous discussion on overcoming objections for strategies you can use to analyze the rhetorical situation and anticipate possible reader objections.

The email in Figure 9.4 is a diagnostic persuasive message. Read the message, noting the annotations that highlight the organizational pattern used to develop and present the argument. You must understand your reader's perspective to anticipate possible objections to your proposal or idea, as well as to demonstrate how both of you benefit from your solution. For example, in Figure 9.4, Ms. Singh notes in the third paragraph that the amount of space that their division receives is directly related to how often they all use the space. For the survey research team to continue to enjoy their spacious office area, they need to schedule their work in it. If the space appears to upper management to be underused, it will be reallocated to another division. Ms. Singh reminds them that they all benefit if they all use the office space, the underlying goal of her message.

Subject:	Scheduled appointments for February
Date:	Fri, 24 Jan 2020 13:33:18-0500
From:	Amarita Singh <asingh2@innovativemarketsurveys.com>
To:	In-person Interview Team <sales.associates.inperson@innovativemarketsurveys.com>

Thanks to all who have sent in your appointment schedules for February. If you have not done so, please send your appointment schedules as soon as possible. Clients have been arriving at the office looking for sales associates, and we were often unable to let them know where and when they could find you. From the information you have sent, we have created a chart for the month of February that lists who is booked into which appointment room for all scheduled interviews.

1. Opens by establishing common ground.

2. Describes shared problem.

3. Explains solution to the problem (stated impersonally).

An accurate appointments schedule for the 4th floor is important for two reasons. First, please note that your contract requires you to keep us informed of your appointments with clients. In addition, the "Information for Sales Associates Fall/Winter 2019–2020" document (attached) requires that you notify us of all pre-arranged appointments. If you have scheduled fewer than the minimum appointments for February (15 per day), please email Penny Xi with an updated schedule as soon as you complete your arrangements.

Second, we need to demonstrate that we are using our new office space to justify the amount and location of our offices. Please schedule your interviews to use the appointment rooms on the 4th floor. In the next month or two, the plans for renovating our building will be finalized, and if we do not show that we are using our space well, we may find ourselves in smaller quarters after the renovations are finished.

4. Explains why the requested action is needed. Also shows how team benefits from writer's proposal.

If you have already sent in your appointment schedule, thanks for your prompt response. If you have not, please do so by Friday at 4 p.m. I look forward to having the opportunity to talk with you in person next week at our monthly staff meeting.

5. States clearly what writer wants reader to do.

Figure 9.4 An example of a diagnostic persuasive email message asking employees to use new office space to conduct market survey research.

The message in Figure 9.4 uses a standard pattern of organization for diagnostic or problem-solving messages. Address these topics in this order:

1. Open by establishing or building common ground between writer and readers
2. Describe the problem shared by you and readers
3. Explain the solution to the problem (use neutral language to keep the discussion impersonal)
4. Explain why the proposed action is necessary and how readers benefit from this solution
5. Explain clearly what you want readers to do

For complex persuasive situations, you may need to devote a paragraph to each of these steps; in more straightforward situations, a sentence or two may accomplish your goal. Adapt the pattern to fit your purpose and audience as you write.

Rhetorical Situation 9.2: Please Hang Your Winter Gear in the New Company Cloakroom

Gerry Michaels has asked Adam Zeleski to solve the winter coat problem before Gerry gets back from his sales trip. Gerry wants him to figure out the best solution and write a memo to everyone telling them to fall in line. Gerry is heading to the airport for a two-week trip around the southern United States to line up new customers for Elite Swimwear. Elite Swimwear has surprised everyone by becoming a successful designer and manufacturer of high-end swimwear, when industry commentators swear that Idaho-based fashion design and manufacturing can't compete globally. Located in the thriving city of Hidden Springs, Idaho, its success isn't obviously assured, although it is located just north of Boise in the Rocky Mountain foothills and a patchwork of lakes and parks. However, through the hard work, shrewd business sense, and design flair of the co-owners, Elite Swimwear is a flourishing (if improbable) success.

One of the problems Hidden Springs has is snow—lots of it. Given the amount of snow that falls on the town most winters, many of Elite Swimwear's employees leave their cars at home and cross-country ski, snowshoe, or drive their snowmobiles to work. Snowmobiles in the parking lot instead of cars aren't a problem, but storage of all the employees' winter gear associated with these modes of transportation is a problem. The coat racks are groaning under the weight of snowsuits, scarves, ski pants, and coats; and boots and shoes everywhere make walking through the office difficult.

As he left, Gerry asked Adam to find a solution to the outerwear problem before someone injures themselves falling over someone else's ski boots. Adam considered several solutions, including installing an army of coat hooks and boot racks along the hallway leading to the company offices. A major objection to this solution, he concedes, is that, although workable, it will clutter the spacious hallways and create a potentially negative first impression for visitors to the company. Then Adam has an inspiration: an old storage closet at the end of the hallway can be cleared out and made into a cloakroom. Coat hooks will hold the snowsuits, ski pants, and winter coats; a shelf above the coat hooks will store helmets, hats, and gloves; and a series of low racks will support boots and shoes, organizing them and raising them off the floor so that they can dry quickly. A bonus is that one sweep of the cleaner's mop will clean up the dirt and snow as it dries off the footwear. Employees, who enter mainly through the front door, can strip off their travel gear and change into their street shoes in the cloakroom before making their way to their desks or the plant. They can even build a rack for skis and a series of hooks for snowshoes in one corner.

Adam proposes the solution to Rachel Fielder, company CEO, who enthusiastically endorses the idea. A quick phone call to Gerry secures his approval. Gerry also directs Adam to a carpentry company that has completed several earlier jobs for the company. MacDuff Framing and Carpentry can start on the project right away. Before Adam knows it, the cloakroom is nearly ready for use. All that remains is to announce the new facility to company employees. Adam thinks it is the kind of message that should be spread orally, but Gerry wants every employee to receive an email directing them to the cloakroom and explaining any rules associated with it, and he has asked Adam to draft the email.

Exercise 9.3: Overcoming Reader Objections: Using the Company Cloakroom

As noted earlier, reader objections generally originate from three areas:

- practical reasons
- misunderstanding or misinformation
- emotional reasons

1. Using these three general areas, brainstorm a list of objections that employees at Elite Swimwear might have for using the new company cloakroom. To do this, you will need to determine and evaluate the perspectives of the different groups of employees. First, determine whether office staff, sales staff, and warehouse staff may have differing perspectives. Also consider whether their mode of transportation (car, snowmobile, snowshoe, cross-country skis) might affect their perspectives on using the cloakroom.

2. Next, generate a list of benefits that employees and the company will share if everyone uses the cloakroom. You can develop these benefits based on the counters to the objections that you listed in item 1.

3. Using both your list of objections and your list of benefits, generate a corresponding list of arguments or reasons that you could use to overcome the employees' various objections.

4. As your instructor directs, write a one- to two-page memo to the instructor that summarizes the best ideas from your three lists. Expand the ideas into mini-arguments, as appropriate, to help you see how these ideas can help you better reach different segments of your audience of employees at Elite Swimwear (for example, will sewing-machine operators have different objections from the office staff?).

Analysis: Please Use the Cloakroom

Adam knows that several of the company's employees will probably object to using the new cloakroom, so before he begins drafting the memo to inform them of the new policy, he spends a few minutes generating a list of possible objections based on the three areas that generally give rise to objections: practical reasons, misunderstanding, or emotional reasons. He suspects that most of the objections that his coworkers may have to using the cloakroom will be practical or emotional reasons such as fear of personal items being stolen or resistance to changing habits. He will have to counter such objections in his explanation so he jots down some potential solutions he can offer to relieve his readers' concerns.

Once he is ready to begin writing, he identifies one or two possible points he can make to establish common ground with his coworkers/readers. It is going to be easy to describe the problem, Adam decides, because nearly everyone has complained about tripping over boots or skis. They will all understand the necessity of maintaining a safe working environment. He decides he will probably not need much detail to describe the solution because most of his readers are already familiar with the renovation and its purpose.

Adam knows that he also needs to highlight for his readers several ways in which they are all going to benefit from having the new cloakroom available, so everyone will finish reading the email feeling good about the cloakroom and happy to make use of it.

 Professional Communication Challenges 9.2

1. Write the email announcing the opening of the new winter-wear cloakroom

Writing as Adam Zeleski, draft the email message to all employees regarding the use of the new employee cloakroom. Because employees are used to the current system where three or four of them share a coat tree near their desks, some have voiced concerns about not being able to keep an eye on their belongings and equipment while they work. Other employees who drive to work have a minimum of items to hang up, and they want to continue the current system, since they did not cause the problem the cloakroom is designed to fix. Rachel and Gerry have drafted a list of rules to communicate to all employees about cloakroom use (see Figure 9.5). Include those rules, as appropriate, in your draft.

Purpose: To convince all employees at Elite Swimwear to hang their winter outerwear in the new company cloakroom

Audience: All employees at Elite Swimwear, including designers, cutters, sewing-machine operators, and office staff, who may or may not snowmobile, snowshoe, or cross-country ski to work regularly

Genre: Email

Rules for Cloakroom Use

All employees will use the cloakroom to store their outerwear while they are working at Elite Swimwear.

All footwear should go on the lower racks and not on the floor.

All helmets, etc. should be stored on the shelves above the coat hooks.

All equipment must be stored using the racks and hooks provided for that equipment.

Employees may store shoes on the boot racks for use when they arrive each day.

Figure 9.5 **Rules of cloakroom use.**

2. Request an exception

You are an Elite Swimwear employee who works in the company plant. Your spouse drops you off at work every day, so you do not have the winter gear that has contributed to the clutter around the premises. You want to be able to leave your coat on the hook near your workstation so that you can quickly put it on when you have to supervise incoming or outgoing shipments, which occur at least three times a week (and sometimes more often). You have found that when you have to walk to the front of the plant to get your coat each time, it slows down this step of production. You spoke to Adam Zeleski about an exemption from using the cloakroom, but he said you would have to make your case in writing to Gerry Michaels and Rachel Fielder yourself because they had said "no exemptions." Make your case.

Purpose: To explain how using the cloakroom will inhibit you from doing your job and to offer an alternative solution that solves the problem

Audience: Gerry Michaels, president of Elite Swimwear, and Rachel Fielder, CEO of Elite Swimwear, both of whom now hang their winter wear in the new cloakroom

Genre: Email

CHAPTER SUMMARY

- Direct request messages overcome objections by giving practical reasons, clarifying misunderstandings or misinformation, and responding to readers' emotions.
- Organize a direct-request message by giving the background to the problem, asking for the solution, giving the reader the information they need to act, creating incentives for the reader, and countering objections.
- Diagnostic or problem-solving persuasive messages aim to convince readers that the proposed solution is good and to get readers to behave differently to solve the problem.
- Organize a diagnostic message by establishing common ground, describing the shared problem, explaining the solution to the problem and why the requested action is needed, and showing how readers benefit from writer's proposal.

CHAPTER 10

Proposals

 LEARNING OUTCOMES

1. Think of proposals primarily as persuasive documents
2. Use logic, credibility, and emotion to convince your audience to accept your proposal
3. Structure unsolicited proposals using a problem–solution model
4. Organize and format a proposal document

GETTING STARTED

Proposals share a common purpose: they attempt to persuade people that your idea is a good one. Proposals range from high stakes ("Will you marry me?") to much lower (a text suggesting you get together with some friends at a bar). Even résumés are a kind of proposal: you are proposing that a company hire you. All of these share the essence of written proposals in business contexts: a good idea that you try to get others to join in on.

To write a successful proposal at work, you need to establish that you are worth listening to (credibility), create logical reasons (logic), and generate enthusiasm (emotion) for your idea. Solicited proposals generally state the problem that needs to be solved; these kinds of proposals argue in favor of your solution to the problem. Unsolicited proposals, however, must argue that there is a problem before identifying how to solve it. As you prepare to write a proposal document, make sure you know which of these two kinds of arguments you are writing.

The Douglas Mountain Recreational Equipment Rhetorical Situation offers an example of a solicited proposal: the president of the company identifies the problem and asks for solutions to it. In Rhetorical Situation 10.2, Alyssa Kelin-Moore sees a need for an operations manual: she needs to argue that the need exists, which is a hallmark of an unsolicited proposal. Jacob Horne, in Rhetorical Situation 10.3, finds himself in a situation where he is responding to a municipal government request for a proposal (an example of a solicited proposal).

WRITING PERSUASIVE PROPOSALS

 Think of proposals primarily as persuasive documents

Writing a good proposal is writing a persuasive proposal. Proposals are all about convincing your reader to say yes. Proposals present an idea or plan to do something, often to solve a problem or provide a service or product. In a competitive situation, you have to show how your idea, solution, and abilities are superior to those being offered by the writers of competing proposals. **Solicited proposals** (where someone has requested proposals be submitted—that is, has circulated a Request for Proposals, or RFP) generally result in a competitive situation, where only one or two successful ones will be chosen, but not always. For example, in Rhetorical Situation 10.1, the president of Douglas Mountain Recreational Equipment has distributed an RFP for internal proposals. In this Rhetorical Situation, if the ideas proposed are all appropriate, they will all be accepted. In other noncompetitive situations, you may be submitting a proposal that you were motivated to write by observing a problem that needs a solution. This is an **unsolicited proposal**. In this case, your reader is not expecting the proposal, so you will have to convince her or him that the problem you have identified really does exist and is significant enough to need a solution. In situations where every proposal is likely to be accepted, you are still writing a persuasive document because you need to show readers that your idea is worthwhile and you have the expertise to complete the project.

solicited proposals: Proposals that have been requested by an organization via a Request for Proposal (RFP)

unsolicited proposal: A proposal that you prepare without being asked to by a potential client

Business Communication: Rhetorical Situations

When someone has requested a proposal, you won't have to convince the requester to accept it. Nevertheless, RFP set criteria for acceptable projects, so you will need to show how your team's proposed projects are suitable and fit those criteria. If you are suggesting an activity that doesn't fit the criteria well, you will need to make a well-supported argument to show why the requester should consider your idea. By presenting a clear, well-developed argument, you can persuade readers that your idea is still valid and worth pursuing.

Proposal Writing and Persuasion

 Use logic, credibility, and emotion to convince your audience to accept your proposal

Proposals achieve persuasion when they convince readers to act: to select your proposal from among competing solutions to their problem, approve your proposed project, and get started. To persuade readers in a proposal, use a logical argument supported by evidence, a demonstration of your credibility, and an emotional appeal to help readers feel the importance of your argument. This section shows you how and when to use these appeals in a proposal to make it as effective as possible.

LOGIC

Logic refers to the series of claims and supporting evidence that you develop and organize to discuss your solution to the problem. You will need to provide logical arguments in both solicited and unsolicited proposals. In a competitive solicited proposal, the point of the argument is to show readers how the writer can develop and deliver the solution described. The logic should also explain the benefits of the writer's particular solution and emphasize how this solution is superior to other possible solutions.

Below is an example of a logical argument in a grant proposal. Note the supporting evidence that strengthens the logical claim that the group has experience. Note also how the numerical details that are provided add credibility to the argument: they are specific, and that conveys the detail-oriented values of the people proposing this project.

> **What do we do?** Community Gardens Group has extensive experience planning and running our community garden. The growers and members have planted over 4,010 linear feet of annual crops and over 1 acre of 3 varieties of potatoes. In addition to growing produce for our members on the 6 acres we cultivated, this year we distributed over 3,000 pounds of organically grown produce to the Youth Emergency Shelter, City Food Bank, University Students Food Bank, and Meals on Wheels.

Figure 10.1 **Logic and credibility in a grant proposal.**

CREDIBILITY

Credibility is essential in a proposal because the proposal can only persuade readers if they trust the writer and respect what he or she has to say. You can create trust and respect on the part of readers in four ways:

1. Show readers that you are knowledgeable about your subject matter
2. Include a thorough and detailed discussion of the issues relevant to the topic
3. Provide details about your qualifications and the resources available to you on this project
4. Submit a work schedule that is realistic and detailed

Show Your Knowledge of the Topic. Part of your credibility in a proposal grows out of the logic of your argument: if your ideas are reasonable and your evidence provides solid support, then your readers will grow to trust that you are competent and trustworthy. When you use some of the vocabulary appropriate to your topic, you also demonstrate your knowledge and "membership" in the group of experts on that topic. It is important, however, to strike a balance between using technical terms appropriate to the subject and the knowledge of your readers, who may not be experts in that area. Define technical terms and use only the vocabulary you need.

Include a Discussion of Issues Relevant to the Topic. You also demonstrate your expertise and trustworthiness on your topic by accurately presenting the right amount of information about your topic. Be concise while including details that your reader both needs and wants to know. State and develop ideas appropriately and then stop. When readers find what they need to know in your discussion, they will feel that you are a credible speaker on your topic.

Provide Details about Your Qualifications and Resources. Another aspect of your credibility is the experience, expertise, and track record that you bring to the project. Describing your background and your record of success on previous projects instills confidence in your reader about the proposed project. Include details that build your credibility by showing that you have the skills and the resources to successfully complete this project as well. For example, if you need expertise in an area that you don't currently have, you could name contacts you already possess who will provide that expertise for you. When you show that you can anticipate potential problems as well as access the connections that allow you to supply missing elements, you build a strong ethical appeal that improves the persuasive power of your proposal.

Submit a Realistic and Detailed Work Schedule. The fourth area that helps build credibility is in the work schedule you provide with the proposal. Take the time you need to accurately and thoroughly project the various stages of the project. When readers assess your planning, they see that you have thought through the project and accurately evaluated the time it will take to complete. If you show that you have a reasonable plan for hitting your deadlines, you are more likely to convince readers that you *will*, in fact, hit those deadlines.

EMOTIONAL APPEAL

The emotional appeal in a proposal refers to the legitimate use of readers' emotions or feelings to engage their minds and build assent. Persuasion is not complete until readers do more than say, "Yes, you have a point." Detached interest is not persuasion. You want readers to move beyond uncommitted interest to actually doing something, even changing their behavior. In the case of proposal writing, you want readers to select your proposal, approve your ideas, and allow you to start the project.

Emotion is the main tool that helps readers become invested in your project and that moves them from interest to assent or action. It's not unethical to show readers why your ideas are important and set up opportunities for them to become invested in your proposal, but it is unethical to use emotional appeals that are unconnected to your subject matter to evoke a response in your reader. For example, advertisements that propose purchasing a product as a solution to consumers' insecurities (in other words, "drink this beer to become more attractive to others") aim to manipulate viewers into choosing their product. In a proposal, you should focus on showing readers how the solution you propose will benefit them and be superior to other possible solutions. If you make readers feel the truth of your statements, you are likely to persuade them to choose or approve your proposal.

Here are two ways to create an effective emotional appeal in a proposal:

- use concrete examples and vivid details
- incorporate figurative language, including comparisons, where appropriate

Figure 10.2 provides an example drawn from a grant proposal.

I am president of the Springfield Organic Growers Cooperative, a small non-profit group with the goal of creating a sustainable community culture focused on public education and active participation of growing crops. Our humble gardens serve the volunteers that work there because they provide access to experienced gardeners and fresh produce. We also serve the surrounding community by providing free and fresh produce to food banks and other organizations. Currently, we have more than 100 members drawn from a wide cross-section of economic and social groups devoted to providing equitable access to nutritious food. I am writing to request a donation of $500. This donation would be used to buy a variety of gardening equipment, including tomato cages, various hand tools, and a cultivator.

Figure 10.2 **Emotional appeals work through specific and vivid language.**

Paul Steinberg, manager of a recreational equipment retail outlet, Douglas Mountain Recreational Equipment (DMRE), looks down at his notes and announces that the last item on the meeting agenda is that corporate head office wants each store to put together a proposal outlining ideas for community service projects for next year. Eyebrows rise around the table. Every year the employees at DMRE devote several weekends to raising money for a local charity. In the past, the employees at each store have decided what group they want to support independently of the head office, so the request for proposals is a notable change to the initiative.

Paul explains that Doug Black, the president of DMRE, feels that the company is straying too far from the corporate image in what employees are choosing to support. For example, last year one store in Southwestern Ontario did a series of fundraising projects for the local cancer center. No one actually objected to them supporting such a good cause, but Black has decided this directive will encourage everyone to pursue more sports- or fitness-related activities that better fit with the company's vision and mission. Paul explains that this change makes sense because that is what DMRE does—sell recreational equipment. Black feels it is important to show company employees living active and healthy lifestyles as well as helping their communities. Paul catches glimpses of a few eyes rolling, but he isn't surprised. His team is a group of particularly independent-minded young people. He knows they enjoy giving back to the community, but he also knows some of them will resent this interference from the company president.

Julia Ke is an enthusiastic and energetic member of his team who is particularly adept at identifying groups in the community which most need support. Paul knows that some of the projects they had taken on in the last year or two are the result of her instigation, like putting a new roof on the Denise Carr Women's Shelter. However, these projects have also been tenuously related to DMRE's mission. After much discussion, the team had decided the shelter's need outweighed corporate's preference. He is bracing himself for her reaction, but she surprises him.

"I don't think that's out of line," she says, "since Doug gives us time off for these projects. If he's going to compensate us the way he does, I guess it makes sense that he should have some say in what we do. But I *also* think reroofing the women's shelter last year was worthwhile, even if the public didn't associate our work with DMRE." Julia then asks the group what they want to do this year that is more recreational-equipment related.

Paul suggests that the group brainstorm some ideas and see what most people are in favor of doing. He points out that once the group has picked out a project they will have to submit a written proposal to the president. A few groans meet these words. Paul explains that the president wants a written proposal so that he can give feedback to ensure that it fits the company's goals.

"I know what we can do," exclaims Frances. Everyone turns to her. "Let's sponsor a dragon-boat racing meet! That would be so much fun! We can form our own team, but also invite some of the businesses around town to start teams and compete with us. We can also invite racing teams from other cities in the area as well. We can use the meet to raise money to support something like the Boys and Girls Club. They organize sports activities for underprivileged kids in the city. That should fit Mr. Black's criteria. We could hold the meet right here on Clear Lake."

Tran thinks that is a cool idea. He explains that his cousin is on a dragon-boat racing team that practices on Lake Winnipegosis. He has also seen one that trains out of Nanaimo Harbor, and he says that it looks like a lot of fun.

Kelly suggests that they can run or sponsor a marathon or a rock-climbing event for adolescents. Several other ideas are quickly suggested, and the meeting quickly transforms into an uproar as staff members make suggestions and speak over one another. Paul calls the meeting back to order and asks for a volunteer to write the proposal. Julia raises her hand meekly. He thanks Julia before instructing everyone else to email their suggestions to her. Julia will compile a list, send it around for everyone to vote on, and then take the top three favorites, research them, and outline how they may work as service projects for next year.

 ## Professional Communication Challenges 10.1

1. Proposing three service projects for the DMRE sales team

Take on the persona of one member of the Douglas Mountain Recreational Equipment sales team and write a proposal describing three possible service projects that the sales team could undertake for the following year. This Rhetorical Situation is not obviously set in any particular region, so locate it in your area and develop three of the ideas proposed by members of the sales team for service projects that are appropriate to your location (see Figure 10.3). Be sure to select ideas that are related to sports and recreational activities, as requested by the company president.

Direct your proposal to Doug Black, the president of DMRE. Of course, Paul Steinberg is your initial and secondary audience.

Use all available resources (Internet, library, etc.) to research your three activities so that you can clearly and completely describe them in your proposal. Use the discussion in this chapter on writing proposals to help you develop your ideas, organize your arguments, and present them clearly, concisely, and convincingly.

Audience: Doug Black, the president of DMRE

Purpose: To persuade Black to approve your proposal

Genre: Proposal

Dragon-boat racing meet to raise money for a local group (need suggestions)

Hold a marathon

Organize a rock-climbing event for adolescents and young adults

Participate in local walking/running/biking event sponsored by someone else

Organize spring cleanup drive for Clear Lake (or Thunder River)

Hold mountain bike ride to raise money for low-income families in city

Hold a golf tournament to raise money for local group (need suggestions)

Habitat for Humanity—help build some houses?

Set up a program to collect used sports equipment at the store to donate to local children's groups or underprivileged young people

Organize and run Environmental Awareness weekend at the mall

Figure 10.3 **Sales team suggestions for possible service projects.**

2. Write a proposal that suggests service projects that do not fit the corporate image

Writing as one of the employees in Rhetorical Situation 10.1, draft a proposal in which you suggest three service projects that aren't clearly related to fitness and recreation. In this case you are going to have to make well-developed and supported arguments as to why your ideas are appropriate and should be approved even though they aren't directly related to the president's recent mandate.

Use all available research sources to collect information about the three projects you propose and situate them in your local area so that your evidence and arguments are concrete, specific, and compelling. In your proposal, focus on showing Mr. Black how these projects will benefit both DMRE and the local community. If you want to show how the projects are indirectly related to fitness and recreation, go ahead.

Audience: Doug Black, the president of DMRE

Purpose: To persuade Black to approve your proposal

Genre: Proposal

Analysis: DMRE Supports an Active Local Community

Use Concrete Examples and Vivid Details. Use descriptive verbs and adjectives to create a compelling experience for readers. Include information that helps to make your subject matter come alive. For example, if Julia Ke is arguing that the proposal to organize a spring cleanup of local waterways is most appropriate because it fits the company environmental stewardship program, she can make her argument more or less compelling by adding or omitting vivid details. Of these two versions, which one do you find most interesting?

> *Version 1:* We propose to organize a weekend spring cleanup scheduled for April to invite community members to join the staff in collecting garbage from the waterways around our city. This cleanup project will fit well with DMRE's environmental steward-ship program.

> *Version 2:* This year we will invite community members to don their rubber gloves and boots to join us in our 1st Annual Waterways Spring Cleanup in April. Armed with decom-posable garbage bags, rakes, and shovels, we will gather on the shores of Clear Lake, Thunder River, and Burrow Creek and work together to restore the pristine beauty of our local waterways. This project represents a new and innovative direction for our team, which has not, in the past, participated in DMRE's environmental stewardship program.

Although version 2 is longer, it includes more information about the proposed project and some specific details that help readers better imagine the shape the activity will take. Black will also know which waterways the team plans to work on and the type of work they intend to do dur-ing the cleanup (pick up garbage, etc.).

Incorporate Figurative Language, Including Comparisons, Where Appropriate. Although many people associate figurative language with literary texts and poetry, it is equally useful in business and professional communication. You can use apt comparisons as well as rhetorical figures to help readers feel the significance of your ideas. For example, of these two statements, which one creates the most impact on you, as a reader?

> *Version 1:* We will all enjoy the garbage-free banks of the local lakes and rivers later in the summer.

> *Version 2:* On those hot, sultry afternoons in July, our novice canoe classes will paddle quietly *like the Indigenous peoples of this area through an unspoilt wilderness.*

The simile, *like Indigenous peoples of this area through an unspoiled wilderness*, expands on the verb *enjoy* from version 1, painting for readers the picture of local waterways as they were before widescale human development, which has made necessary the proposed environmental cleanup. The simile links Julia's argument for this being a worthwhile project to the company's image as environmentally conscious. It also invokes the company's adherence to the "Leave No Trace" principles of environmental ethics in a way that should be an effective emotional appeal to the company president.

HOW TO WRITE UNSOLICITED PROPOSALS

 Structure unsolicited proposals using a problem–solution model

Unsolicited proposals present different rhetorical challenges to ones that your boss or instructor will ask you to write. One important part of such a proposal is showing readers that the problem exists and is significant enough to need solving. You can define *significance* in financial terms—for example, the cost or lost income that the problem represents for the organization. You can also define significance in terms relating to corporate image—for example, the problem generates bad publicity or public criticism for the company. The point is that you want to show readers that the problem is an issue and it needs a solution. Choose whatever terms you think will have the best impact to persuade your reader.

The second part of the challenge in writing this type of proposal is describing your solution to the problem and showing readers why it is the best option. What may be obvious to you is not necessarily obvious to readers, so explain what makes it the best solution. Show readers how your solution will benefit them and/or the organization. When readers share your view of the problem, they are more likely to agree with your analysis and conclusion.

Use this pattern to organize the argument in this type of proposal:

1. What is the problem? (Define and explain it)
2. Why should we solve this problem? (Why is it significant?)
3. What should we do to solve this problem? (Describe your solution)
4. Why should we choose the solution you propose? (Emphasize its benefits)

By the end of the proposal, you should have convincingly answered all of these questions.

 Rhetorical Situation 10.2: "Would You Please Show Me How to Fill Out These Forms?"

Alyssa Klein-Moore looks at the two forms that she has pulled from the drawer. Both have "Client Information" printed at the top, but a quick glance tells her the questions on each are different. She searches the form for a publication date to determine whether one is an updated version of the other. No such luck. The instructions don't indicate when to use each form either. She will have to ask someone, again. She sneaks a peek at Mrs. Chato, who is waiting patiently for her to hand over the form. Alyssa looks around the office but everyone is busy. Surinder, the middle-aged office manager, is on the phone; Jorge, a 40-year-old assistant dental technician, is meeting with a client, and she remembers that Munir Abbasi, the summer student intern, is on a coffee run. Alyssa's training would be much smoother if she had a training manual so that she doesn't have to ask someone about everything.

Alyssa likes working as an administrative assistant at Gleam Dental Clinic, but without any training procedure or manual, it is hard and delicate work finding out what she needs to know to do her job. Everyone is so busy and she constantly has to interrupt someone to ask simple questions. She jots everything down that she learns in her notebook, but the list of new duties seems endless.

She remembers a suggestion that her dad made on the phone the previous evening when she was describing her first two days to him. "Why don't you offer to make a training manual for the office?" he said. "That way you can learn how to do everything, you will have a reference if you forget something, and it will be useful for the next person they hire who won't have to rely on everyone else in the office to teach them the way you have to do."

She wonders if the dentists in the office will agree to her spending some time putting the manual together. Will they object to paying her to do it? It will be more productive if she can look things up rather than waiting until someone is free to ask. The manual may actually save the practice money in the long run because other new employees can use it too. They can even take it home and study it at night so that they can figure out in advance where to find the information quickly and efficiently.

Surinder hangs up the phone and turns to Alyssa, indicating which form should go to Mrs. Chato. Surinder notes that the office really must get rid of the old files, but everyone is too busy to clear them out. There is no way Alyssa can do this during normal working hours—maybe coming in on a Sunday would be necessary.

"What we need is an employee training manual," says Alyssa. "Do you think Dr. Watson would be willing to let me put one together, Surinder?"

Surinder responds that this is a good idea. She pauses for a moment and then suggests that rather than talking to him, Alyssa write up a proposal. That way she can explain the financial advantages thoroughly—calculate how many hours the established staff lose helping new employees, how many weeks it takes for new people to become completely productive, and how a manual may shorten that time. Then Dr. Watson can circulate the proposal among the other doctors. Surinder points out that Alyssa is likely to get approval fairly quickly if she can show how the manual will save the practice time and money.

Just before lunch, Alyssa manages to seize a few moments to talk to Dr. Watson about her idea. He agrees that the office can definitely use a more systematic method of training new staff.

"We also need to see some numbers," he notes. "If you can show us why a manual is the best solution and also quantify the savings for us, I expect the other dentists will agree to making the training manual a part of your duties during down periods in the office until the project is finished. Yes, I do think the written rationale is the way to go here."

 Exercise 10.1: Identify the Problem

Part A: Use Rhetorical Situation 10.2 as the basis for the discussion in this exercise. With one or two of your classmates, draft some ideas that could be useful in writing an unsolicited proposal for Dr. Watson. Generate a list of statements or phrases that help you 1) define the problem that Alyssa identifies at Gleam Dental Clinic, and 2) demonstrate the significance of the problem.

Remember to define the problem in terms that will make sense to the dentists at the clinic, rather than to Alyssa herself or some of the other staff members. When you are discussing the significance of the problem, generate as many different terms of significance as you can to help you view the problem from many different angles, including financial (see Figure 10.5), customer service, and corporate image. The more angles you take, the better you can consider which terms of significance will be most compelling for Dr. Watson and his colleagues.

Part B: When you feel that your discussion has exhausted the possibilities for analyzing the problem and its significance, use some of the statements or phrases generated during your discussion to write one-paragraph drafts of your argument for the problem section of the proposal. Add evidence where appropriate to support your claims. As you draft, pay attention to your credibility as a writer for this project and the emotional appeal that is a companion to your logical argument.

 ### Exercise 10.2: Describe a Solution

With one or two of your classmates, discuss Rhetorical Situation 10.2, paying particular attention to the range of solutions that are possible to solve the problem that Alyssa Klein-Moore (or your group from Exercise 10.1) identified at Gleam Dental Clinic.

Cover these topics in your discussions and make notes of useful ideas that are suggested:

1. What solutions are possible to train new employees at Gleam Dental Clinic?

2. Which solution(s) is/are most appropriate for Gleam Dental Clinic?

3. In your group's estimation, which are the top two solutions to the problem as you (or Alyssa Klein-Moore) define it and why?

In your discussion, aim to generate as many possible solutions to the problem as you can. When you have created a list that gives you a range of interesting possible solutions (expand on those suggested in Figure 10.4), evaluate each suggestion with an emphasis on how well it fits the context of Gleam Dental Clinic (small office, busy, wide range of ages of employees). How appropriate does your group think a wiki might be for new and existing employees at the clinic? Decide on the top two solutions and explain what makes you rate them as the best.

Possible formats for training information:

Manual (print: easily updated, may become outdated quickly; electronic: easily updated, easily accessed, easily lost if employees can't find file; new employees can print off .pdf to take home or access on home computer ... what else?)

Video (problem: production values; is this best way to present information? Need a script, video camera; how easy is this for new employees to use? View on computer screen? No way to make print copies ... what else?)

Wiki (electronic entries, easily updated, downside is employee knowledge needed to use it ... what else?)

What other new technology could I use? (must take into account demographic of employees, technical abilities, etc.)

Figure 10.4 **What is the best format or genre for training materials?**

FORMATTING A PROPOSAL

 Organize and format a proposal document

The preceding section described what kinds of arguments you should make in an unsolicited proposal as you write it. Figure 10.5 outlines a format for structuring unsolicited proposals. Use the headings given in the figure—they are standard and readers will look for them as a way to conceptually organize your information. Note that in the first two sections, you both describe and explain the problem and then you describe and explain your proposed solution. In these first sections you grab and hold your reader's attention through the persuasiveness of your descriptions of the problem and the solution. If you do not successfully convince readers of the validity of the problem, the information that you present in the rest of the proposal will be less compelling.

1. Problem Statement
   - describe problem
   - demonstrate why it needs a solution

2. Solution Description
   - describe solution
   - show why it is the best solution
   - demonstrate how it benefits the reader/organization

3. Methods
   - explain how you will solve the problem

4. Qualifications and Resources
   - show why you are the person to solve the problem

5. Work Schedule
   - timeline for completing the project

6. Budget
   - estimate costs for solving problem/completing the project

7. Call to Action
   - request approval to move forward with project

Figure 10.5 **Outline for structuring an unsolicited proposal.**

Sections 3 to 7 provide details about your actual plan for solving the problem, as well as a timeline and budget. Readers who are persuaded that the problem and solution you describe are valid will find this additional information useful to decide whether to give you permission to proceed.

Exercise 10.3: Describe the Benefits of the Solution

Using one of the top two solutions that your group chose in Exercise 10.2 and through discussion with one or two classmates,

1. Generate a list of benefits that you can see in the solution that your group chose. (Make sure to consider ways in which the solution benefits new employees who would be using the training material and the organization as a whole. Designate someone in the group to record the useful ideas that come out of the discussion.)

2. Evaluate how effective you think the benefits that your group has generated will be in convincing the various potential readers of your proposal.

3. Develop the argument for each benefit by drafting (collaboratively or individually) a paragraph for each one. As you draft, think about which benefit is most persuasive or attractive for your potential readers. Also think about which ones might be most useful (even if it is not the newest or current technology) when you draft the proposal to create the training material.

Professional Communication Challenges 10.2

1. Write the proposal to create training material for new employees at Gleam Dental Clinic

Writing as Alyssa Klein-Moore, write an unsolicited proposal to Dr. Watson and the other dental partners and associates making a case for the necessity of creating training materials for new employees at Gleam Dental Clinic. Explain the problem that you see and why it is necessary to solve this problem. Use the information supplied in Figures 10.4, 10.6, and 10.7 as evidence to support your arguments quantifying the amount of time and money that the training information would save the practice. Include an explanation as to why the manual (or some other approach, if you think there is a better one) is the best solution to the problem. You can argue for using either a print or electronic (or both) version of the manual based on which format you think would be most useful in the office.

Financial savings

Hours spent learning

Day 1: 7 hours × $17.00/hr. = $119.00

Day 2: 7 hours × $17.00/hr. = $119.00

Day 3: 6 hours × $17.00/hr. = $102.00

Total for 3 days: $340.00

Projection: 3.5 weeks of learning @ 4.5 hours a day: 4.5 hours x 17.5 days × $17.00/hr. = $1338.75

Hours spent teaching

After 3.5 weeks, staff will have spent approximately 62 hours teaching procedures (**N.B.** Staff use fewer hours because new employee spends time alone practicing new procedure): 62 hrs × $17.00/hr. = $1054.00

Total training costs for one new employee: $2392.75

Figure 10.6 **Financial cost of training one new employee.**

Hours spent learning procedures (based on 30 hours): estimate for proposal budget

Hours spent creating materials (based on 30 hours): estimate for proposal budget

Hours spent designing materials (based on 20 hours): estimate for proposal budget

Hours spent testing materials (based on 20 hours)

Hours spent revising materials (based on 10 hours)

Figure 10.7 **Estimate costs of creating training materials (hours × $17.00/hr. wage).**

Audience: Dr. Watson and the other medical partners

Purpose: To persuade Watson to approve your proposal

Genre: Proposal

2. Write an unsolicited proposal offering to solve a problem that you observe at work or at school

Identify a problem at work or on your school campus that you have some ideas about how to solve. Find out who would approve a proposal for solving such a problem, and address your unsolicited proposal to that individual. Use the information in this chapter, especially the information in the following sections, to help you organize and present your ideas so as to convince your reader(s) that the problem is significant enough to require a solution and that you have a well-thought-out plan for how to do it.

Audience: You must specify this

Purpose: To persuade your audience to approve your proposal

Genre: Proposal

HOW TO WRITE A PROPOSAL IN RESPONSE TO A REQUEST FOR PROPOSALS (RFP)

Request for Proposals (RFP): A document that outlines what a vendor is looking for in a proposal to solve their business problem

When responding to an **RFP**, consider the needs expressed by the issuer in the proposal. These needs will form the backbone of the criteria for evaluating submissions. Unlike most class situations, only one proposal will be chosen—there is only one passing grade to be handed out! Information on the Contracts Canada website notes that bidders may not contact the organizations requesting the bids without compromising the bid process. This warning means that you must interpret the RFP without feedback from the issuer, making a careful and accurate analysis essential. A careful analysis of the RFP also helps you understand what information should be included in the proposal.

Government contracting in the United States is a large topic, but the overall process is similar. You must read and respond to the "Contract Opportunity," read the details for the bid you must prepare, and prepare the proposal documentation. A good place to start for background on how it works is the Introduction to Federal Government Contracting website: https://www.usa.gov/government-contracting-for-beginners.

Here are three steps to use in analyzing an RFP:

1. Determine what kind of proposal is requested
2. Identify the evaluation criteria outlined in the RFP
3. Determine what information to include in the proposal

Determine What Kind of Proposal Is Requested

Under the heading "Requirements" (see Figure 10.8), the RFP specifies that one contractor will be selected ("a Contractor"). It also states the deliverable requested—"an innovative creative advertising and social marketing campaign"—and the length of the contract—"one year with potential for extension for two additional years." Our analysis of this section of the RFP reveals that this is a competitive bid with a creative marketing campaign being produced. In contrast, when an instructor in one of your classes requests a proposal, the situation is noncompetitive, because every student's proposal will be accepted, if he or she proposes a reasonable and well-thought-out idea for a paper or project.

Requirements

Municipal Services is seeking a Contractor to update existing marketing materials or develop new materials, for an innovative advertising and social marketing campaign. The campaign will last one year with potential for extension for two additional years provided the initial campaign meets our objectives and budget. The successful bidder will provide a campaign strategy including an innovative approach, media partners, social media strategy, and an overall plan that includes a detailed critical path that covers the implementation time frame for each media product and the proposed budget breakdown.

Figure 10.8 **What kind of proposal is requested?**

Evaluation Process

The successful bidder must satisfy all of the criteria in the Request for Proposal, including: providing an example of one national integrated campaign that includes print and one other media; providing an example of one national multimedia campaign that includes TV and social media; and listing the personnel who would lead work in the major project categories and their prior accomplishments; complying with the certification requirements described in the RFP; and providing hourly rates; and evidence that the bidder has provided verified proof of financial resources to perform the work.

Bidders that meet all criteria will proceed to a second round of evaluation where quality of the proposal will be evaluated using a point system.

Figure 10.9 **Identify the criteria outlined in the RFP.**

Identify the Evaluation Criteria Outlined in the RFP

In the RFP partially reproduced in Figure 10.9, the criteria are described in the section titled "Evaluation Process." The mandatory criteria (in other words, the information that must be supplied in the proposal) are the following:

The products
1. One sample national integrated campaign that includes print and one other medium
2. Example of one national multi-media campaign that includes TV and social media

The personnel

3. List the personnel who would lead work in the major project categories and their prior accomplishments

4. Hourly rates of these key people

The organization

5. Evidence from the organization that it is financially capable of developing these campaigns and delivering these products

Other

6. Once bidders make the initial cut (the proposal includes 1 to 5), quality of the proposals will be evaluated by a point system

It is fair to assume that those items listed first are the most important criteria to the evaluators. In this case, the sample products appear first, not surprisingly. Proposal readers are immediately interested in the type and quality of campaign ideas submitted by the bidders. After they have reviewed the sample work proposed, evaluators are secondly most interested in assessing the members of the team assembled to produce the creative work. They want to know that the team members are qualified and capable of completing this project. Third, evaluators are interested in a breakdown of costs for developing the proposed products, and fourth, they want a commitment from the bidding organization that it can and will meet its financial obligations in developing these products.

Determine What Information to Include in the Proposal

The third step in analyzing the RFP is to determine what information needs to be covered in the proposal. This step is similar but not identical to identifying the evaluation criteria. For example, often the team that you assemble offers strong support for your ability to complete the project you propose. In this case, you want to describe your (or your team's) qualifications and certifications to do the work. Discussing qualifications includes both formal education and some description of previous creative projects you may have completed.

This analysis gives us useful information about the criteria and priorities of the evaluators of the RFP. The next stage of proposal development is to pull together the team and actually generate the deliverables stipulated in the RFP criteria. Once you've outlined your ideas for the potential solution, you should select a format for the proposal. Often, a partial format may present in the criteria stated in the RFP (see the next section for more information on formatting this kind of proposal). Once you have drafted the proposal, review your analysis of the RFP to ensure that you have not gone off track anywhere and that you have included all relevant information and criteria.

Jacob Horne, an up-and-coming Client Relationship Manager at Tennant and Marshall Marketing, stops by his mailbox on his way to his cubicle. There is a stack of papers and envelopes, but one in particular catches his attention because it has a bright yellow sticky note on it with his supervisor, Ron Tennant's, scrawl across it: "I think we have a shot at this one. Look through it and drop by my office to talk before you start the draft." Jacob removes the note so he can see the two pages underneath. He skims the title: "Varscona County Community Get Fit!"—it is a Request for Proposals from Varscona County Municipal Services (see Figure 10.10). He briefly rifles through the other papers in his mail to see whether there is anything else he needs to attend to right away, but it all appears to be routine. There are no other yellow sticky notes from Ron. As he passes Ron's office, he asks him if he has time to talk about the RFP from Varscona County Municipal Services. Ron asks Jacob to read the request and come by in 20 minutes or so.

Ron begins by suggesting that Jacob can be the lead person on this proposal because he had great success with the last government contract. Jacob replies that while this is true, Monique contributed important work to that project, too. He asks if she can be assigned to this proposal as well. Ron points out that Monique is mired on a federal government contract right now, so she may only be able to contribute ideas and not much text, at least until the end of the month. Jacob and Ron talk for 10 or 15 minutes about the requirements discussed in the RFP. Together they identify the key personnel from Tennant and Marshall Marketing who have the expertise to create this advertising campaign. Jacob takes notes as they talk (see Figure 10.11). Ron suggests that Jacob check the federal government website for details or any changes about the bidding process and suggests a deadline of a week's time for the draft.

Trade Agreement: NONE
Tendering Procedures: The bidder must supply Canadian/American goods and/or services
Attachment: None
Competitive Procurement Strategy: Best Overall Proposal
Comprehensive Land Claim Agreement: No
Nature of Requirements:
ADVERTISING SERVICES
Prentice, James
Telephone No. - 123-123-1234
Facsimile No. - 123-123-1230

THERE IS NO SECURITY REQUIREMENT ASSOCIATED WITH THIS SOLICITATION.

VARSCONA COUNTY COMMUNITY GET FIT!

REQUIREMENT

Varscona County is seeking a Contractor to update existing marketing materials or develop new materials, for an innovative advertising and social marketing campaign. The campaign will last one year with potential for extension for two additional years provided the initial campaign meets our objectives and budget. The successful bidder will provide a campaign strategy including an innovative approach, media partners, social media strategy, and an overall plan that includes a detailed critical path that covers the implementation time frame for each media product and the proposed budget breakdown.

OBJECTIVES AND PURPOSE

This campaign (part of Municipal Services' larger social marketing campaign) supports the Varscona campaign to increase the use of the county recreational facilities in an effort to improve overall health outcomes for the county. Over the long term (3–5 years+), the campaign, together with other initiatives, seeks to create an active citizenry and build favorable health outcomes. For the 2020–21 fiscal year, the goal remains the same; that is, to encourage citizens of Varscona county to engage in physical activity. For Option Year 1 (FY 2021–22) and Option Year 2 (FY 2022–23), objectives and requirements will be similar to those of FY 2020–21.

EVALUATION PROCESS

The successful bidder must satisfy all of the criteria in the Request for Proposal, including: providing an example of one national integrated campaign that includes print and one other media; providing an example of one national multimedia campaign that includes TV and social media; and listing the personnel who would lead work in the major project categories; complying with the certification requirements described in the RFP; and providing hourly rates; and evidence that the bidder has provided verified proof of financial resources to perform the work.

PERIOD OF THE CONTRACT

The period of the Contract will be from date of award to March 31st, 2021 with the first Option period running from April 1st, 2021 to March 31st, 2022 and the second Option period running from April 1st, 2022 to March 31st, 2023.

BASIS OF SELECTION

The responsive bid with the lowest cost-per-point will be recommended for award of a contract. Delivery Date: Above-mentioned

The Crown retains the right to negotiate with suppliers on any procurement.

Documents may be submitted in either official language of Canada.

Figure 10.10 **Example of a Request for Proposal.**

Business Communication: Rhetorical Situations

Creative team members: Me, Monique, and Rita

Media choices: Ron suggests billboard (+print) and Internet (+television)

   - Must discuss with Monique and Rita to decide if these are the right ones

Ask Fred Marshall for financial workup to show T&M Marketing can finance development of campaign

Pull résumés for Rita and Monique for qualifications section (see Figure 10.12)

Draft due week Monday (April 13)

Figure 10.11 Jacob Horne's notes from his discussion with Ron Tennant about the Varscona County Municipal Services RFP.

Analysis: Formatting a Solicited Proposal

When Jacob sits down at his desk to work on the RFP from Varscona County Municipal Services, the first thing he does is analyze the RFP carefully to determine what information James Prentice, the issuer of the RFP, wants in the proposal. The RFP contains the criteria that Prentice and the selection committee will use to evaluate and choose from among the proposals. In a competitive situation such as this, only one proposal will be chosen. More information is available on the Doing Business with Government (Canada) website, (https://www.canada.ca/en/services/business/doing-business.html) or the Introduction to Federal Contracting (US) website (https://www.usa.gov/government-contracting-for-beginners). Note that bidders may not contact the organizations requesting the bids without compromising the bid process. This warning means that Jacob has to interpret the RFP without feedback, making a careful and accurate analysis essential. If he is successful, he will bring at least $25,000 and a year (or longer) of new business to Tennant and Marshall Marketing.

Our analysis of the RFP reveals a partial outline for the organizational structure of the proposal: two sample campaign ideas; personnel, qualifications, and certification; and budget. This structure is a variation on the standard generic format for a proposal (see Figure 10.14). Jacob will likely adapt this generic format to the implied format from the RFP. In other words, he will add the sections not specified in the RFP, as appropriate, to ensure readers have the complete information they need to evaluate the proposal. Instead of the "Problem Statement/Background," he uses two headings adapted to the subject matter of the project: "Sample Print and Billboard Campaign" and "Sample Television and Internet Campaign" (or whichever of the second media his team chooses in each case). He will evaluate whether a discussion of methods or procedures for developing the campaigns is appropriate to his readers' needs, as identified in his analysis. He can adapt the "Qualifications/Resources" headings to his situation and call it "Personnel: Qualifications, Certification, and Commitment." In this section he describes the qualifications and credentials of the creative people working on the campaigns. This information he compiles from the staff résumés kept on file for proposal writers (see Figure 10.12). Because the RFP highlights budget information (the hourly wages of personnel and a legal commitment from Tennant and Marshall that it can finance this project), Jacob may consider moving the budget discussion before the work schedule in the proposal. Prentice has requested atypical information as part of the financials, so Jacob thinks about whether this part of the discussion should be highlighted rather than relegated to the end of the proposal, as is standard.

If your analysis of the RFP does not suggest a format for the proposal, use the standard format presented in Figure 10.14.

QUESTIONS A PROPOSAL MUST ANSWER

A proposal is an informative document, and readers come to it expecting to gather complete information about the project that you are proposing to create. They have specific questions that they want you to answer. The following list summarizes the questions that readers expect to have answered when they finish reading your proposal:

- *What problem will you solve?* Answer this question in the problem statement section.
- *How will you solve the problem?* Answer this question through your discussion in the problem statement and methods sections.
- *What will you produce for the reader?* Answer this question in the problem statement.
- *Can you accomplish what you propose?* Answer this question through your discussion in the methods, qualifications and resources, and work schedule sections.
- *What benefits do you present?* Talk about how the reader benefits from selecting your proposal in the problem statement and the qualifications and resources discussion.
- *When will you complete the project?* Your work schedule answers this question.
- *What will it cost?* The budget discussion answers this question.

Of course, you are not just answering these questions; you are also constructing a persuasive argument to convince readers to choose your proposal. For example, to answer the question "Can you accomplish what you propose," Jacob will sketch out a clear and detailed work plan so that readers can imagine his team working through the project stages of the four marketing campaigns specified in the RFP. He also plans to emphasize his team's history of meeting or exceeding deadlines in earlier projects. This provides evidence to support his claim that they will complete the campaign designs as promised. Without evidence, the claim is an assertion (a statement without proof); he adds evidence to make it into an argument. The following exercise helps you turn the answer to one of these questions into a persuasive argument.

Exercise 10.4: Writing an Argument with Evidence

In groups of two or three, place yourself in Jacob Horne's position (or one of the other two members of his creative team, Monique Ducharme and Rita Sharma) and discuss possible benefits that the creative team at Tennant and Marshall can offer to James Prentice and Varscona County Municipal Services. At least one person in your group should record the group's ideas. In your discussions, come up with ideas that answer the question "What benefits do you present?" When you have brainstormed a number of good benefits (such as the educational backgrounds of your team members, past success with similar projects), decide where they would fit best in the proposal: in the problem statement, in the qualifications and resources section, or somewhere else in the proposal.

When you feel you have exhausted the possibilities for discussion, either individually or collaboratively draft two paragraphs that include both claims and evidence that you could use in a draft of the proposal. In one paragraph, develop benefits that will fit in the problem statement/ background section. In the other paragraph, discuss benefits that will fit in the qualifications and resources section. If you identified benefits that fit other parts of the proposal, develop them into suitable paragraphs as well. Ensure that you include evidence to make your case convincing.

As your instructor requests, hand in drafts of the paragraphs with the names of everyone in the group who participated.

Professional Communication Challenges 10.3

1. Write a solicited proposal for Varscona County Municipal Services RFP

Use the information in the next section to help you, writing as Jacob Horne, to draft a proposal that responds to the Request for Proposals (RFP) in Figure 10.10. If you have a background in marketing or advertising, you may already have enough knowledge and experience to develop a publicity campaign. If not, conduct some Internet or library research to gather enough background (aim for some plausible ideas at this point) to develop ideas for a social marketing campaign. Also check out the Doing Business with Government (Canada) website (https://www.canada.ca/en/services/business/doing-business.html) or the Introduction to Federal Contracting (US) website (https://www.usa.gov/government-contracting-for-beginners) for information about writing proposals for government business. Use information from Figures 10.10, 10.11, and 10.12 to write your proposal.

Audience: James Prentice

Purpose: To persuade Prentice to award the contract to Tennant and Marshall Marketing

Genre: Proposal

Points to Emphasize about Creative Personnel

Monique Ducharme
Concordia University, BFA 2016
Centre des arts visuals, 6 courses (graphic design, figure drawing, animation, etc.)

$40.00/hr.

Experience:
- Dove Real Women (National), 2017
- Public Works, Clean Water Campaign, 2018

Rita Sharma
Ontario College of Art and Design, EMDes 2015
OCAD, BFA 2012

$65.00/hr.

Experience:
- Featured artist, McClure Gallery, Boston, MA, 2019
- Public Works, Clean Water Campaign, 2018
- Ride Public Transit, 2017

Me
UBC, BComm (Marketing), 2016

$35.00/hr.

Experience:
- Public Works, Clean Water Campaign, 2018
- Outstanding Marketing Project for 2019 (awarded by Tennant & Marshall)
- Pulse Marketing Board of Canada, Saskatoon, SK 2017

Figure 10.12 **Jacob Horne's notes summarizing qualifications and credentials of his creative team.**

2. Write a solicited proposal for Gleam Dental Clinic

Reread Rhetorical Situation 10.2. Dr. Grant Watson (the practice owner) has requested that you develop training materials for the office. He has asked two employees to come up with ideas, but he intends to accept only one of the two proposals. Writing as Alyssa Klein-Moore or Munir Abbasi, develop a proposal to create training materials for the office that Dr. Watson will want to use. Draw on the information in Rhetorical Situation 10.2 and the proposal criteria in Figure 10.13 for your draft. Use the standard generic proposal format in Figure 10.14 to structure your proposal.

Audience: Dr. Watson and the other medical partners

Purpose: To persuade Watson to approve your proposal

Genre: Proposal

The training materials must be

- easy to update
- compact and usable
- accessible in all parts of the practice

- clear, concise, and complete
- inexpensive to produce and update

Figure 10.13 **Proposal criteria for Gleam Dental Clinic.**

- problem statement/background
- methods/procedures
- qualifications/resources

- work schedule
- budget

Figure 10.14 **Standard generic format for a proposal.**

CHAPTER SUMMARY

- There are two main types of proposals: solicited proposals (Requests for Proposals) and unsolicited proposals.
- Good proposals use a combination of logical arguments, credibility, and emotional appeals to persuade readers that their proposals should be accepted.
- Writing unsolicited proposals requires that writers show that the problem exists and is significant in addition to offering the best solution to the problem.
- Analyzing an RFP requires that writers determine what kind of proposal is requested, identify the evaluation criteria outlined in the RFP, and then determine what information readers want to see in the proposal.
- A proposal must answer the following questions:
  > What problem will you solve?
  > How will you solve the problem?
  > What will you produce for the reader/client?
  > Can you accomplish what you propose?
  > What benefits do you present?
  > When will you complete the project?
  > What will it cost?

© Monkey Business Images/Shutterstock

CHAPTER 11

Informal and Interim Reports

 LEARNING OUTCOMES

1. Define activity, status, and progress reports and organize one appropriately

2. Describe the purpose and audience for an activity report

3. Identify the information that should be present in a trip report and organize that information appropriately

4. Describe the purpose and audience for a trip report

5. Define a meeting report and demonstrate how to structure one appropriately

6. Describe the purpose and audience for a meeting report

GETTING STARTED

The majority of your writing at work will involve writing informal or short reports: activity reports, trip reports, and meeting reports. When we think of reports, we often imagine the thick, heavy, massive texts that are every worker's nightmare—if they have to write them. Success as a writer at work, though, may very well depend on your ability to master the short report: write clearly, concisely, and quickly about work-related topics. Developing your skills in these genres depends on learning about how they are structured and what kinds of information readers expect in them.

The first section of this chapter begins with activity reports, which detail your accomplishments for the month. This section presents the information you need to know to write an informative and persuasive activity report. The middle section of this chapter introduces you to trip reports. Trip reports are filed following employee travel at the organization's expense. This section discusses your purpose in writing the report, the content it presents, and your audience. The third section of this chapter looks at meeting reports or minutes. Meeting reports are usually kept by the administrative assistant of an organization, and they serve as a permanent record of what happened at the meeting. They showcase the decision-making and analytical skills of those who attended the meeting and act as a legal and official report of the meeting. This section also includes a generic structure for a meeting report that you can adapt to your specific situation.

The three Rhetorical Situations in the chapter describe contexts for writing each kind of report. Martin Dasher must write a status report on the progress of usability testing while also positioning himself for a return to programming computer code. Casey MacLean attended a seminar on how to use OrderNow software; her trip report provides the details of the seminar and trip to management. Arthur Banda, a member of the executive at the Daily Bread Food Bank, is responsible for writing the minutes of their most recent meeting.

WHAT ARE ACTIVITY, STATUS, AND PROGRESS REPORTS?

 Define activity, status, and progress reports and organize one appropriately

 Describe the purpose and audience for an activity report

Activity or status reports—also known as progress reports—are required at many organizations from all employees as a way to track company and employee productivity, either generally or on specific projects. These reports also allow employee input and enable them to comment on their past and future activities.

Content
The following information is normally included in an activity report:

- details of completed work
- description of problems encountered

- summary of solutions to problems
- outline of work remaining to be completed

The terms *status*, *activity*, and *progress reports* are sometimes viewed as interchangeable, but there are subtle differences between them. At the same time, these distinctions are not cut in stone; different organizations evolve different traditions of naming, so if you are asked to write one of these reports at a new organization, ask a few questions about the content and emphasis so that you can decide which area to emphasize in your report.

Introduction or project description:

- summarize the project you are working on
- summarize your progress
- briefly identify obstacles you overcame
- assess whether your project is on time and on budget

Work completed:

- detail task by task what you have done
- evaluate your progress against the plan
- describe any problems encountered in greater detail and how you solved them
- note what you've learned that may benefit others

Work remaining:

- assess remaining work against the plan
- detail tasks remaining before completion
- anticipate possible problems and offer potential solutions

Cost (if budget is involved):

- report on what budget you have spent, what remains, and why any discrepancies exist (for example, unforeseen costs associated with solving problems)

Assessment of progress so far; conclusion and recommendations:

- assess whether you will complete the project as planned
- propose any necessary revisions to the schedule or plan

Figure 11.1 **Typical structure for a progress or status report.**

As the name suggests, a status report often focuses on one large project, with the discussion reporting where the writer is in the process of completion (in other words, what is the status of this project?). A progress report is very similar to a status report in that the writer emphasizes what has been accomplished so far and what remains to be done before the project is complete.

The progress report may not focus on just one project, however; it may report on a series of projects in mid-process. The activity report is generally used by organizations to keep track of what employees are doing day to day or week to week. It includes reporting on all of an employee's activities rather than the effort toward completion of a single project.

Informal reports (in fact, *all* reports) have goals from both the organization's perspective and the employee's perspective. While demonstrating their competence on past work, employees can also shape their future work by making suggestions or offering solutions to problems raised in the report.

Figure 11.1 outlines a progress or status report structure. Use it if your organization does not have an established format.

Readers expect to gain specific information from a progress or status report. They want these points:

- a descriptive title announcing report content
- an executive summary to skim for project context or background
- a discussion of how this work contributes to the organization's larger goals (its relevance)
- a report on positive and negative project developments so they can learn from your solutions

Note that your readers want to learn from the discussion in your report.

Rhetorical Situation 11.1: Accounting for Your Productivity at Afoyalan Pharmaceuticals

It is the 29th of the month, and Martin Dasher realizes that his first project of the day should be a status report to summarize his accomplishments for the month. It is due tomorrow. Martin doesn't have to review his notes to know that he has spent all of April working on a nonprogramming project: he has been user testing the newly developed online employee training materials. Developing and running the usability tests has been a huge stretch for him, and although he feels he has done a great job, he is tired of document production and wants to get back to his real job before he gets too far behind on his own projects.

He took over for Nirmala Eko, Afoyalan's technical writer, when she left on maternity leave just as the beta version of the training materials was finished; she won't be back until July 1. Megan Korrigan, the human resources department head, and Sefu Afoyalan, the company president, had insisted that the training materials for the new system come online as soon as possible. Mr. Afoyalan had decided that Martin knew the most about the new program, so he should take over the user-testing phase.

One of the things that excited Martin when he started at Afoyalan Pharmaceuticals 18 months ago is the relatively small size of the company. With only two programmers in the IT department, he can work on aspects of information technology beyond programming. Although the user-testing project wasn't exactly what he had in mind, it has been interesting. At the same time, he wants to get back to programming. He decides to write his status report to accomplish two goals (in this order): 1) to convince Sefu Afoyalan that it is time he returned to programming, and 2) to demonstrate the great job he has been doing in Nirmala's place.

A quick look at his notes shows Martin that he has lots of details to cite in recording his progress over the month (see Figures 11.2 and 11.3). He adds his main persuasive goals for the report to his notes as a way to focus his thoughts. The big question is how to convince his boss that he is more valuable as a programmer than as a user-testing coordinator.

Summary of problems found in modules 1 through 4

- Three problem areas in module 1:
    1. Wrong visual in Figure 1.8 (original didn't show the crucial detail on screen)
    2. Unclear phrasing in step 1.3; changed "add ellipses between elements" to "insert 'period space' three times between elements"
    3. Added glossary to define delimited terms of program

- One problem area in module 2:
    1. Deleted steps 2.1 to 2.3 from first draft because no one used them

- Four problems in module 3:
    1. Added definition of "repeated selection" to glossary because users didn't see its specialized use
    2. Added three more figures to steps 3.3–3.5
    3. Added callout detail to Figure 3.7 to highlight relevant information
    4. Corrected two broken links in step 3.8

- One problem in module 4:
    1. Ambiguous phrasing in step 4.3; changed "add three spaces between elements" to "hit 'enter' three times"

- Additional problem in module 2:
    1. Deleted Figure 2.3 to end user confusion generated in step 2.4

- Additional problem addressed: redesigned the "repeat selection" icon

Figure 11.2 **Martin Dasher's notes on progress over the past month.**

April Status Report
Martin Dasher

Persuasive Goals for this Report:

1. Convince Sefu that I should get back to programming right away (calculate $$ saved by eliminating several steps from inventory control process)
2. Show that I worked hard on this user testing and did a good job, even though this is not related to my training or usual job responsibilities (I'm a good team player!)
3. Show why Valerie can finish user testing and meet May 18 for full operations

Main points to make:

1. **What we got done:**
   - first and second phase testing completed
   - identified and corrected 11 problems in modules 1 through 4

2. **What we still have to do:**
   - final phase testing for modules 3 and 4

3. **Budget:**
   See Megan for exact figures, we are not over projection (we weren't two weeks ago). Then we had spent $8,000 of our $15,000 budgeted for this process. We should be close to $10,000, but I have to check this.

4. **Projection for hitting deadline:**
   - not much left to do: final test of modules 3 and 4
   - users are lined up (Becky, Todd, Mira, Amir)

We should hit May 18 launch date.

Figure 11.3 **Martin Dasher's notes for writing his April status report for Afoyalan Pharmaceuticals.**

Re: Budget for Employee Training Materials on New World Order program
From: megan.korrigan@afoyalanind.com
To: martin.dasher@afoyalanind.com

Hi, Martin,

Here are the budget figures: the project has spent $9,741.32, as of April 27. You have $5,258.68 left to complete the project. Note that any funds spent between April 27 and today (Apr. 29) have not reached me yet, so you should subtract them from these figures if you want exact amounts.

Cheers,
Meg

Figure 11.4 **Email from Megan Korrigan about the usability testing budget for the employee training online learning modules.**

Business Communication: Rhetorical Situations

Moving Martin out of Nirmala's position will create a problem—there is no one left to run the testing—so he will also need to suggest who can complete the testing in his place. He also needs to reference an important neglected project to add urgency to his reassignment. He had been working on an important project before he was reassigned. He will just have to reacquaint himself with the details of that project. As for his own replacement, Valerie McCorkindale from human resources has been helping him; she can easily coordinate the final tests. Martin has them set up so they do not need technical expertise, and she is better than he is with people. Martin opens the status report template (see Figure 11.1 for the template structure) and fills in the basic financial details (Figure 11.4).

Analysis: Martin Aims to Return to Programming

Martin Dasher writes an activity report every month. In part, his report for April will assess the status report of user testing new training materials for the company. Martin's boss wants to know whether this project is on schedule to launch as planned. In addition to showing the project is on schedule, Martin also wants his boss to remember that Martin's assigned work has been neglected over the past month. He wants Sefu Afoyalan to send him back to his programming work.

Purpose

 Describe the purpose and audience for an activity report

Martin hopes to accomplish several goals with his activity report:

1. to ensure he returns to programming
2. to showcase his activities in user testing, although not his area of expertise
3. to update his coworkers and company president, Mr. Afoyalan, on the status of the employee training materials
4. to reassure the reader that all the training materials will come online May 18

Audience

The audience for a status or activity report is broader than you might think. The **initial audience** (and the primary audience) for Martin's report is Sefu Afoyalan, the company president, who supervises all employees at the small company. In addition, Martin will send a copy of the report to Nirmala Eko so that she can follow the training materials' progress while on maternity leave. Megan Korrigan is another reader who wants the training materials online quickly in order to train employees who will work with the new program. Martin may also CC his coworkers who are helping to test it so that everyone knows where they are in the process. The report will be archived for other employees to refer to it later.

initial audience: The first person to whom you send your completed work; often, there are many other audiences who will also read it

Persuasive Goals

Another interesting aspect to this status report is the persuasive element by which Martin aims to get his programming job back as soon as possible. Martin notes the need for a convincing case if he is to move back to his former job. He suggests that he will include an estimate of the money to be saved when he finishes his proposed "fix" for the company database. Providing good reasons will encourage Mr. Afoyalan to decide in Martin's favor.

Exercise 11.1: What Is the Difference between an Activity Report, a Status Report, and a Progress Report?

As a discussion among groups of two or three people or individually as a writing exercise, discuss or draft answers to the following questions:

- If the terms "activity report," "status report," and "progress report" refer to the same kind of document presenting the same kind of material, why do you think these three different terms have developed?
- What differences in content or purpose can you infer from the three different terms?
- Would you organize your discussion in, say, an activity report differently from a progress report? Why or why not?

Professional Communication Challenges 11.1

1. Write a draft of Martin Dasher's activity report

Using the information from the case; the information in Figures 11.2, 11.3, and 11.4; and the discussion on activity, status, and progress reports, write a draft of Martin Dasher's activity report for the president of Afoyalan Pharmaceuticals. In your draft, try to accomplish the persuasive goals that Martin identifies in his notes in Figure 11.3, as well as including all relevant information drawn from the case to demonstrate that Martin is a conscientious and hard-working employee who earned his paycheck last month. Remember that your primary goal in writing this report is to ensure that Martin is returned to his original position as a company programmer.

Audience: Company president Sefu Afoyalan; fellow employees at Afoyalan Pharmaceuticals

Purpose: To show your competence as a worker and to have someone else take over user testing the training materials so you can return to your original work

Genre: Activity report

2. Write an activity report for your business communication instructor

Write an activity report for your business and professional communication instructor to report on what you accomplished this week (or over the last two weeks) toward the reading and assignments in your business and professional communication class. Your goal in writing this assignment is to show your instructor how hard you have been working on the course and to convince him or her that you will complete the rest of the assignments in this course in a timely fashion.

Audience: Your business and professional communication instructor

Purpose: To demonstrate your hard work and learning so far in this course

Genre: Activity report

TRIP REPORTS

 Identify the information that should be present in a trip report and organize that information appropriately

 Describe the purpose and audience for a trip report

Many organizations require employees to write trip reports when they return from travel on company business. Sometimes the trip report is a form with blanks to fill in, but some organizations request a written document to establish that the trip was taken. A trip report is usually a short (250 to 500 words) memo report and records the trip's date, destination, and purpose. It includes details to prove the writer took a productive trip where he or she represented the organization effectively and accomplished the goals set out for the trip. It also itemizes trip-related expenses. From the primary reader's perspective, the trip report should prove the employee took the trip and completed the work that motivated the trip. Secondary readers want the report to summarize the main functions of the trip. Consider who else besides your immediate boss might read your trip report.

Content

The content of a trip report varies depending on the business trip's length. The headings allow you to describe the trip's general intent and its outcome or success. Attachments include original receipts for travel (boarding passes or taxi receipts), food (restaurant or credit card receipts), and accommodation (your hotel bill), if your organization reimburses travel expenses after the trip. Attachments may also include documents (for example, brochures, reports, other types of information) relevant to the purpose for the trip.

 Rhetorical Situation 11.2: How I Spent My Training Seminar

"So how was the course you took in Toronto?" asks Midori Fujioka as she passes the door, her arms loaded with file folders. Casey MacLean replies that it had been great, if a bit overwhelming. She gestures to a pile of brochures, papers, and handwritten notes about the inventory control program *OrderNow*. She describes how the instructors went over the basics the first half of each day but then after lunch got into how to use the functions that Casey and her colleagues need for tracking and updating inventory at Parsons Electronic Superstore. Casey had spent part of the previous week at a two-day workshop learning how to use *OrderNow*, recently purchased by Parsons Electronics. Casey went to the workshop as the only full-time employee in charge of store inventory. Midori had decided the best way to learn the new program was to send Casey for training and have her teach her part-time counterparts, Lim Kuang and Frank Delacroix, who shared inventory management responsibilities for the store on the late, weekend, and holiday shifts.

Midori is happy that the course worked out, and she asks Casey to arrange a meeting with Lim and Frank to teach them what she has learned. Midori notes that she will also need a trip report as soon as Casey can write it, but by Friday at the latest.

Casey agrees and asks if she should include copies of her notes and the instructional materials. Midori says no, not this time, and asks Casey to file the handouts they gave her in the educational materials filing cabinet. Midori asks Casey to just summarize the highlights in her report so the office has a record of what she learned.

Casey turns to her filing drawer, deciding that she will start the trip report immediately. Flipping through her files, she finds what she needs: a copy of a report from an earlier trip. It will be a good model. It has the correct headings, and best of all, as Casey remembers, Midori had said it was a good report. She locates the earlier report file in her documents folder and saves the file with a new name. Then she deletes most of the information, leaving only the headings. She fans the papers from her trip across the desk and pauses for a moment, debating. She had actually missed the morning session of the second day because of a bout of food poisoning. "How should I handle that in the trip report?" she wonders.

Analysis: Casey Reports on Her Training Trip

From the writer's perspective, the trip report shows that the trip was taken as planned and that work was accomplished on the trip. In Casey MacLean's case, she wants to show that she attended the training seminar and learned the main functions of *OrderNow* that Parsons Electronics needs to properly manage its inventory. If problems arose or the trip was less successful than hoped, the writer has a more challenging task in writing the trip report. For example, because Casey got food poisoning at dinner on the first day, she had to miss the first half of the second day. She has to report this absence and explain what course material she missed. She also needs to explain how she plans to or has compensated for her absence. For example, she may outline a plan to learn what she missed by self-study or attending a second seminar later in the month. Midori Fujioka is interested primarily in two points: 1) Casey learned the functions that Parsons Electronics most needs to manage its inventory, and 2) Casey can train the other employees using what she learned at the seminar.

 Professional Communication Challenges 11.2

1. Write a trip report for Casey McLean

Writing as Casey McLean, draft a trip report using the information provided in the case, the format in Figure 11.5, and the previous discussion on writing trip reports. Write to Midori Fujioka as your primary audience, keeping in mind that other employees and even the owner of the company, Bill

Parsons, may read your report in the future. Include detail to show that Casey did attend the training seminar and learned the information she needs to use the newly purchased inventory control program *OrderNow*.

Audience: Midori Fujioka

Purpose: To persuade your readers that the trip was worthwhile

Genre: Trip report

Trip date and destination

Purpose of the trip

Background of the trip

Details of the trip
- who went
- what happened
- outcome/results
- implications

Conclusions/recommendations

Any follow up

Attachments

Figure 11.5 **Generic format for a trip report.**

MEETING REPORTS

 Define a meeting report and demonstrate how to structure one appropriately

 Describe the purpose and audience for a meeting report

Meeting reports are informal reports that record details about a meeting to provide a permanent record of what happened, who attended and said what, what decisions were made, and what work remains for subsequent meetings. Sometimes called *meeting minutes*, meeting reports are often kept by the secretary of an organization or the administrative assistant of the division and circulated before the next meeting for participant review. A first order of business at the next meeting is often to discuss the previous meeting report, revise it if necessary, and vote to accept the report as an accurate record of that meeting.

Purpose

A meeting report accurately and concisely records what happened at an organizational meeting. It acts as an official and legal record of the meeting discussion in the event company records are subpoenaed for a court case or other legal proceeding (commission, inquest). Readers of meeting reports can vary. Some readers read to discover what happened at the meeting because they could not attend. Others review the report because they were present and must approve it for accuracy. From the organization's perspective, meeting reports provide a historical record of its work and important decisions.

As a writer of a meeting report, you likely want to accomplish several goals: 1) to show that your group makes well-thought-out and significant decisions, 2) to demonstrate that the group works hard and accomplishes things, and 3) to illustrate the proficiency and accuracy of your own communication skills.

Committee or group name/date of meeting/location

Summary of follow-up actions and individuals responsible for follow up by date

Individuals present (also those absent)

Agenda items

Discussion of each agenda item
- background to item
- discussion of item
- outcome/decision/action plan

Next meeting date and proposed agenda

Figure 11.6 **Generic structure for a meeting report.**

Content

As noted, meeting reports briefly summarize the items on the meeting agenda and the discussion about each item. Generally, these reports record the committee or group name, the date of the meeting, and its location. They often summarize the follow-up action that was chosen, the person selected to take action, and the deadline for completing it. Meeting reports also record who attended the meeting, as well as those who should have but did not attend. Next, the report records any discussion about agenda items and the outcome or decision reached about each. It ends by identifying the date and time of the next meeting and any agenda items that were identified for it. Figure 11.6 outlines a generic structure to use or adapt for a meeting report at your organization.

Audience

Meeting reports are archival documents (they record the events of a meeting for later reference or review) rather than transactional documents (documents generated to accomplish a specific action with a group of readers). Readers for a meeting report can vary widely, and they are often far distant from the meeting itself. They can include 1) members of the committee, those who attended and those who did not (the **initial audience** for the report); 2) administrative staff evaluating the work of the committee or group (the **gatekeeper audience**); 3) others who want to verify action taken at the meeting; 4) the new head of a committee interested in those issues the committee or group has handled in the past (**secondary audience** for the report); and very occasionally 5) legal teams who investigate ethical problems to determine whether specific issues were discussed and when (a version of the **watchdog audience**, but with more power than watchdog audiences usually have).

gatekeeper audience:
Readers who decide who else will read your document

secondary audience:
People who will read your document for different reasons than the primary audience

watchdog audience:
Readers who may obtain your document and read it for political, legal, or social reasons

▲ **Rhetorical Situation 11.3: The Daily Bread Executive Board Meeting**

"Hello, everyone," says Helen Bean, smiling at her assembled staff. There are six people altogether who comprise the executive of the Daily Bread Food Bank. Today they have one newcomer to their monthly meeting, Paul Gonzalez. He is a student at the local college and as part of his program he hopes to write a grant to raise money for the Food Bank. Helen introduces Paul to the rest of the team. On Paul's right is Marci Aziz, the chief fundraiser. Helen notes that Paul will be working closely with her. Beside Marci sits Jin Han, the head driver and ace mechanic. He supervises other volunteers on food pickup and does minor service on the fleet. Helen continues by introducing Eamon O'Malley, who does the accounting books, and Arthur Banda, who manages the food bank. She points out that Arthur also acts as the scribe at the food bank's meetings because he has the most legible handwriting. Helen then notes that one more member of the executive, Ivan Alexandrov, cannot attend the meeting.

Paul is then asked to introduce himself. He describes how he has volunteered a lot with literacy programs and raising funds at the canvassing level but has never had the chance to write grants to raise money. He explains that he is a second-year business student also doing a minor in service learning.

Marci welcomes Paul and describes how she is connecting with local businesses such as restaurants and grocery stores to gather donations for the food bank. That keeps her pretty busy, she says, and as a result she is not finding time to locate sponsors for their transportation end, which is almost as important as having food on the shelves. Jin agrees, noting that without trucks the food doesn't get onto shelves, but they also don't need trucks if there is no food to transport.

Helen says that they do have one more thing on the agenda. In February, Eamon offered to meet with local car dealership owners to see what kind of deal they might give the food bank if the executive decides to purchase a new van. He reports on that meeting, explaining that he visited all the local dealerships and gathered both official and unofficial prices for a van. He notes that Robson Motors has offered to give the food bank a van from their leased fleet and charge them a fraction of the original price, but in exchange Mr. Robson also wants his dealership logo splashed all over the van. Eamon says he told Robson that the Daily Bread executive would need to discuss this generous offer. He then distributes a half-sheet of paper with dealer names, van information, and prices on it. Everyone sits quietly for a few minutes studying the figures.

Eamon, after a minute, asks Jin how he feels about advertising Robson Motors as the volunteers make their rounds. Jin shrugs and says that he thinks it doesn't matter so long as the Food Bank logo and name also figure prominently on the van. He then asks about the mileage on the used van, pointing out that this, as well as its maintenance and repair records, are more important than the paint job. He notes that a beat-up van could cost the organization money in towing and repair charges way above the low price, not to mention the inconvenience of breaking down by the roadside. The others around the table nod at Jin's comments.

Arthur says that Robson is offering them a good price. He suggests that maybe they can get more information about the specific van and if it is in good shape, accept the offer. Paul suggests that Robson may also be willing to include some warranty for maintenance and repairs as part of the deal.

Helen thinks that is a great idea. She also suggests that maybe they can apply for a grant to cover capital costs. She asks Paul if he has found any funding possibilities that may cover these types of expenses in his preliminary research. Paul responds that those grants are rare. Marci suggests that they can make a convincing argument to one of the agencies that having roadworthy vehicles is central to Daily Bread's mission.

Helen agrees. She then ends the meeting by asking Marci and Paul to research potential funding sources more fully, Eamon to gather more information about the use history of the van offered by Robson Motors, and Arthur to circulate the minutes of the meeting so that Ivan can read them.

 Professional Communication Challenges 11.3

1. Write the meeting report for the Daily Bread Food Bank executive committee

Writing as Arthur, the food bank manager, or Shelley, his assistant and a food bank volunteer, draft a copy of the minutes for this meeting of the executive committee of the Daily Bread Food Bank. The minutes or meeting report will bring a sixth member of the committee, Ivan, up to date on the group's discussions at the meeting, and it will also serve as a record of the group's activities. The meeting report will record the start of Paul's activities with the food bank as well as the organization's efforts to update its van fleet for collecting food donations around the city. Use the information in the preceding section of this chapter to help you write an informative meeting report for the Daily Bread Food Bank.

Audience: Ivan Alexandrov, the members of the Executive Committee, and the members of the board of directors of the Daily Bread Food Bank

Purpose: To accurately and concisely record what happened at the meeting and what action was taken or decided on

Genre: Meeting report

2. Write a meeting report for a group to which you belong

If you are a member of a school or work committee, record notes at the next meeting so that you can write a report of that meeting. Use the discussion in this section to help you format and draft an accurate and appropriately detailed account of the meeting. Your report should be a document that other members of the committee could approve as an accurate record of the meeting and that will inform individuals who could not attend the meeting about the main items discussed and the actions or decisions that were made or approved.

Audience: The other members of the committee meeting, your instructor, and classmates who may be interested in the activities of this committee

Purpose: To accurately and concisely record what happened at the meeting and what action was decided on or taken

Genre: Meeting report

CHAPTER SUMMARY

- Activity or status reports document two types of activities: employees' general productivity, and progress on a specific project.
- Activity and status/progress reports include descriptions of what work has been completed, problems encountered (and overcome), solutions to problems, and what work remains.
- Trip reports are short and document trip dates, destination(s), purpose for the trip, who went, what happened, results, reflections on trip's outcome or success, and receipts for trip expenses.
- Meeting reports or minutes are a permanent record of what happened at a meeting and include who attended, what they said, what decisions they made, and what work remains for later meetings.

CHAPTER 12

Research Reports: Recommendation, Analytical, and Informational

LEARNING OUTCOMES

1. Describe what a research report is and explain how to gather information to write one

2. Identify how to find and evaluate print and online published sources

3. Prepare for, conduct, and complete an interview

4. Create and administer survey research and evaluate and analyze survey data

5. Format and draft a research report

6. Understand and manage the political elements of writing a business report

GETTING STARTED

Reports are the engine that drives the modern organization, providing the power required to make good decisions about the future of an organization or business. For example, the municipal government might notice a rise in vandalism cases involving 12- to 15-year-olds in your town in the later afternoon, after school ends and before many parents finish work. The members of city council might discuss the role the city should play in developing activities or programs targeted to this age group to prevent bored teenagers from getting into trouble—in a similar case in Stettler, Alberta, the council voted to fund a skate park. Generally, the solution to problems like this is proposed in the form of a written report that outlines the problem, examines the potential solutions, and often recommends the best solution to the decision makers.

In this chapter, you learn about writing formal reports that require some type of research to find the best solution. The different types of reports (informational, analytical, and recommendation) refer to what writers do with the research they gather. An informational report examines a subject in depth but generally does not recommend solutions to the problem it examines. Analytical reports go a step beyond informational reports by providing discussion and analysis; they might even include several recommendations for readers to choose from, but they stop short of identifying one best solution. Readers of analytical reports have to choose the best solution for themselves. Recommendation reports, then, go beyond analytical reports by seeking to solve the problem and recommend the best solution. If you are unsure of which report your readers are expecting, ask questions until you are clear about the purpose for your report.

Most research reports grow out of a question or problem that needs a solution. Many problems can have several solutions, but careful research can help you decide which one is the best solution. This chapter introduces you to the basic methods of report writing research: using published sources, interviewing experts, and creating surveys. Interviewing and survey research are primary sources; published documents and website materials are secondary sources. Primary research in report writing focuses on people as a source of information (interviews or surveys). Secondary research includes published sources of information, including books, journal or magazine articles, reliable Internet websites, and .pdf documents. Next, the chapter shows you how to transform your research findings into a draft report. You learn the basic components of a formal report and the rhetorical considerations for each section. This is followed by useful information about repetition of text in research reports and the shifts in the discourse used from section to section. The chapter ends by considering the political implications of report production and addressing the ways in which even a report authored by one person should be a collaborative project if it is to achieve its goals.

The Rhetorical Situations in this chapter offer opportunities to write two different types of reports. Kay McKenzie asks Josh Irvine to write a recommendation report to help her decide if she should open a new location for new business. An Kim, a part-time worker at the Ritchie Community Center, has been asked to conduct a survey of teenagers at the Center and write an information report based on the results. These reports form the basis for decisions that decide what the organizations will do next.

GENRES OF THE RESEARCH REPORT

 Describe what a research report is and explain how to gather information to write one

Research reports address real questions to which people need good-quality answers. If answers are immediately obvious, no report is needed. When a report is assigned, it is because a lot of research must be done to identify a range of possible answers or solutions. In the context of business and professional communication, primary research refers to the report writer working with people to find answers. Generally, report writers use interviews or surveys to collect information (opinions and ideas) from people. Secondary research refers to published texts. Vast amounts of published information are available in libraries and online.

Research reports come in three main genres or types:

- *Information report* (collect and present information on a subject): A writer who has been asked to *explore* a problem chooses an information report format. Information reports introduce the topic, explain relevant background, assemble research on the topic, and end by interpreting and summarizing the problem. Information reports do not recommend solutions.
- *Analytical report* (collect, analyze, and present information on a subject; offer a range of solutions): A writer who has been asked to *study* a problem and devise a series of possible solutions chooses an analytical report. Analytical reports explore the topic or problem, collect data and research to explore potential solutions to the problem, and identify several solutions for readers to consider and choose from.
- *Recommendation report* (collect, analyze, and present information on a subject; recommend the best solution): A writer who has been asked to *solve* a problem chooses a recommendation report. Recommendation reports allow the writer to examine the problem in depth, analyze the data and research related to the problem, and discuss possible solutions to the problem, and they empower the writer to judge and recommend the best solution of those considered.

Formal and Informal Research Reports

Reports can be formal or informal, depending upon the nature of the problem and the level of formality of the organization. Formal reports are usually many pages long, bound into a permanent cover, and include traditional sections and front matter such as a cover letter, an executive summary, and appendices. Informal reports are usually shorter, do not contain front matter or appendices (although they may include a references page), and may be formatted as a memo directed to the writer's supervisor.

RESEARCH METHODS: SECONDARY SOURCES

 Identify how to find and evaluate print and online published sources

Online Keyword Search

The simplest way to begin a search online is to type keywords linked to the topic into one of the many Internet search engines: Google, Firefox, or Bing, among others. A keyword search using *business plan* brought up over 5,800,000,000 hits, far too many, suggesting that the search terms are too broad and need to be refined. However, at the beginning of a research project, the first few screens of links will likely provide ample starting points. You can also use metasearch engines to locate information that may be useful to your project. **Metasearch engines** allow you to search for more focused content. For example, globalspec.com searches websites for engineering materials and specifications.

As search results appear on your screen, evaluate the sites themselves and the information they contain to determine the reliability and trustworthiness of each. Sites that exist mainly to sell products or services are less reliable than government- or educational-sponsored websites. Figure 12.1 summarizes some tips for evaluating the credibility or trustworthiness of the information that you find online and in print.

Remember to keep records of the citation information for all of the sources that look useful. Save the URLs for or bookmark reliable sites and record the date that you visited the site; you will need that information later for citation purposes.

Figure 12.2 identifies the information that you should record for each website. To save headaches later, record this information for sites that seem less useful, but that you might use in the future.

metasearch engines: Web search engines that compile results derived from several other search engines

Considerations	Print Sources	Online Sources
General trustworthiness	If library sources, they have already been evaluated for credibility and purchased. Library sources have a high rate of dependability.	Anyone can post anything. Most websites have no screening mechanism for content. Material can range from highly credible to highly suspect.
Author	What information can you find about the author? What else has the author published? What have other writers said about this text or author (book reviews, review essays, texts published in response)?	Is there an author identified? What additional information can you find about this person? What are their credentials on this topic and generally? What organization(s) is he or she affiliated with? Can you find reviews or evaluations of this writer's work?

Considerations	Print Sources	Online Sources
Publisher	Who published the document?	Check the site URL.
	Is it a reputable and recognizable publishing house?	Websites associated with the government or postsecondary educational institutions (.gov, .gc. ca, .edu, .uschoolname, etc.) are more trustworthy than commercial sites (.com, .net, etc.). Nonprofit-sponsored websites (.net, .org, etc.) can vary in their reliability.
	What kinds of other publications does this publisher issue?	
Date or timeliness	How recent is the text?	When was the website last updated?
	Is timeliness important to your topic? Historical documents don't lose credibility with age; in contrast, research on extended reality (XR), for example, should be as current as possible.	Does the website acknowledge recent developments on a topic?
		If sources are included, how recent are their publication dates?
Bias of content discussion	What perspective does the text or writer take on the topic?	What perspective does the writer take on the topic?
	To what extent does the writer maintain a neutral stance towards the topic?	Does the writer try to sell you a product or service or specific point of view?
	Can you detect a political or philosophical slant to the ideas?	Does the writer maintain a neutral attitude towards the topic (reporting rather than commenting or evaluating)?
	How does this slant affect the information in the text?	
	How will your use of this information affect the text that you are writing?	What political or philosophical slant can you detect towards the discussion of the ideas?
		How might this slant affect the information on the site?
		How will your use of this information affect the text that you are writing?

Considerations	Print Sources	Online Sources
Evidence and quality of sources	What evidence does the writer use to support his or her argument or position?	What evidence does the site use to support the position it advances?
	Did the writer conduct primary or secondary research to support his or her views?	Is the information based on credible research or published sources?
		Does the site provide sources for statistical or proprietary information?
	Does the text have a bibliography and citations?	How credible and recent are the sources cited on the website?
	How credible and recent are the sources cited by this writer?	Lack of or out-of-date sources can seriously undermine credibility for some topics.
	Lack of or out-of-date sources can seriously undermine credibility for some topics.	

Figure 12.1 **Tips for evaluating the trustworthiness of print and online sources.**

Figure 12.2 **To document your sources accurately, record as much information from the page as you can for each source you use.**

Source: https://articles.bplans.com/how-to-write-a-business-plan/ (Bplans.com)

Business Communication: Rhetorical Situations

Kay McKenzie bustles through the front door, her arms filled with boxes and bags. She just returned to her store, Secret Garden Treasures and Gifts, the night before and is anxious to show her sales team the new products she has found. She has with her items from six artisans who work along the west coast of Vancouver Island. She unwraps a Haida carving of the sun with inlaid mother of pearl and delicate patterns of ash and cherry wood. The artist who created the mask is going to send more pieces. They are expensive, but amazing. She then lifts a life-size yellow and green glass banana slug out of the box. "Aren't these great?" she exclaims.

Kay pulls out several more unique pieces that Josh Irvine thinks are well chosen for the store. It caters to a discerning clientele in the city's hottest urban redevelopment area, the Docks. At first there had been mostly nightclubs and bars around Secret Garden, but elegant residential towers and unique shops are drawing increasingly larger crowds and more wealthy visitors and residents to the area. Business has certainly picked up in the last three years, and Kay is constantly thinking about how to grow her business and bring in more unique products and appreciative customers. She has suggested that Josh return to school for some business credentials to help with her plans. She has even paid for part of his tuition, an incentive that he couldn't refuse, although he hadn't planned to return to school.

In fact, he was thrilled to join Secret Garden as an assistant manager after he graduated because he needed a break from books and teachers. Kay had to talk him into hitting the books again, but he has to admit it has been a terrific idea. Josh enrolled in the School of Retail Management, and he was pleased to see that the information is relevant and useful to the business. Kay thinks that a city on the west coast might be perfect to set up a second Secret Garden. Although Josh agrees that a second location is a good idea, he isn't sure what may be the right location—the west coast is too far away, and neither he nor Kay knows any of those potential markets well.

Kay thinks that Josh can take over the current location temporarily while she does some research and scouts locations. Her plan isn't to do anything right away but to explore the opportunity of opening a second location. With so many artists and artisans on the Gulf Islands, Vancouver Island, and along the coast from Seattle southward to northern California, she feels they can collect some amazing stock. Some of the stock can be shipped eastward, adding to their current location's unique offerings.

Kay feels that Josh's business studies background should be useful to determine if this idea is feasible. She asks him to do research on the best locations, digest what he can find, and report what she should do to expand Secret Garden. She asks him to identify the hottest location in the city and look for a neighborhood that feels similar to the Docks. She says that she wants the answer to these two questions: 1) should she open a second location on the west coast, and 2) what would be the best location for the new store?

Josh asks if she wants him to scout possible sources of merchandise. Kay feels that she has enough ideas about that already. She wants him to look at the small business situation there: What help do the state/provincial governments offer new start-ups? What government-sponsored programs can they apply for? How does renting compare to buying based on per-square-foot costs? What sales will they need to generate to make a profit and keep the location open? How many employees will they need? She stresses that she doesn't want him to just describe; she needs his advice to evaluate the information he finds.

Josh scribbles some notes while he and Kay are talking. He realizes he needs an outline of what topics to cover in the report. He will do that right away and get Kay's approval before she leaves the store.

Analysis: Considering a West-Coast Location

 Prepare for, conduct, and complete an interview

In Josh Irvine's case, Kay McKenzie has requested a recommendation report (she asks him to study a problem and recommend a solution). To study the problem, he conducts some research to identify what topics to cover in the report. He knows he has several options for gathering information:

- print and online sources (secondary sources)
- interviews (primary source)
- surveys (primary source)

Josh decides to start with trade books, textbooks, business magazines, journals, and websites to learn what topics to cover. Then he will choose one or two professors at the university with expertise in these areas to interview. He will also consider other contacts (family members, friends, and acquaintances) who may offer insight and advice. After brief consideration, he decides that surveys of the general population to collect opinions, preferences, and shopping habits will be much less useful to his report. He decides not to do survey research on this project: "I can see developing a survey as we get closer to analyzing the clientele for this new store, but for this report I need basic information on opening a new location." He then decides to start his research on the Internet. Figure 12.3 shows the results from this initial search. After that, he will research textbooks at the school bookstore and then end up at the library. He thinks that a librarian at the information desk can help him identify good sources and help him find some of the sources he has seen but can't track down.

After Josh reads the information on business plans from several sites that turned up in his search, he has a better idea of the topics he should research for his report. Topics might include describing the business opportunity, locations in the city, how the finances would work (including start-up costs for the new location), and an appendix with background information from the local Business and Community Association. He also eliminates several topics because he is not creating a business plan for Kay McKenzie but rather a document more closely tailored to her question about whether to expand into a west-coast city. This report will, in fact, precede a business plan. He decides to also collect data to use later for a convincing business plan that Kay can take to her bankers.

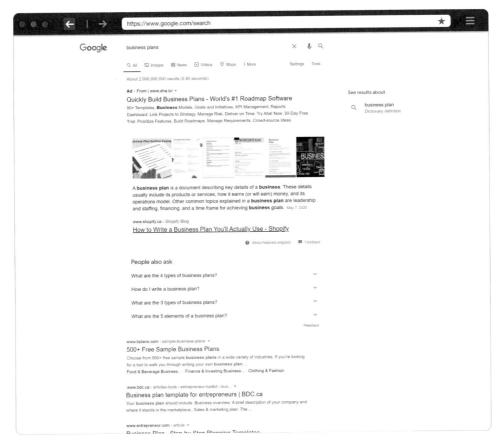

Figure 12.3 An initial search for information on business plans using Google brings up some useful links that help Josh get started.
Source: Screen capture of results from the Google search engine.

Once he knows what topics he should research for the report, Josh realizes that his job has barely begun. He also needs to research the local and provincial/state business scene. He can use the Internet to search for government- and business-related websites, as well as real-estate and financial websites, to gather the raw data he needs about the city as a site for Kay's business. He also hopes that he can figure out what areas of the city may be the best choices of location for a new unique gift shop.

ONLINE DATABASE SEARCH

Josh's review of the information on various business websites has given him a great starting point. However, he isn't going to stop with a review of websites; he will also search the databases at his school library to locate trade publications and academic journals for articles relevant to his project. He will search for business-related publications in one or two of these databases:

- ArticleFirst (FirstSearch)
- Factiva (Dow Jones)
- LexisNexis Academic (LexisNexis)

Access these databases by visiting your school library's webpages. You may need your school user ID and password to do the search. Some of these databases have full-text articles online; others contain abstracts of the articles. You will have to visit the library to find these journals or books from your online search.

Professional Communication Challenges 12.1

1. Write a report recommending whether Kay McKenzie should open a new store in a city of your choice on the west coast

Adopting the persona of Josh, write a research report for Kay McKenzie that evaluates whether she should open a second branch of Secret Garden Treasures and Gifts in the city you have chosen. As your instructor directs, write your report as either an analytical report (you make several recommendations based on your conclusion but do not specifically recommend one course of action) or a recommendation report (analyze the data and recommend to Kay McKenzie what you think she should do). Use the information in the case as well as the discussion in the chapter to help you write the report. Collect information from reputable websites to research the prospects for new businesses in the city, and use this information to help you decide what to recommend to Kay. Include relevant data about start-up costs, projected time period to profitability, and details about potential local, regional, or provincial programs that may help Kay develop her business. Also include graphs and charts, where appropriate, to display the costs and benefits of her proposed plan.

Audience: Kay McKenzie, owner of Secret Garden Treasures and Gifts

Purpose: To show her why the city you have chosen is/is not a favorable location for her new store

Genre: Formal report (analytical or recommendation)

2. Write a status report for Rhetorical Situation 12.1

Writing as Josh Irvine, write a status report for your boss, Kay McKenzie, reporting on the progress you've made so far on your research report. A status report is a persuasive document that demonstrates your competence, hard work, and ability to solve problems as an employee of the organization.

Audience: Your boss, Kay McKenzie

Purpose: To demonstrate to her that you are doing a good job of looking into the feasibility of opening a second store location in the city you chose on the west coast

Genre: Status report (for information on writing status reports, see Chapter 11)

Conduct two online searches, one using Internet search engines such as google.ca, yahoo.ca, or ask.com and one using three databases from your school library. Locate at least three useful website sources and three useful articles or books drawn from your database search. Use these sources to create an annotated bibliography. An annotated bibliography consists of two parts:

- citation information for each source
- summary and analysis of the useful content in each source

To create an annotated bibliography, carefully record the citation information for each source.

- *For print sources:* author, title of publication, publication information, publication date, page numbers
- *For online sources:* title of page, author (if listed), sponsoring organization, date page was posted, date you accessed the page, page numbers (if listed), complete URL

For the annotations, write at least two paragraphs:

- summarize the main content or argument of the webpage or article.
- analyze the ways in which you expect this source will be useful or is relevant to your project.

The sources that you select for your annotated bibliography should cover a variety of topics related to your report, including the specific content that you will need to write your report.

RESEARCH METHODS: PRIMARY SOURCES

Interviews

After he has collected as many relevant and useful print and online secondary sources as he can use, Josh Irvine decides to talk to some experts. People with expertise in the areas he has chosen will help him tailor the general information from the secondary sources to his specific situation—in this case, Kay's proposed business venture. He considers whom among his contacts he might talk to.

Whom to Interview: People with expertise are another potential source of information for any project. Josh generates a list of everyone he knows who is a good source of expertise, including acquaintances. He has taken several business courses in his program, so he identifies those instructors as individuals who can help him review the content to discuss in his report. However, they are busy people, so he must prepare carefully before the interview to ensure that it runs efficiently and on target. He also recalls that some websites from his earlier search had email or chat connections to ask an expert questions about business law and regulations in the state or province, entrepreneurship, and other topics. These contacts can also help him answer specific questions that arise as he assembles and interprets his data about business in the city.

---

80 per cent of a good interview is preparation:

- learn the basics of the subject matter
- learn your interview subject's areas of expertise
- write down an organized list of questions to direct the interview

---

Figure 12.4 **Prepare for interviews.**

The Interview Process: Josh had taken a journalism class in high school, so he knows the basics about interviewing (see Figure 12.4). He knows the three stages to a successful interview:

- preparing for the interview
- conducting the interview
- using the interview information

Educate Yourself: To prepare for the interviews, Josh considers what he wants to learn from each person during the interview and prepares a list of questions for each interview subject. He realizes that he must also do more research before the interview. If he goes into the interview already knowing the basics of, for example, business plans, he won't need to waste valuable time having his interview subject teach him. That way he can focus on asking more advanced questions that will improve his report quality. With background knowledge, he can generate more effective follow-up questions. As he thinks about gaps in his knowledge and whom to ask about which topic, Josh realizes that he doesn't know much about each person's areas of expertise. He decides to do a quick Internet search on each person to learn more about their interests and specialties so that he can make the best use of the interview time.

Prepare a List of Questions: When Josh feels knowledgeable about his subject matter and his interview subjects, he is ready to draft questions to help direct each interview (see Figure 12.5). He starts with the basic journalists' questions: Who? What? Where? When? Why? How? These general questions help generate more specific questions about the topics. Then he reviews his notes, assessing what he has omitted.

When he has exhausted his ideas about possible questions, Josh reviews the list and reorganizes the questions until they progress logically and smoothly through his research areas. Preparing his questions on the computer rather than writing them out by hand allows him to compose, arrange, and print the list to make a legible handout for the interview.

- ask questions that cannot be answered with a simple "yes" or "no"
- ask questions that you cannot find answers to somewhere else
- ask questions to help you understand difficult ideas or concepts
- include background, where necessary, to provide context to your questions

Figure 12.5 **Strategies for asking good questions.**

After filling in the blanks he saw after reviewing the project as a whole, Josh decides his list is ready:

1. He can cross out the questions as he works through them
2. He will use this list to control and direct the conversation to collect the information he needs
3. He has extra questions in case his interview subject answers efficiently and there is ample time at the end

When Josh feels prepared, he decides to schedule the interview. First he calls Dr. Spengler, the professor who taught his Issues and Innovations in Retailing class. When he connects to Dr. Spengler's voicemail, Josh leaves a clear, concise message requesting the hour-long interview, summarizing the subject of the interview and leaving his cell number to return the call. After disconnecting, Josh decides to email Dr. Spengler in case he doesn't check his messages regularly. Email will also give Josh the opportunity to more fully describe his goals for the interview.

 Exercise 12.2: Write an Email to Dr. Spengler Requesting an Interview

As Josh Irvine, draft an email to Dr. Spengler requesting an interview and explaining why you want to talk to him. Remember that Dr. Spengler is a busy person and may not feel he has an hour to talk to you, so consider and include some type of motivation to convince Dr. Spengler to agree to the interview.

Audience: Dr. Spengler, a business professor from a class you took last term

Purpose: To persuade him to grant you an hour-long interview

Genre: Persuasive email message

Length of the Interview: Josh asks Dr. Spengler for an hour-long interview because he has several complex topics to learn about. Josh feels he can persuade Dr. Spengler to talk to him for an hour, but any longer will be too great a time commitment. In addition, an hour of directed conversation, careful listening, and note taking is mentally draining. After an hour, neither he nor Dr. Spengler will be at their sharpest, and it is important not to waste his interviewee's time. If they have topics left to discuss at the end of the hour, Josh decides, he can schedule a follow-up interview.

Note Taking during the Interview: "Should I take notes or record these interviews?" Josh asks himself. Digitally recording an interview is much easier, especially if you have a digital recorder. Josh knows he can borrow a digital recorder from his cousin, but he also knows that it always takes 10 or 15 minutes to train the device to recognize the speaker's voice, and he isn't sure that his interview subjects will want to spend this time to get organized. "Do I want to take that time from my interview to set this up?" reflects Josh. However, the digital recorder will also eliminate transcribing time by converting the audio file into a text file, and it is easier to skim a printed page than handwritten notes to extract the important points from the interview. Then Josh remembers from an earlier class that the instructor had urged them to always take notes, whether they are recording an interview or not, in case the equipment fails. Josh finally decides that if he can borrow a digital recorder for the interviews, he will. Otherwise, he will take detailed notes during the interview.

Conducting the Interview: Josh makes sure he arrives at his interview with Dr. Spengler five minutes early. "Thanks for agreeing to talk to me, Dr. Spengler," he says as he shakes his former professor's hand. "I really appreciate you giving me a few minutes of your time to help me with this project for work. I have registered for your class on starting a small business in the fall term, but unfortunately I need to know more about it now."

"Well, I always enjoy seeing former students continue on with the work after they leave my class," says Dr. Spengler. "Why don't you check out the books that I've ordered for that class as possible sources for your report? A couple of them are really good and one even uses some examples from business in BC and in Washington."

"Great, I definitely will. I will also have a jump on the fall reading," notes Josh. "Let's start by me describing where I'm going with this report. Then I have some questions, but if something occurs to you while I'm talking, please interrupt me." He briefly describes Kay McKenzie's request; then he poses his first question: "Dr. Spengler, what would you say are the top three things someone starting up a new business should be wary of?"

As the other man talks, Josh listens carefully, noting in a word or two the important points being made. Josh decided to take notes and go back and fill in details as he remembered them immediately after the interview. He is careful to look up frequently, making eye contact with Dr. Spengler and nodding and smiling to convey that he is listening, he understands, and he is finding the information important. This kind of response is called *active listening*, and it lets the speaker know that you are engaged with their words (see Figure 12.6).

Josh is busy during the interview, listening carefully, thinking about what is said, formulating follow-up questions, and ensuring they cover the areas that he had identified in his preparation. Several times, when Dr. Spengler seems to drift off topic with a particularly complex point about economic theory, Josh tactfully brings him back to the main point, "Wow, Dr. Spengler, listening to your explanation of risk theory shows me how much I still have to learn. It is a fascinating area, isn't it? But what your explanation makes me wonder is whether and how we can use this predictive theory to minimize risk for the small business owner."

Josh is startled to see that his hour is up. He still has a few more questions, but a brief glance shows that he has answers already embedded in earlier questions. "This has been fantastic, Dr. Spengler. You have helped me so much, not only with what I need to know for this report, but what I want to know as I continue in this program. Thanks again for your time and your valuable expertise."

"You're very welcome, Josh," replies Dr. Spengler. "I have enjoyed thinking about some of these subjects in the context of an actual business in a real location."

"I think I understood everything you said pretty well," adds Josh. "But if I have questions as I look over my notes and try to apply your ideas to my research, would it be okay if I contact you for one or two things?"

"Yes, certainly," answers Dr. Spengler. He explains that he will be out of town the following week, however, so Josh should email him for a faster response.

"Again, thank you." Josh gathers his notes and papers as he leaves.

- make eye contact
- smile and nod
- where appropriate, rephrase what the speaker has said to show you understand his or her point

Figure 12.6 **Strategies for active listening.**

Using the Interview Information: Josh leaves Dr. Spengler's office and heads to the library. While details of the interview are still fresh, he reviews his notes and fills in points. After half an hour, he has recorded everything important that he can recall from the interview. He numbers all the pages and then writes Dr. Spengler's full name, official title and position, and the interview date on each page so that he can cite this information on his references page. He still needs to interview a second professor, as well as check out the books that Dr. Spengler mentioned. Then he will explore the online information he has gathered about small business regulations and incentives in the state/province in the context of ideas from the interview.

When Josh begins drafting his report, he uses the interview data collected in several ways:

- as evidence to support decisions he makes about how to proceed
- as a credible source, cited to support his recommendations about opening the new store location
- as an expert defining technical terms related to the report topic
- as summary of the method he chose to assemble his research

He reports some of his interview subject's comments directly through citations. He also summarizes the responses as background to clarify technical concepts or explain his process in answering Kay McKenzie's question.

Josh Irvine decides that survey research won't help him answer the question posed by Kay McKenzie. We turn now to a different scenario in which survey research is the only way to answer a supervisor's question. In the following case we meet An Kim, who is charged with determining the best choices for literacy events for young adults at a local community center.

Surveys

 Create and administer survey research and evaluate and analyze survey data

Surveys are useful for gathering opinions and ideas from a wide variety of people so that the survey results can be quantified (or counted) and, if possible, compared to other surveys. This is why, in Rhetorical Situation 12.2, Mr. Joshi suggests to An Kim that she survey the young adults in the local community. The advantages to using a survey are that you can reach a large number of different people, ask them the same questions, and count and compare their responses. Disadvantages to survey research are respondents' unwillingness to fill out the survey, their concerns about the confidentiality of their responses, and loaded survey questions that distort respondents' answers (see Figure 12.11). Unless you have a budget for conducting survey research that allows you to pay respondents, you have to consider how to motivate people to fill out your questionnaire. Think about the ways in which your gathering of information may benefit them so that they will donate their time and opinions.

One way to create an online survey is to use one of the websites listed in Figure 12.7 or one that you may already be familiar with. These websites allow you to generate a survey quickly and easily. With some providers (for example, SurveyMonkey, Qualtrics, SurveyGizmo), a basic survey of 10 questions is free; more advanced features may be purchased. The site's services include collecting and analyzing responses. You can create a mailing list inviting participants to complete your survey, and when you have finished gathering the data, you can download it in a spreadsheet or results report. Although they make parts of survey creation relatively simple, they do not create good survey questions for you, so you should know how to write good questions to gather the information needed for your report.

The following online survey sites allow you to create free trial versions or free short surveys of up to 10 questions:

SurveyMonkey: www.surveymonkey.com

Checkbox Technologies: www.checkbox.com

ESurveysPro: www.esurveyspro.com

ESurveysPro also offers a free trial version of their more expensive service.

Figure 12.7 **Online websites that offer free trial versions or free short survey options.**

Writing Good Questions: The heart of good survey research is writing good questions that get answers to help with your research. There are two types of questions to ask: **closed-ended questions** and **open-ended questions**. Closed-ended questions offer respondents a list of possible answers from which they can choose. You control the answers and respondents choose the one that best fits their situation. Open-ended questions ask respondents to use their own words and to explain why they hold the views they do. Open-ended questions allow respondents to give surprising or unanticipated answers. Figure 12.8 presents examples of open-ended and closed-ended survey questions.

closed-ended questions: Questions that require respondents to choose one of several answers provided by the survey

open-ended questions: Questions that leave a space for the respondent to fill in an answer in their own words

Open-ended survey questions	Closed-ended survey questions
1. What is the best gift that you've ever received?	1. How often do you visit a gift store to buy a present for someone? ☐ More than once a week ☐ Once a week ☐ Once a month ☐ Several times a year ☐ Never
2. Why was that gift the best one you've ever received?	2. What types of stores do you usually shop at to buy gifts for other people? ☐ Department stores ☐ Electronics stores ☐ Clothing stores ☐ Home furnishing stores ☐ Gift stores ☐ Other—Please list:_____

Figure 12.8 **Examples of open-ended and closed-ended survey questions.**

You can see from the examples in Figure 12.8 that closed-ended questions are the easiest to tabulate; you just count up the responses for each choice. The open-ended questions are more challenging because you have to decide how best to categorize and count many, perhaps quite different, responses. At the same time, open-ended questions give you more accurate information because respondents can choose the answer that best suits them; closed-ended questions force respondents to choose one predetermined answer that may not match their experience well.

Remember as you create survey questions that the more questions you ask, the more likely it is that respondents will not complete or return the questionnaire. Similarly, open-ended questions take more time and effort for respondents because they have to formulate an answer and write it down. Checking boxes is much faster and easier. To increase the chance that more people complete your survey, limit your use of open-ended questions. Use them to identify the most important information that you need to know.

DOs AND DON'Ts FOR QUESTION WRITING

Do Use Plain Language to Ask Questions: Avoid complex sentence structure and use **plain language** to make questions easy and fast to understand. In Figure 12.9, the first question uses undefined technical terms yet asks responders to make a choice. Some people would have to guess at their answer. The revised question explains without technical language the choices open to the respondent.

Too technical: (Check one.) Would you prefer an employee pension plan with

_____ a defined benefit or

_____ a defined contribution?

Better: (Check one.) Would you prefer an employee pension plan that

_____ sends you a check for a specified amount of money each month after you retire?

_____ deposits a set amount of money each month before you retire into a mutual fund that you select?

Figure 12.9 **Undefined technical terms can produce inaccurate responses.**

Do Ask Specific Questions: Ask questions that respondents know how to answer. Vague or ambiguous questions force them to make up answers or abandon your survey because they do not understand what you want. Figure 12.10 forces readers to stop and consider the question.

Ambiguous question: Do you ride the bus because it's too far to walk, because of bad weather, or safety concerns? Yes _____ No _____

Clear question: Which reasons apply to your decision to ride the bus? (Check all that apply.)

_____ I ride because it is too far to walk.

_____ I ride when the weather is too cold or too wet.

_____ I ride to ensure my personal safety.

Figure 12.10 **Ask questions clearly.**

Loaded question: Have you ever received a single gift that you liked?

Neutral question: Generally, how happy have you been with most of the gifts that you have received?

Figure 12.11 **Use neutral language to gather unbiased responses.**

Don't Ask Loaded Questions: Loaded questions are ones that signal to your respondents how you want them to answer. In Figure 12.11, the first question steers respondents to respond critically; the revised second question uses neutral language. Neutral language gathers unbiased responses.

Don't Ask Several Questions in One Sentence: Do not phrase questions so they ask more than one thing in the same sentence. Such questions often offer one area of response so respondents cannot tell to which part of the question the answer corresponds (see Figure 12.12).

Multiple questions in one: Should Secret Garden stock more gift ideas or more artwork?

Multiple questions subdivided:
- gifts
- artwork
- books

Figure 12.12 **Multiple questions should be asked separately.**

Creating Good Responses: The second half of writing good survey questions is creating suitable responses. Of course, you only need to provide responses with closed-ended questions. Choose from several options for responses:

- yes/no answers
- rating scales
- comparative rating scales
- category scales

Yes/no answers require respondents to check "yes" or "no" in response to the question. Figure 12.13 presents a list of options that respondents can answer "yes" to by checking the box or "no" by leaving it blank. As you can see in this example, you can obtain a lot of information from one question if you use some ingenuity and format it as a list.

1. Which types of stores have you shopped at in the last year to buy a gift for someone? Check all that apply.

☐ department store

☐ electronics store

☐ clothing store

☐ home furnishing store

☐ gift store

☐ bookstore

☐ other—please list:_____

Figure 12.13 **Yes/no questions generate a lot of information.**

Rating scales enable respondents to represent their responses using numbers. The number represents the strength of their response. Scales allow these options:

■ choose one of the listed numerical responses
■ give a number to the responses listed
■ select among a range of numbers
■ select a number that corresponds to a word or phrase that describes the response

Likert scales (a kind of rating scale) traditionally use a five-point range, although other ranges, such as seven and nine, are also possible. Represent the intervals as a list or on a line graph with numbers. Figure 12.14 shows two Likert scales, one that uses a numbered line and the other a numbered list.

2. This neighborhood needs more specialty stores.

1. Strongly agree
2. Agree
3. Neither agree nor disagree
4. Disagree
5. Strongly disagree

1	2	3	4	5
Strongly agree	Agree	Neither agree nor disagree	Disagree	Strongly disagree

Figure 12.14 **Two layouts for a Likert scale response. The first one is a numbered list; the second one is a numbered line.**

Business Communication: Rhetorical Situations

Comparative rating scales allow respondents to rank their responses. Figure 12.15 is an example of a comparative rating scale.

3. Please rate your three favorite types of gifts to give:

_____   Books

_____   Music

_____   Clothing

_____   Travel

_____   Kitchen items

_____   Tools

_____   Furniture

_____   Cash

_____   Artwork

Figure 12.15 **A comparative scale asks respondents to identify the types of gifts they prefer to give.**

Categories provide general ranges of answers for people to select. For example, you may not be able to calculate exactly how many gifts you give in a particular month, but you likely have a general sense and could fit yourself into a scale that identifies categories such as "frequently," "occasionally," or "almost never."

Choose Your Survey Medium: You have several choices for distributing your survey. You can post it online using a site such as SurveyMonkey.com, you can distribute print copies, or you can use telephone conversations. Whichever method you choose, prepare your questions so they are clear and easy to understand. Use the tips in Figure 12.16 to prepare your questionnaire.

Reporting Survey Data: After creating your survey, you need to locate those people who will respond to it. If you use a print survey, you can leave copies of it in a public place for respondents to pick up and fill in. Be sure to include information on how to return the form to you. If you want to survey a particular population, you must decide how to contact those people and how many you can afford to contact. Keep track of who returns the survey so you know what your response rate is. The higher the number of people who respond to your survey, the better quality your data will be.

Open-ended survey questions produce **qualitative data**—data that are not easily counted but add important details. To tabulate qualitative data, read through the answers looking for patterns and group similar responses together. Qualitative data give a context to the numeric patterns arising from quantitative data. If many respondents give you the same answers to a question, these data are considered quantitative because you can count them. Answers to closed-ended

qualitative data: Data that answers research questions through words, stories, and observations

quantitative data:
Data that can be represented in numbers, tables, and charts

questions are **quantitative data** as well. For closed-ended questions, count the totals to each answer and write the totals directly onto a blank survey sheet. Look for patterns in your data that help you generalize your results. When you use quantitative data in your report, present the data in a table or graph so readers can see the patterns that you think are important.

- Give the survey a title.
- Write a short introduction to encourage respondents to finish the survey.
- Order your questions from easy or factual to more complex to create the feeling that the survey will be fast to answer.
- Leave space for respondents to write answers to open-ended questions.
- Edit the survey form to include only questions you really need answers to.
- Leave lots of white space so the form looks inviting.

Figure 12.16 **Tips for preparing survey forms.**

Look for ways to present data from surveys that illustrate the points you want to argue in your report. Graphs and charts compare survey answers so your readers can see the significance of your findings.

Exercise 12.3: Create a Survey to Identify the Gift-Giving Practices of People in Your Age Group

In groups of two or three people, create a one-page survey that helps you gather information about the gift-giving practices of students at your institution. Use the information in the previous section to help you design a persuasive, easy-to-fill-out questionnaire that respondents want to answer.

Audience: Your classmates as potential respondents

Purpose: To create a well-designed survey

Genre: Survey

Rhetorical Situation 12.2: Collecting Survey Data to Write a Report for a Nonprofit Organization

An Kim, who works part time at the Ritchie Community Center and is a full-time Humanities major at Ritchie College, says hello to the center manager, Mahavira Joshi. Mahavira asks how her day is going and thanks her for going out of her way to find him. He says he has just heard that the Ritchie Community Center has been awarded a $3,000 government grant to hold a series of events for young adults at the drop-in program at the center.

Business Communication: Rhetorical Situations

An is tempted to offer Mahavira a high five in celebration but thinks better of it. Instead, she offers an exuberant "Congratulations!"

Mahavira appreciates An's enthusiasm. He then explains the terms of the award: that any events paid for by the grant have to be related to literacy in some way and they have to bring young people ages 15 to 20 (more or less) to the center. He says that he has no idea of the interests of this age group, so that's where he hopes An can help with research. His idea is that a survey of this group may help to find out what they think is cool, what may bring them to the center.

An agrees, noting that there are several online survey sites they can use, such as Qualtrics and SurveyGizmo. Mahavira says he likes the idea of an online survey, thinking that it might fit that age group—that it is free is a big benefit too. Mahavira asks if An can prepare a report on the survey results for the board of directors. He doesn't want a big report, just an informal but informative one to circulate in advance of the board meeting to be held next month. He wants to present the members with a range of options so they can make the final decision.

An says that she can email the survey to some of the students at her school, maybe also put it out to some of her social media contacts. If it is a short survey, An says that she thinks most of her group will be likely to fill it out right away.

This sounds good to Mahavira. He suggests that perhaps she can work with Ben Dunwoody on this. Mahavira thinks that between An and Ben they can brainstorm some initial suggestions for activities for the survey. He adds that perhaps their friends on social media can also add input on what would be exciting to generate even better ideas. An thanks him for the suggestion and says she will look for Ben.

Mahavira tells An that he is looking forward to reading the report, noting that it is great to have the grant money to promote the center's mission. He adds that if An has any problems or questions to let him know and he will do what he can to help.

 Exercise 12.4: Create a Survey for Ritchie Community Center

Writing as An Kim or Ben Dunwoody, create a one-page survey that you can use to gather information about literacy-related social activities that 15- to 20-year-olds would find appealing. If you wish, you can use one of the web survey sites to create an online survey for this exercise (see Figure 12.7). Use the information on creating good survey questions to help you develop a survey that this demographic would want to fill out and that will provide you with insights as to the activities this group would want to support. Make sure your questionnaire will provide you with information that would help you write the report described by Mahavira in Rhetorical Situation 12.2.

Audience: 15- to 20-year-olds who are interested in cool literacy-related activities

Purpose: To persuade this demographic to give you useful and interesting ideas for activities they would spend time attending

Genre: Survey (up to 10 questions)

WRITING THE REPORT

 Format and draft a research report

Analyze the Research Results

When you have gathered the information you need, the next step is to analyze it to find a solution. You may have already developed a sense of the solution to the problem as you did your research. In Rhetorical Situation 12.1, Josh Irvine has two questions to answer: 1) Should Kay McKenzie open a second location on the west coast?, and 2) What would be the best location for the new store? Josh likely already has a sense of the first answer based on his research, but the answer to the question about location may or may not be obvious. Without actually visiting the areas, he can only guess, but telephone conversations with two or three commercial real-estate agents about possible hot locations in the city will give him some expertise to draw on.

You may already have a strong sense of what you want to say in the report, but you should still study your research carefully to ensure that you recommend the best solution. Set up criteria as you analyze your information to ensure you remember the top priorities for the solution.

Identify Appropriate Evidence

A report is an argument to persuade readers of the validity of your recommendations, so identify persuasive evidence in your results that supports your discussion. Even information reports use financial and other types of data to develop graphs or charts that illustrate and support their conclusions. If appropriate, include photographs or drawings to illustrate details that build your case. Reports should offer multiple ways for readers to understand the information that you've gathered. For example, Josh Irvine can include maps of the neighborhoods he recommends as well as graphical representations of financial data to support his recommendations.

Draft the Report

The report does not have to be drafted in order. Start with whatever topic seems easiest to write about. Once you have written a complete draft, you can work on making the sections fit together coherently.

FORMATS FOR RESEARCH REPORTS

Direct Organizational Pattern

A research report is a multi-page document that presents the information that readers need in order to understand the problem and solution that you propose. It consists of conventional sections that accomplish different goals. These sections should be ordered according to your readers' attitudes toward your report and its findings. For example, if readers have a positive attitude toward your subject matter (say, your boss has followed your project, approved early suggested results, and now eagerly awaits your final recommendations), choose a direct pattern of organization that places conclusions and recommendations up front in the report, immediately following the executive summary.

Figure 12.17 shows a direct organizational pattern. Use this pattern if you believe readers will respond positively to your report. For example, if Josh Irvine decides that Kay McKenzie should definitely open a new location for Secret Garden in Vancouver, he would likely use a direct pattern of organization because he can expect, from her initial enthusiasm, that she supports this recommendation. If, however, he decides to recommend against a Vancouver location, he might use a different organizational pattern to show her why the expansion is a potentially bad idea. In this case, he would use an indirect pattern.

- executive summary
- conclusions/recommendations
- introduction/purpose/problem
- background
- research methods
- findings or results
- implications (what does this mean?)
- appendices (sources; raw data; supplementary charts, graphs, or tables; etc.)

Figure 12.17 **A direct organizational pattern for an analytical or recommendation report.**

Indirect Organizational Pattern

An indirect pattern of organization defers the conclusions and recommendations of the report until the logical end. This indirect pattern allows you to work through the problem, analyze your data and research, and demonstrate in a clear, logical manner that your conclusion is solid and not easily refuted by opposing viewpoints. This pattern shows and persuades readers at the same time that the outcome they resist supporting is, in fact, the best one. See Figure 12.18 for an example of an indirect pattern of organization for a report.

- executive summary
- introduction/purpose/problem
- background
- research methods
- findings or results
- implications (what does this mean?)
- conclusions/recommendations
- appendices (sources; raw data; supplementary charts, graphs, or tables; etc.)

Figure 12.18 **An indirect pattern of organization for an analytical or recommendation report.**

REPORT SECTION CONTENT

Whether you use a direct or indirect pattern of organization for your report, include the following types of information in sections of the report as listed. This overview follows an indirect pattern of organization, presenting the writer's conclusions and recommendations at the end, after they have made the case for the analysis presented.

- The *executive summary* or *abstract* briefly summarizes the report subject. It presents the recommendations made in the report and the reasons for these recommendations. It briefly describes the topics discussed in the report and the depth to which you discuss them. As you organize the information in your abstract, choose a method that fits the information you want to convey in this section.

- The *introduction/purpose/problem* is part of the main body of the report that summarizes the project. It explains the report's purpose and describes the problem that the report solves.

- The *background* updates readers on the history of the problem and relevant information that helps them understand your discussion and your solution(s) to the problem.

- The *research methods* section describes the methods used to collect the information presented in the report. If you used interviews or surveys to gather information, this section of the report provides the details that readers need to evaluate the validity of your results. This section should convince readers that you've used sound research principles so that they can feel confident about the reliability of the solution(s) you recommend.

- The *findings* or *results* section presents the information you found. Often this section includes graphical representations of data to display trends and insights based on your research. Use graphs to show patterns to readers and to turn the raw numbers into information that readers can easily process and understand. If you conducted a survey or interview, present the data or information relevant to your solution. See Chapter 13 for more information about turning raw data into visuals that readers can understand. Usually this section does not interpret or explain your data. The explanation and interpretation come in the next section of the report, the implications. This pattern borrows from that used in scientific research reports, where results are discussed separately from the arguments about their significance. This separation allows readers to assess the results without having the writer overtly shape those results. Include relevant results, but not every result. Be aware that readers look for mention of negative results as well as positive ones. They want to learn from what you have done so they can avoid making similar mistakes.

- The *implications* section interprets your results and explains what they mean. If necessary, repeat or refine charts and graphs to highlight the significance of your results. When you explain why they are significant, you transform your information into knowledge that readers can use to shape their actions. Also describe any limitations on your results.

- The *conclusions* and *recommendations* may be discussed together or separately. The conclusion does not usually introduce new ideas or insights; instead, it summarizes the main points of the report. Use paragraphs or a numbered list to remind readers of the important conclusions reached in the report. When discussing your recommendations, list the action items you recommend to solve the problem. Your action items are new information, so explain why you chose this course of action and why it will be effective. Readers also expect you to use your experience on this topic to recommend actions on related decisions and to comment on future research or activities related to this project, so don't cut your discussion of recommendations short.

- *Appendices* include information supplementary to the report, such as completed survey forms, analyses of data, lists of works cited, references, or notes. If your material for the appendix is extensive, consider subdividing it into several appendices for quick reference. One appendix is sufficient if the only item in it is a reference list.

FORMATTING CONCLUSIONS AND RECOMMENDATIONS

As you draft your conclusions and recommendations, consider the best way to format these on the page to draw your reader's attention to them. Consider pulling out one or more bullet points that concisely summarize the main points. Readers can skim the bullet points to decide whether to read further.

Format your recommendations as bullet points or a numbered list. If the conclusions are self-explanatory, the list may be all you need. However, if readers need additional information or you want to persuade them to accept your recommendation, include some concise elaboration to accompany the bullet point. Figure 12.19 shows examples of both formatted and unformatted conclusion and recommendation sections. Consider which one a busy reader would prefer to receive.

The underlying persuasive message of your report should demonstrate your knowledge of correct research methods, your ability to follow those methods to collect accurate and useful data, and your ability to organize and interpret this information. Aim to communicate the reliability of your research so that readers trust it as a foundation for good decisions.

Example 1

Conclusions and Recommendations

This report demonstrates that we can solve the problem of budget overruns on department photocopying if we monitor more closely who is making copies and how many copies each person makes. Though it is impractical to have individuals self-report their photocopying usage (we have tried this approach but found large discrepancies between the hand-recorded numbers and the electronic tally on the machines) or to assign an employee to oversee photocopying, we can install a device that requires user ID and password before individuals can access the machine. The device will track who makes copies and how many copies they make. Barb can oversee this usage, query those who make excessive copies, and monitor the copy budget. We recommend the purchase of either a tracking device that is compatible with our current photocopier (see appendix A for two choices available) or the purchase of a new photocopier that has this software already installed (see appendix A for machines available).

Example 2

Conclusions

- We must monitor photocopier usage more closely.
- Self-reporting and employee surveillance have been unsuccessful in the past.
- Purchase of new technology will enable electronic monitoring and recording of copier use.
- Our choices:
  a. Buy a device to restrict copier use that fits on our current copier.
  b. Purchase a new copier with limited access software installed.

Recommendations

1. Purchase limited access software that is compatible with our current copier.
2. Issue user IDs and passwords to all employees.

Figure 12.19 Example 1 buries conclusions in a paragraph, whereas Example 2 highlights the main ideas in bullet points.

The Languages of the Report Genre

Reports are a genre (type of document) that employs different discourses or kinds of language in each section. For example, the executive summary uses the discourse of the generalist, giving a concise overview of the highlights of the report. This means that readers need no specialized or technical knowledge of the subject matter to understand the report abstract. When readers move to a different part of the report, however, they may have to know more about the subject matter. For example, the discussion of research methods (how the writer gathered the data presented in the report) requires writers to speak as researchers by employing the technical terms necessary to show their methods of collecting data are sound. Therefore, when reading the research methods, readers must also read as a researcher so they can evaluate the writers' methods.

The language of a report shifts again in the results and findings section when writers speak as scientists. They discuss the important data and results and use graphs and charts to highlight the relationships that are relevant to the report subject matter.

In the implications section of a report, writers switch their language again to use the discourse of finance. They talk about what the statistics and graphs in the results section mean to demonstrate that the solution they propose is both feasible (it can be done) and superior (it is better than other possible solutions). Financial language allows writers to highlight the cost-effectiveness of their solution (why it makes financial sense to choose the recommended solution). In situations where money is not the primary factor—for example, in government or nonprofit organizations—report writers use the language of ethics to highlight the moral soundness of the proposed solution(s).

Assess how well you've made these changes in discourse as you evaluate your draft in the process of revisions. You want to become skilled at shifting among different types of language, because the more smoothly you do so, the more convincing your readers will find your argument.

Another characteristic of the report genre is that it uses repetition. Reports summarize the same information at specific points throughout. For example, the abstract summarizes report highlights. Readers skim the abstract to discover the main recommendations that also appear in greater detail in the recommendations section. You can use the prose that you've drafted for one section in another section without worrying about repetition; only minor revisions might be needed. Once you have drafted the recommendations, for example, you can reuse your text to write the abstract.

 Exercise 12.5: Analyze the Discourse in Different Sections of an Annual Report

An annual report is a good choice for illustrating how dramatically the discourse shifts from one section of a report to another.[1]

1. Read the three sample texts reproduced from the October 2014 Report of the Auditor for the Government of Alberta. Excerpt 1 (Figure 12.20) reproduces the first three paragraphs of the Auditor General's Message. Excerpt 2 (Figure 12.21) reproduces the Auditor General's discussion of "What we examined" and "What we found." Excerpt 3 (Figure 12.22) reproduces a more detailed discussion from page 204 of the report, where the Auditor General explains specific findings about the SIVPP (Statement of Investment Valuation Principles and Practices). In small groups or individually, examine the different features of discourse that you observe in each excerpt.

---

1   Vijay Bhatia, "Discourses of and in International Arbitration Practices across Cultures and Socio-Political Boundaries," unpublished presentation, Conference of the Canadian Association of Teachers of Technical Writing, Vancouver, BC, 3 June 2008.

Auditor General's Message

We want to reiterate the message from our July 2014 public report regarding the need for improved results analysis reporting. This October 2014 report provides further evidence of that need—seniors care and the joint Canada–Alberta plan for oil sands monitoring.

The purpose of results analysis is to learn from what you do, so that you can do better in the future. Reporting those results helps Albertans understand what the government is achieving and how it might improve. Our July 2014 report provided a framework for three inseparable elements: governance, oversight and accountability for results. We urge users of our public reports to revisit the July 2014 report.

Good leadership encourages a clear analysis of results for significant matters, including priority initiatives. We cannot ask those we audit to tell Albertans whether they are achieving results as planned, if we do not do the same ourselves. We include our Results Analysis Report 2014 in this report (page 217).

Source: October 2014, Report of the Auditor General of Alberta, http://www.oag.ab.ca/webfiles/reports/October%202014%20Report.pdf

Figure 12.20 **Excerpt 1.**

What we examined

Our audit objective was to assess the nature and quality of the first annual report (2012–2013) on the joint plan for monitoring oil sands development. We also assessed whether the results the two governments shared in the report were complete and verifiable, based on evidence that was sufficient and appropriate. To assess the quality of that evidence, we looked at the processes the department used in 2012–2013 to manage the projects for which it was responsible.

What we found

The governments of Alberta and Canada jointly released their first annual report long after the information it contained was current.

The report for 2012–2013 was released in June 2014, 15 months after the March 31, 2013 end of the first year. The 2013–2014 report on the second year of implementation has not yet been released.

The report lacked clarity and key information and contained inaccuracies. The report was not clear on:

- whether overall implementation of the plan was on track
- which of the projects committed to for 2012–2013 were completed, partly completed or not completed
- what remained to be done to implement the governments' key commitments

Source: October 2014, Report of the Auditor General of Alberta, http://www.oag.ab.ca/webfiles/reports/October%202014%20Report.pdf

Figure 12.21 **Excerpt 2.**

Similar to the accounting standards, the SIVPP also requires that day-one gains only be recognized where management can support the valuation increase through comparison to similar transactions in an observable market. We concluded that management's practice of revaluing the life settlements immediately after purchase did not comply with AIMCo's SIVPP.

All of the $325 millions of unrealized gains on these investments, up to December 31, 2013, originated from revaluing the investments through a change to the discount rate, which was different than the internal rate of return implicit in the purchase prices. Management and their agents were unable to provide adequate support for the change to the discount rate that is required by the accounting standards.

Aside from the discount rate, life expectancy is another key variable in estimating the value of the life settlements. Management has not yet reviewed whether the life expectancy assumptions underlying the valuations should also be updated.

Source: October 2014, Report of the Auditor General of Alberta, http://www.oag.ab.ca/webfiles/reports/ October%202014%20Report.pdf

Figure 12.22 **Excerpt 3.**

2. Answer the following questions:

- Who is the audience for this passage?
- What is the purpose of each passage?
- What does each passage tell you about the genre of annual report? In other words, what can you learn about the reports as a genre or type of document based on this example?
- What kind of language is used in each excerpt? In other words, what voice does the writer use in each excerpt? Does he/she speak as an expert? A generalist? A researcher? A scientist? Does this voice change from one excerpt to the next?
- Do you need any kind of specialized knowledge to understand the discussion? Identify specific technical terms that the writer uses. What does this vocabulary tell you about the writer, the subject matter, and the writer's relationship to the reader?
- How does the language change from one excerpt to the next?
- Why do you think this change in language is important to the annual report as a genre?

3. As your instructor directs, either record enough details from your group's discussion to summarize the main points that came up in your group and present them to the whole class, or write a one-page analysis of your comparison of the discourse used in each excerpt. Make sure you answer the questions listed in item 2 above and hand in your analysis as your instructor requests.

© Antonio Guillem/Shutterstock

1. Write the informal analytical report for Ritchie Community Center Board of Directors

Distribute the survey that you created in Exercise 12.4 to the young adults at your school or at a local shopping area to gather responses. Aim for a total of 25 to 30 completed surveys. Use the discussion in this chapter to help you tabulate and analyze your survey responses. Write the informal report requested by Mahavira Joshi, using the responses generated by your survey. As your instructor directs, create an analytical or recommendation report. Direct the report to the members of the Ritchie Community Center Board of Directors. As Mahavari requested, describe, summarize, and analyze the responses of your respondents. You should evaluate the options suggested in the survey results and recommend several courses of action, but do not recommend one best activity to the board (unless your instructor directs you to do so). Provide enough information about the options that the board can make an informed and wise choice in spending the grant money (or feel secure that your recommendation is the best choice).

Audience: Mahavira Joshi and the members of the Ritchie Community Center Board of Directors

Purpose: To present the results from the survey in a report format that will allow members of the board to make good choices on how to spend the $3,000 grant money

Genre: Formal report (analytical or recommendation, depending on your instructor's choice)

2. Write an informal informational report on gift-giving practices

Distribute the survey that you created in Exercise 12.3 to a selection of students on your campus. Aim for a total of 25 to 30 completed surveys. Use the discussion in the earlier section of this chapter on analyzing survey data to help you tabulate and interpret your survey responses. Using the information in the earlier sections on writing a report, write an informal information report describing and analyzing the gift-giving practices of the students at your institution. Direct this report to your instructor and classmates.

Audience: Your instructor and classmates

Purpose: To provide readers with information and insight about the gift-giving practices of a selection of students at your post-secondary institution

Genre: Informal information report

RESEARCH REPORTS AND OFFICE POLITICS

 Understand and manage the political elements of writing a business report

Report writing never takes place in a vacuum. Even if the report is written by one person, it should be a collaborative effort to be successful. Collaboration comes into play through two avenues: first, most report writers need information from other employees for their research (e.g., An must work with Ben to develop the survey at Ritchie Community Center); and second, the writers want fellow employees to support their ideas. In most workplaces, business proceeds smoothly if the right people are consulted on a project. If you are writing a report, do not write it in isolation. Study your organization to identify whom you should consult at each stage of the development process. Should your boss see a draft of the report, or should you discuss your findings with him or her as you develop them? If you need input from fellow employees, what is the most persuasive way to ask for their help? Discuss your ideas with colleagues so they can contribute if they want to.

If you are solving a problem in the report, your coworkers will implement the solution. If they don't support your ideas, they will not act. If you bring them into the process, even at an advisory level, you help ensure that they stay involved and have chances to provide feedback. They are likely to welcome your solution because they helped develop it. Inexperienced writers who single-handedly solve a problem often find their report collecting dust on a shelf because, although their work is excellent, it ignored the office hierarchies that promote or suppress good ideas. As you write your report, consult others. If you develop a plan that they may have to act on later, discuss the plan with them early to gain their approval and support. Another bonus is that your solution is likely to improve when your coworkers offer feedback and suggestions that force you to think harder about your ideas.

CHAPTER SUMMARY

- Research reports pose a problem or question that needs a solution or answer. Solve the problem and answer the question through the use of print and online sources, interviews with subject-matter experts, and surveys of the population to gather opinions and preferences.
- Record complete citation information as you locate sources.
- Evaluate the reliability of your print and online sources.
- Surveys allow you to gather opinions and ideas from a variety of people so that you can count the results and compare them to other survey results.
- Analyze the research results, identify appropriate evidence, and draft and format the research report.
- Shift discourses as you write the different sections of a research report.
- Repeat information as necessary throughout the report.
- Work with others to build support for your report.

CHAPTER 13

Design and Visuals in Business and Professional Communication

LEARNING OUTCOMES

1. Design and present information effectively
2. Select appropriate stories for presentation through visuals
3. Present visual information accurately, ethically, and effectively

GETTING STARTED

A useful component of business and professional communication is page design, which structures information visually so that readers can easily skim the document and locate key information. This chapter introduces you to four useful techniques for presenting information effectively: the effective use of white space, descriptive headings, lists for multiple ideas, and visuals to highlight data and concepts. All four of these techniques are essential components of business and professional communication documents.

The first Rhetorical Situation introduces you to George Morawska, who realizes that a fact sheet would help him serve customers and boost sales at his YourPhone Kiosk location. Good fact-sheet design requires attention to several important aspects of document and information design, including choosing the correct format for information and knowing the basic aspects of designing documents.

In the second Rhetorical Situation you will meet Sen Wang, a forestry student and summer intern with the federal government, who needs to create a brochure to educate members of the general public about the pine-beetle infestation in parts of western North America and what they can do to help prevent the beetle's eastward spread. This section shows you how to translate scientific information into visual images to ensure it reaches the broadest possible audience. Visuals include graphs, charts, tables, photographs, drawings, and so on. To communicate visually with readers, writers should choose a story to communicate through each visual. This section helps you understand how to select appropriate stories and graphs and to present information accurately and ethically.

DOCUMENT FORMAT AND DESIGN IN PROFESSIONAL COMMUNICATION

 Design and present information effectively

Basic Components of Document Design

In business and professional communication, attend to how you place information on the page. Each document you write has a purpose, and readers pick the document up with a goal in mind. How you present your information directly affects whether you and your readers achieve your goals.

Here are four techniques for presenting information that will help your readers quickly grasp your meaning:

1. use white space to emphasize important points
2. use headings that stand out
3. use lists to emphasize multiple ideas
4. include visuals that make data and concepts easily accessible

USE WHITE SPACE

White space refers to the parts of the page that do not contain text or visuals. Arrange headings, visuals, and text on the page so that the white space around them makes them stand out. For example, the fact sheet in Figure 13.1 uses space between the columns, around the bullet point list, and around the photographs to emphasize the information in each grouping. Figure 13.2 uses white space around the text, images, and table so that it is easy to see the different parts of the information sheet. Visually, it makes you want to review the figures and learn more about "Youth Risk Behavior."

white space: The parts of the page that do not contain text or visuals

USE HEADINGS THAT STAND OUT

Subdivide your information into chunks and put a descriptive heading at the beginning of each chunk. The headings should tell readers what the section covers.

Choose a typeface for your headings that contrasts with the main text typeface and that is easy to read. Type is organized into families:

- Serif
- Sans-serif
- Slab serif
- Script
- Decorative

Serif typefaces include Times New Roman, Garamond, and Baskerville. Their distinguishing feature is that each letter sits on little feet, or serifs, that clearly define the ends of the letters. Serif typefaces are the easiest to read in a print document.

Sans-serif typefaces are those such as Calibri, **Arial**, Century Gothic, and **Helvetica**. These typefaces lack the feet, or serifs, of the serif typefaces. These typefaces give a cleaner, crisper look than serif ones, but they are harder to read in print. Online, sans-serif typefaces are easier to read and are therefore preferable in that environment.

Slab serif typefaces have broad, heavy serifs. For example, **Cooper**, American Typewriter, and `Courier` are slab serif typefaces.

Script typefaces are the ones that look like handwriting or printing—for example, *Apple Chancery*, *Brush Script*, and *Bradley Hand*. Script typefaces can add character and tone to your document, but some script typefaces are hard to read, so choose carefully.

Decorative typefaces are the ones that are eye-catching but difficult to read, for example, 𝔘𝔫𝔦𝔣𝔯𝔞𝔨𝔱𝔲𝔯 𝔐𝔞𝔤𝔫𝔲𝔱𝔦𝔞, **Braggadocio**, and *Zapfino*. Never use a decorative typeface for more than a word or two in a document. Because of their illegibility, they are not a good choice for your title and headings, but they can add style and pizzazz if you use them properly.

How do you choose? To create an attractive contrast between the text of your document and the titles and headings, select a typeface from one "family" for the text and one from a different family for the title and headings. Research has shown that serif typefaces, such as Baskerville and

Times New Roman, are good choices for the body text of a document because most people are easily able to read them. Typefaces from the other families are more difficult to read. So choose an attractive serif typeface, such as **Cambria** or Garamond, for the body text, and then choose a more dramatic typeface such as *Apple Chancery* or **Helvetica** for your headings. When making your choice, always consider the purpose of your document, the context for your communication, and your readers. For example, a typeface like **Bradley Hand** adds an informal touch to your document—is an informal touch appropriate to the situation for which you are writing? Make a choice that suits your message.

Typeface choices can be contrasting (they are visually different from each other) or conflicting (they are slightly different from one another). A contrasting choice means choosing typefaces from different font families (serif, sans serif, slab serif, script, or decorative), such as Garamond (serif) and *Apple Chancery* (script); they are VERY different. A conflicting choice means choosing two typefaces from the same font family (e.g., two different script fonts) so they are only slightly different and not significantly different (for example, **Bradley Hand** and *Cavolini*), leaving readers to wonder whether the writer clicked on the wrong choice when formatting the document text.

Exercise 13.1: Identifying Typeface Families

Which typeface family does each of the following belong to? Serif? Sans Serif? Script? Decorative?

1. Courier
2. **COPPERPLATE**
3. Harrington
4. **Bradley Hand**
5. **Playbill**
6. Baskerville
7. *Brush Script*
8. **Blackoak**
9. Eurostile

Exercise 13.2: Evaluating Contrasting or Conflicting Typefaces

Do these typeface combinations contrast or conflict? Identify which typeface family each word belongs to, and then decide whether the choices contrast or conflict (contrast is good; conflict is bad). Which typeface family does each of the following belong to? Serif? Sans Serif? Script? Decorative?

1. *Free* **STUFF**
2. **Blissful Ignorance**
3. Delicious **Garbage**
4. Recommended **Solutions**
5. *Willfully* Inadequate
6. Surprisingly **Interesting**

Business Communication: Rhetorical Situations

USE LISTS TO EMPHASIZE MULTIPLE IDEAS

One habit to form in business and professional communication is to format the text as a list whenever you place three or more items in sequence. For example, Figure 13.1 uses a bulleted list for the seven areas where genetically modified organisms are allowed for use in Australia. The formatting emphasizes the permissible uses through the bullet mark and the surrounding white space.

Note the conventions for formatting lists:

- If the order of the items in the list is important, number them
- If the order doesn't matter, use bullet points

USE VISUALS

Visuals are an essential part of business and professional communication. Look for places in your document where you can place a visual (an image, graph, diagram, or drawing) to improve your reader's understanding of your subject matter. You can use these to improve the overall look of your document by adding visual interest. But visuals are so much more useful than just acting as decoration in business and professional communication. Use them as part of your argument—facts and statistics are often much clearer when presented in a graph or table. When you depict statistics in a graph, for example, you make choices about what parts of the data to emphasize by adjusting the scale of the x and y axis. See the second half of this chapter for more information on creating and using visuals.

Exercise 13.3: Evaluating Page Layout in Business and Professional Documents

Collect four or five examples of business and professional writing documents. Examine each one and analyze the use of the following:

- white space
- contrasting headings
- lists
- visuals

Write two or three paragraphs evaluating how effectively the various elements are used in laying out the document. Include specific examples of layout that you think are well done, as well as specific examples that could be improved.

Document Formats: Information or Fact Sheet

An information or fact sheet displays and compares the relevant features of several different types of items. But what does an information sheet look like? What would be the best design to display the information? If you check out the document templates that came with your word processing program, you may or may not find something that will work. If you do a quick search on the Internet, you will find dozens of examples of different types of sheets, depending on

Australian Government
Department of Health
Office of the Gene Technology Regulator

Genetically modified organisms in Australia

Gene technology is widely used in Australia: in agriculture, in research, in health and medicine, in education, and in industry.

When gene technology is used to create a genetically modified plant, animal or other living thing (an organism), the use of this genetically modified organism (GMO), for example growing GM canola, is regulated by the Gene Technology Regulator to protect people and the environment.

You may not create, use or import a GMO in Australia unless you have the appropriate approval.

The Gene Technology Regulator (the Regulator) is appointed by the Governor General of Australia to administer the national regulatory system for gene technology. The Regulator is assisted by the Office of the Gene Technology Regulator (OGTR).

OGTR factsheets explain what GMOs are, how they're used in Australia, how to get permission to import or use them, and how the regulatory system works to protect Australia.

Using GMOs in Australia

The current uses of genetically modified organisms in Australia include the following.

- Three genetically modified (GM) crops are grown in Australia: canola, cotton and safflower. Other crops are undergoing field trials. Read more about GM crops in agriculture.
- GM blue-flowered carnations are grown in Australia and imported from overseas
- Researchers use genetically modified bacteria, plants, animals and other organisms in their

research. They use a range of techniques including adding, modifying or turning off genes to study what the genes do.

- Genetic modification is widely used to make medicines such as insulin, and vaccines such as Gardasil. A small clinical trial of an oral cholera vaccine was held recently in Australia.
- Genetic modification is also used to make medicines and vaccines for animals such as the Hendra vaccine for horses.
- Schools use GMOs in biology classes
- Individuals are starting to use GMOs for personal research.

Importing GMOs

Internationally, genetically modified organisms are more widely used than in Australia. For example, about 80 GM crops are grown around the world.

You may not import any live GM plants, animals, and other organisms unless you have approval under the relevant biosecurity and gene technology legislation. For example, you need permission from the Gene Technology Regulator to import GM grain and you may also require an import permit from the Department of Agriculture and Water Resources. You will also need permission from the Regulator to import GM bacteria for research, or GM 'glow in the dark' aquarium fish. Some approvals are delegated to institutional biosafety committees and are then reported to the Regulator. Read more.

Regulating GM products

Food Standards Australia New Zealand is responsible for the safety assessment of genetically modified

foods. The use of GM products as human therapeutics is regulated by the Therapeutic Goods Administration. The Australian Pesticides and Veterinary Medicines Authority regulates the use of GM products as pesticides or animal medicines.

Other factsheets

What is gene technology?

Who needs to apply to import or use (deal with) a GMO

Information for importers of grain and laboratory/research supplies

GM kits in schools

Biohacking and community science

Public participation in assessing gene technology

Reporting misuse of genetically modified organisms

Don't import glowing fish unless you have authorisation

Oral trial of cholera vaccine in Australia

How we regulate the intentional release of GM crops and other GMOs into the environment

| Version 1 | June 2018 |
| Version 2 | September 2018 |

Contact us: ogtr@health.gov.au, www.ogtr.gov.au, phone 1800 181 030, or post: Office of the Gene Technology Regulator MDP 54, GPO Box 9848, Canberra ACT 2601.

Figure 13.1 Fact Sheet on genetically modified organisms from the Australian government Department of Health website.

Source: http://www.ogtr.gov.au/internet/ogtr/publishing.nsf/Content/9AA09BB4515EBAA2CA257D6B00155 C53/$File/01%20-%20Genetically%20modified%20organisms%20in%20Australia.pdf

whether you search for "feature sheet," "fact sheet," or "information sheet." Figure 13.1 is one example of a fact sheet on genetically modified organisms in Australia. A quick glance highlights several characteristics of the fact sheet layout:

- a title
- headings
- images

The information about genetically modified organisms is organized under the headings, and the photographs add visual interest. The title informs readers about the subject of the fact sheet.

Figure 13.2 shows a second model for a fact sheet. It highlights other characteristics of information sheets, including:

- topic title and logo
- organization logo and name
- headings
- brief introduction to topic
- labeled tables of information

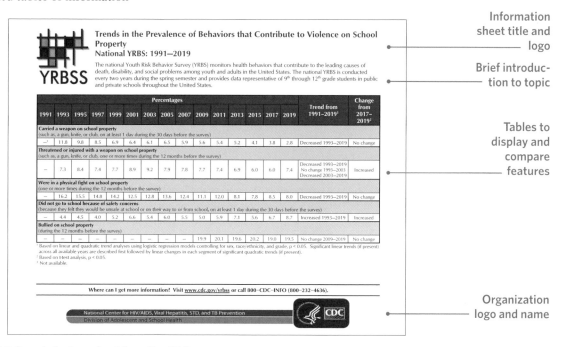

Information sheet title and logo

Brief introduction to topic

Tables to display and compare features

Organization logo and name

Figure 13.2 Sample feature sheet from the CDC.
Source: Trends in the Prevalence of Behaviors that Contribute to Violence on School Property, National YRBS: 1991–2013, Centers for Disease Control, http://www.cdc.gov/healthyyouth/yrbs/pdf/trends/us_violenceschool_trend_yrbs.pdf

Researching and Selecting Document Formats

genre: The type of document used in a workplace to accomplish the goals or purposes of work

template: An example version of a file that shows the format or structure of a document

Decide which format is best for your document. Should you use a fact sheet? A letter? A report? A proposal? Your choice will depend on your purpose for writing, your audience, and the situation or context. Different situations call for different types or **genres** of document. Once you have determined which genre best suits your situation, you can decide how to format and structure the document by choosing a **template** from the options supplied with your word processing program. The template supplies basic formatting to use as you compose. However, some genres are not covered in the template collection. In this case, an Internet search can help you find examples of the type of format you should use. Examine five or six different examples to see the range that is possible. Look for variations that can help you present your information most clearly and effectively. Use these samples as models for structuring and presenting your writing.

Exercise 13.4: Find Examples of Three Fact Sheet Layouts

Using the Internet or library, find three different examples of layouts for fact or information sheets and make printouts or photocopies. Write a half- to one-page memo to your instructor that covers the following:

- identify the features of each example that you think are effective in the fact sheet
- explain what these features contribute to displaying the pertinent information effectively

Rhetorical Situation 13.1: YourPhone Kiosk: Using Visuals for Effective Product Presentation

Working at the YourPhone Kiosk in the Lakeside mall provides some income, especially in the summer months when it is hard to find full-time employment in an air-conditioned environment. Even though it is a dry heat, 45° C in the valley is still hot. George Morawska likes the phone business well enough. A constant stream of shoppers provides an interesting backdrop.

The mall traffic lightens considerably as the post-lunch crowd thins out. George glances down at the latest iPhone. The last customer at the end of the lunch rush asked some good questions about what phone would be best for her. She has an old LG phone—nothing special—and a contract that expired two years ago. George knows he has a shot at selling her something better and earning a decent commission, but the difficulty of comparing devices made it impossible to make the sale today. What was her name, again? He glances at the business card she'd left: Fatima Noor.

Fatima was interested in the new LG because several people at her workplace have them, but she also knows many people who have iPhones and various Samsung Android phones. It isn't at all clear to a nontechnical person which one is a good fit for her.

George had started by asking her if she would use it mostly as a phone. He knows that many customers haven't really thought out how they will use the device, and until he gets them to talk about this, he is just wasting his time.

Fatima replied that she needed a phone, of course, but she also needed to keep up with her email. She noted, "I sell real estate and more and more of my clients are using email to communicate with me." She liked the idea of having a keyboard on the phone itself, which is why many of the other realtors had chosen LG. She had seen them using the predictive typing feature and thought that it might work for her.

George confirmed that this was a big advantage for those phones. He pointed out, though, that all of these devices had pluses and minuses. What Fatima would choose depended on what she would use it for most of the time. Fatima replied that she would also rely on it for her calendar and to take photos of some properties to help remember them.

George noted that most of the high-end smartphones could do all of these things, and the reviews for the best ones were more or less even. Even battery life was now pretty consistent, with the best units having enough power to get through a workday under normal circumstances. And because Fatima was a real-estate agent who spent a lot of time in her car, she could always use a power adaptor to charge the phone while driving from one appointment to another.

Just then Fatima's old phone had started ringing. "Oh—that's my office," she said, glancing at her phone screen. "I've got to go, but thanks for your help. I really appreciate it. You seem to know everything about them, and it's hard for me to keep them all separate. Do you have anything that I can take with me?"

"No, but I'm here quite a bit if you want to come back. Here's my card."

"And here's mine," she said, handing it to him. "Thanks again."

As he watched her walk down the mall toward the food court, he thought to himself, what I need is a sheet—nothing fancy—that I could hand out to customers like that. If they could see the advantages and disadvantages of each phone quickly and clearly, they would be much more likely to make a decision on the spot. And that would mean I would get credit for the sale.

Professional Communication Challenges 13.1

© F-Stop boy/Shutterstock

1. Create a fact sheet for three or four smartphones

Create a one-page, 8.5 × 11-inch sheet that George can use to hand out to customers such as Fatima Noor. Use different fonts for headings and for the text in the sheet. Leave plenty of white space so that readers can quickly skim and compare one device with another.

Visit a commercial website such as the following to see how they organize comparisons of different devices:

- verizonwireless.com

- www.pcworld.com
- www.bell.ca
- www.telus.com
- www.pcmag.com

Audience: Customers such as Fatima Noor, who would like to buy a new phone but lack time to research and compare their options

Purpose: To highlight the key features of three or four types of smartphones

Genre: Information fact sheet

2. Recommend one particular device that best meets Fatima's needs

Analyze the information that Fatima Noor gave George to determine her needs in a cell phone and write an email that George could send her recommending which particular device would best fit her needs. Use the Internet or visit a cell-phone retail outlet to research the various options, then decide which one would best fit her requirements from the perspective of initial cost, ongoing expenses, service, learning curve, and features. In your message, include at least two visuals.

Audience: Fatima Noor, who would like a new cell phone but lacks the time to research and compare the main brands' features

Purpose: To recommend one brand over the others as the best fit for Fatima's needs

Genre: Email report

USING VISUALS IN BUSINESS AND PROFESSIONAL COMMUNICATION

 Select appropriate stories for presentation through visuals

Many people may think of visuals as decoration, but they are far more useful than that. Charts, diagrams, and tables can translate complex information into stories that readers can more quickly process and understand than textual descriptions and numbers. For example, in Rhetorical Situation 12.2, Dal Blackfoot emphasizes to Sen Wang that she should use images rather than text to tell the story of the pine beetle in her brochure. He means translating the scientific data that she finds into tables, graphs, or charts so that her readers can quickly understand the importance of the information. Paragraphs of text discourage readers, especially in a brochure. Tables of data can also turn off readers when they are expected to draw their own comparisons. But graphs that clearly and dramatically compare data for readers communicate with impact.

Many people enjoy learning and learn more easily when you use narratives or stories. Stories can also be persuasive because they demonstrate "why." Good visuals also tell a story clearly and concisely. But don't include a graph or chart simply for visual appeal. Also avoid using charts and figures to tell stories that everyone already knows. Instead, study your data or statistics to find something interesting and unexpected. Create a graph or chart that will accomplish a goal: it may surprise readers or it may teach them something.

For example, Figure 13.3 lists the figures for the top trading partners with the United States in 2020. This presentation of data allows readers to assess the total amount of trade and with the US trade deficit with each country over this period. As general information, this table is interesting, but each reader who examines it will notice and take away something different.

Top 5 US Trade partners (2020)	Total value of trade (in billions $)	Trade deficit (in billions $)
Mexico	615	102
Canada	612	27
China	559	346
Japan	218	69
Germany	188	67

Source: https://www.thebalance.com/trade-deficit-by-county-3306264

Figure 13.3 **US Trade Deficit with top five trading partners (2020).**

Here are three interesting "stories" that we saw in these data:

1. Although China is known as a major exporter to the United States, Mexico and Canada are significantly larger trading partners.
2. Canada exports almost as much to the United States as it imports, and it is thus a more equal trading partner than the other countries.
3. Japan and Germany have smaller trading imbalances than China but larger than Mexico or Canada on a percentage basis.

If you want readers to note something specifically from the table, you need to either point it out directly to them or choose a different method of presentation.

To show the story in item 1, instead of using a table, the comparison is more quickly and effectively displayed by using a bar chart (see Figure 13.4).

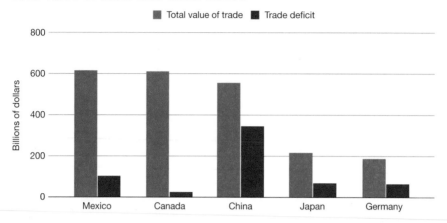

Figure 13.4 Bar chart comparing trade values for the five largest US trading partners.
Source: Graph created by R. Graves, http://www40.statcan.ca/l01/cst01/envi27a.htm

In contrast, Figure 13.5 has Japan and Germany removed from the comparison so that it emphasizes the numbers of the top three US trade partners.

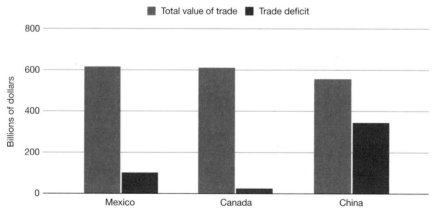

Figure 13.5 Bar chart comparing the imbalance of trade with the US for the top 3 trade partners.

As you can see, it is important to choose the right visual for telling your story.

How to Choose the Right Visual for a Story

Each type of visual is best suited to presenting a different type of information or a particular relationship between data. Here are nine types of visuals:

- bar chart
- line graph
- pie chart
- dot chart
- Gantt chart
- table
- map
- photograph
- drawing

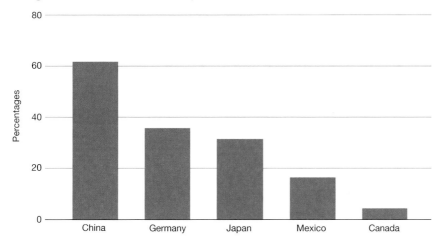

Largest Trade Deficit for Top 5 Trade Partners

Figure 13.6 **Bar graph emphasizing trade deficits.**

Bar Chart. Use a bar chart to

- compare items
- show change over time
- show frequency or distribution
- show correlation

Bar charts can show comparisons—for example, the five largest trading partners with the United States, as in Figure 13.6.

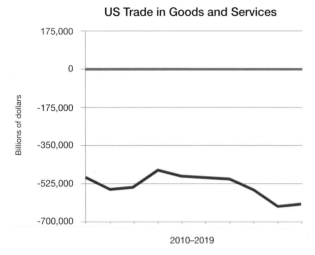

Figure 13.7 Line graph comparing item over time (i.e., increase in US trade deficit).

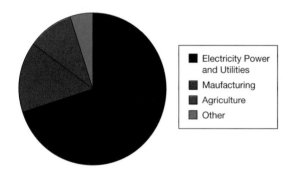

Figure 13.8 Pie chart showing the percentage of water used by each industrial sector.

Source: Graph by R. Graves. http://www41.statcan.ca/1762/ceb1762_000_e.htm

Line Graph. Use a line graph to

- compare items over time (as in Figure 13.7)
- show frequency or distribution
- show correlation

A line graph is useful to emphasize the comparison between the figures that you want to illustrate. In Figure 13.7, the gentle curve of the line graph emphasizes the fact that the value of the trade deficit went up and down over the ten-year period. Why might you want to graph these particular numbers?

This type of chart might be useful in a news report to show readers the increase in the trade deficit after the 2016 election. The information it presents could be persuasive to readers by showing readers why trade deficits interact in complex ways with trade agreements and the overall strength of the economy.

Pie Chart. Use a pie chart to show how one part or several parts are related to the whole.

To use a pie chart, your total has to add up to 100 per cent. Pie charts are useful because they allow your readers to visually compare groups. They can clearly and effectively make a point about quantities. For example, in Figure 13.8, the pie chart format forcefully shows that electricity power and utilities are the largest users of water in the industrial sector. In comparison, manufacturing, agriculture, and other sectors use half that consumed by utilities and power generation.

Dot Chart. Use a dot or density chart to show frequency or correlation.

Figure 13.9 is a dot chart that shows the approximate locations of coffee shops in the greater Toronto Area prepared as part of a business plan to open a Tea Emporium in the downtown lakeshore area of the city. The distribution of dots illustrates both the number and distribution of potential competitors to a proposed tea shop across Toronto generally as well as in the target neighborhood. The graphic gives an immediate sense of market penetration. In addition, the range of specific coffee shops that are named also informs readers as to the relative proportion of these shops that are chains/franchises compared to independent retailers. This graphic provides a quick overview of the data that would enable readers to understand the overall trends in this market.

Gantt Chart. Use a Gantt chart to show a timeline—for example, a schedule in a proposal or progress report. A Gantt chart is a visual display of a timetable of activities for a project or idea.

Figure 13.10 is a Gantt chart for a weekly status report, which requires employees to account for how they spent their time during the previous week. The employees' boss may use the status reports for recordkeeping.

The arrows visually depict the amount of time that each step took to develop the brochure. Viewers can easily see which stages of the project were most and least time consuming. They can also evaluate whether the amounts of time indicated are realistic or not.

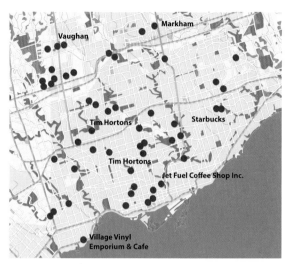

Figure 13.9 **Dot chart showing coffee shops in and around Toronto.**

Activity	Mon. 04/06	Tues. 05/06	Wed. 07/06	Thurs. 08/06	Fri. 09/06
Find sources on pine beetles	⟷				
Read sources on pine beetles and take notes		⟷			
Decide what information to include			⟷		
Choose visuals for brochure				⟷	
Create sample page layout for brochure					⟷

Figure 13.10 **Gantt chart documenting an employee's work on a brochure.**

Table: Use a table when the exact amounts are important. For example, if you are showing measurements to two decimal places, a table is the appropriate way to present the figures.

Brand	Number of coffee shops
Tim Hortons	249
Starbucks	151
Second Cup	83
Coffee Time	63
Timothy's	48
Country Style	41

Figure 13.11 **A table showing the number of coffee shops by brand in Toronto.**

Figure 13.11 presents a table that shows the number of coffee shops by brand in Toronto. Because it's a visual from a business plan for a new tea shop, readers will want to know the exact number of each rather than an approximate number, so the table is the appropriate choice.

Map. Use a map to

- show location
- compare two items

Figure 13.12 uses a map to show the location of the Morice Timber Supply Area in western British Columbia, the area studied by researchers Nelson, Boots, Wulder, and Carroll. Using a map accurately pinpoints the location of the area under study. The authors also give the geographic coordinates (54° 24' N, 126° 38' W) for the Morice Timber Supply Area for even greater precision.

Figure 13.12 **A map showing the location of the Morice Timber Supply Area in western British Columbia where the pine beetle infestations appeared.**
Source: T. Nelson, B. Boots, and M. Wulder. Large Area Mountain Pine Beetle Infestations: Spatial Data Representation and Accuracy. Mountain Pine Beetle Initiative Working Paper 2006 – 02, Canadian Forest Service. http://www.for.gov.bc.ca/hfd/library/documents/bib97020.pdf

Photograph. Use a photograph to

- reproduce exact detail
- show something being used

In the case of the pine beetle brochure that Sen Wang needs to create in Rhetorical Situation 13.2, a photograph of the actual beetle would help readers identify the creature if they came across one. The photograph gives great detail about the beetle that would be difficult to convey through words alone.

Drawing. Use line drawings to

- emphasize details
- show dimensions

In Figure 13.14, the schematic engineering drawing shows specific dimensions and details.

Figure 13.13 A photograph of a pine beetle.
Source: Natural Resources Canada

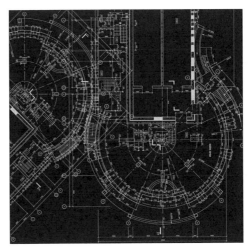

Figure 13.14 A sample line drawing.
Source: Nasri.3d/Shutterstock

Conventions for Visuals

 Present visual information accurately, ethically, and effectively

Use the conventions associated with visuals so that you are presenting the required information with them. The following are important conventions for a visual:

- *Title.* Use a descriptive title with each visual so that readers know what it represents, for example, "Figure 13.6: Largest Trade Deficit for Top 5 Trade Partners."
- *All units are labeled.* If you are using graphs or charts, make sure that the x-axis and the y-axis are clearly labeled with the units of measurement. If you include a legend, make sure that these items are also listed clearly and legibly.
- *Source of data.* If you are using data or statistics created by someone else, make sure that you include the source so that users can evaluate its validity.
- *Source of visual.* If you are using a visual that someone else created, include the source. This means at the least you should include the URL where you found the visual, if located online. If you are using the visual for purposes that are not educational (that is, associated with a school assignment), you must have permission to use it. Contact the original creator of the visual and request permission to reprint it. Sometimes you will need to pay a fee to reproduce it; other times you need only obtain written permission.

Exercise 13.5: Find an Interesting Story and Create a Graph to Tell It

Explore the US Census website (www.census.gov/en.html) or Statistics Canada website (www.statcan.ca /menu-en.htm) until you find some data that you think are interesting and unexpected. Use a graphing function within a spreadsheet file (Google Sheets, for example) to create a chart or graph to display the interesting story that you have found. Make sure that you select the most appropriate graph to represent your data. Include all conventional labels for your graph, such as title, legend (if appropriate), data labels, source, and figure number and caption. In addition to your graph or chart, add a paragraph or two that explains the point of your visual.

Ethical Use of Visuals

Visuals should clearly and accurately represent the subject matter they are presenting. It is possible to create visuals that mislead viewers, and you should know a little bit about these techniques so that you can recognize a visual that is not giving you the straight story. Examine the bar chart in Figure 13.15. It reports the differences in opinion between students who support postsecondary tuition fee increases and those who oppose them. At first glance, the graph measures a huge disparity of opinion. However, if you look more closely, you can see that the actual range between students supporting fee increases and students opposing them is only 16 percentage points, not that far outside the survey's margin of error. It also makes it appear that many students oppose the increases, yet they are, in fact, outnumbered slightly by those who either don't know or support the increases.

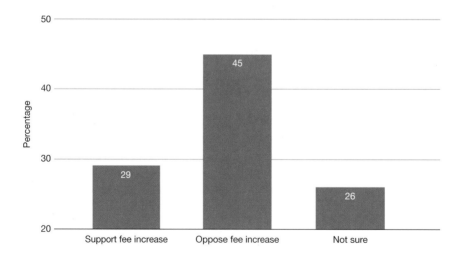

Figure 13.15 **A misleading bar chart exaggerates the differences of opinion among three groups.**
Source: © Pearson Education, Inc.

Business Communication: Rhetorical Situations

The exaggeration is created by representing only 30 percentage points on the graph. At the same time, this misleading presentation diverts our attention from the fact that nearly 30 per cent of students support fee increases. The misleading representation of these survey findings leave you with exactly the opposite impression from the truth: that there is a big difference of opinion on this issue among students.

TECHNIQUES FOR MISLEADING PRESENTATION OF DATA

Y-Axis Does Not Start at Zero. Visuals can be misleading when the y-axis does not begin at zero. Unless they look closely, viewers may assume the graph starts at zero, so they may not recognize that the differences between the data are being exaggerated through an inaccurate presentation.

If you want to omit some of the numbers on your graph, you should start your graph at zero but create a visual break between the zero and the numbers that are relevant to your data. The break draws your readers' attention to the fact that some of the numbers in the y-axis have been omitted.

Chartjunk that misrepresents the degree of increase. Sometimes writers try to jazz up a graph by using icons or drawings—called **chartjunk**—instead of traditional bars or lines. Often this tactic can obscure or misrepresent the data being presented.

chartjunk: Graphics added to charts to add visual interest but that distract from the data

Figure 13.16 uses icons instead of standard bars to illustrate the increase in pet adoptions at Stone River Animal Rescue Center. Although the graph is visually interesting, the cat images prevent readers from estimating any but the most general figures.

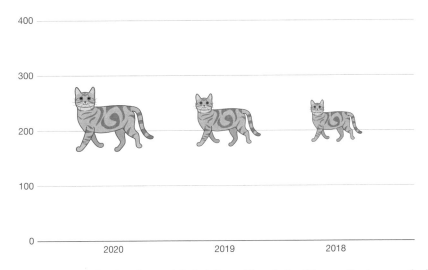

Figure 13.16 Pet adoptions have tripled at Stone River Animal Rescue Center over the last three years.
Source (cat): © Studio Ayutaka/Shutterstock

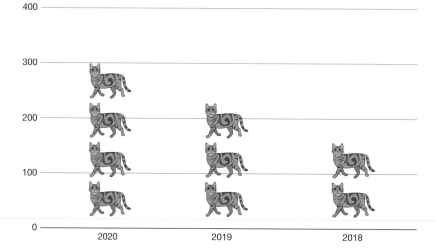

Figure 13.17 Stone River Rescue Center has successfully rehomed an increasing number of cats over the past three years.

Source (cat): © Studio Ayutaka/Shutterstock

It is difficult to determine the proportions between the icons to evaluate the data depicted. Similarly, the use of cat icons may distract readers from recognizing that this graph describes *all* pet adoptions, including 150 dogs, 15 rabbits, a peacock, and a pot-bellied pig in 2020.

Figure 13.17 uses uniformly sized icons to more accurately represent the increase in the number of cat adoptions at the Stone River Rescue Center. The data that it presents have been amended to show only cat adoptions so that viewers will not be misled by the choice of icons. The revision is a clearer and more accurate representation of the data being presented.

By examining other writers' visuals carefully, you can gain valuable information about how to present visual information clearly, usefully, and ethically.

Of course, sometimes the data or information that you have to present does not reflect well on your organization. In such a case, you should discuss with your supervisor the best way to approach such a situation. You will have to decide for yourself whether you are comfortable with the solutions that your supervisor may advise.

Exercise 13.6: Evaluating the Ethics of Some Sample Visuals

Using the Internet, find a selection of five or six visuals and evaluate the ethical presentation of the data. Alternatively, use a selection of visuals supplied by your instructor for your analysis. Examine the validity of the data supplied in each example. Assess whether the data are presented ethically. What kinds of changes would you need to make to ensure that the visual presents its data clearly and ethically? Write a memo of several paragraphs in which you include a copy of the visual as well as your analysis and evaluation of its flaws and how to correct them.

Rhetorical Situation 13.2: Pine Beetle Infestation: Presenting Technical Information to a Public Audience

With 70,000 students and only 8,000 jobs, getting hired as a summer intern student at Forestry Resources was a long shot—really lucky, given the lottery selection system—but it worked for Sen Wang. As a forestry student, she needs this break to get a foothold in the profession. Now the fun begins.

The summer internship location at the Western Forestry Center means she flew in with just a weekend to find somewhere to live. She lucked out when the office turned out to be not too far from the local university campus; there is plenty of cheap student housing nearby. Maybe this will work out after all.

The first couple of weeks have been, well, boring. Lots of training videos and meeting people and trying desperately to remember names and faces—and attach the right names to the right faces. But that changed with her first project: researching and preparing a draft of a brochure on the pine beetle.

While she knows about the problem with the pine beetle in a general way, Sen hasn't really studied it until this past week. Natural Resources has thousands of scientific publications in its database about the beetle; finding information has not been difficult. But she now realizes why the administrators at the Western Forestry Center want an information brochure: almost all of the information is too technical for most people to follow.

She has found one publication that might help her get started: "Mountain Pine Beetle Mania: A Junior High Science Resource" (http://nofc.cfs.nrcan.gc.ca/bookstore_pdfs/26052.pdf). Most of it details how to teach kids about the pine beetle, but the section defining pine beetles gives her somewhere to start. The back of the booklet lists some web resources that also promise to provide information.

Her supervisor, Dal Blackfoot, explains, "We want to produce a brochure that brings the public up to speed on the problem and identifies the solutions currently being considered. We don't want you to bury readers in details. In fact, the real problem is to convey the basic information in as few words as possible and, if possible, through images. Use the images to tell a story about how widespread the problem is too, so include a map or graphic that shows this."

"Okay," responds Sen. She makes a note on her worksheet.

"At this point you are only producing an internal document," notes Dal. He explains that her work will be the basis for a graphic designer to work from if the center decides to distribute her brochure widely. This plan means that Sen should include images that she finds on the web, but with citations so that the graphic designer can locate the original later.

When he asks if Sen has any questions, she asks about the audience. She thinks "the general public" sounds too broad: will there be a group that may be more likely to see this brochure than others? Like employees of logging companies? Or homeowners? Would people in nearby cities need this information?

"Well, that's the problem," says Dal. He explains that they want everyone who may come in contact with the pine beetle to have some idea of what it is. The goal of the brochure is to have readers take precautions to try to contain the pest where it is and prevent further spread.

"I see," responds Sen. "Okay, well, this should be fun. Thanks, Dal."

1. Create a draft of the pine beetle educational brochure

Create a draft of Sen Wang's brochure. Use the links in Figure 13.18 to find information about the pine beetle. Include images that you find on the web, but remember to cite the source of the image in an attachment. You want to reach as broad an audience as possible and educate them on how best to contain the pine beetle's spread. Your brochure should include a map that shows the spread of the pine beetle so far. It should also present statistical information that will help to convince readers that the pine beetle is a serious problem in forests and that they should do what they can to help.

Government/Public Information

https://www2.gov.bc.ca/gov/content/industry/forestry/managing-our-forest-resources/
forest-health/forest-pests/bark-beetles/mountain-pine-beetle

https://csfs.colostate.edu/forest-management/common-forest-insects-diseases/
mountain-pine-beetle/

https://www.nrcan.gc.ca/our-natural-resources/forests-forestry/
wildland-fires-insects-disturban/top-forest-insects-diseases-cana/
mountain-pine-beetle/13381

https://www.fs.fed.us/research/invasive-species/insects/southern-pine-beetle.php

Images

www.forestryimages.org

Figure 13.18 Websites that Sen Wang finds with useful information on pine beetles.

To simplify the process of creating the brochure, consider using a document template in the word processing program that you use.

Audience: Aim to reach a broad audience of readers by explaining technical terms and keeping your vocabulary simple

Purpose: To educate members of the general public to take precautions against helping the pine-beetle spread

Genre: Brochure

2. Create a newsletter to educate rural inhabitants

Create a newsletter (two pages, maximum) directed toward rural inhabitants that will persuade them to contribute to the effort to slow the spread of the pine beetle to forests and woodlots. Include information about the current range of the pine beetle, the likelihood that it will spread, and what readers can do to slow or stop its spread. Include images that you find on the Internet, but remember to cite the source of the images in the newsletter.

Consider using a document template from your word processing program to simplify the process of designing the newsletter. Focus your attention on converting some of your information into visuals, drawings, graphs, and charts, which will help your readers understand and respond to the pine beetle infestation crisis. Include both text and visuals in the document.

Audience: Members of the general public

Purpose: To convince them that the pine beetle is a threat to forests

Genre: Newsletter

CHAPTER SUMMARY

- Choose a fact sheet when you want to offer a brief introduction to a topic.
- Choose a genre that suits your subject, purpose, and audience, and search for models of a genre on the Internet.
- Use white space to emphasize important points, use headings that stand out, and include visuals.
- Translate scientific or financial data into tables, graphs, and charts to show readers the importance of the information.
- Use the proper conventions for visuals, including titles, labels, data sources, and sources.
- Use visuals ethically: don't create visuals that mislead viewers by starting the y-axis other than at zero and avoid chartjunk that misrepresents the degree of increase.

PERMISSIONS ACKNOWLEDGMENTS

Page 18: Reprinted by permission of the Capital Comets Dog Sports Club.

Page 47: Reprinted by permission of the University of Alberta.

Page 65: Reprinted by permission of Heather and Roger Graves.

Page 72: Reprinted by permission of the Canadian Cancer Society. Source: https://www.cancer.ca/en/prevention-and-screening/reduce-cancer-risk/can-cancer-be-prevented/?region=ab. Accessed February 26, 2021.

Page 88: Reprinted by permission of the Canadian Automobile Association.

Page 159: Image source: https://www.lifehack.org/articles/communication/top-10-most-inspirational-bloggers-the-world.html.

Page 187: Homepage of the First Nations Bank of Canada. Source: https://www.fnbc.ca/Personal/.

INDEX